SOUL EATER

8

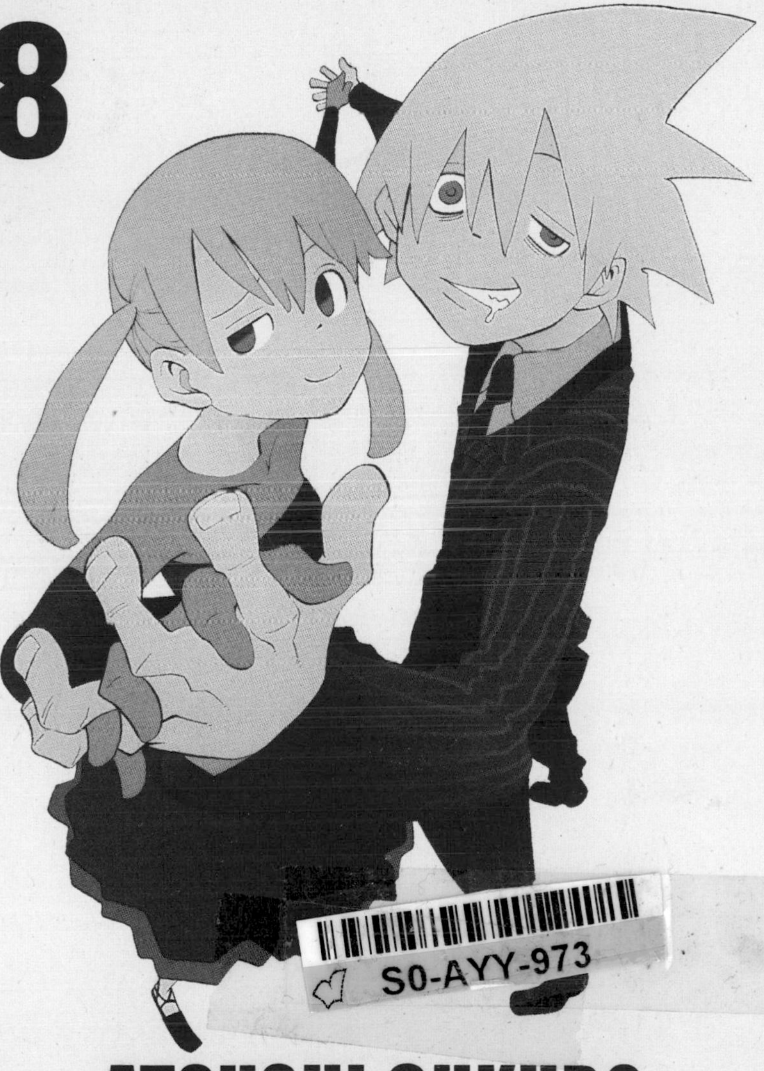

ATSUSHI OHKUBO

WORM: EXPRESS

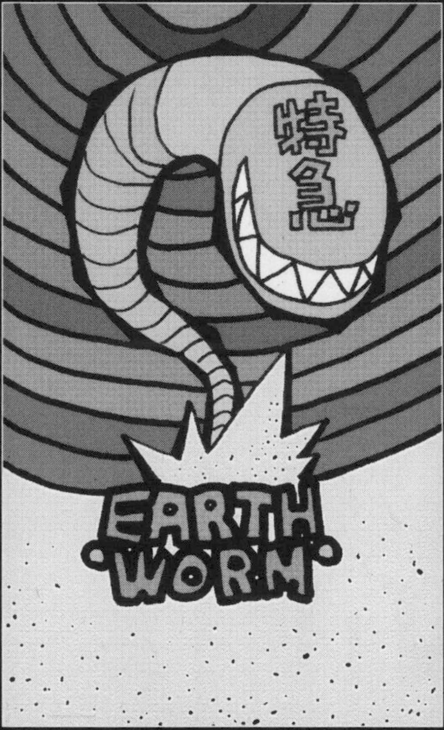
EARTH WORM

OUL EATER

vol. 8

by ATSUSHI OHKUBO

A heart full of motion, A SOUL full of dignity

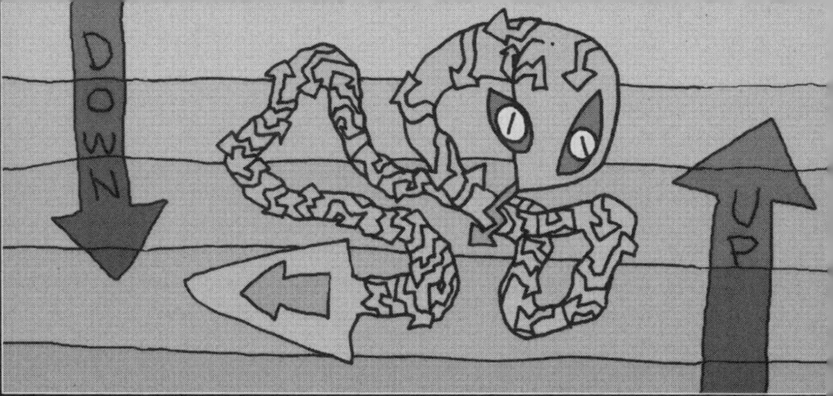
DOWN
UP

CONTENTS

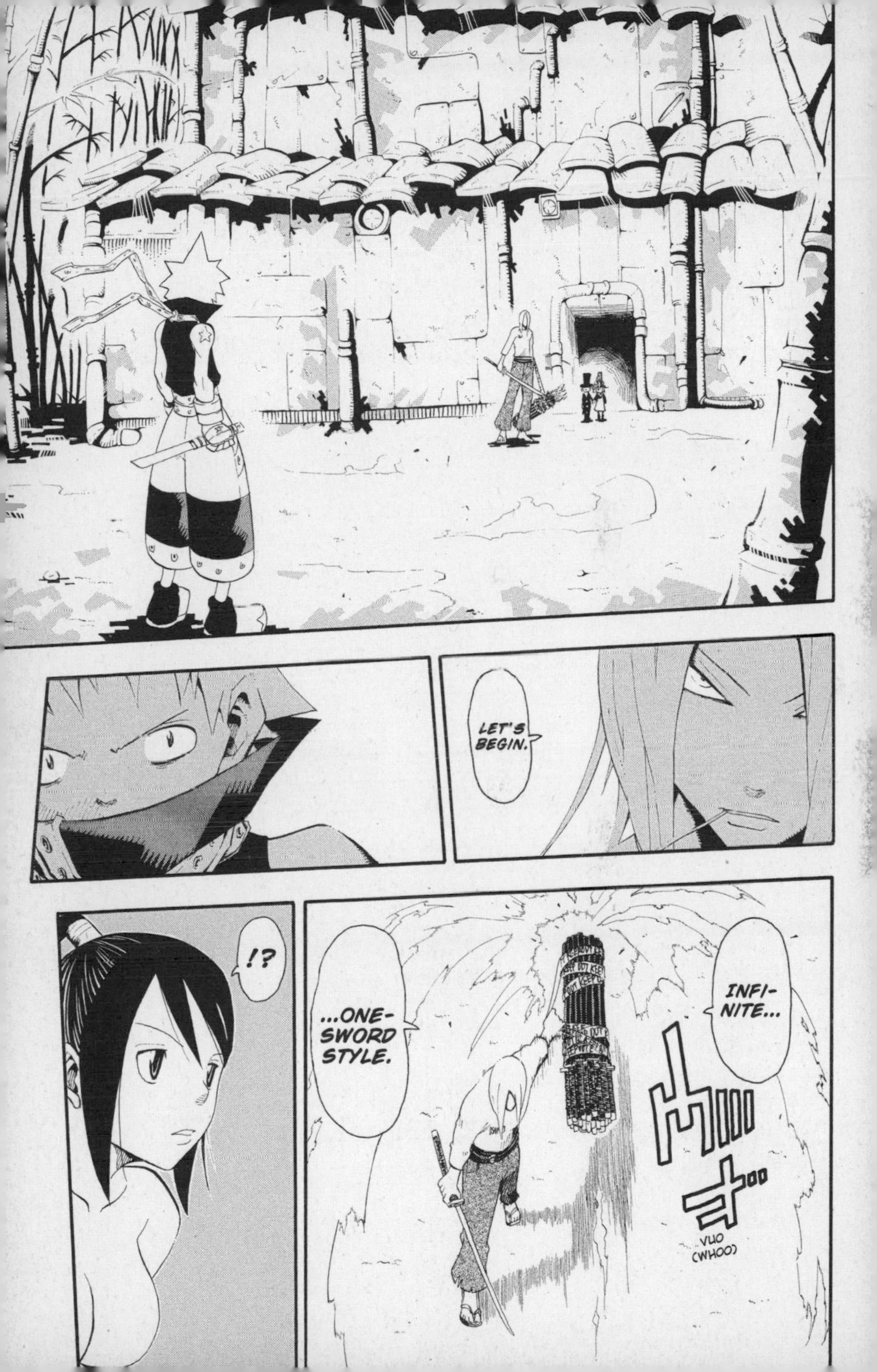
LET'S BEGIN.
INFINITE...
...ONE-SWORD STYLE.
VUO (WHOO)
!?

SOUL EATER

CHAPTER 28: THE BODYGUARD (PART 2)

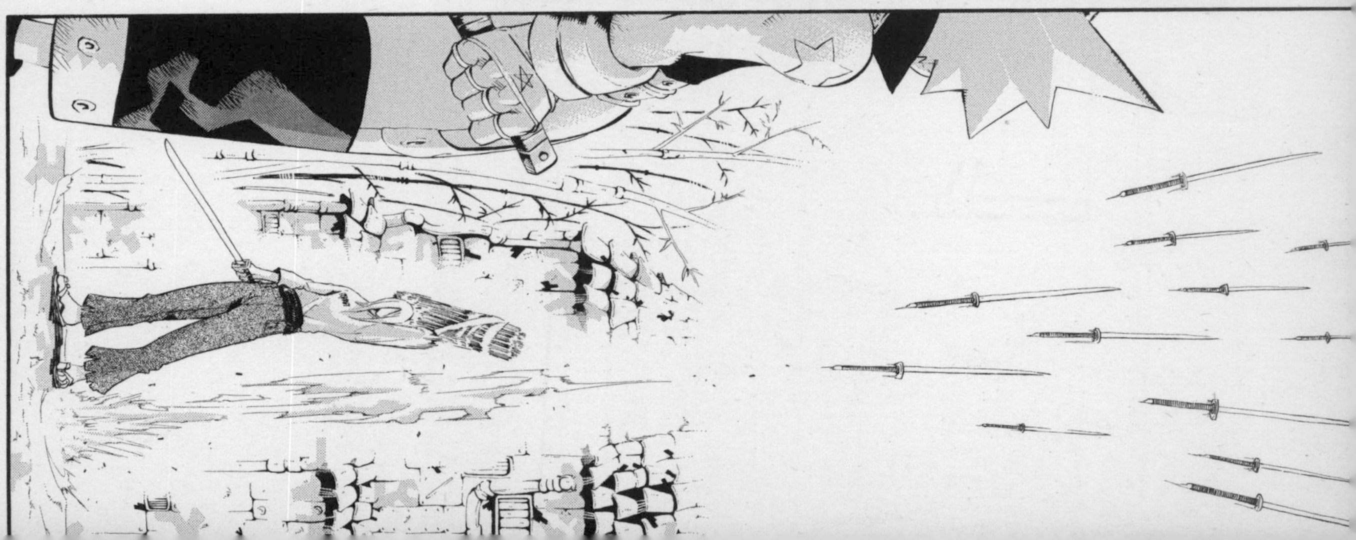

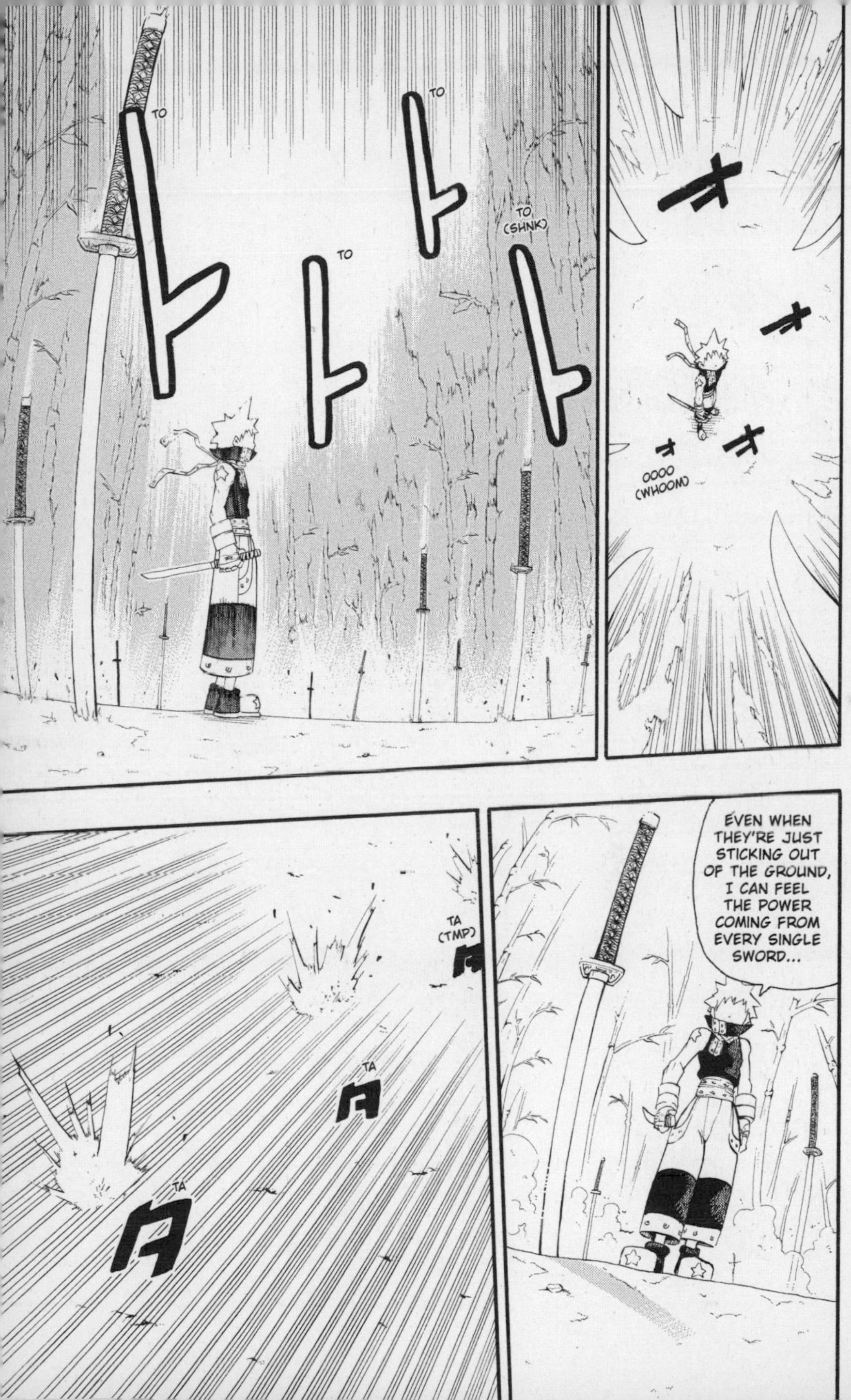
OOOO
(WHOOM)
TO
(SHNK)
TO
TO
TO
EVEN WHEN THEY'RE JUST STICKING OUT OF THE GROUND, I CAN FEEL THE POWER COMING FROM EVERY SINGLE SWORD...
TA
(TMP)
TA
TA

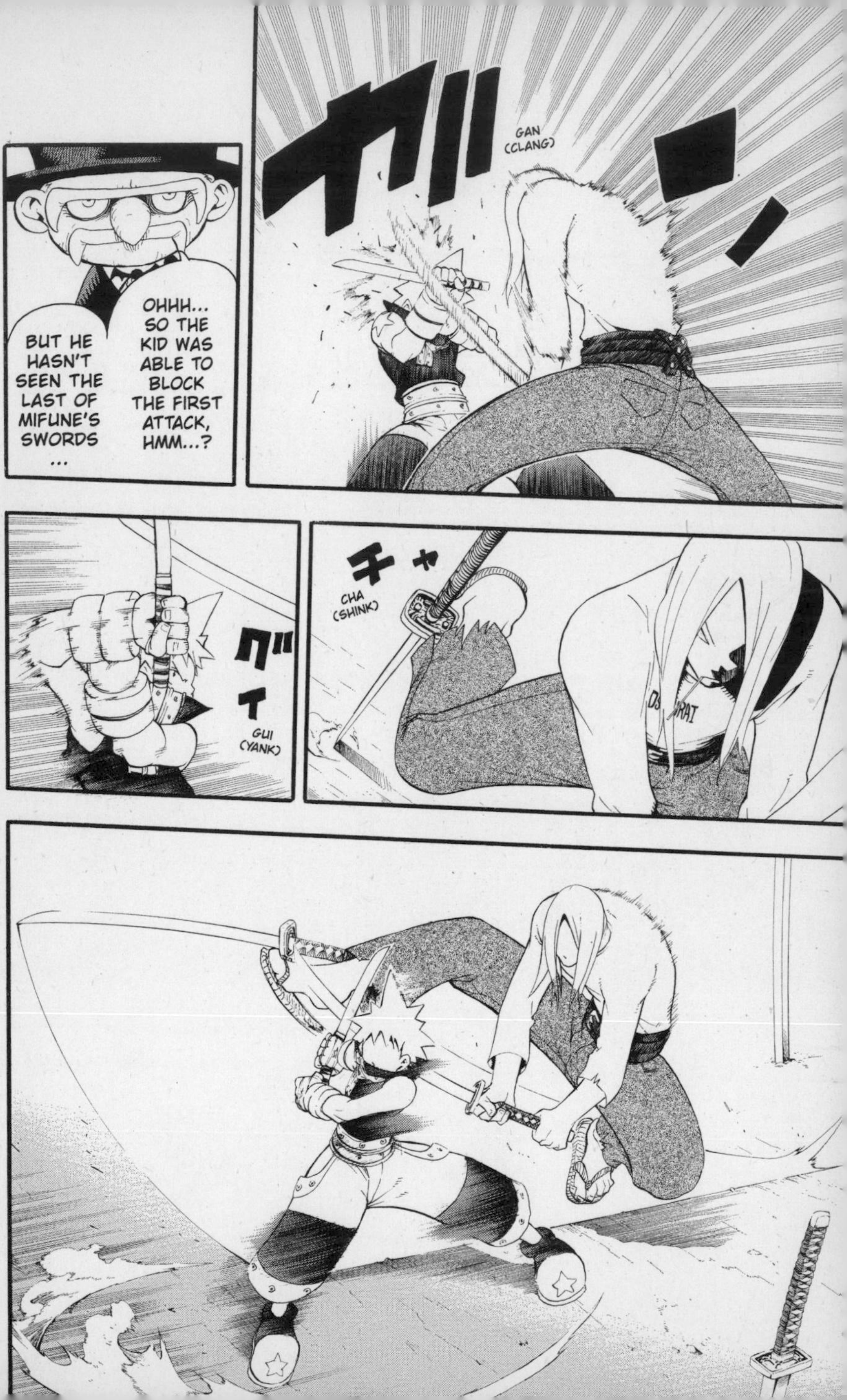
GAN
(CLANG)
OHHH... SO THE KID WAS ABLE TO BLOCK THE FIRST ATTACK, HMM...?
BUT HE HASN'T SEEN THE LAST OF MIFUNE'S SWORDS ...
CHA
(SHINK)
GUI
(YANK)

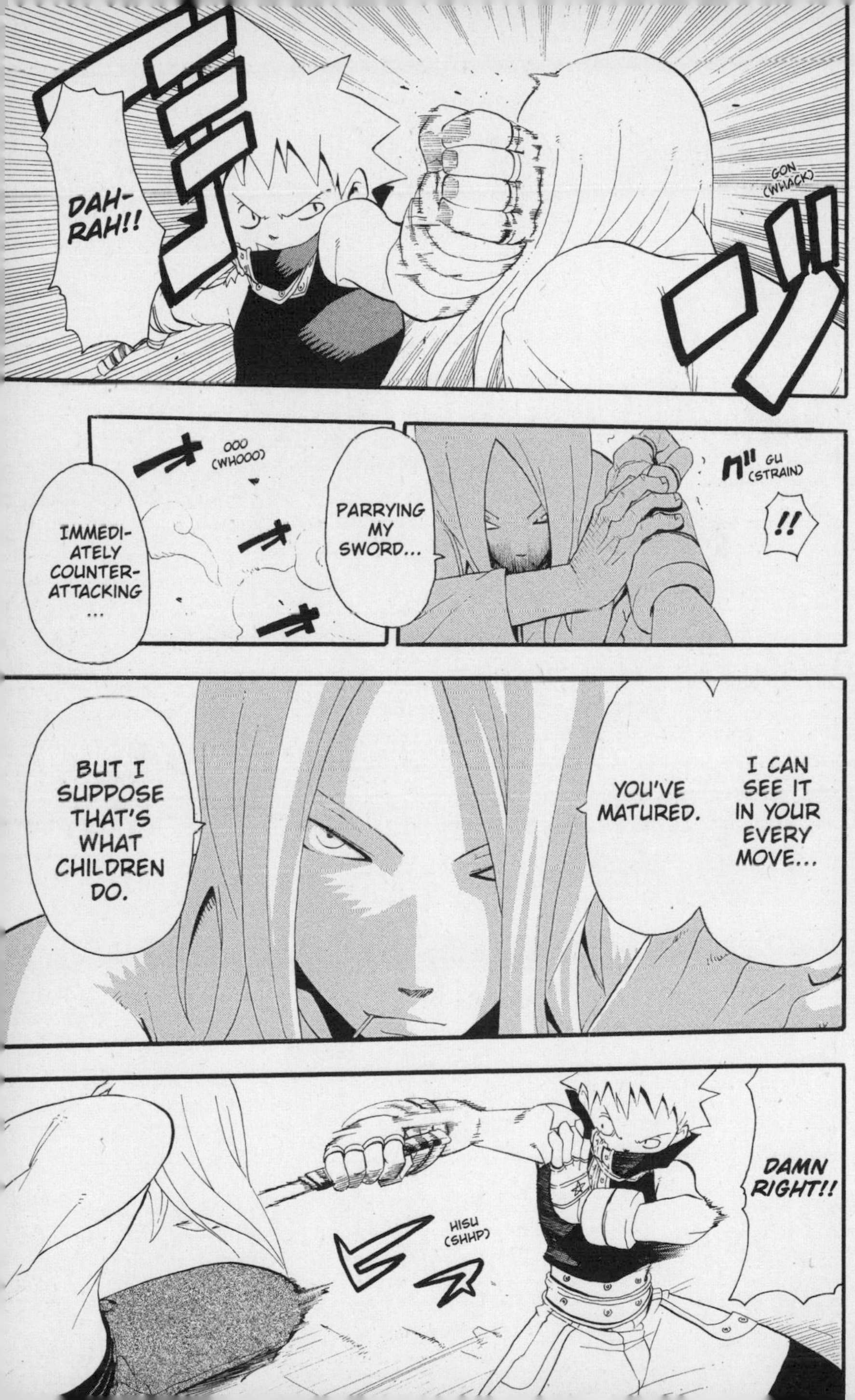
GON (WHACK)
DAH-RAH!!
GU (STRAIN)
!!
PARRYING MY SWORD...
OOO (WHOOO)
IMMEDIATELY COUNTER-ATTACKING...
I CAN SEE IT IN YOUR EVERY MOVE...
YOU'VE MATURED.
BUT I SUPPOSE THAT'S WHAT CHILDREN DO.
DAMN RIGHT!!
HISU (SHHP)

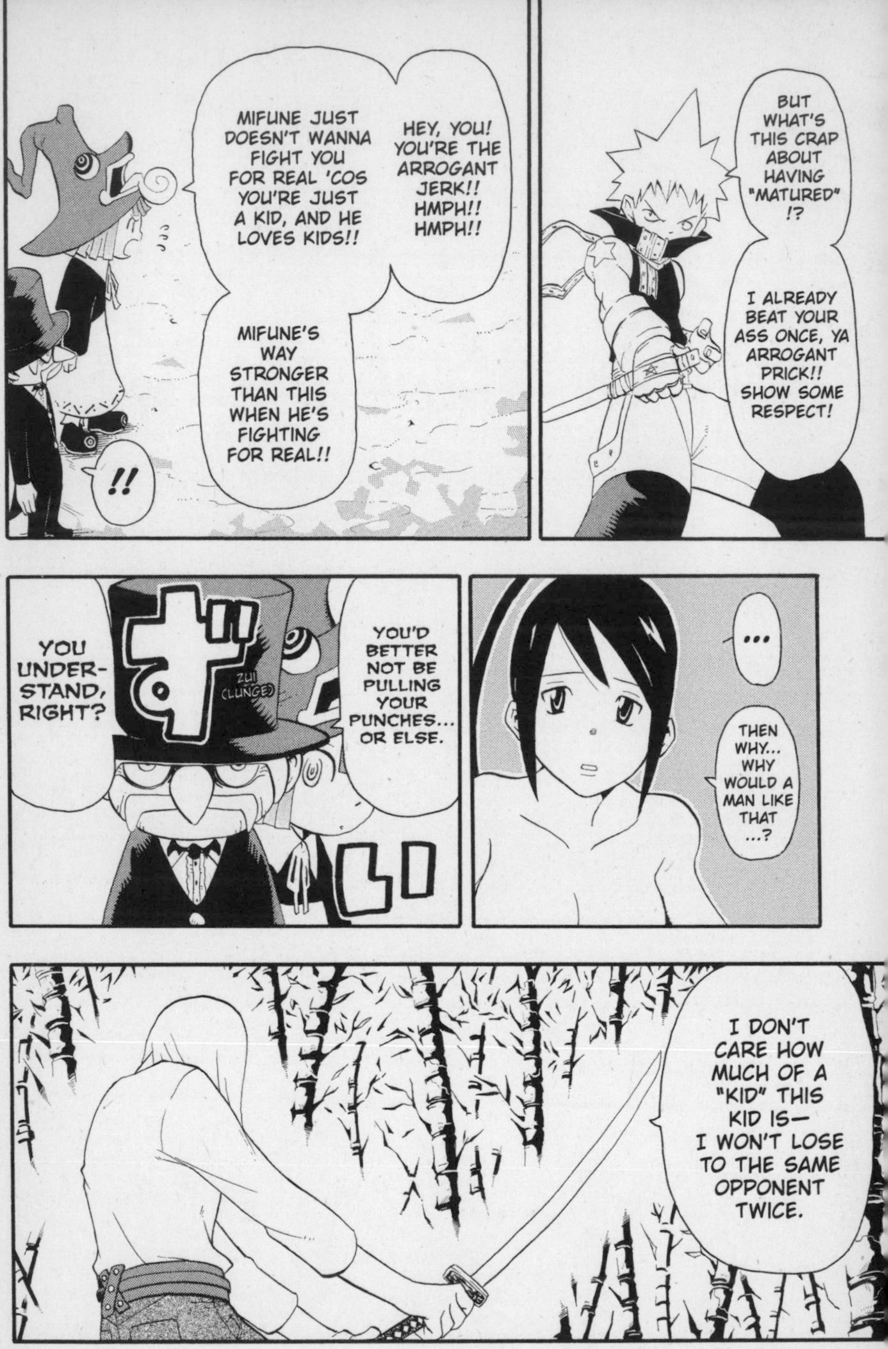
BUT WHAT'S THIS CRAP ABOUT HAVING "MATURED" !?
I ALREADY BEAT YOUR ASS ONCE, YA ARROGANT PRICK!! SHOW SOME RESPECT!
HEY, YOU! YOU'RE THE ARROGANT JERK!! HMPH!! HMPH!!
MIFUNE JUST DOESN'T WANNA FIGHT YOU FOR REAL 'COS YOU'RE JUST A KID, AND HE LOVES KIDS!!
MIFUNE'S WAY STRONGER THAN THIS WHEN HE'S FIGHTING FOR REAL!!
!!
...
THEN WHY... WHY WOULD A MAN LIKE THAT ...?
YOU'D BETTER NOT BE PULLING YOUR PUNCHES... OR ELSE.
ZUI (LUNGED)
YOU UNDER-STAND, RIGHT?
I DON'T CARE HOW MUCH OF A "KID" THIS KID IS— I WON'T LOSE TO THE SAME OPPONENT TWICE.

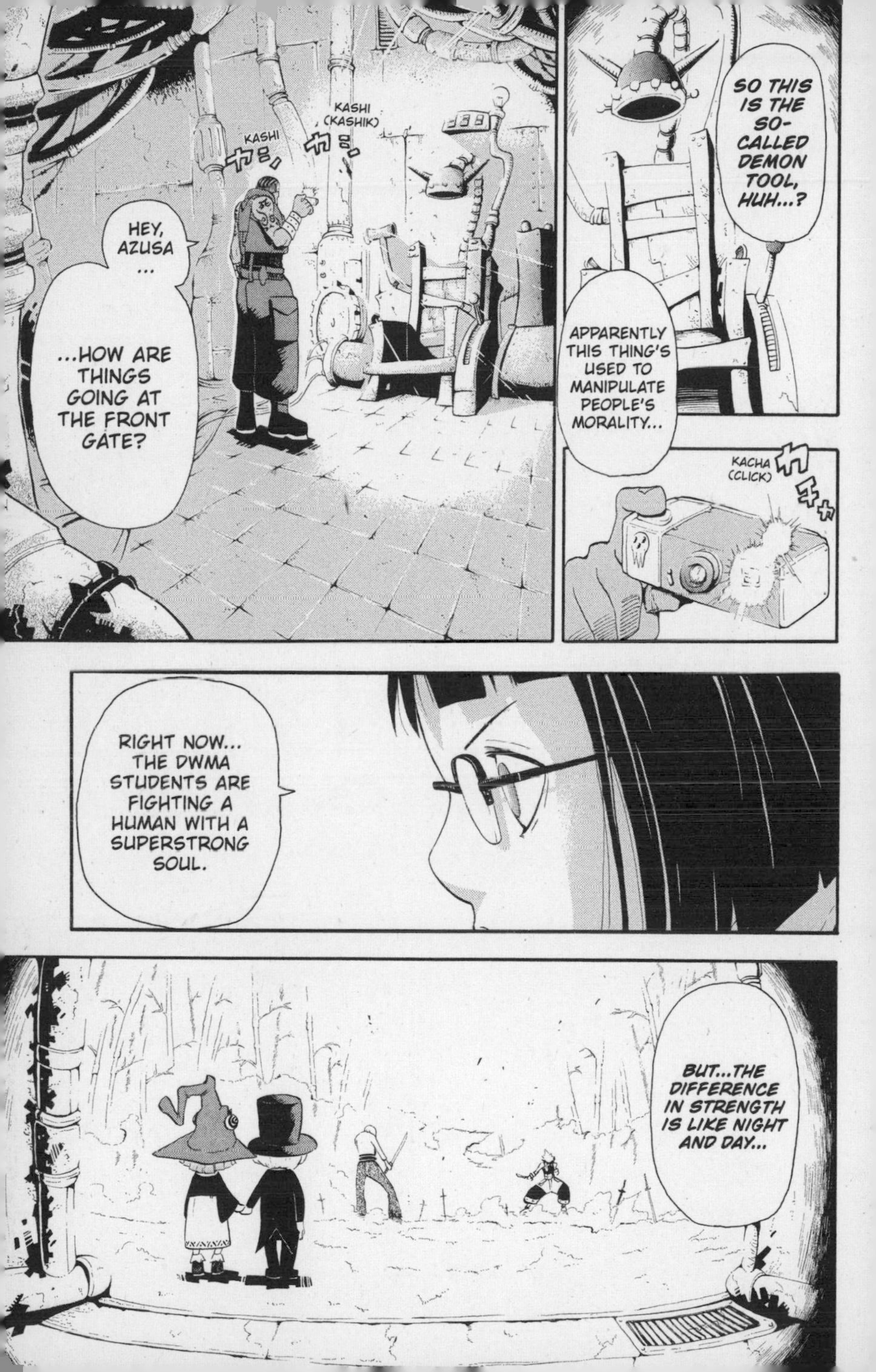
SO THIS IS THE SO-CALLED DEMON TOOL, HUH...?
APPARENTLY THIS THING'S USED TO MANIPULATE PEOPLE'S MORALITY...
KACHA (CLICK)
KASHI (KASHIK)
KASHI
HEY, AZUSA...
...HOW ARE THINGS GOING AT THE FRONT GATE?
RIGHT NOW... THE DWMA STUDENTS ARE FIGHTING A HUMAN WITH A SUPERSTRONG SOUL.
BUT...THE DIFFERENCE IN STRENGTH IS LIKE NIGHT AND DAY...

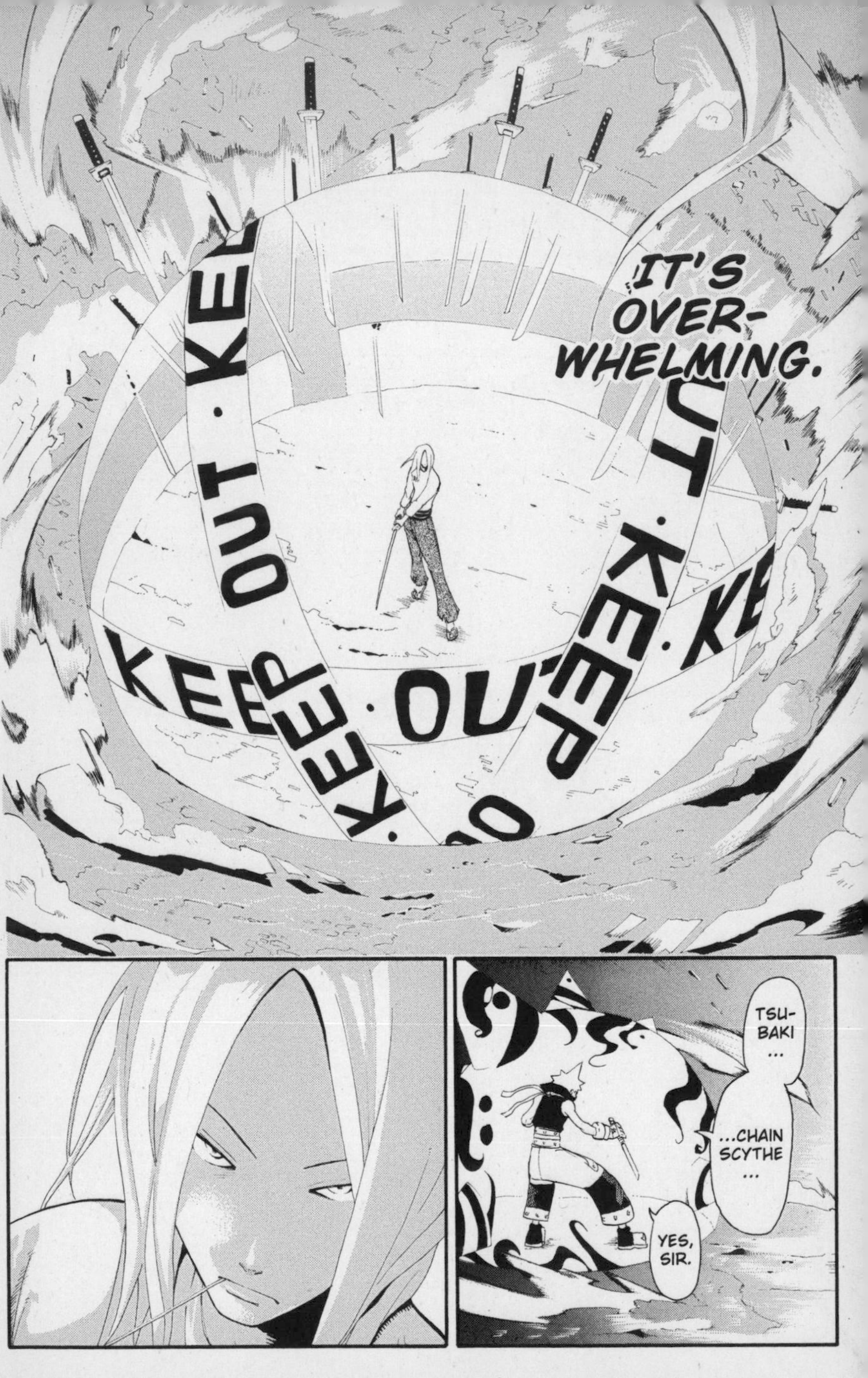
IT'S OVER-WHELMING.
TSU-BAKI ...
...CHAIN SCYTHE ...
YES, SIR.

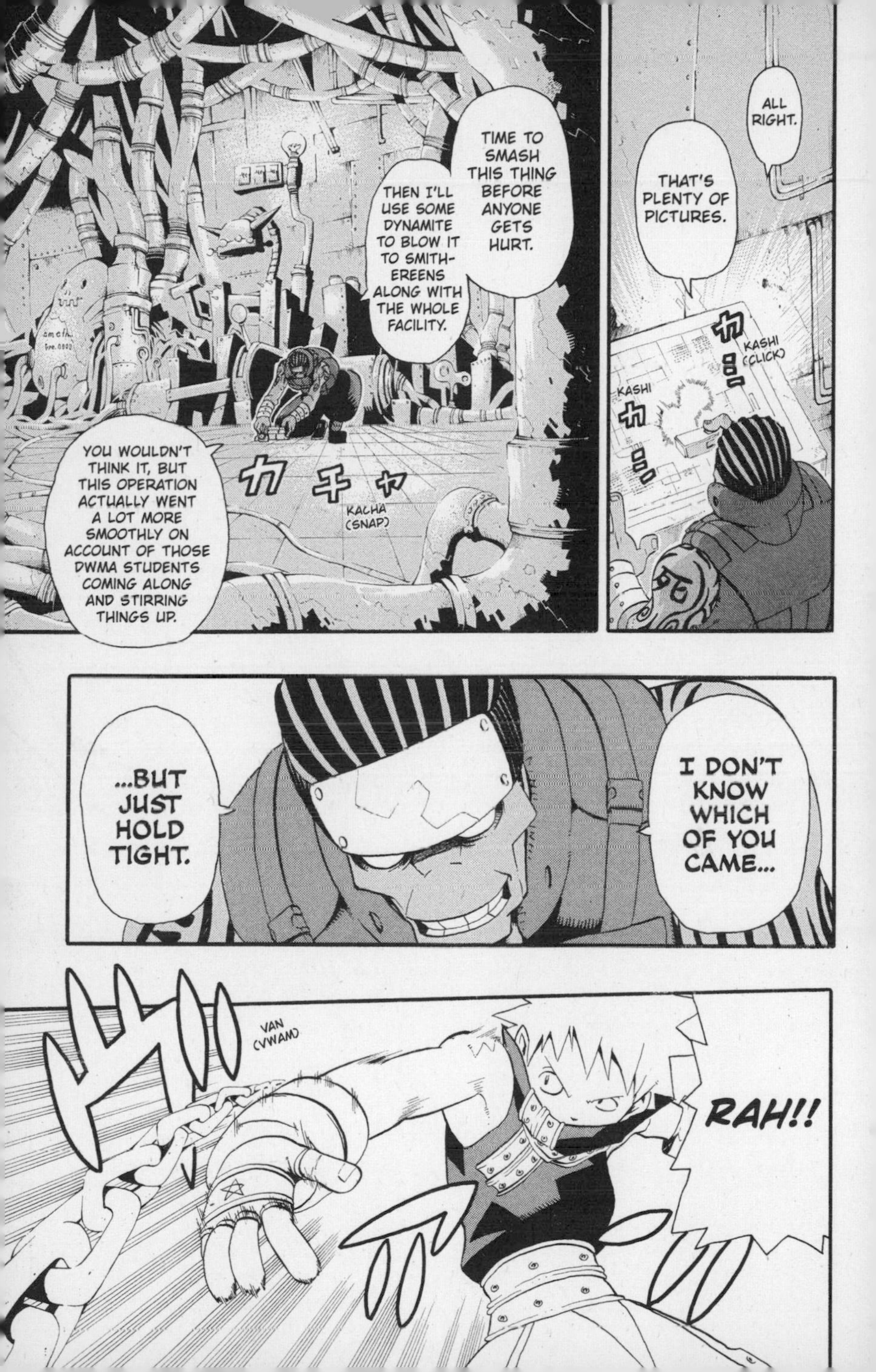
ALL RIGHT.
THAT'S PLENTY OF PICTURES.
KASHI (CLICK)
KASHI
TIME TO SMASH THIS THING BEFORE ANYONE GETS HURT.
THEN I'LL USE SOME DYNAMITE TO BLOW IT TO SMITH-EREENS ALONG WITH THE WHOLE FACILITY.
YOU WOULDN'T THINK IT, BUT THIS OPERATION ACTUALLY WENT A LOT MORE SMOOTHLY ON ACCOUNT OF THOSE DWMA STUDENTS COMING ALONG AND STIRRING THINGS UP.
KACHA (SNAP)
I DON'T KNOW WHICH OF YOU CAME...
...BUT JUST HOLD TIGHT.
RAH!!
VAN (VWAM)

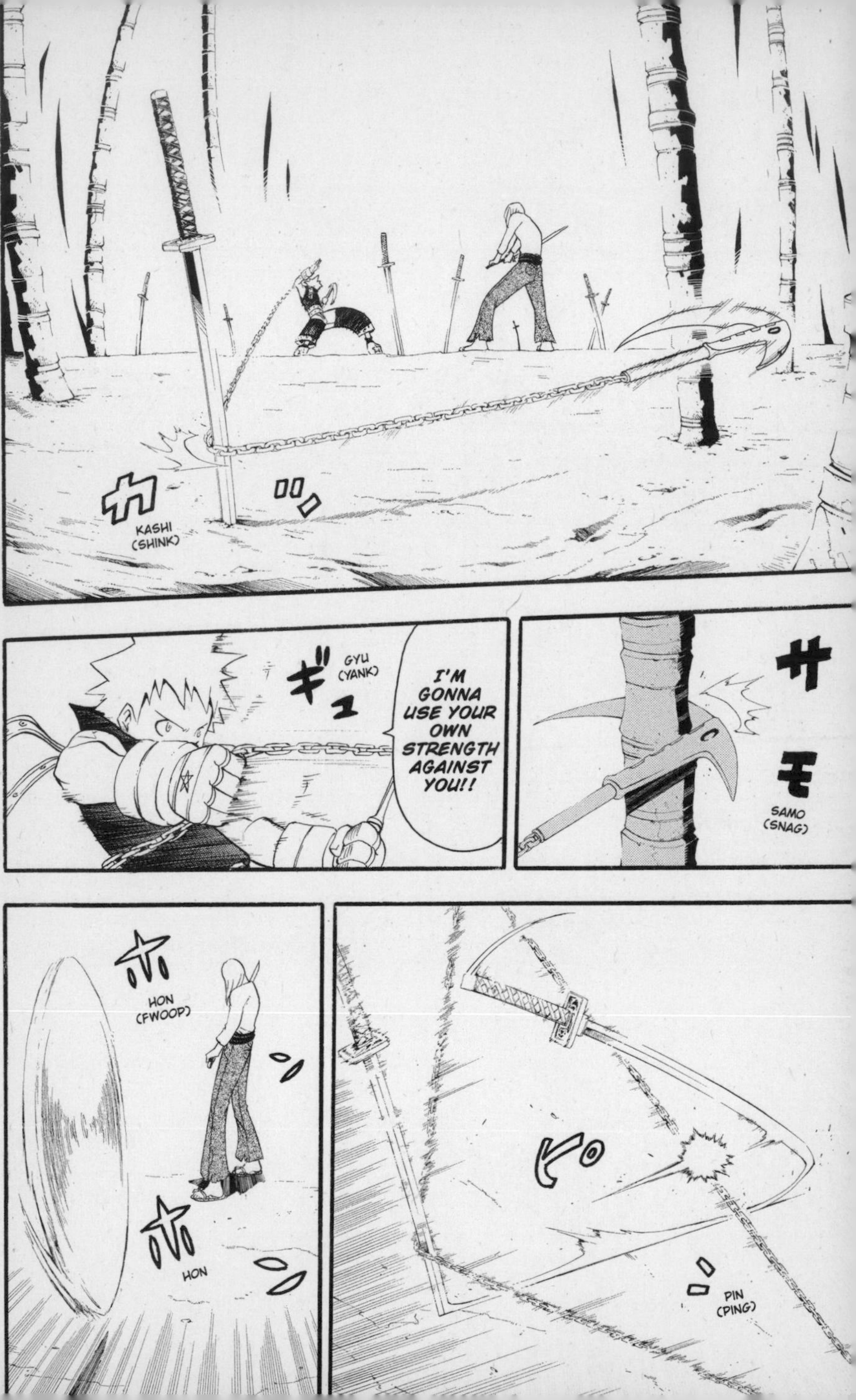
KASHI (SHINK)
SAMO (SNAG)
I'M GONNA USE YOUR OWN STRENGTH AGAINST YOU!!
GYU (YANK)
PIN (PING)
HON (FWOOP)
HON

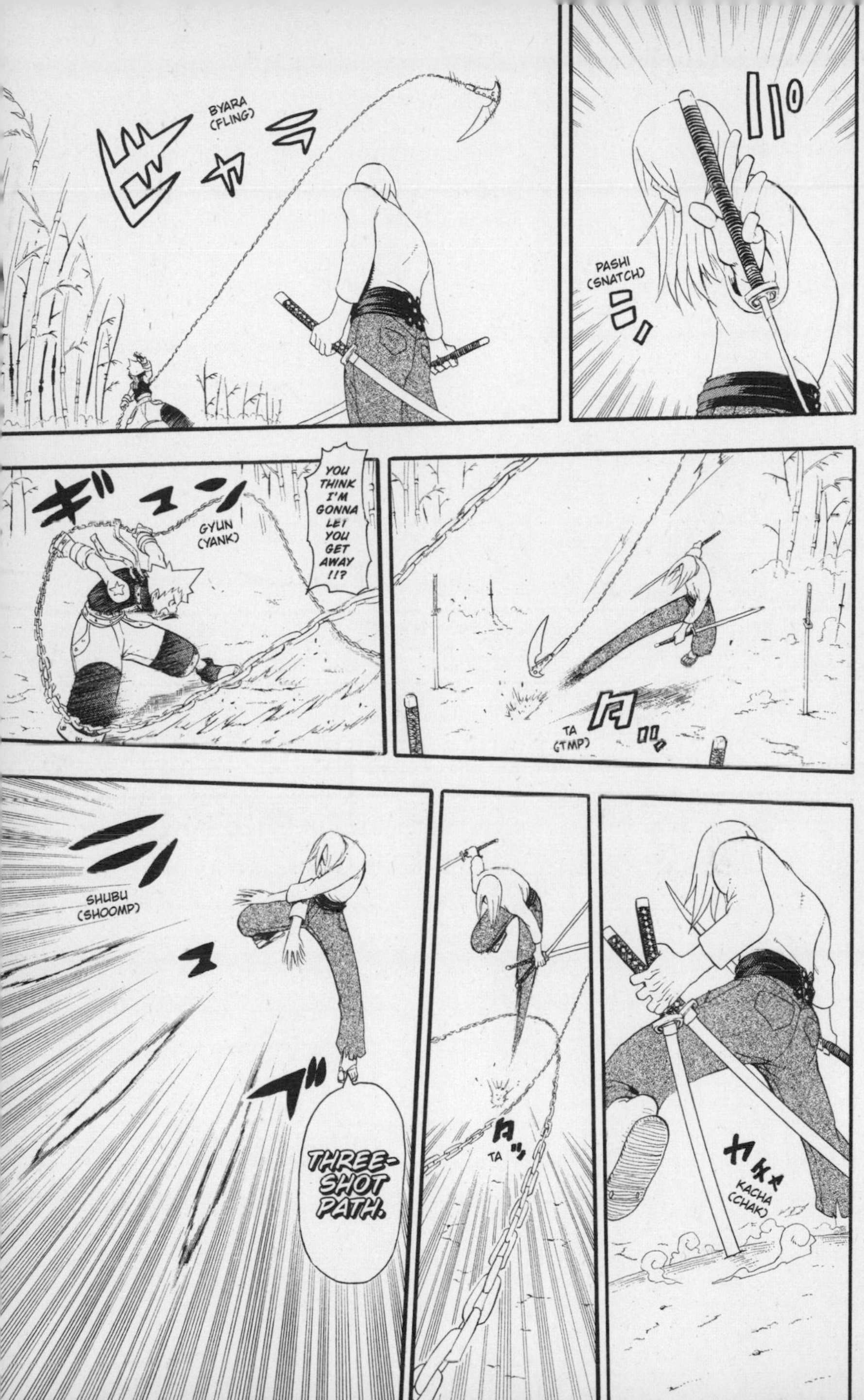
PASHI (SNATCH)
BYARA (FLING)
TA (TMP)
YOU THINK I'M GONNA LET YOU GET AWAY!!?
GYUN (YANK)
KACHA (CHAK)
TA
SHUBU (SHOOMP)
THREE-SHOT PATH.

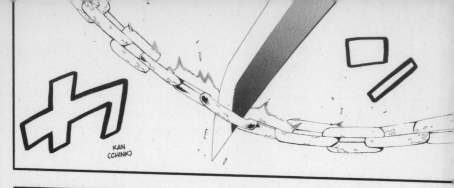

KAN
(CHINK)

WHA!!?

ド゛ ド゛ー゛ド゛
DO   DO   DO
(SHNK)

BLACK☆STAR!!

IN MIFUNE'S HANDS, A SWORD IS MORE THAN JUST SOMETHING YOU SWING, I SEE...

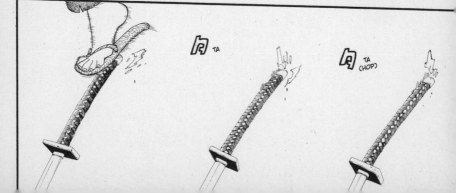

乃 TA

乃 TA
(HOP)

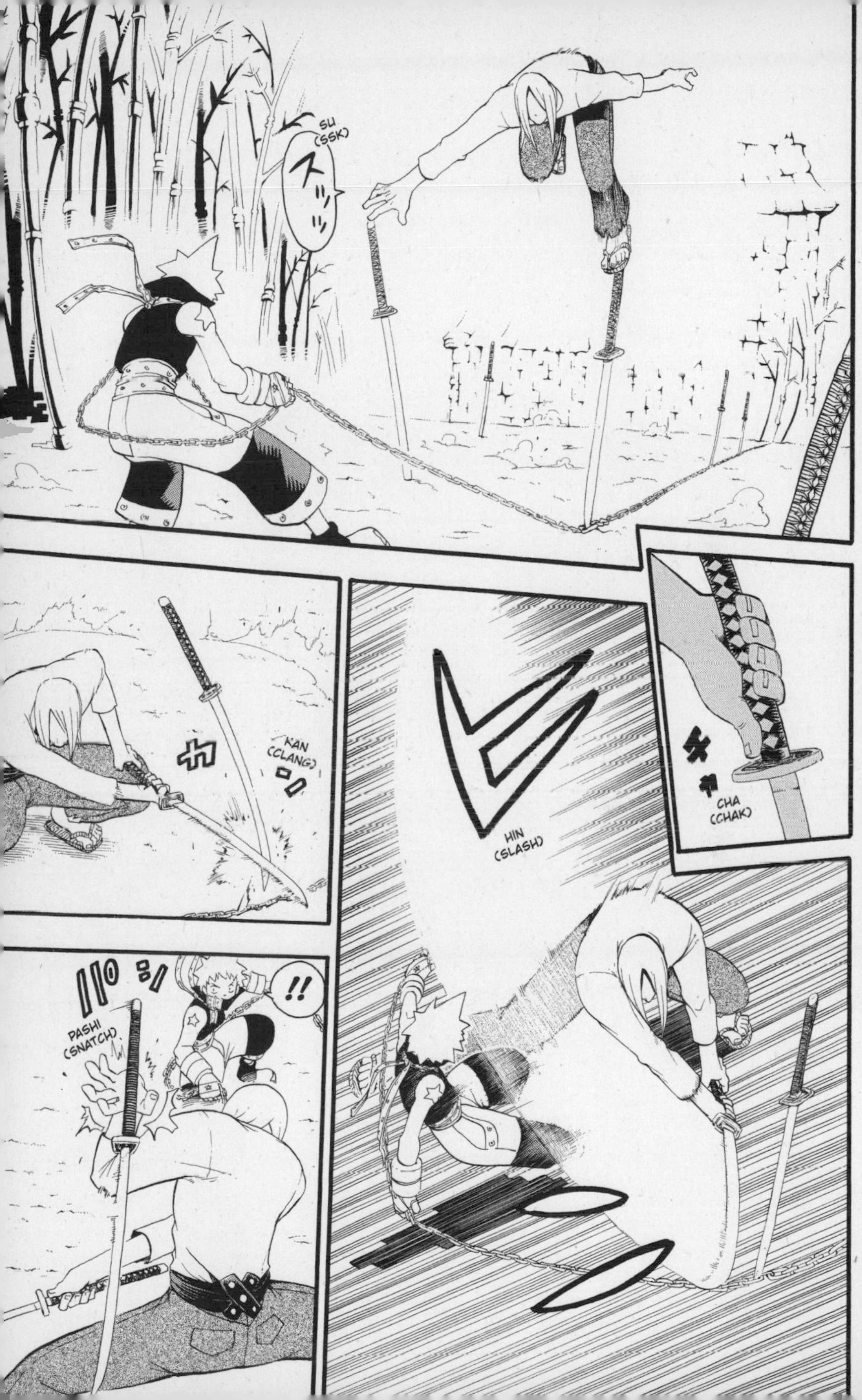

SU (SSK)
CHA (CHAK)
HIN (SLASH)
KAN (CLANG)
PASHI (SNATCH)
!!

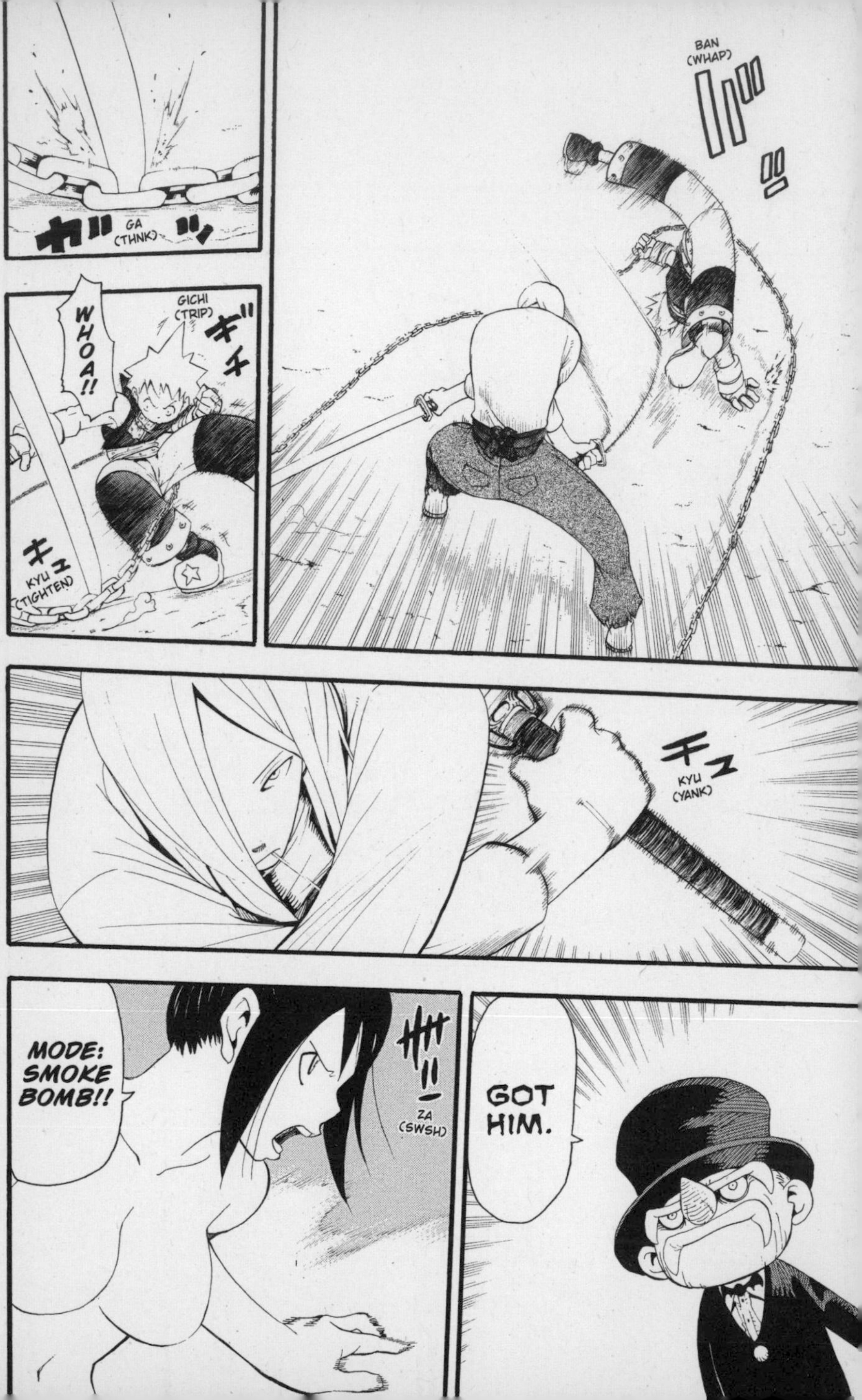
BAN
(WHAP)
GA
(THNK)
WHOA!!
GICHI
(TRIP)
KYU
(TIGHTEN)
KYU
(YANK)
GOT HIM.
MODE: SMOKE BOMB!!
ZA
(SWSH)

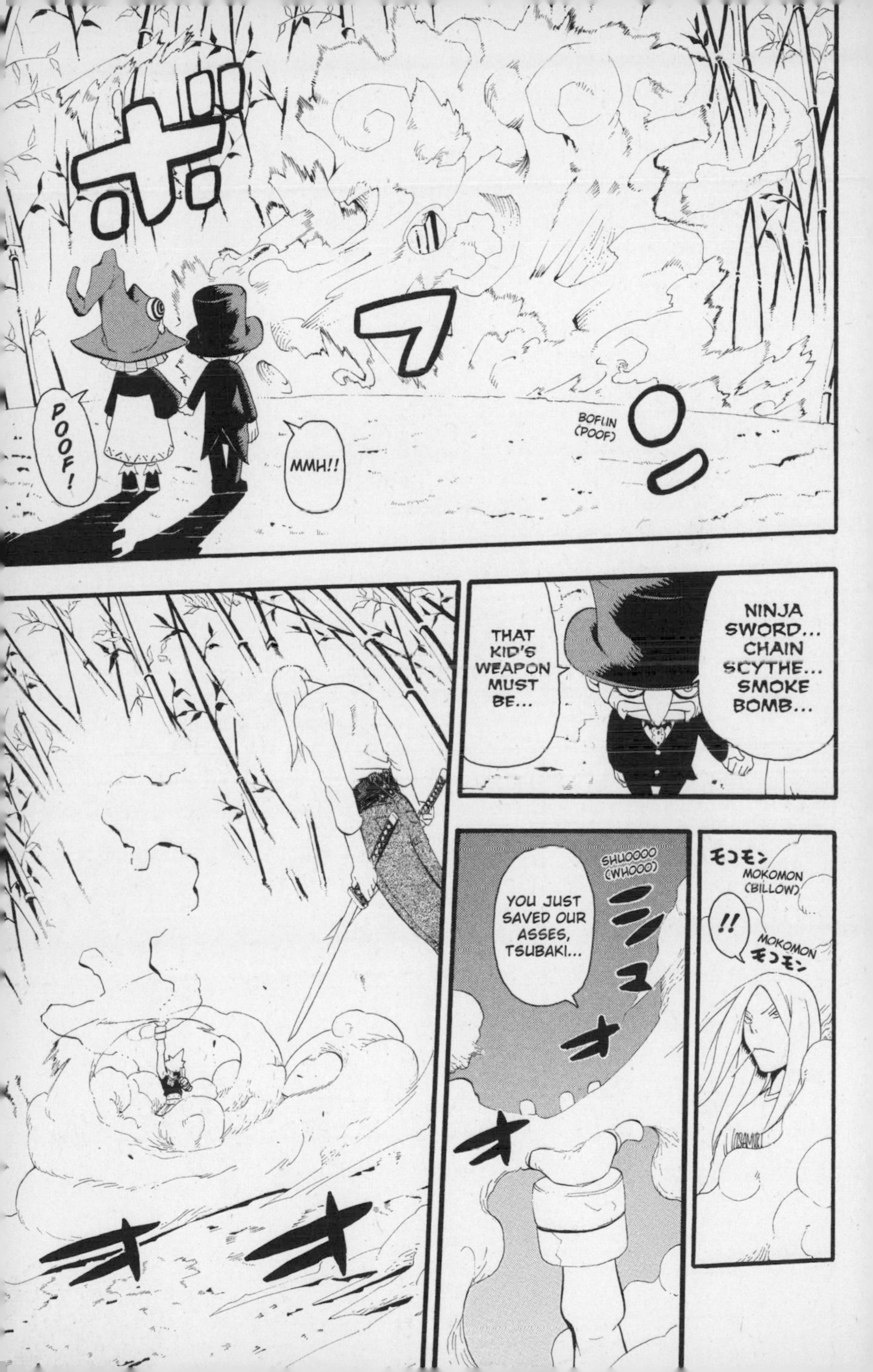
BOFLIN (POOF)
MMH!!
POOF!
NINJA SWORD... CHAIN SCYTHE... SMOKE BOMB...
THAT KID'S WEAPON MUST BE...
モコモン
MOKOMON (BILLOW)
!!
MOKOMON
モコモン
SHUOOOO (WHOOO)
YOU JUST SAVED OUR ASSES, TSUBAKI...

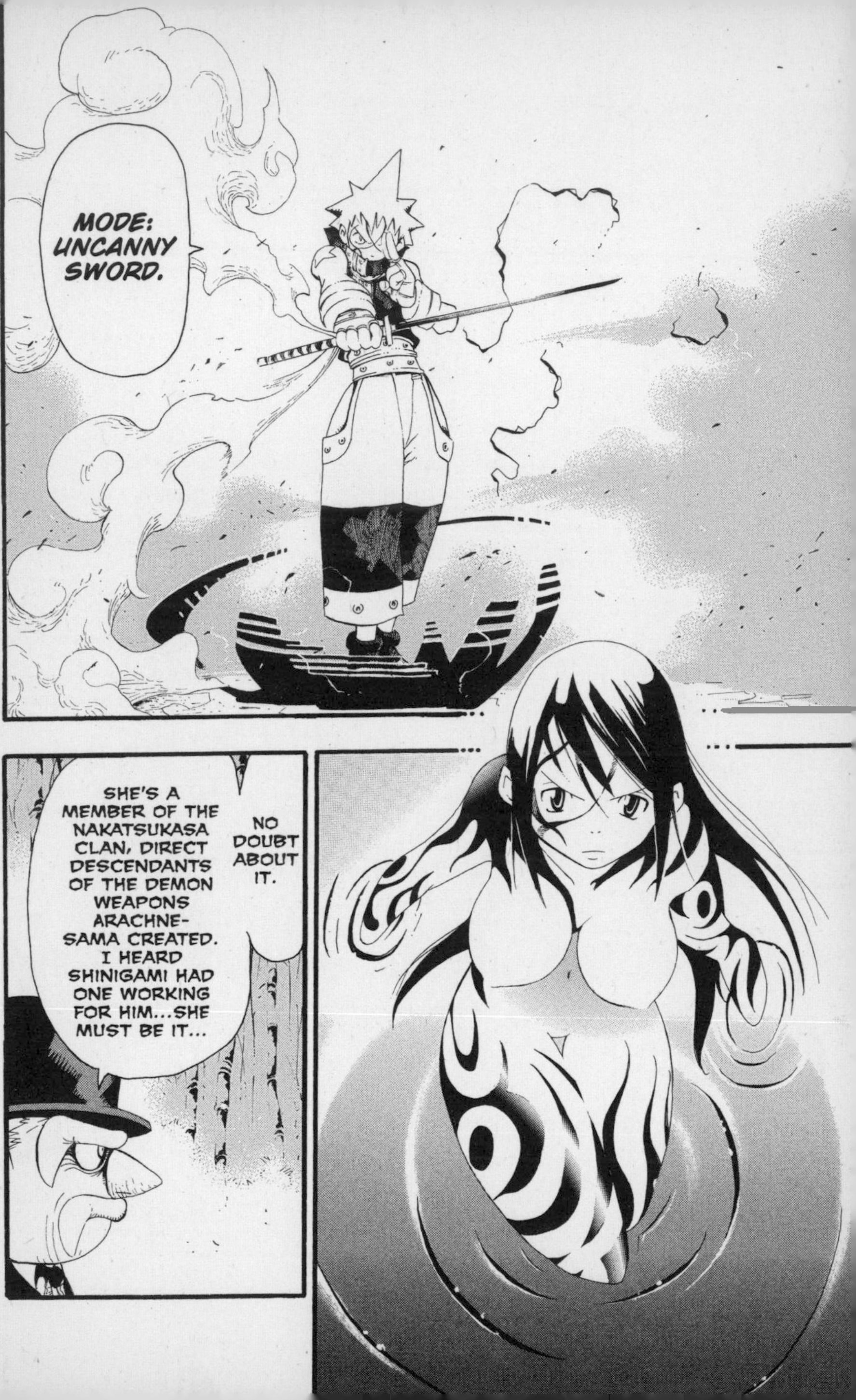
MODE: UNCANNY SWORD.
NO DOUBT ABOUT IT.
SHE'S A MEMBER OF THE NAKATSUKASA CLAN, DIRECT DESCENDANTS OF THE DEMON WEAPONS ARACHNE-SAMA CREATED. I HEARD SHINIGAMI HAD ONE WORKING FOR HIM...SHE MUST BE IT...

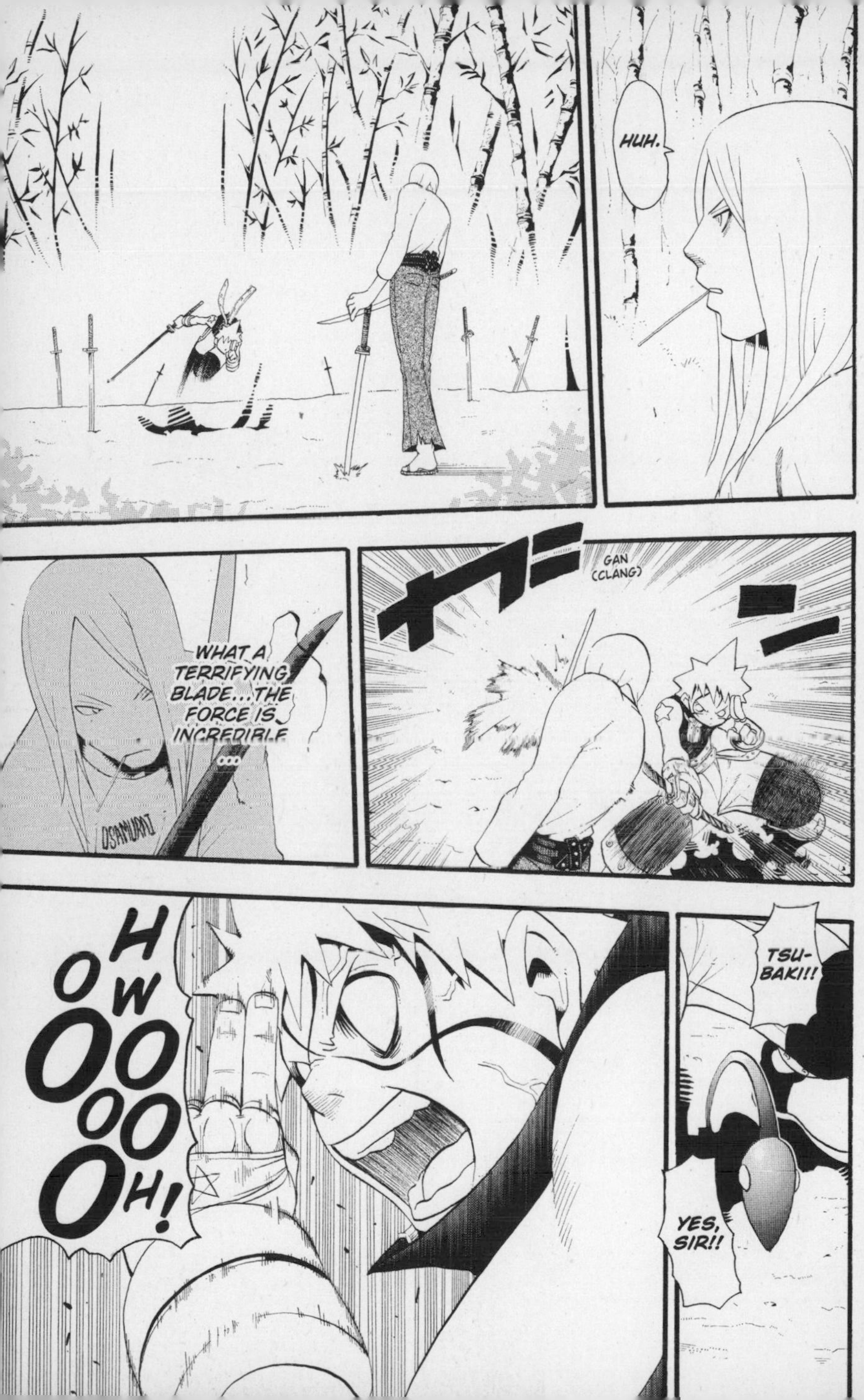
HUH.
GAN
(CLANG)
WHAT A TERRIFYING BLADE... THE FORCE IS INCREDIBLE ...
TSU-BAKI!!
YES, SIR!!
HOWOOOOOOH!

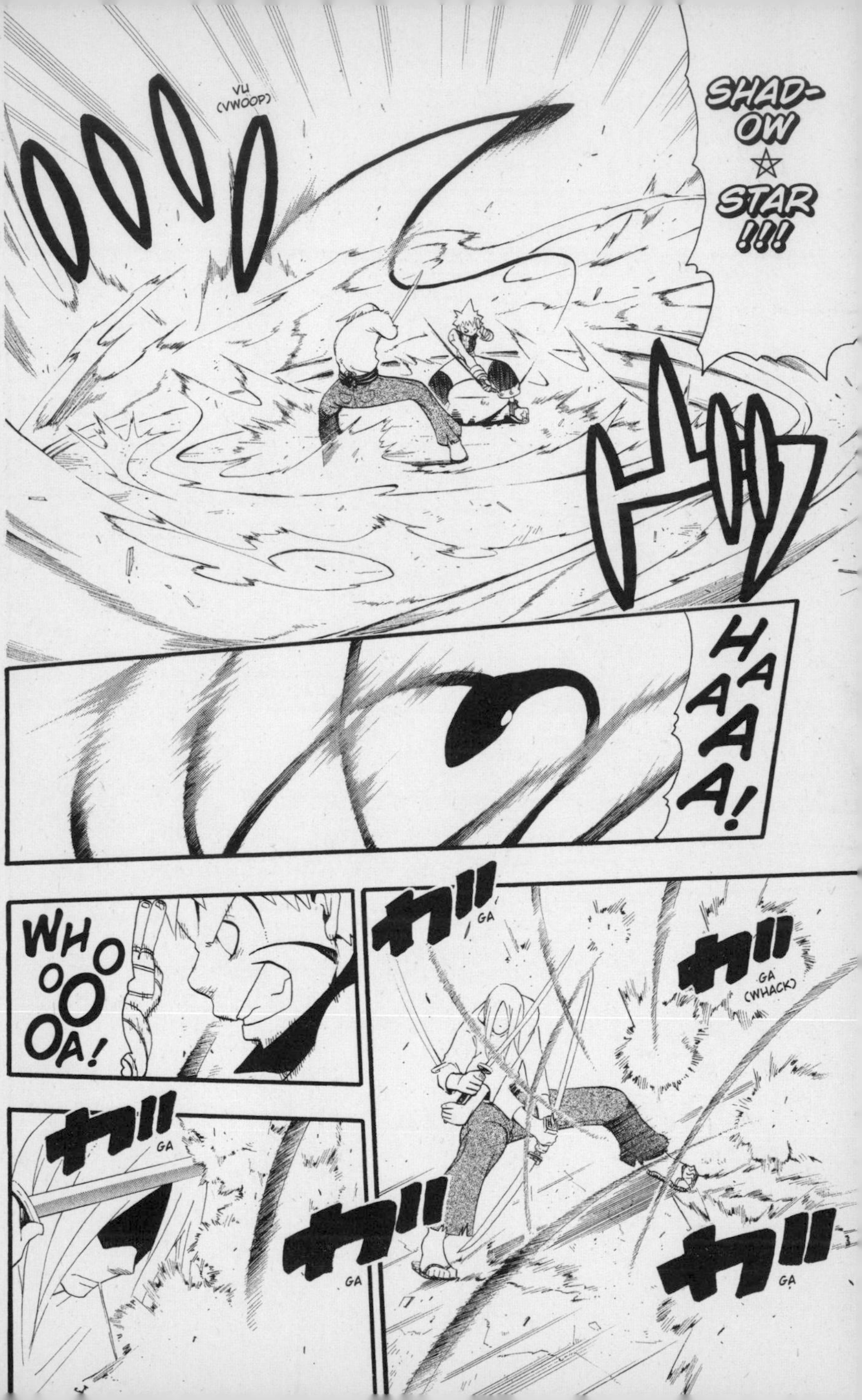
SHAD-OW ☆ STAR!!!
VU (VWOOP)
HAAAAA!
GA
GA (WHACK)
GA
GA
WHOOOOOA!
GA

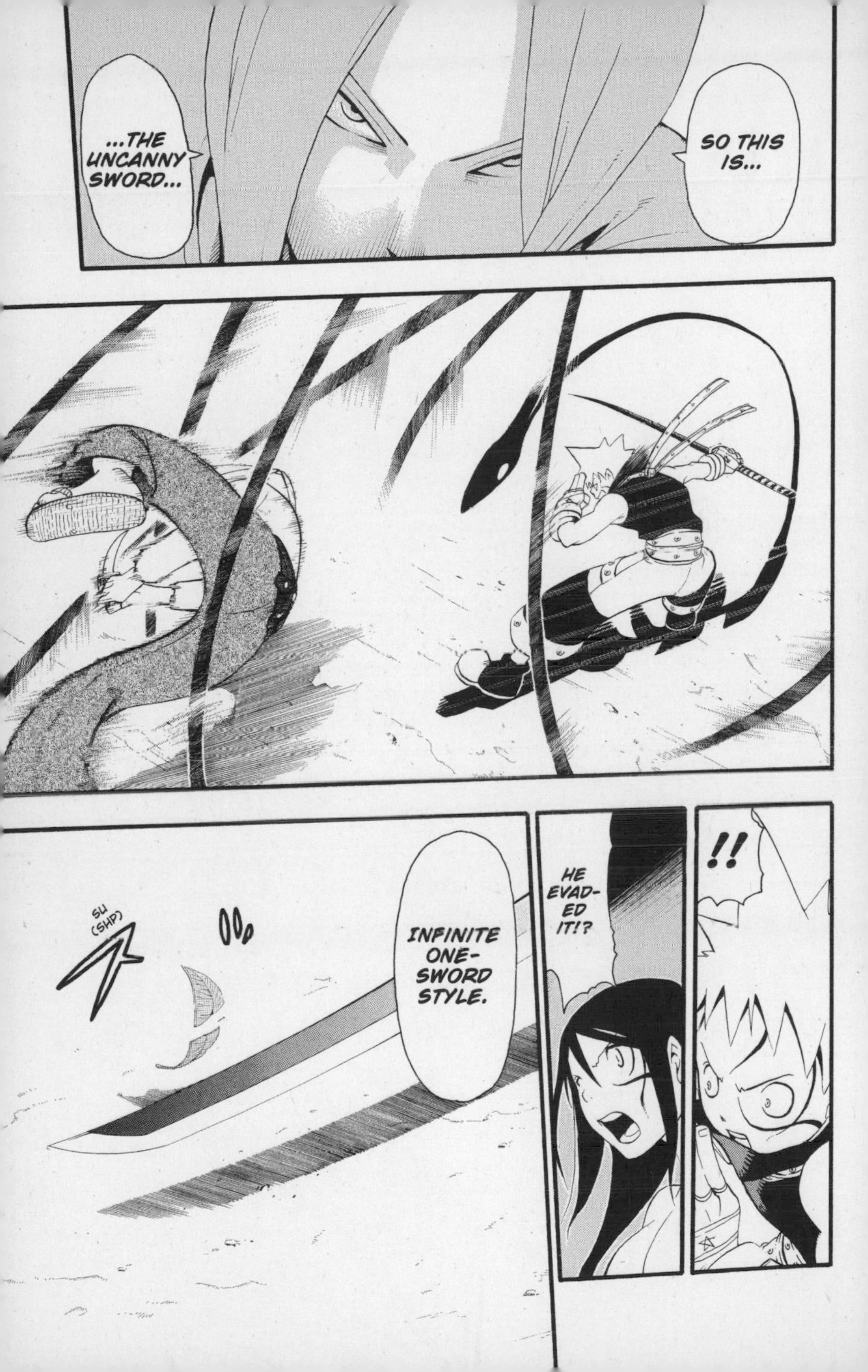
SO THIS IS...
...THE UNCANNY SWORD...
!!
HE EVAD-ED IT!?
INFINITE ONE-SWORD STYLE.
SU (SHP)

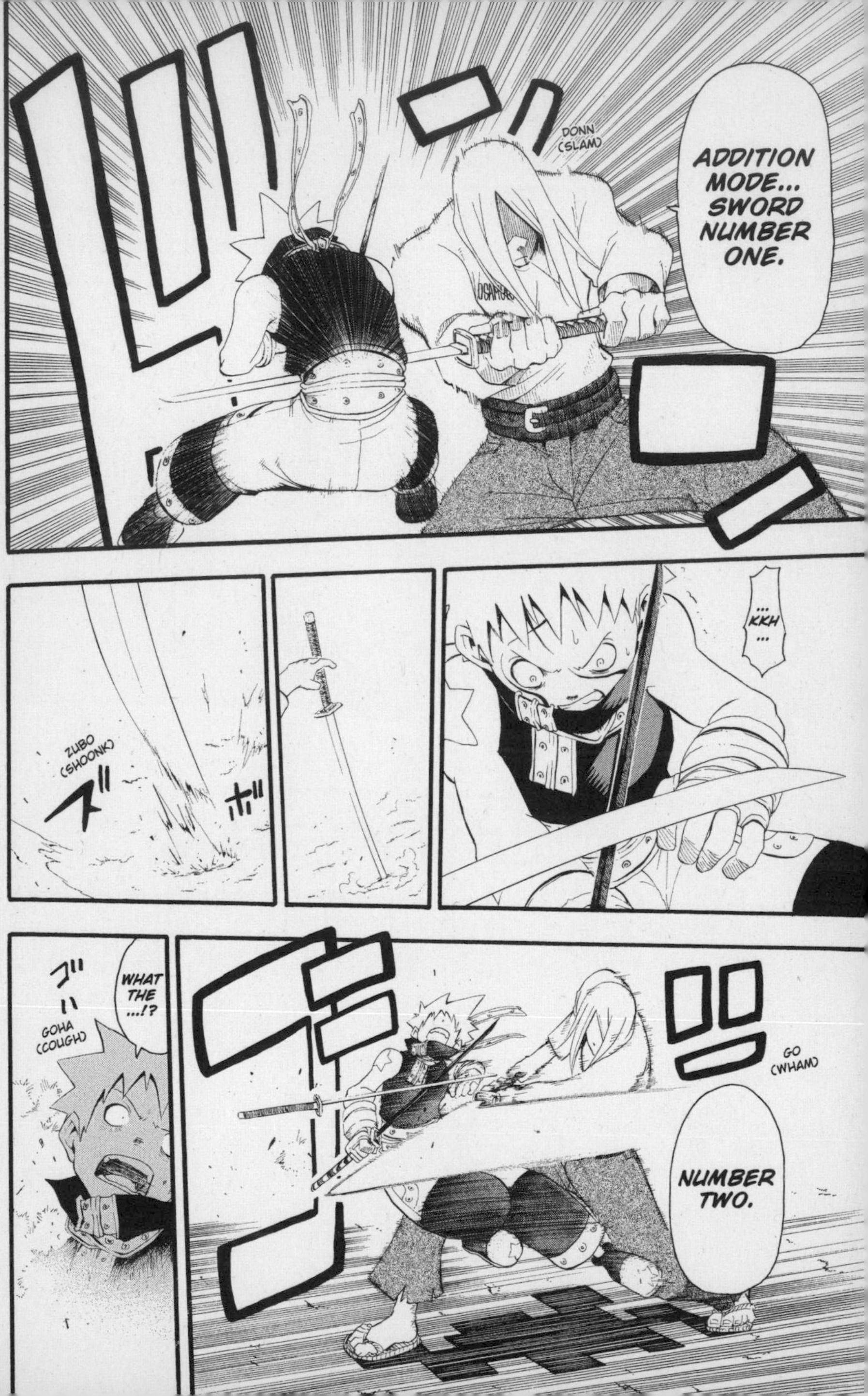
DONN (SLAM)
ADDITION MODE... SWORD NUMBER ONE.
...KKH...
ZUBO (SHOONK)
GO (WHAM)
NUMBER TWO.
WHAT THE ...!?
GOHA (COUGH)

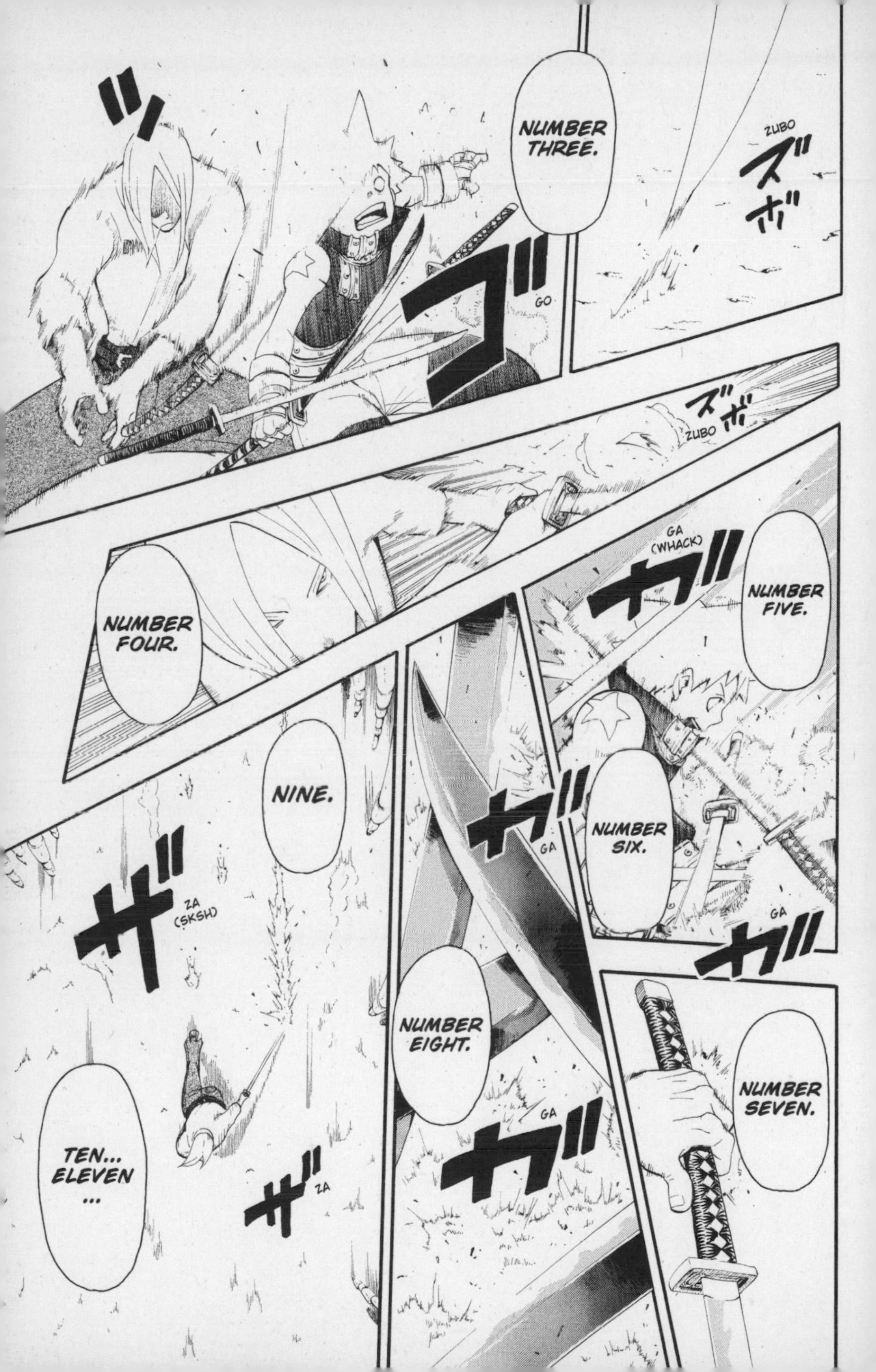
NUMBER THREE.
ズボ
ZUBO
ゴ
GO
ズボ
ZUBO
NUMBER FOUR.
ガ
GA (WHACK)
NUMBER FIVE.
ガ
GA
NUMBER SIX.
ガ
GA
NUMBER SEVEN.
NUMBER EIGHT.
ガ
GA
NINE.
ザ
ZA (SKSH)
TEN... ELEVEN ...
ザ
ZA

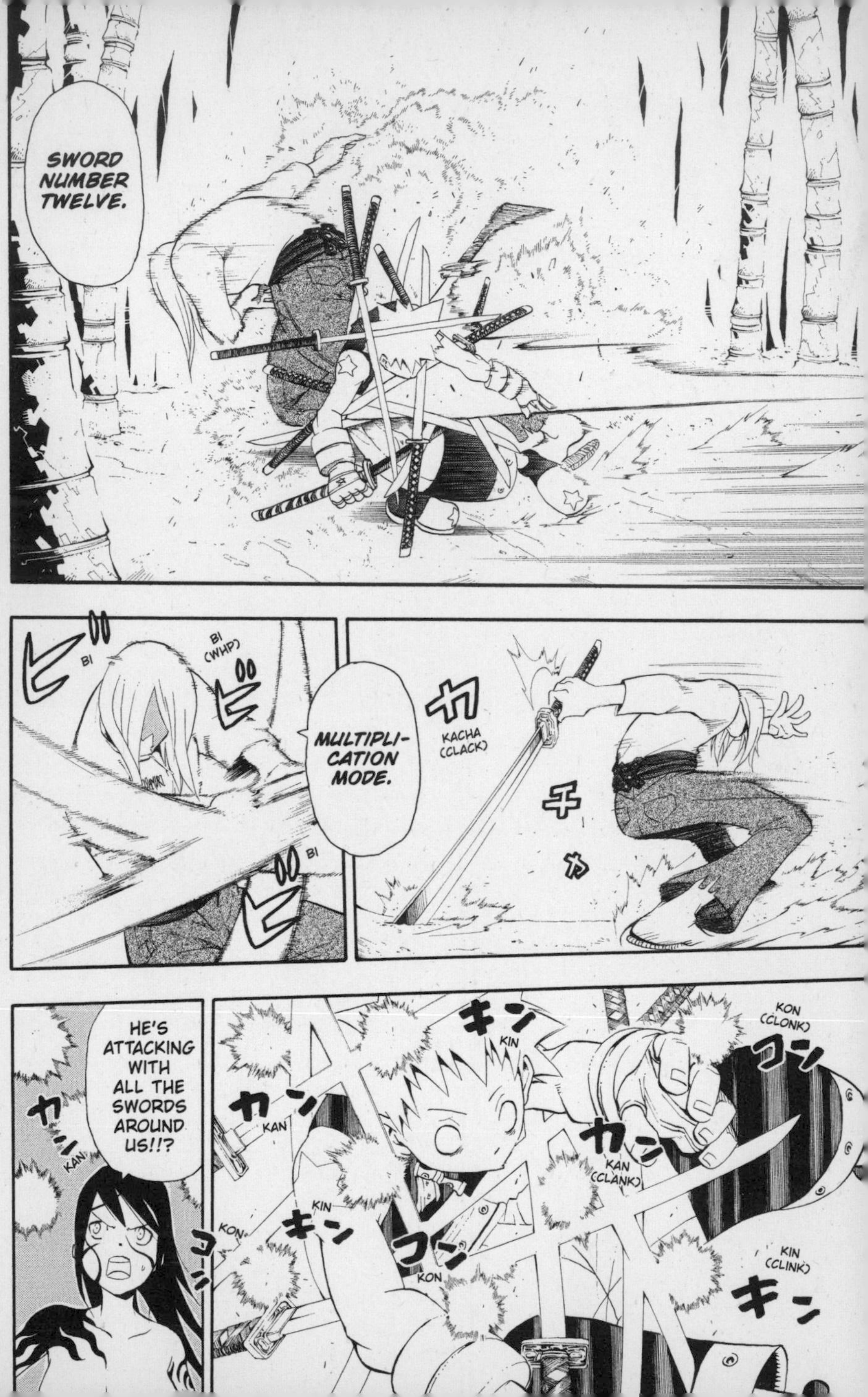
SWORD NUMBER TWELVE.
KACHA (CLACK)
MULTIPLICATION MODE.
BI (WHP)
BI
BI
KON (CLONK)
KIN
KAN
KAN (CLANK)
KIN (CLINK)
KIN
KON
KON
HE'S ATTACKING WITH ALL THE SWORDS AROUND US!!?
KAN

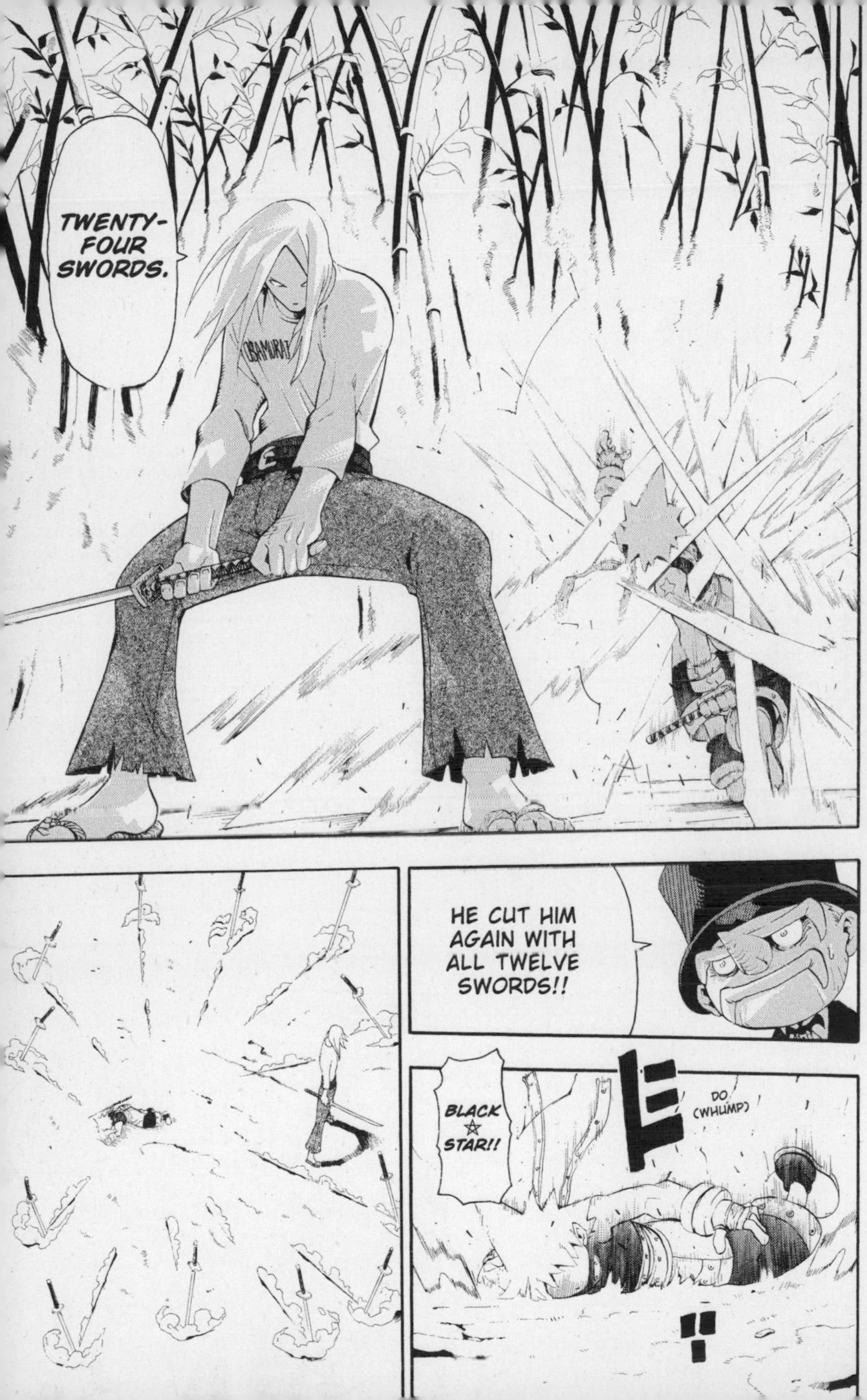
TWENTY-FOUR SWORDS.
HE CUT HIM AGAIN WITH ALL TWELVE SWORDS!!
BLACK☆STAR!!
DO (WHUMP)

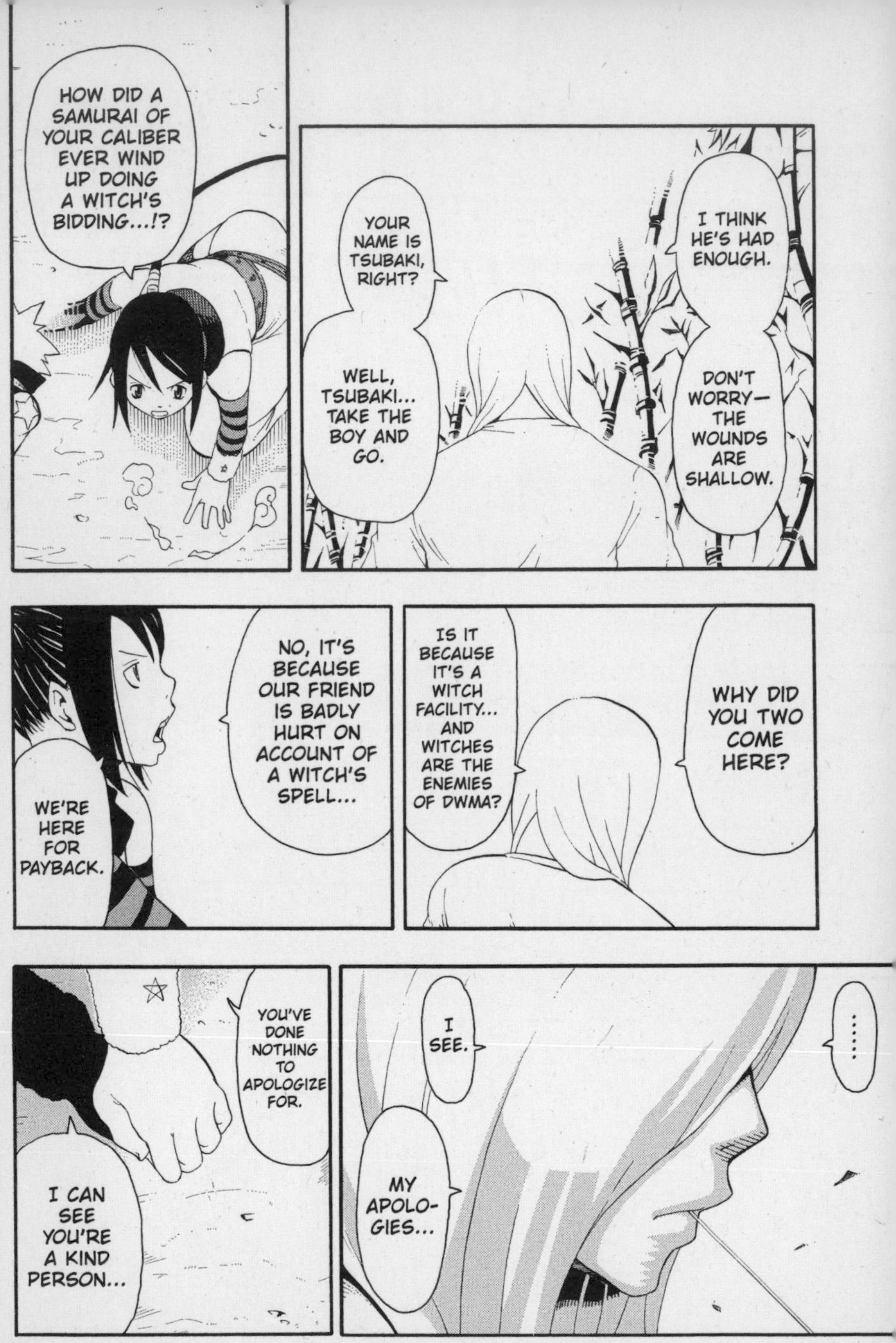
I THINK HE'S HAD ENOUGH.
DON'T WORRY— THE WOUNDS ARE SHALLOW.
YOUR NAME IS TSUBAKI, RIGHT?
WELL, TSUBAKI... TAKE THE BOY AND GO.
HOW DID A SAMURAI OF YOUR CALIBER EVER WIND UP DOING A WITCH'S BIDDING...!?
WHY DID YOU TWO COME HERE?
IS IT BECAUSE IT'S A WITCH FACILITY... AND WITCHES ARE THE ENEMIES OF DWMA?
NO, IT'S BECAUSE OUR FRIEND IS BADLY HURT ON ACCOUNT OF A WITCH'S SPELL...
WE'RE HERE FOR PAYBACK.
......
I SEE.
MY APOLOGIES...
YOU'VE DONE NOTHING TO APOLOGIZE FOR.
I CAN SEE YOU'RE A KIND PERSON...

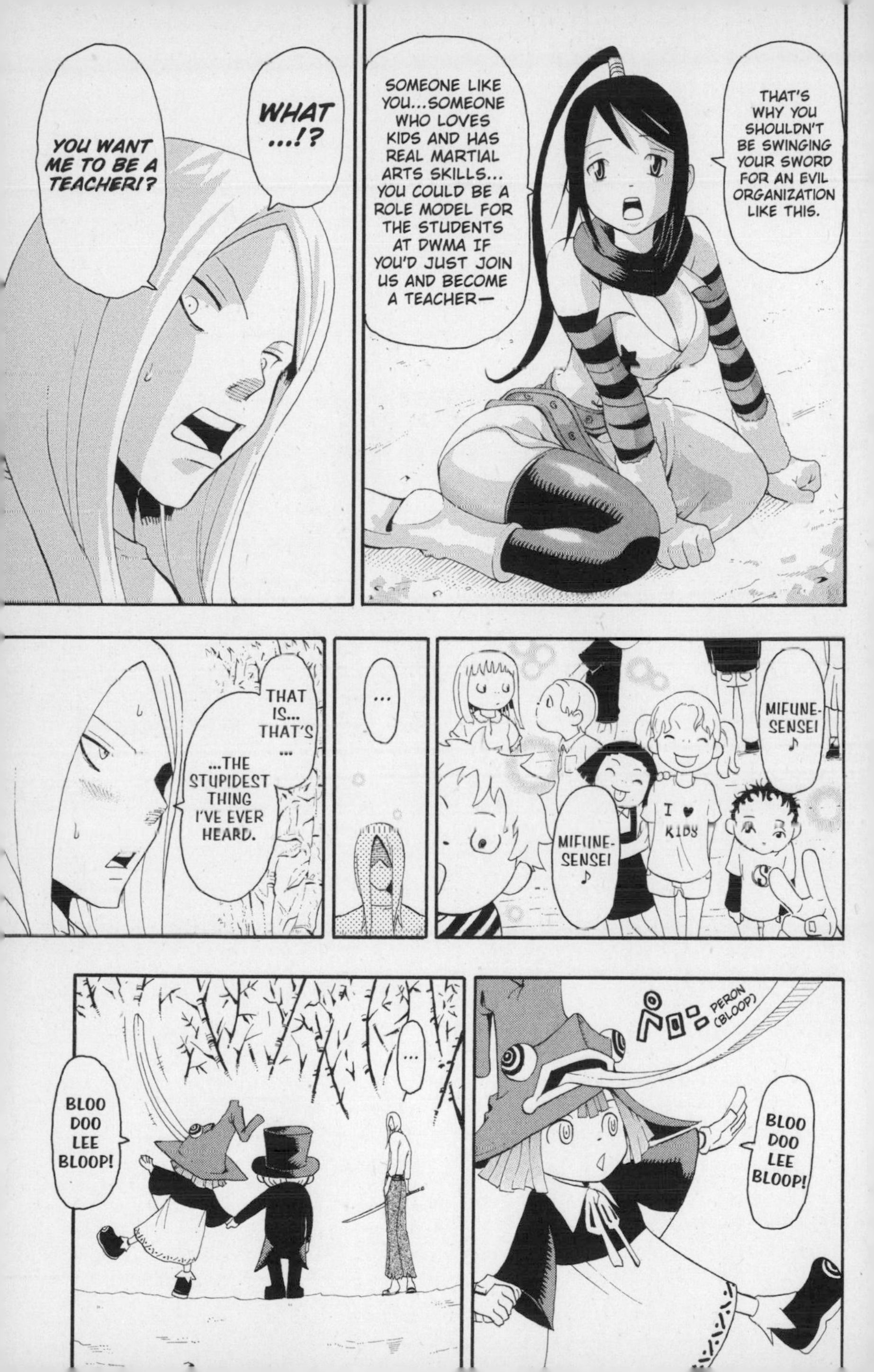
THAT'S WHY YOU SHOULDN'T BE SWINGING YOUR SWORD FOR AN EVIL ORGANIZATION LIKE THIS.
SOMEONE LIKE YOU...SOMEONE WHO LOVES KIDS AND HAS REAL MARTIAL ARTS SKILLS... YOU COULD BE A ROLE MODEL FOR THE STUDENTS AT DWMA IF YOU'D JUST JOIN US AND BECOME A TEACHER—
WHAT ...!?
YOU WANT ME TO BE A TEACHER!?
MIFUNE-SENSEI ♪
MIFUNE-SENSEI ♪
I ♥ KIDS
...
THAT IS... THAT'S ...
...THE STUPIDEST THING I'VE EVER HEARD.
PERON (BLOOP)
BLOO DOO LEE BLOOP!
...
BLOO DOO LEE BLOOP!

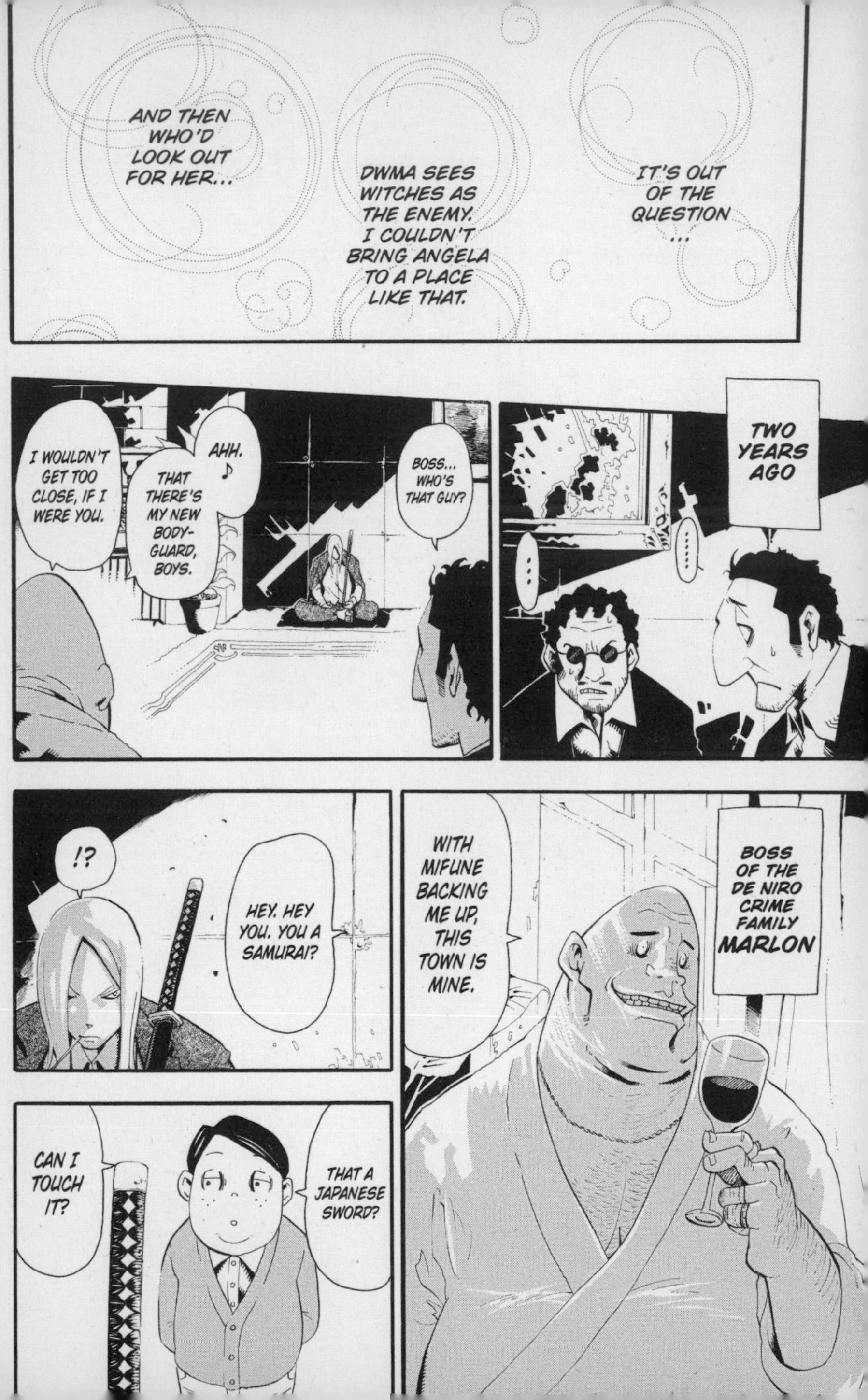
IT'S OUT OF THE QUESTION ...
DWMA SEES WITCHES AS THE ENEMY. I COULDN'T BRING ANGELA TO A PLACE LIKE THAT.
AND THEN WHO'D LOOK OUT FOR HER...
TWO YEARS AGO
......
...
BOSS... WHO'S THAT GUY?
AHH. ♪ THAT THERE'S MY NEW BODY-GUARD, BOYS.
I WOULDN'T GET TOO CLOSE, IF I WERE YOU.
BOSS OF THE DE NIRO CRIME FAMILY MARLON
WITH MIFUNE BACKING ME UP, THIS TOWN IS MINE.
HEY. HEY YOU. YOU A SAMURAI?
!?
THAT A JAPANESE SWORD?
CAN I TOUCH IT?

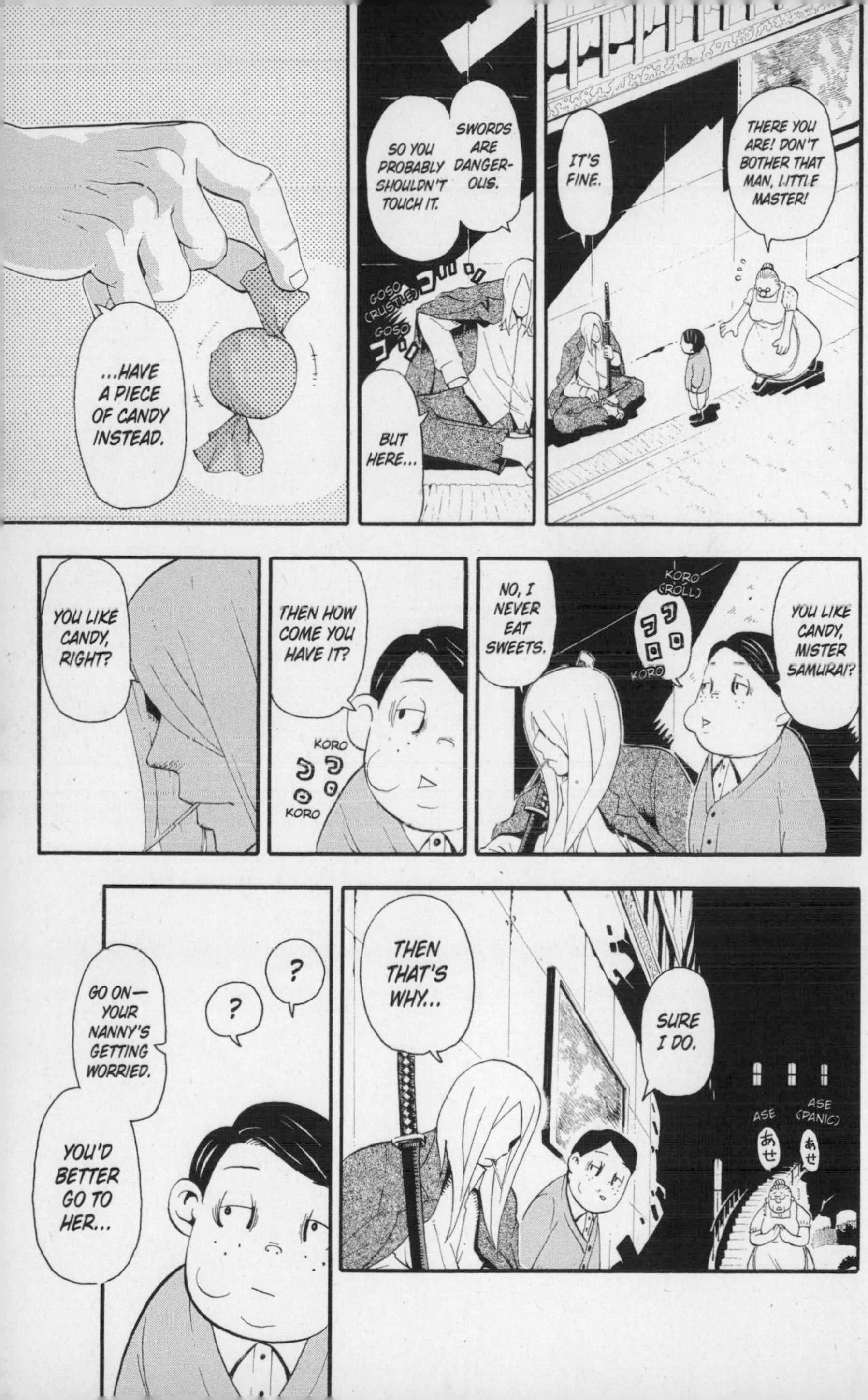
THERE YOU ARE! DON'T BOTHER THAT MAN, LITTLE MASTER!
IT'S FINE.
SWORDS ARE DANGER-OUS.
SO YOU PROBABLY SHOULDN'T TOUCH IT.
GOSO (RUSTLE) GOSO
BUT HERE...
...HAVE A PIECE OF CANDY INSTEAD.
YOU LIKE CANDY, MISTER SAMURAI?
KORO (ROLL) KORO
NO, I NEVER EAT SWEETS.
THEN HOW COME YOU HAVE IT?
KORO KORO
YOU LIKE CANDY, RIGHT?
SURE I DO.
ASE (PANIC) あせ
ASE あせ
THEN THAT'S WHY...
?
?
GO ON— YOUR NANNY'S GETTING WORRIED.
YOU'D BETTER GO TO HER...

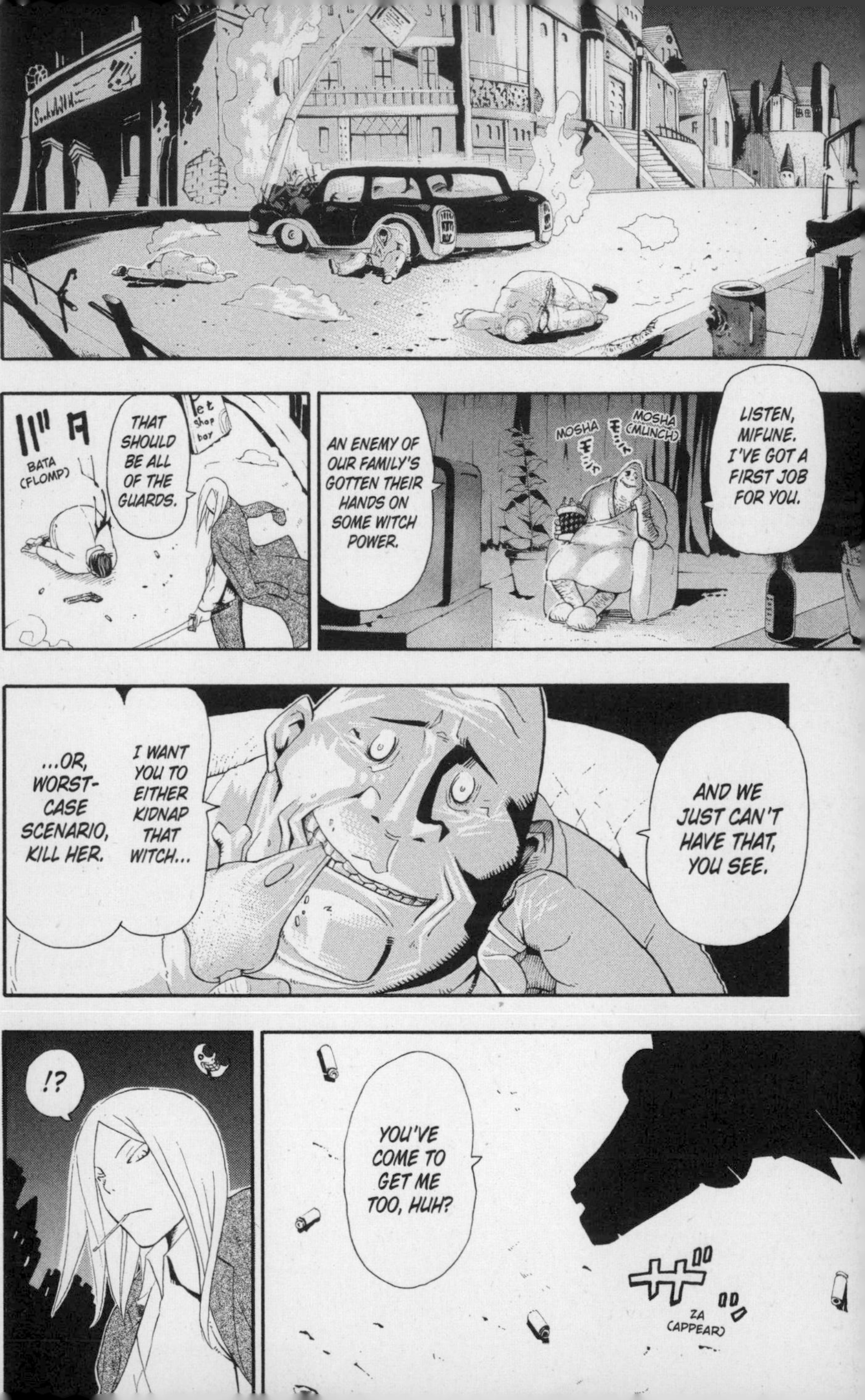
LISTEN, MIFUNE. I'VE GOT A FIRST JOB FOR YOU.
MOSHA (MUNCH)
MOSHA
AN ENEMY OF OUR FAMILY'S GOTTEN THEIR HANDS ON SOME WITCH POWER.
Pet shop boy
THAT SHOULD BE ALL OF THE GUARDS.
BATA (FLOMP)
AND WE JUST CAN'T HAVE THAT, YOU SEE.
I WANT YOU TO EITHER KIDNAP THAT WITCH...
...OR, WORST-CASE SCENARIO, KILL HER.
YOU'VE COME TO GET ME TOO, HUH?
ZA (APPEAR)
!?

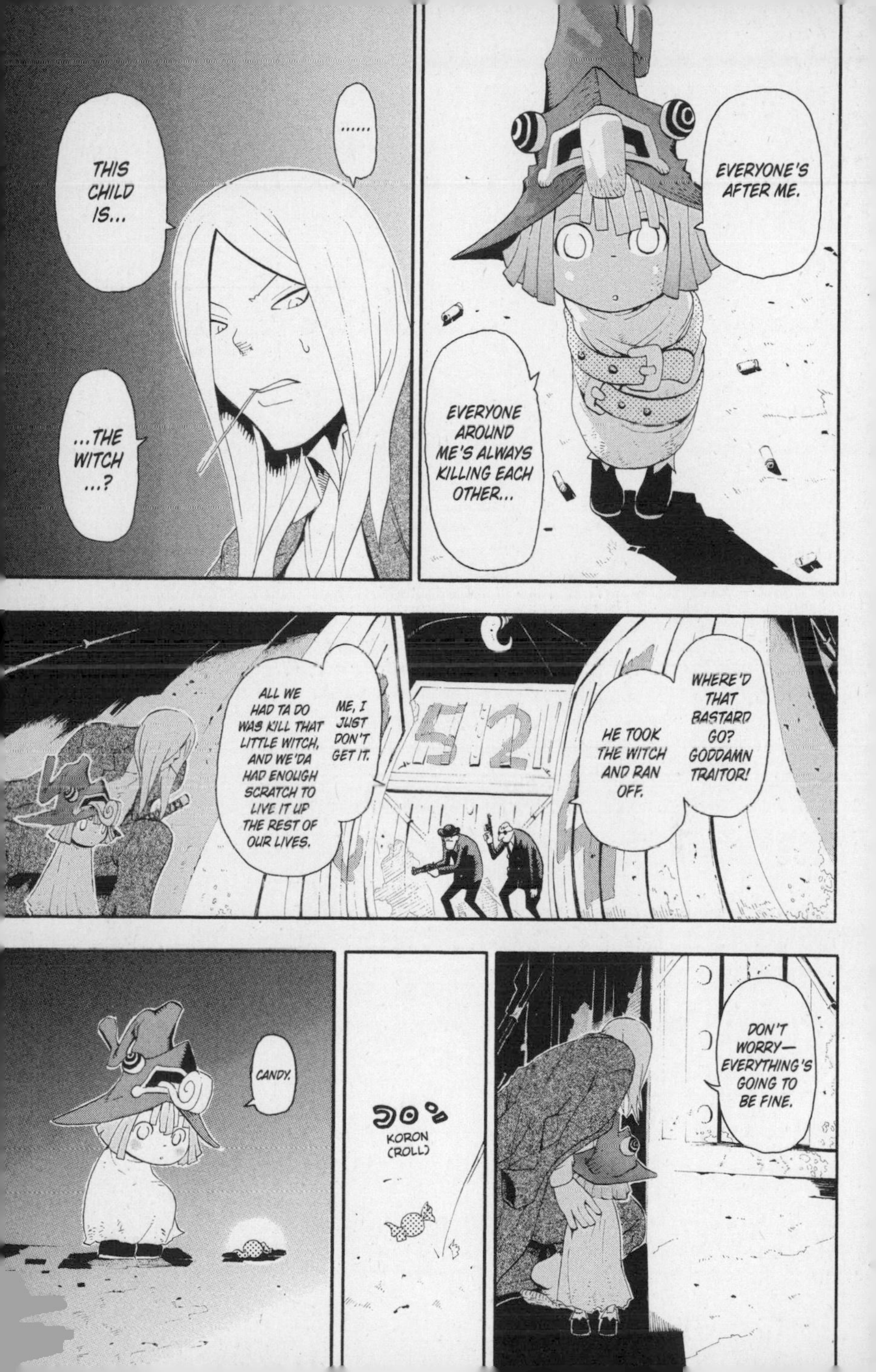
EVERYONE'S AFTER ME.
EVERYONE AROUND ME'S ALWAYS KILLING EACH OTHER...
......
THIS CHILD IS...
...THE WITCH ...?
WHERE'D THAT BASTARD GO? GODDAMN TRAITOR!
HE TOOK THE WITCH AND RAN OFF.
ME, I JUST DON'T GET IT.
ALL WE HAD TA DO WAS KILL THAT LITTLE WITCH, AND WE'DA HAD ENOUGH SCRATCH TO LIVE IT UP THE REST OF OUR LIVES.
52
DON'T WORRY— EVERYTHING'S GOING TO BE FINE.
KORON (ROLL)
CANDY.

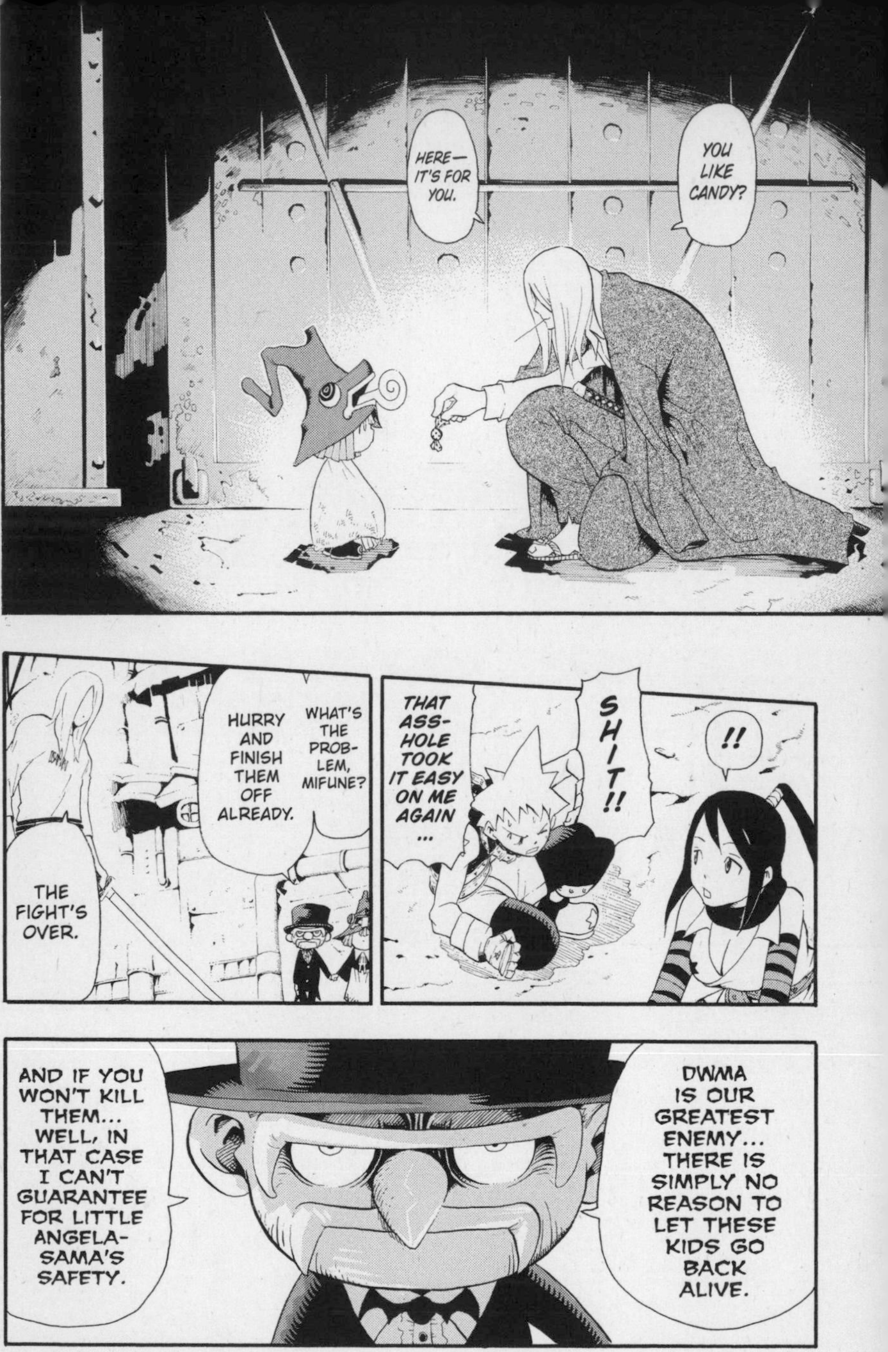
YOU LIKE CANDY?
HERE— IT'S FOR YOU.
!!
SHIT!!
THAT ASS-HOLE TOOK IT EASY ON ME AGAIN ...
WHAT'S THE PROB-LEM, MIFUNE?
HURRY AND FINISH THEM OFF ALREADY.
THE FIGHT'S OVER.
DWMA IS OUR GREATEST ENEMY... THERE IS SIMPLY NO REASON TO LET THESE KIDS GO BACK ALIVE.
AND IF YOU WON'T KILL THEM... WELL, IN THAT CASE I CAN'T GUARANTEE FOR LITTLE ANGELA-SAMA'S SAFETY.

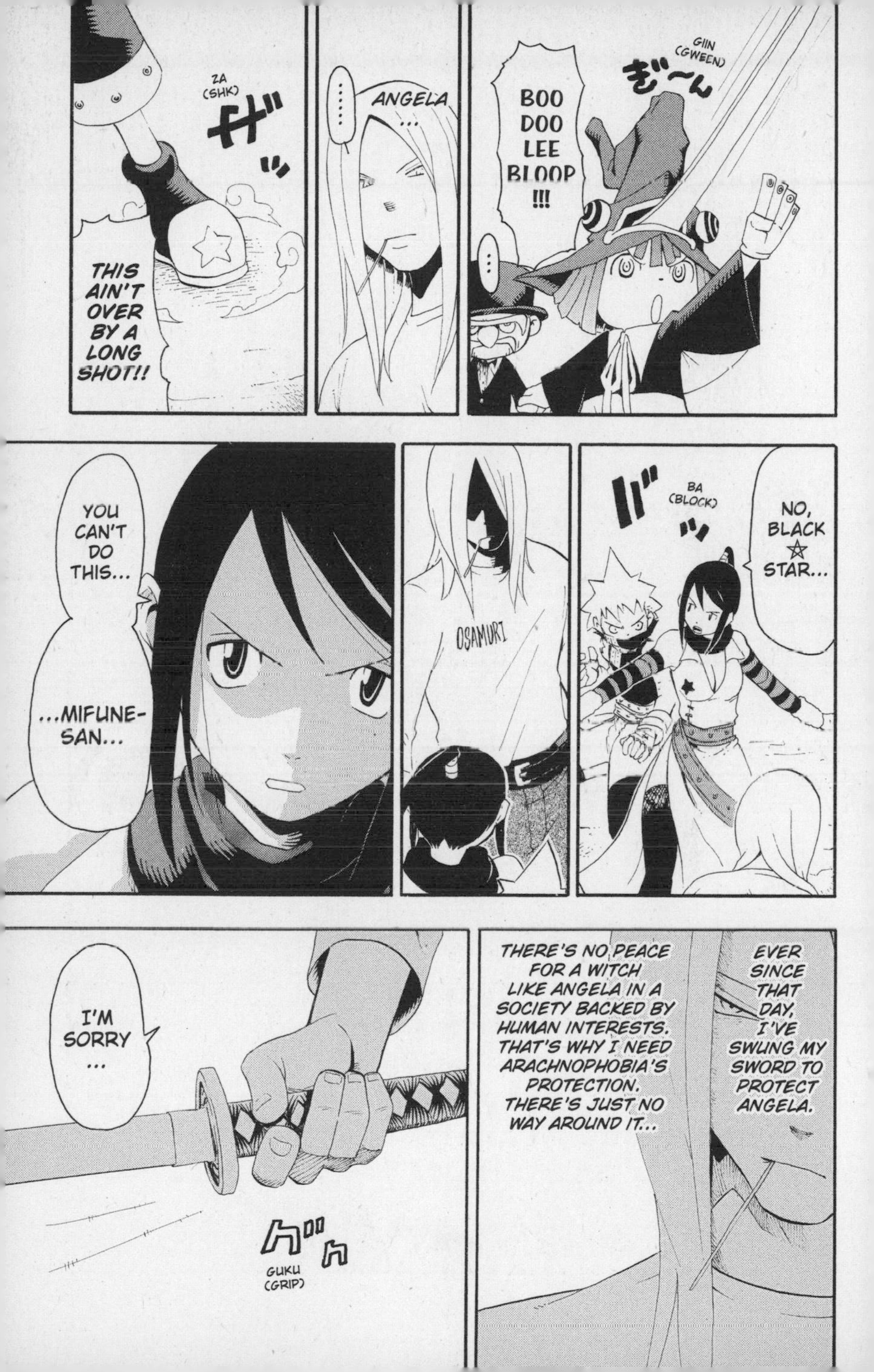
GIIN (GWEEN)
BOO DOO LEE BLOOP!!!
...
......
ANGELA ...
ZA (SHK)
THIS AIN'T OVER BY A LONG SHOT!!
BA (BLOCK)
NO, BLACK☆STAR...
OSAMURI
YOU CAN'T DO THIS...
...MIFUNE-SAN...
EVER SINCE THAT DAY, I'VE SWUNG MY SWORD TO PROTECT ANGELA.
THERE'S NO PEACE FOR A WITCH LIKE ANGELA IN A SOCIETY BACKED BY HUMAN INTERESTS. THAT'S WHY I NEED ARACHNOPHOBIA'S PROTECTION. THERE'S JUST NO WAY AROUND IT...
I'M SORRY ...
GUKU (GRIP)

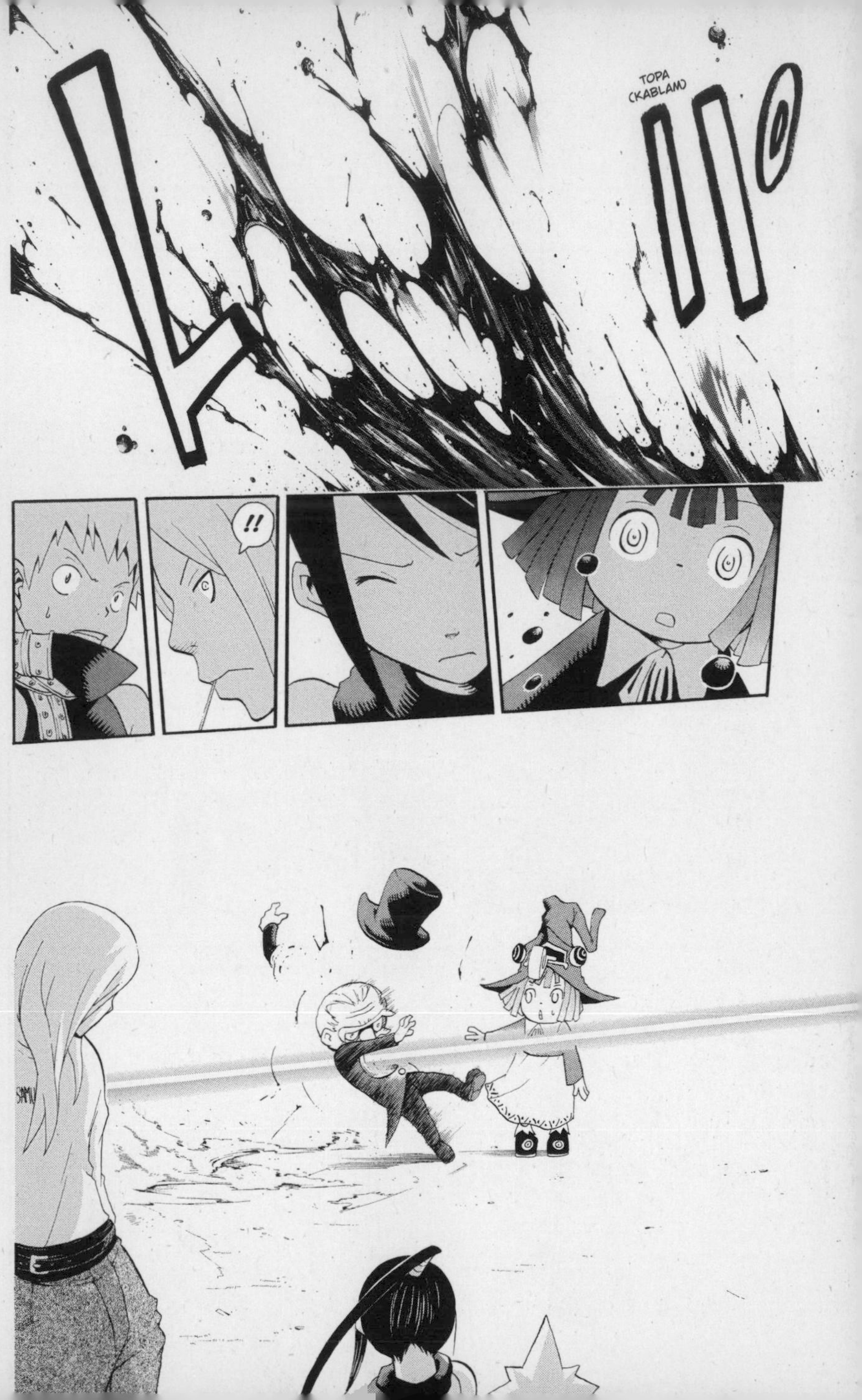
TOPA
(KABLAM)
!!

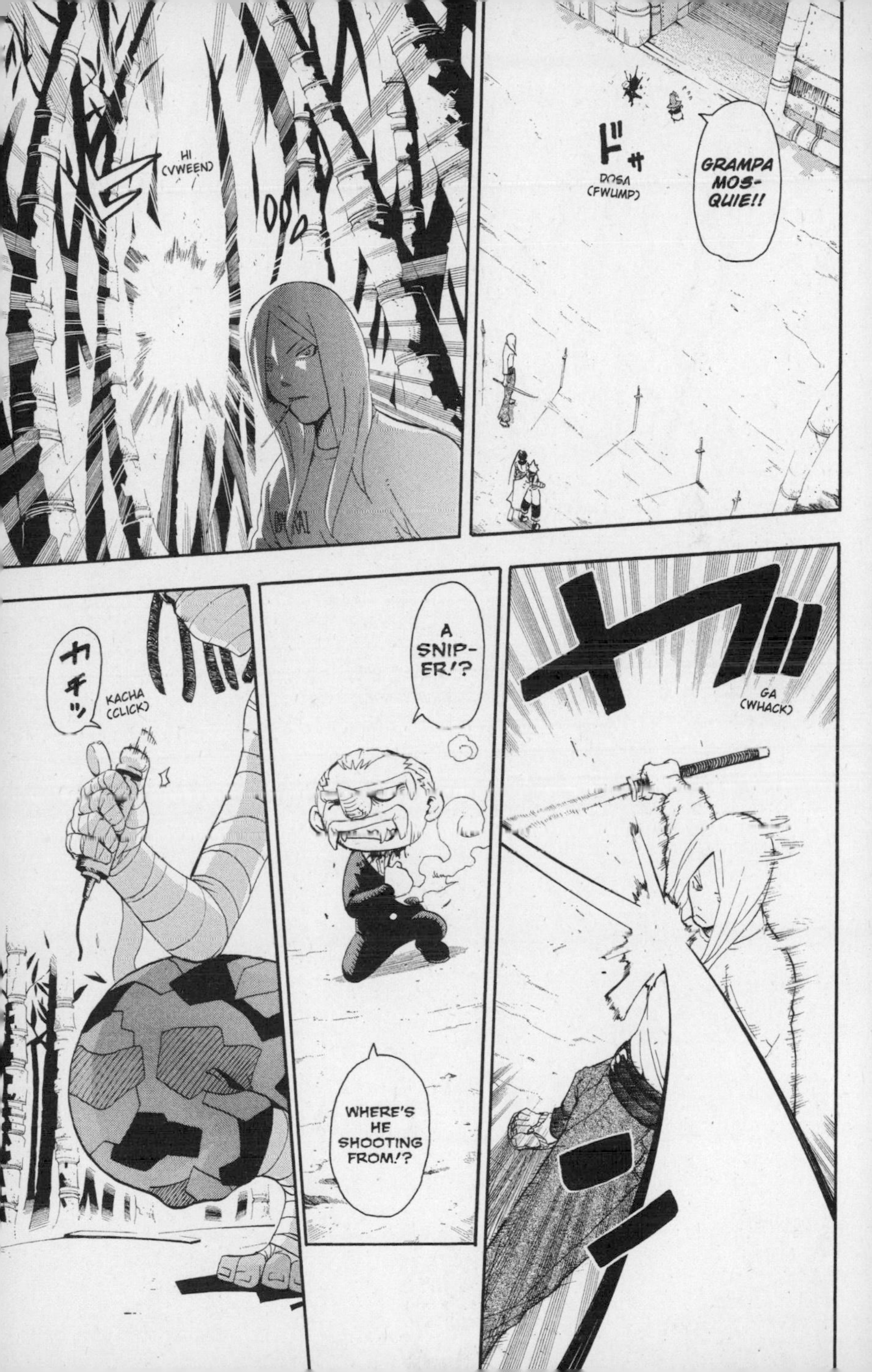
GRAMPA MOSQUIE!!
ドサ
DOSA (FWUMP)
HI (VWEEN)
GA (WHACK)
A SNIPER!?
WHERE'S HE SHOOTING FROM!?
カチッ
KACHA (CLICK)

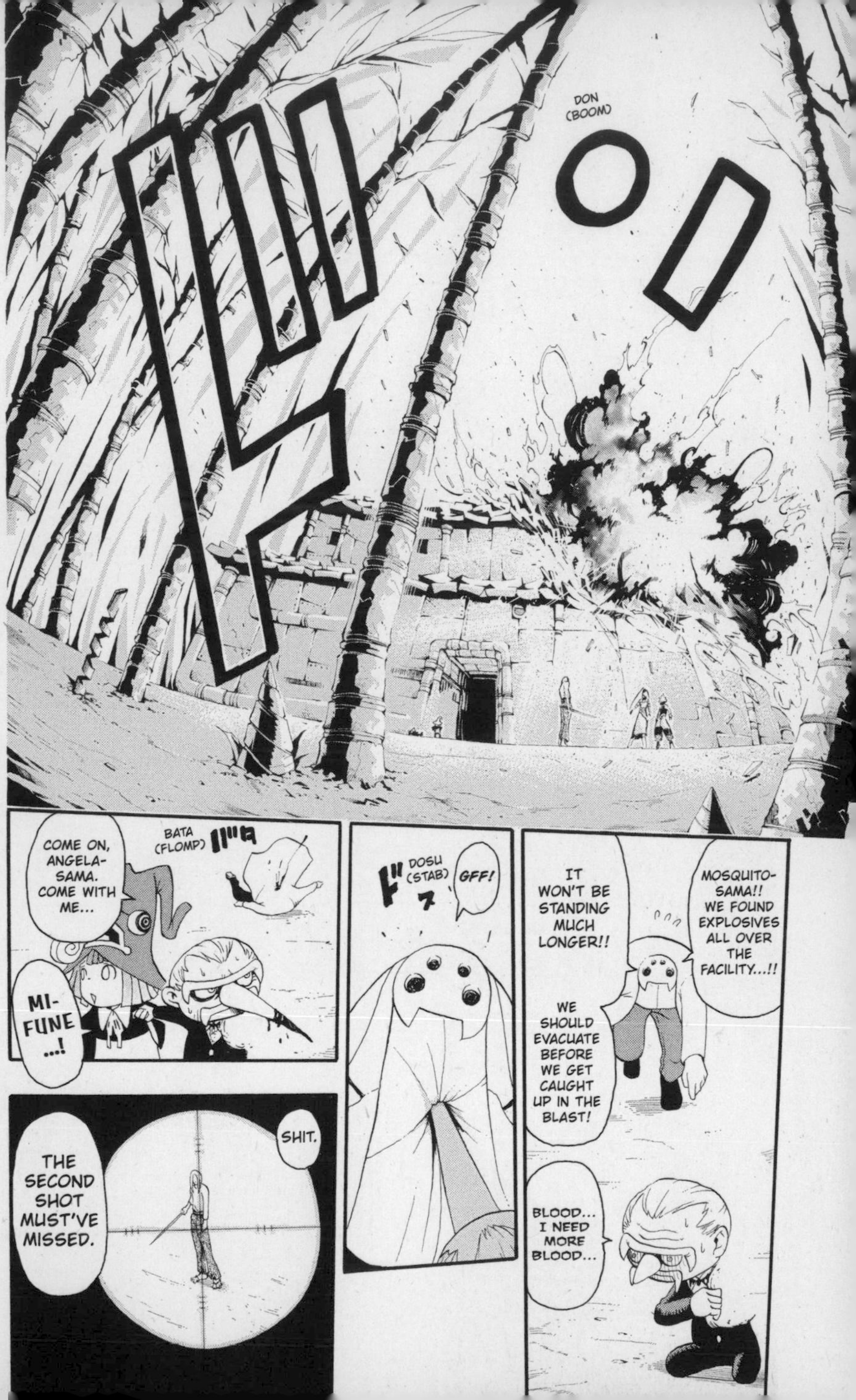
DON (BOOM)
MOSQUITO-SAMA!! WE FOUND EXPLOSIVES ALL OVER THE FACILITY...!!
IT WON'T BE STANDING MUCH LONGER!!
WE SHOULD EVACUATE BEFORE WE GET CAUGHT UP IN THE BLAST!
BLOOD... I NEED MORE BLOOD...
DOSU (STAB)
GFF!
BATA (FLOMP)
COME ON, ANGELA-SAMA. COME WITH ME...
MI-FUNE...!
SHIT.
THE SECOND SHOT MUST'VE MISSED.

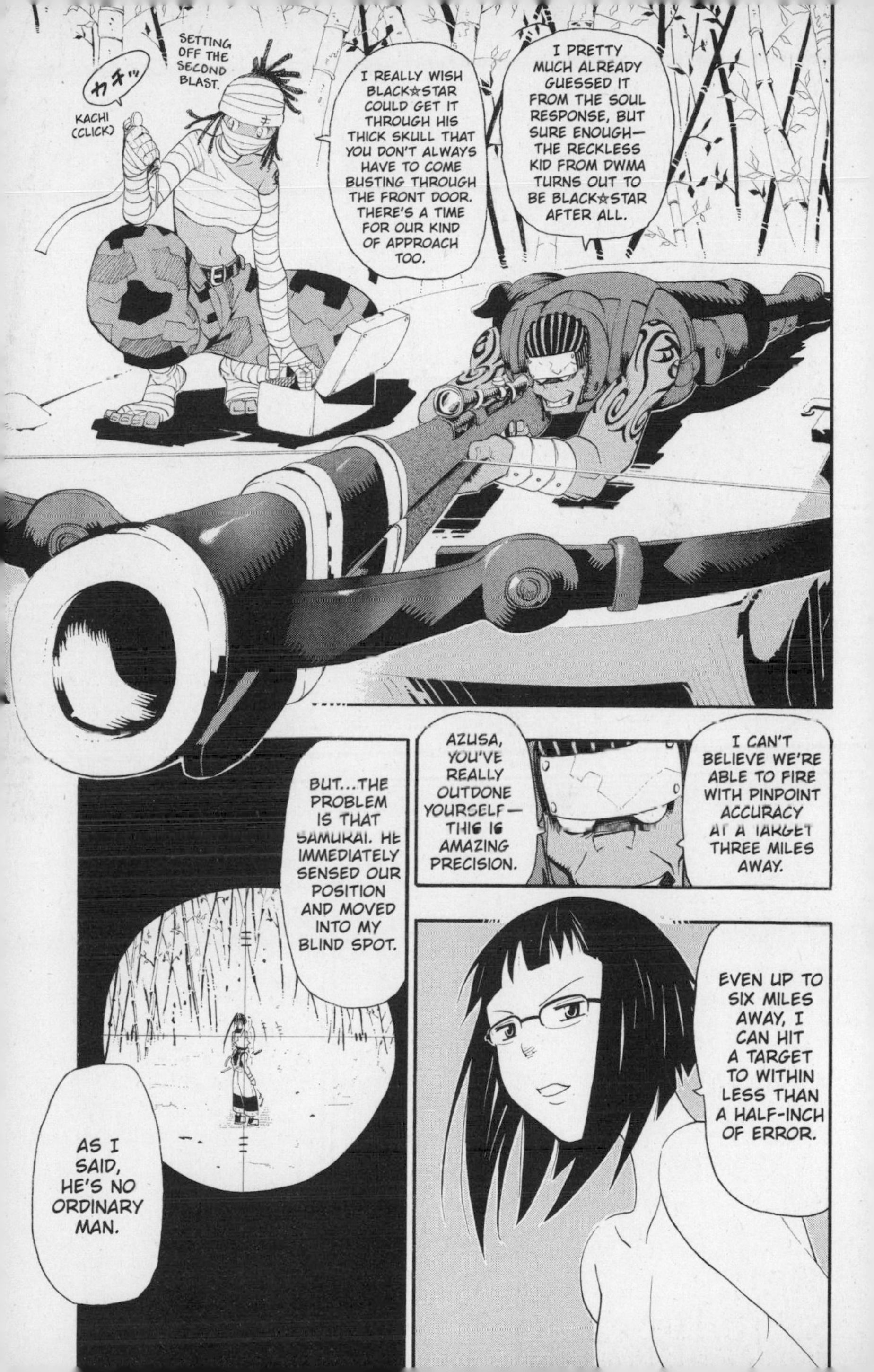

I PRETTY MUCH ALREADY GUESSED IT FROM THE SOUL RESPONSE, BUT SURE ENOUGH—THE RECKLESS KID FROM DWMA TURNS OUT TO BE BLACK☆STAR AFTER ALL.
I REALLY WISH BLACK☆STAR COULD GET IT THROUGH HIS THICK SKULL THAT YOU DON'T ALWAYS HAVE TO COME BUSTING THROUGH THE FRONT DOOR. THERE'S A TIME FOR OUR KIND OF APPROACH TOO.
SETTING OFF THE SECOND BLAST.
カチッ
KACHI (CLICK)
I CAN'T BELIEVE WE'RE ABLE TO FIRE WITH PINPOINT ACCURACY AT A TARGET THREE MILES AWAY.
AZUSA, YOU'VE REALLY OUTDONE YOURSELF—THIS IS AMAZING PRECISION.
EVEN UP TO SIX MILES AWAY, I CAN HIT A TARGET TO WITHIN LESS THAN A HALF-INCH OF ERROR.
BUT...THE PROBLEM IS THAT SAMURAI. HE IMMEDIATELY SENSED OUR POSITION AND MOVED INTO MY BLIND SPOT.
AS I SAID, HE'S NO ORDINARY MAN.

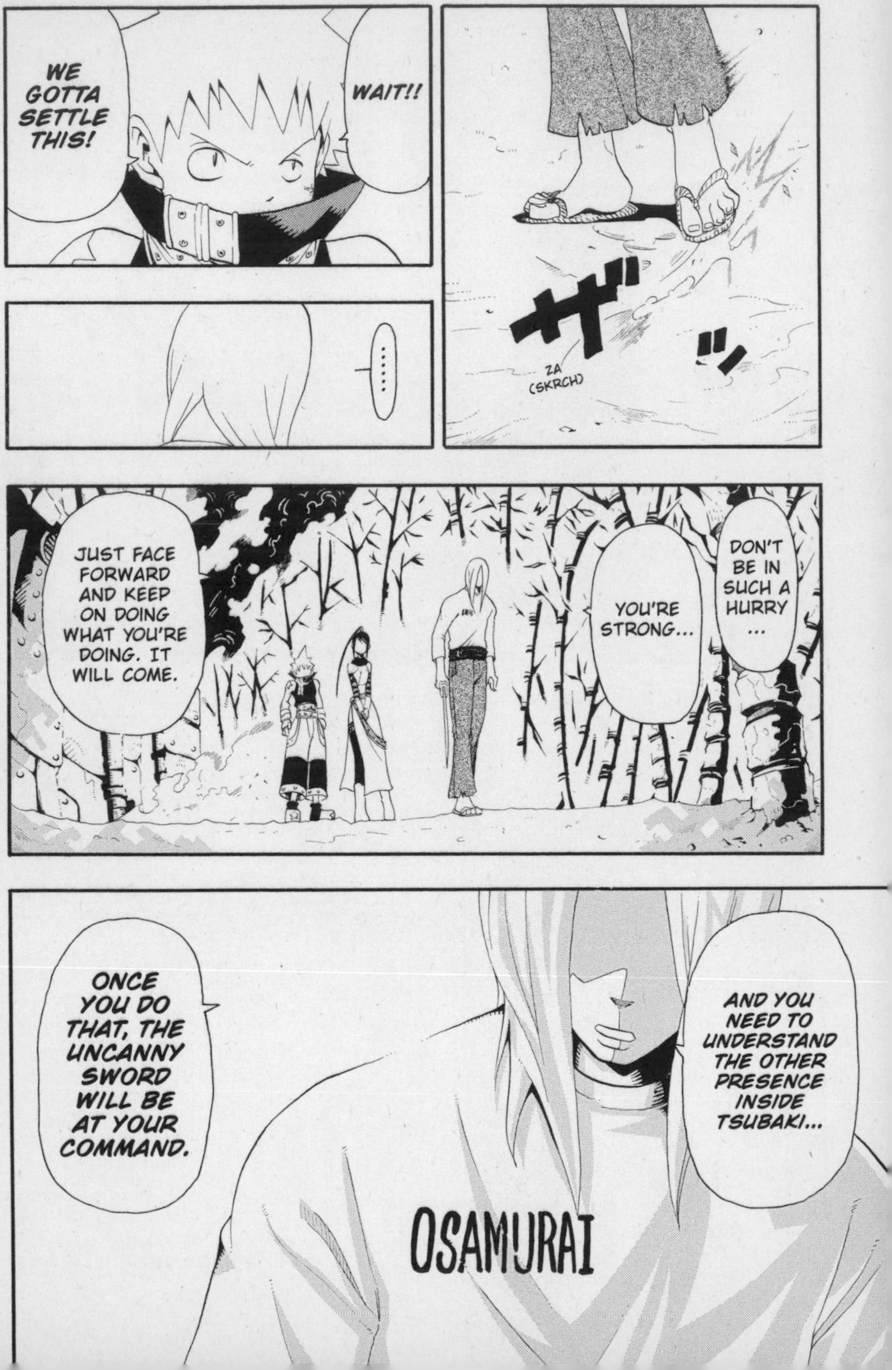
ZA (SKRCH)
WAIT!!
WE GOTTA SETTLE THIS!
......
DON'T BE IN SUCH A HURRY...
YOU'RE STRONG...
JUST FACE FORWARD AND KEEP ON DOING WHAT YOU'RE DOING. IT WILL COME.
AND YOU NEED TO UNDERSTAND THE OTHER PRESENCE INSIDE TSUBAKI...
ONCE YOU DO THAT, THE UNCANNY SWORD WILL BE AT YOUR COMMAND.
OSAMURAI

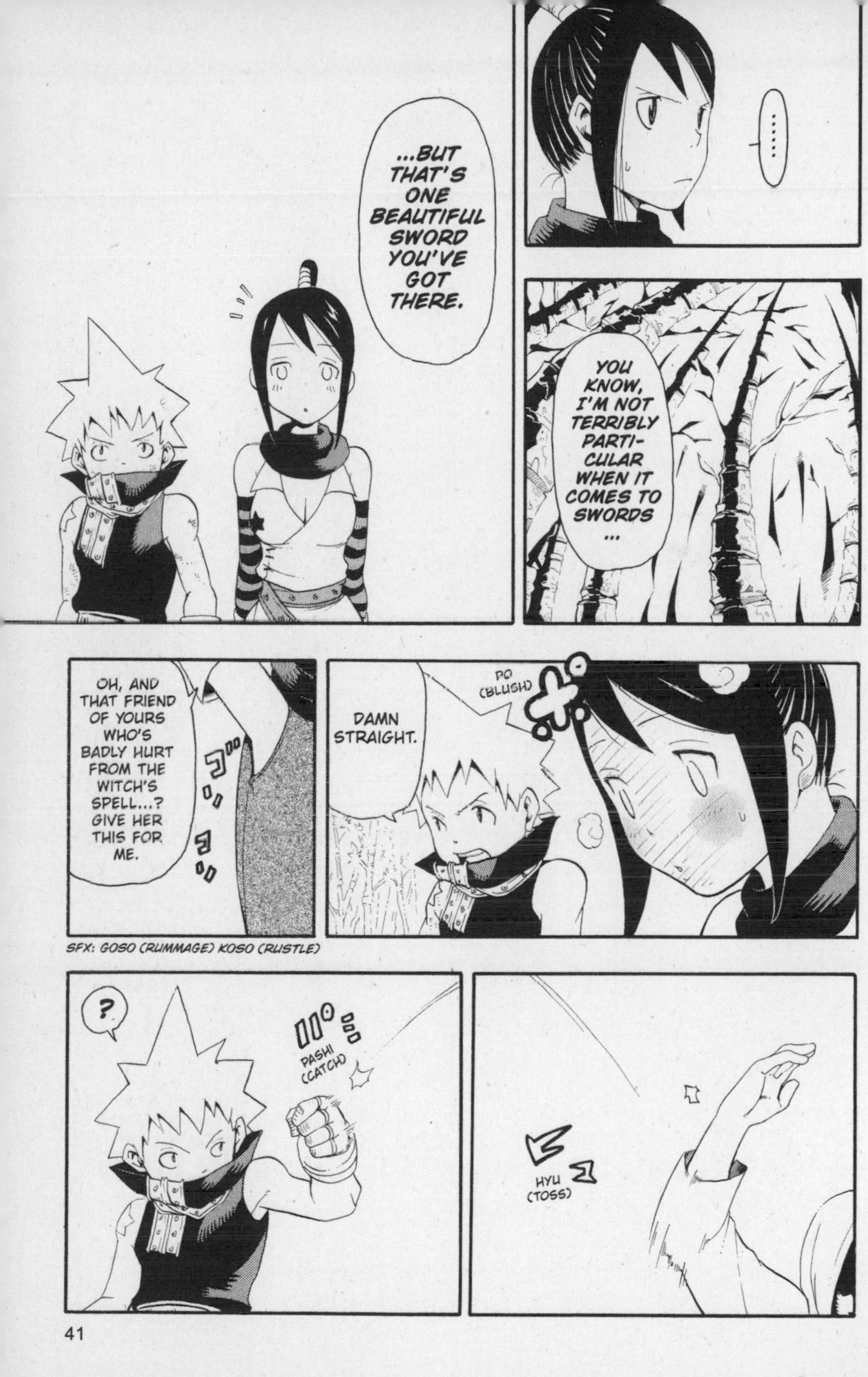
……
YOU KNOW, I'M NOT TERRIBLY PARTI-CULAR WHEN IT COMES TO SWORDS …
…BUT THAT'S ONE BEAUTIFUL SWORD YOU'VE GOT THERE.
PO (BLUSH)
DAMN STRAIGHT.
OH, AND THAT FRIEND OF YOURS WHO'S BADLY HURT FROM THE WITCH'S SPELL…? GIVE HER THIS FOR ME.
SFX: GOSO (RUMMAGE) KOSO (RUSTLE)
HYU (TOSS)
?
PASHI (CATCH)

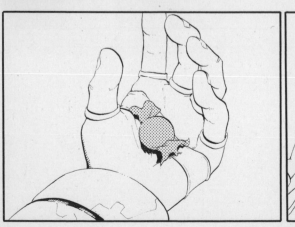

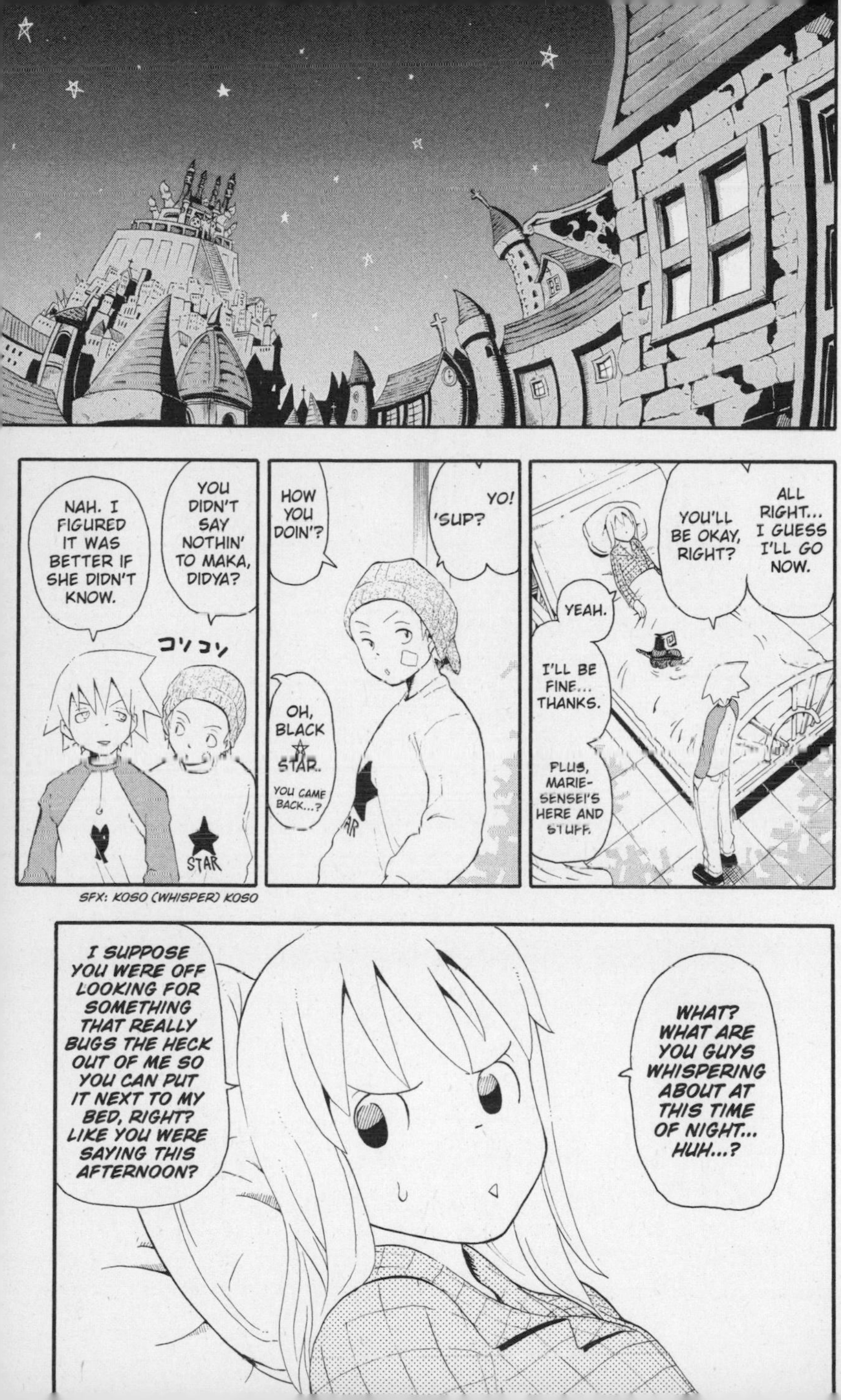
ALL RIGHT... I GUESS I'LL GO NOW.
YOU'LL BE OKAY, RIGHT?
YEAH.
I'LL BE FINE... THANKS.
PLUS, MARIE-SENSEI'S HERE AND STUFF.
YO! 'SUP?
HOW YOU DOIN'?
OH, BLACK STAR.. YOU CAME BACK...?
YOU DIDN'T SAY NOTHIN' TO MAKA, DIDYA?
NAH. I FIGURED IT WAS BETTER IF SHE DIDN'T KNOW.
コソコソ
SFX: KOSO (WHISPER) KOSO
WHAT? WHAT ARE YOU GUYS WHISPERING ABOUT AT THIS TIME OF NIGHT... HUH...?
I SUPPOSE YOU WERE OFF LOOKING FOR SOMETHING THAT REALLY BUGS THE HECK OUT OF ME SO YOU CAN PUT IT NEXT TO MY BED, RIGHT? LIKE YOU WERE SAYING THIS AFTERNOON?

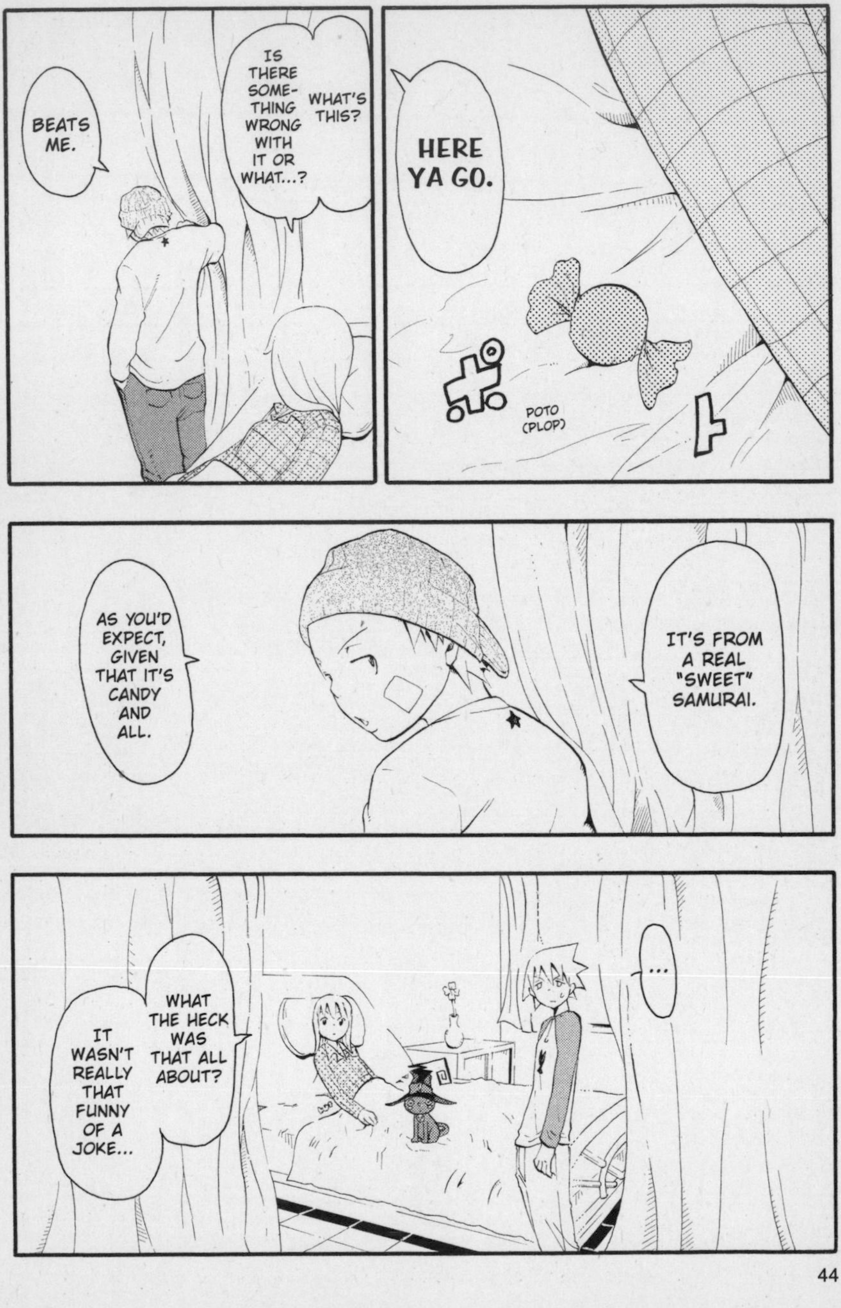
HERE YA GO.
POTO (PLOP)
WHAT'S THIS?
IS THERE SOMETHING WRONG WITH IT OR WHAT...?
BEATS ME.
IT'S FROM A REAL "SWEET" SAMURAI.
AS YOU'D EXPECT, GIVEN THAT IT'S CANDY AND ALL.
...
WHAT THE HECK WAS THAT ALL ABOUT?
IT WASN'T REALLY THAT FUNNY OF A JOKE...

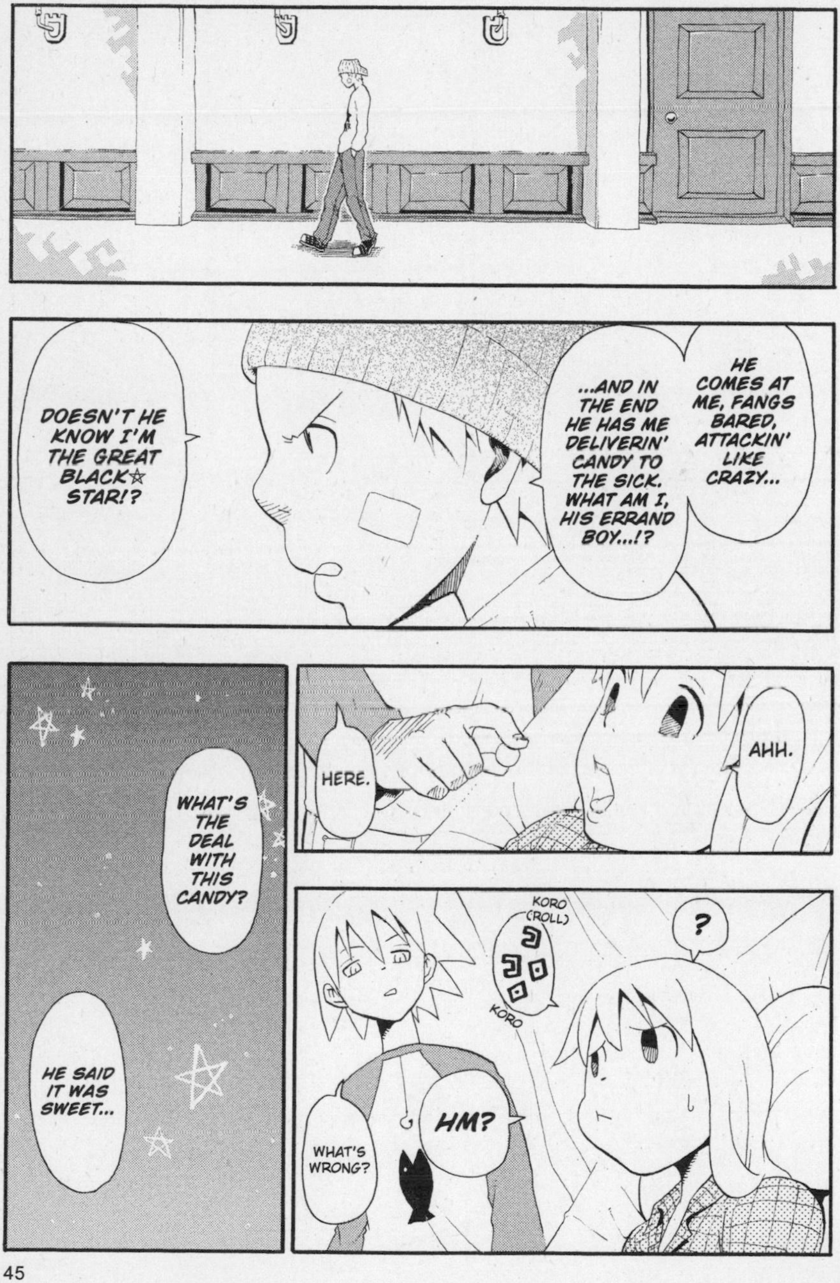
HE COMES AT ME, FANGS BARED, ATTACKIN' LIKE CRAZY...
...AND IN THE END HE HAS ME DELIVERIN' CANDY TO THE SICK. WHAT AM I, HIS ERRAND BOY...!?
DOESN'T HE KNOW I'M THE GREAT BLACK☆STAR!?
AHH.
HERE.
?
KORO (ROLL)
コロコロ
KORO
HM?
WHAT'S WRONG?
WHAT'S THE DEAL WITH THIS CANDY?
HE SAID IT WAS SWEET...

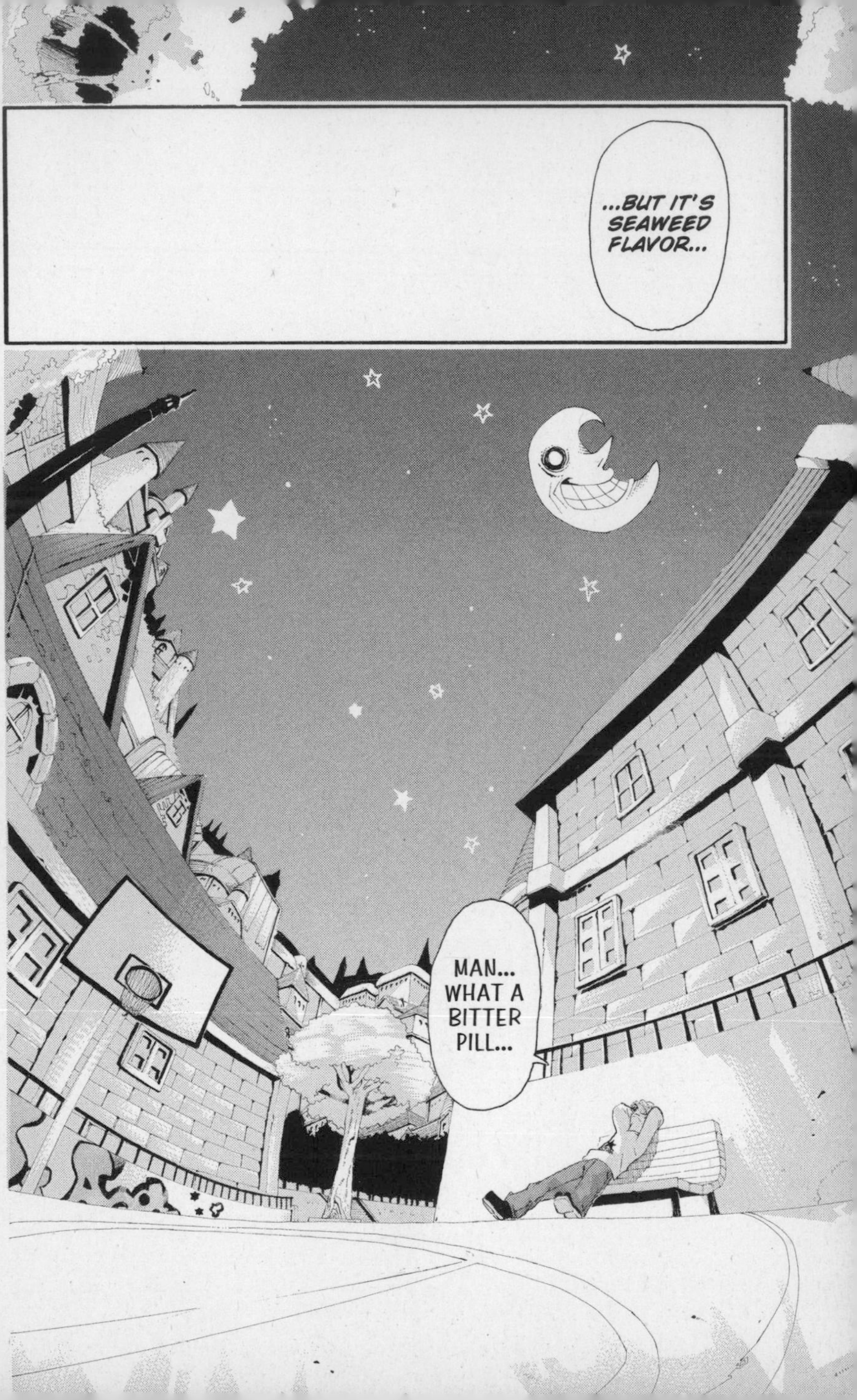
...BUT IT'S SEAWEED FLAVOR...
MAN... WHAT A BITTER PILL...

SOUL EATER

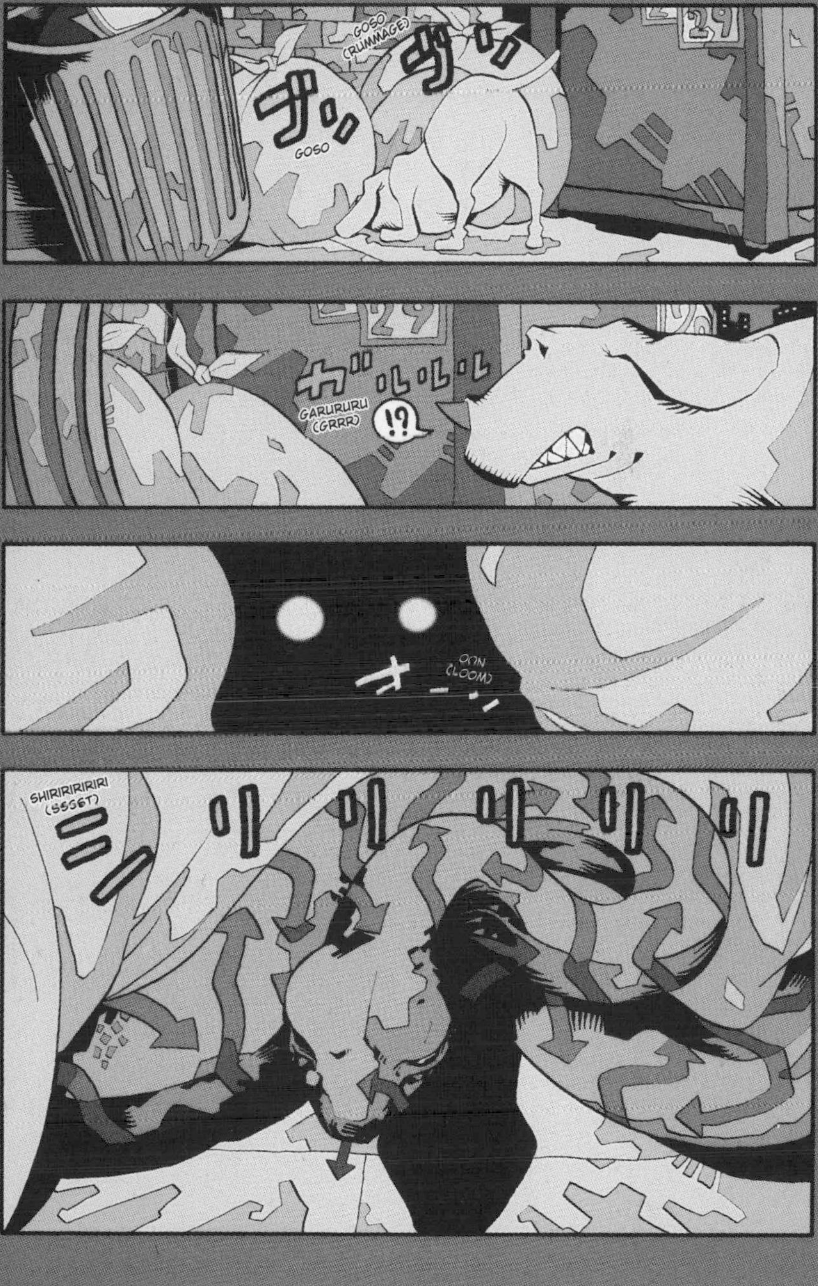
GOSO (RUMMAGE)
GOSO
GARURURU (GRRR)
!?
OON (LOOM)
SHIRIRIRIRIRI (SSSGT)

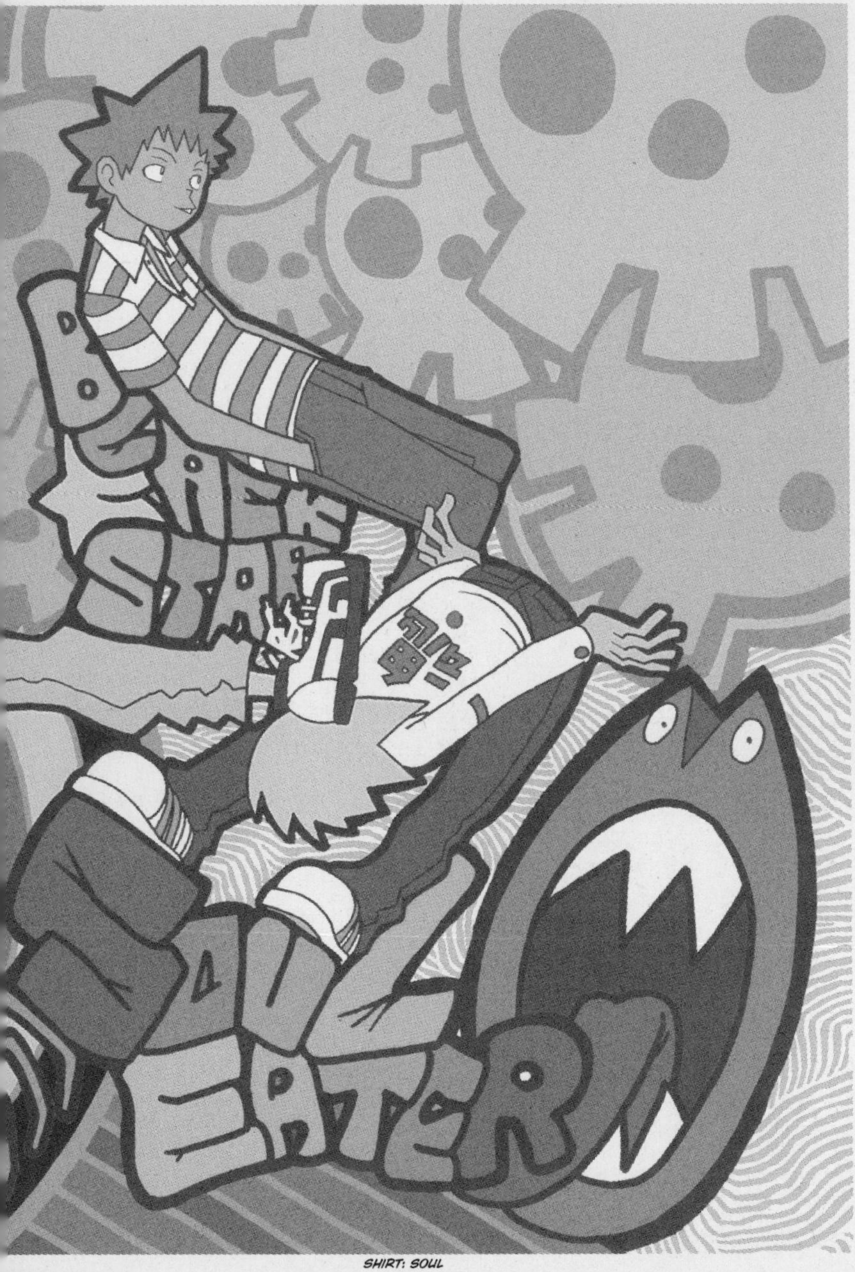

SHIRT: SOUL

CHAPTER 29: SNAKE

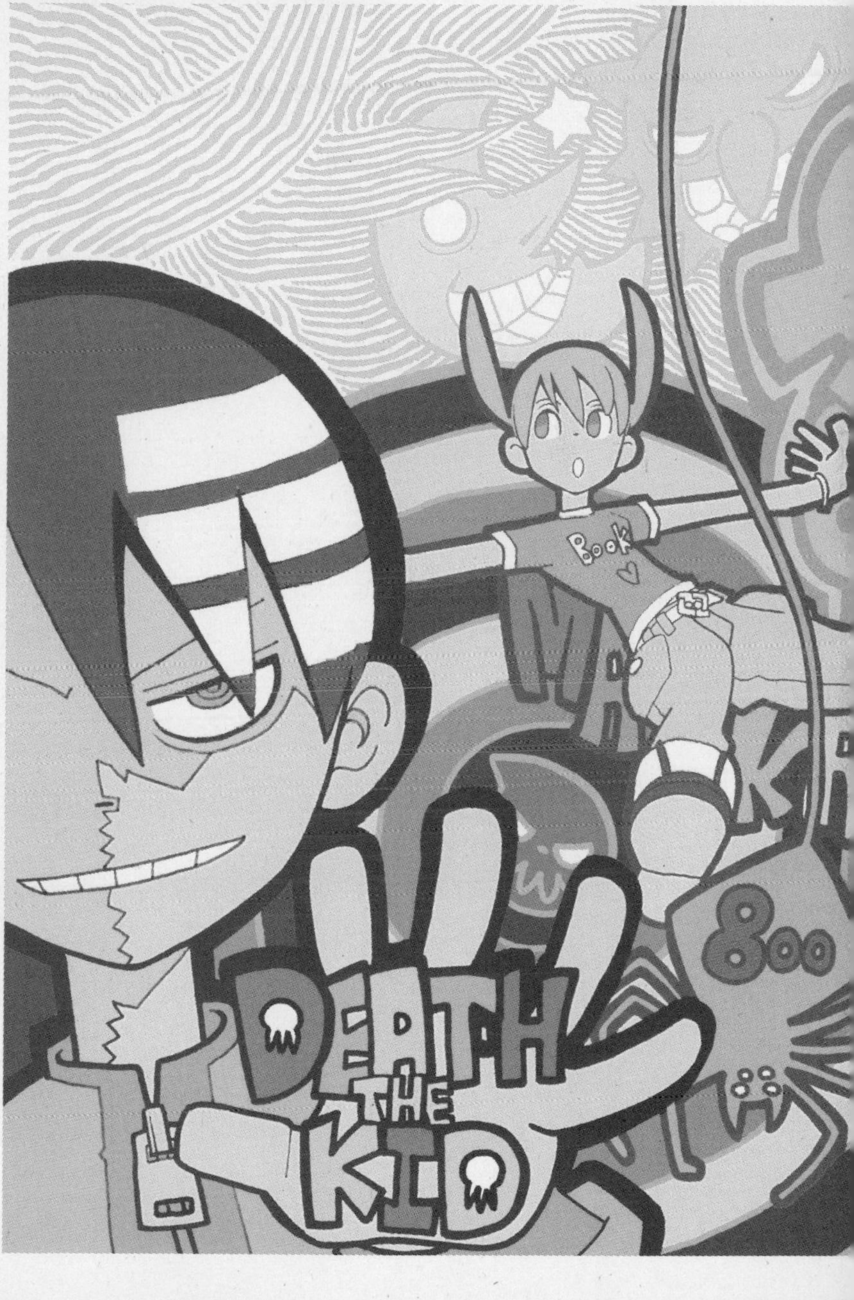
Book
DEATH THE KID

SOUL EATER

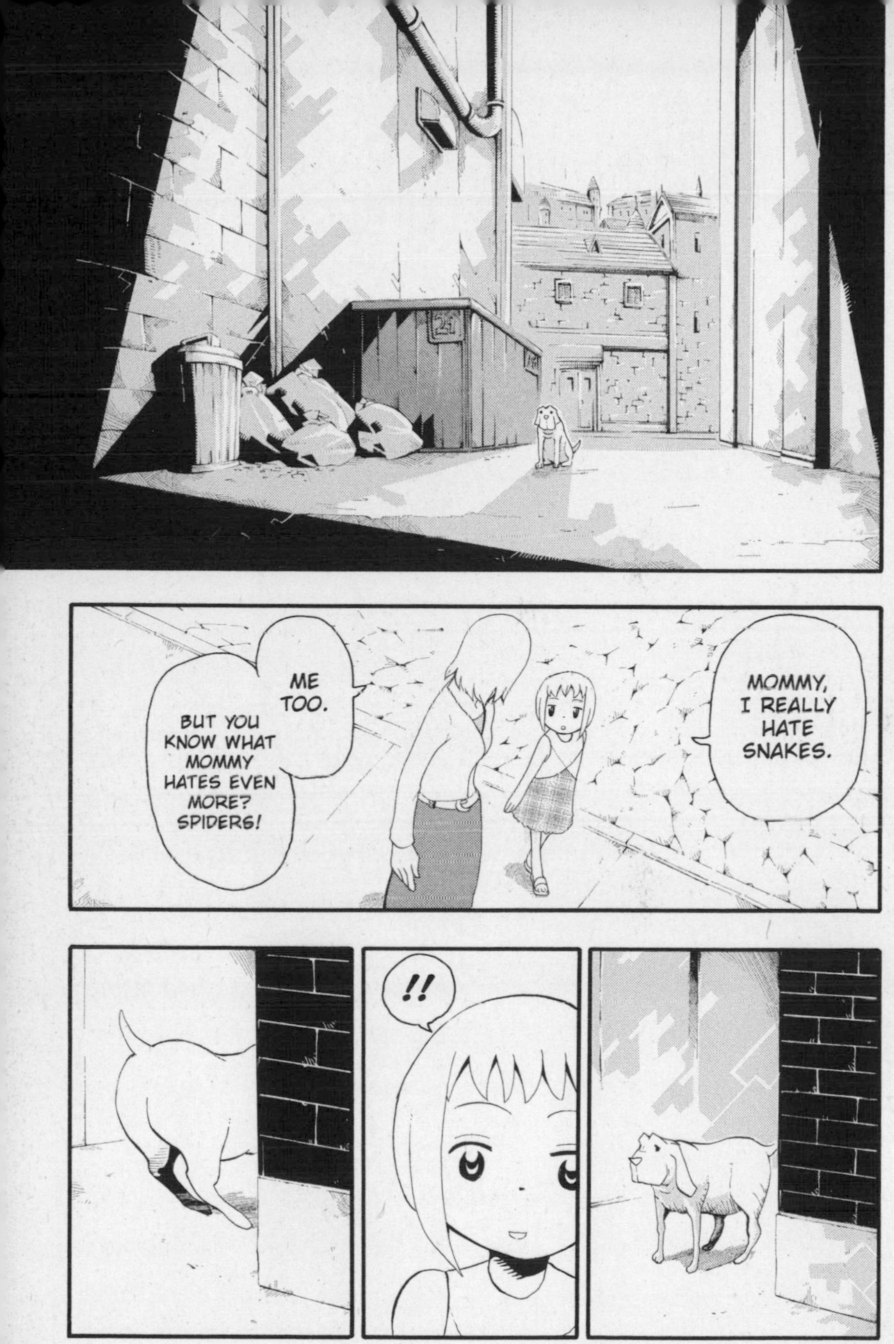

MOMMY, I REALLY HATE SNAKES.
ME TOO.
BUT YOU KNOW WHAT MOMMY HATES EVEN MORE? SPIDERS!
!!

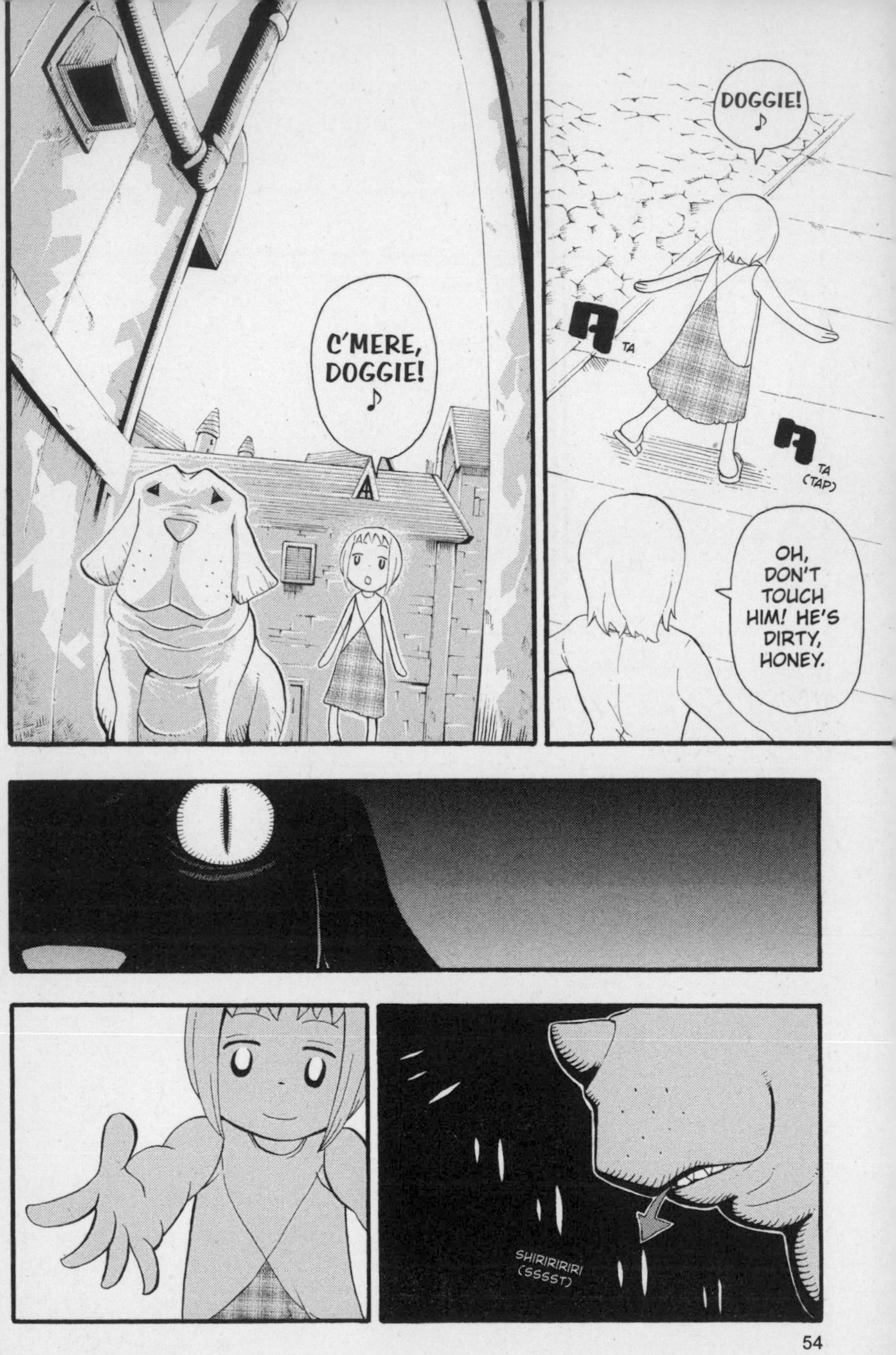
DOGGIE! ♪
TA
TA (TAP)
OH, DON'T TOUCH HIM! HE'S DIRTY, HONEY.
C'MERE, DOGGIE! ♪
SHIRIRIRIRI (SSSST)

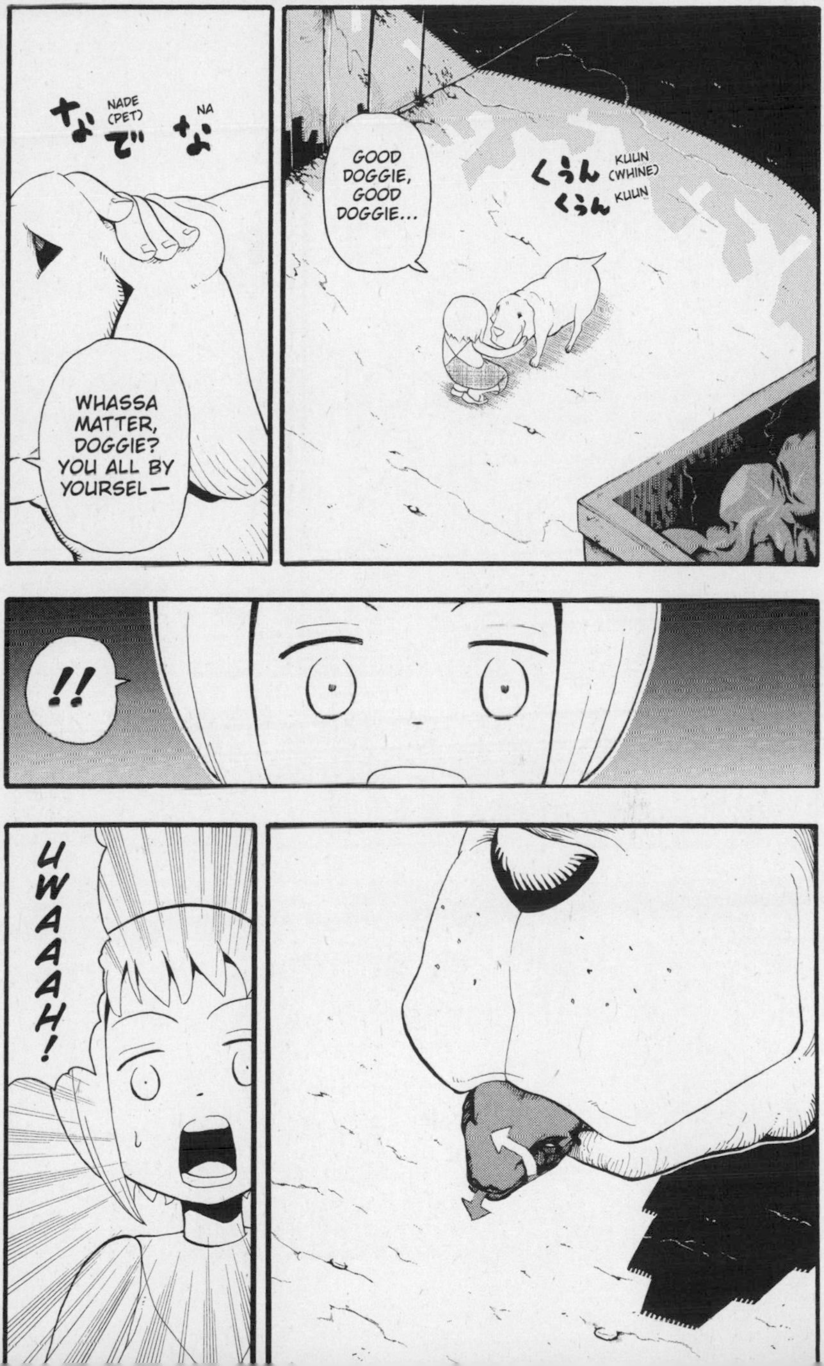
GOOD DOGGIE, GOOD DOGGIE...
くぅん KUUN (WHINE)
くぅん KUUN
なで NADE (PET)
な NA
WHASSA MATTER, DOGGIE? YOU ALL BY YOURSEL—
!!
UWAAAAAH!

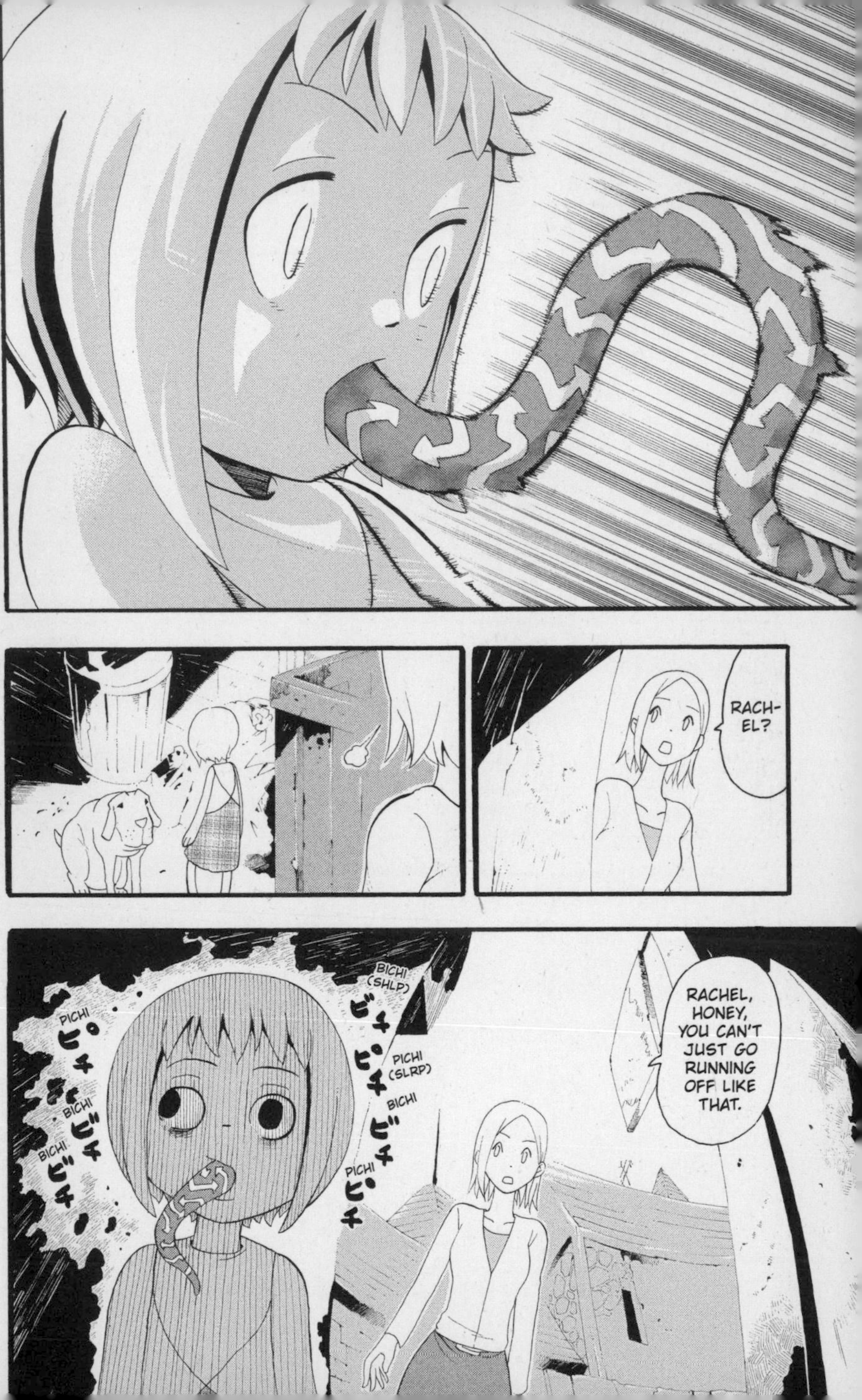
RACHEL?
RACHEL, HONEY, YOU CAN'T JUST GO RUNNING OFF LIKE THAT.
BICHI (SHLP) ビチ
PICHI (SLRP) ピチ
BICHI ビチ
PICHI ピチ
PICHI ピチ
BICHI ビチ
BICHI ビチ

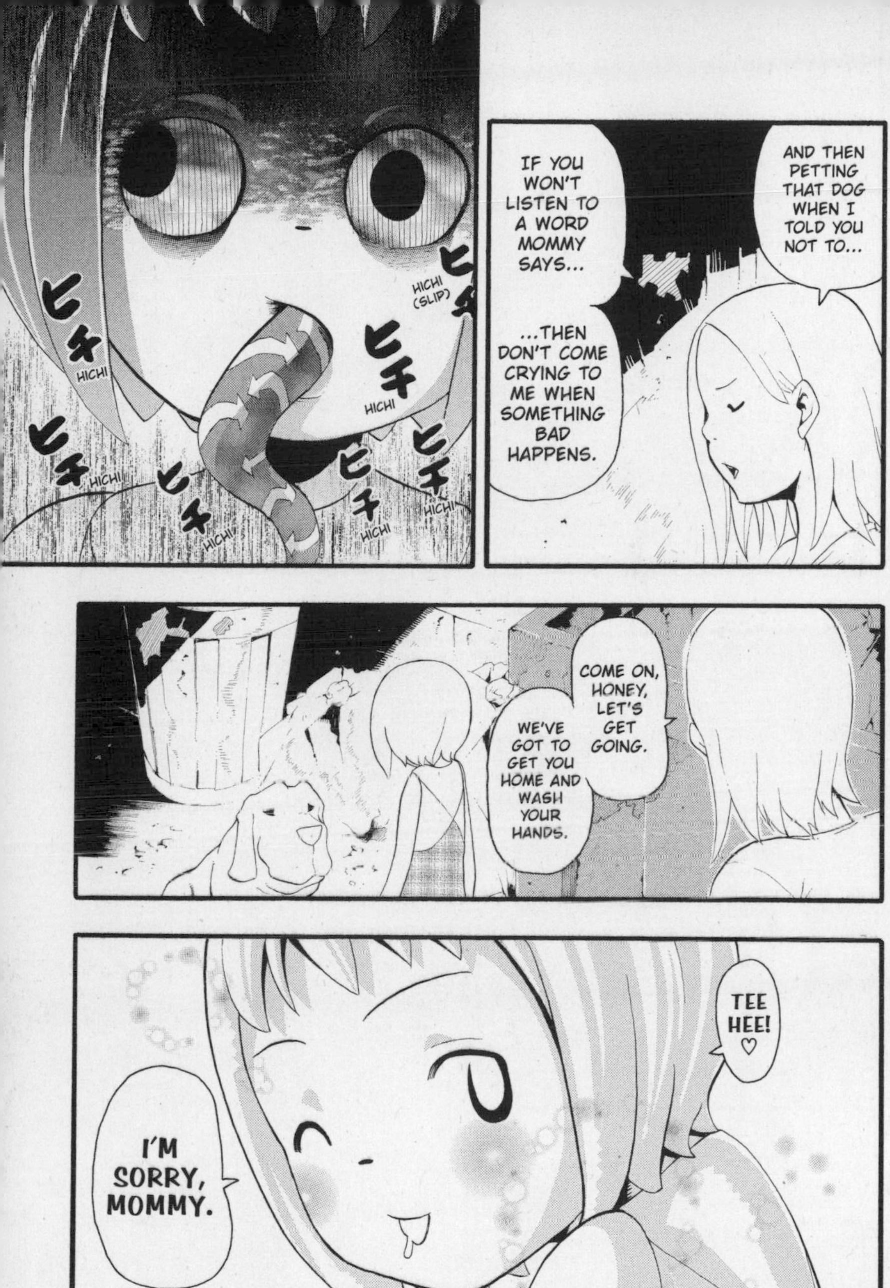
AND THEN PETTING THAT DOG WHEN I TOLD YOU NOT TO...
IF YOU WON'T LISTEN TO A WORD MOMMY SAYS...
...THEN DON'T COME CRYING TO ME WHEN SOMETHING BAD HAPPENS.
ヒチ HICHI (SLIP)
ヒチ HICHI
ヒチ HICHI
ヒチ HICHI
ヒチ HICHI
ヒチ HICHI
ヒチ HICHI
COME ON, HONEY, LET'S GET GOING.
WE'VE GOT TO GET YOU HOME AND WASH YOUR HANDS.
TEE HEE! ♡
I'M SORRY, MOMMY.

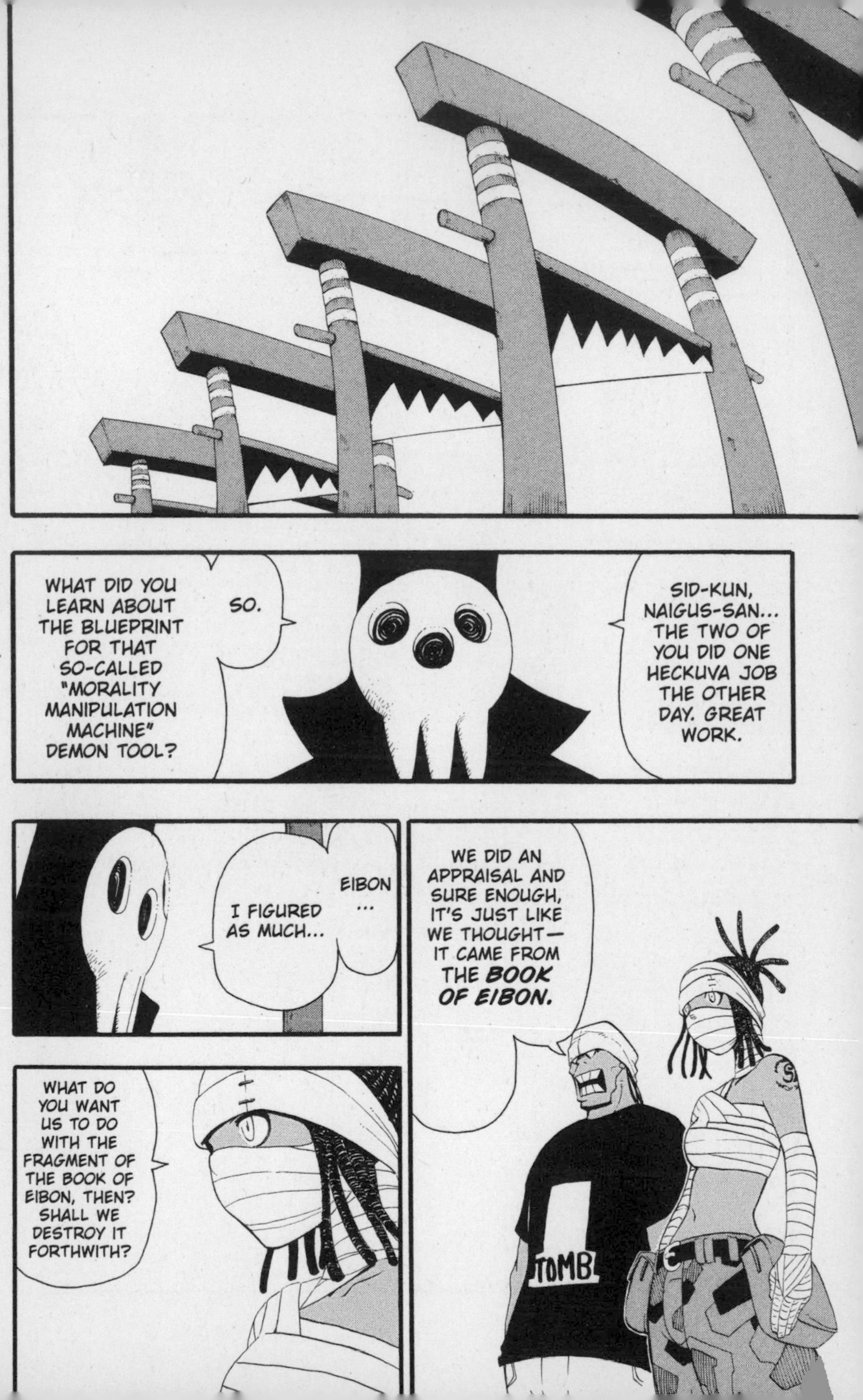
SID-KUN, NAIGUS-SAN... THE TWO OF YOU DID ONE HECKUVA JOB THE OTHER DAY. GREAT WORK.
SO.
WHAT DID YOU LEARN ABOUT THE BLUEPRINT FOR THAT SO-CALLED "MORALITY MANIPULATION MACHINE" DEMON TOOL?
WE DID AN APPRAISAL AND SURE ENOUGH, IT'S JUST LIKE WE THOUGHT— IT CAME FROM THE *BOOK OF EIBON.*
TOMB
EIBON ...
I FIGURED AS MUCH...
WHAT DO YOU WANT US TO DO WITH THE FRAGMENT OF THE BOOK OF EIBON, THEN? SHALL WE DESTROY IT FORTHWITH?

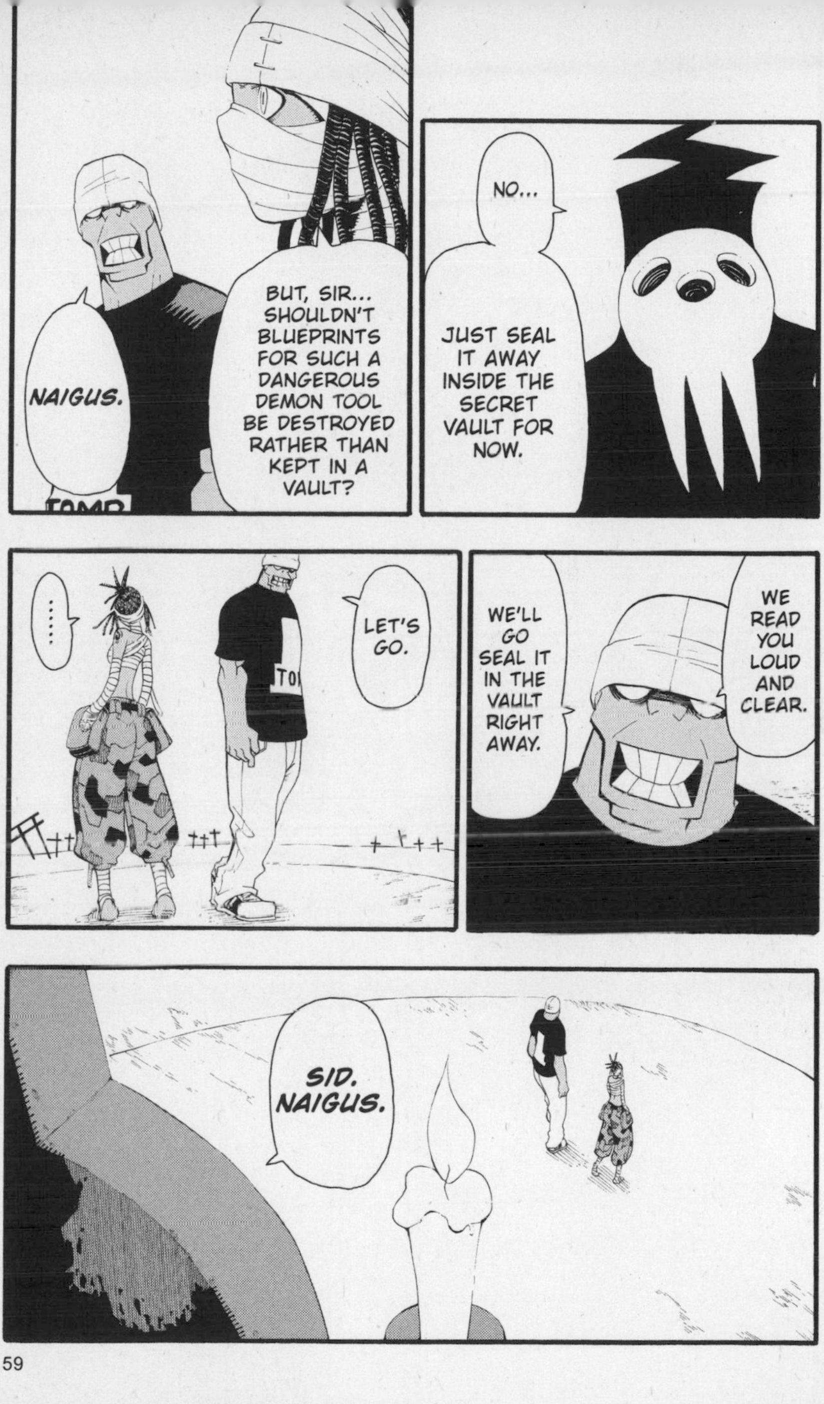
NO...
JUST SEAL IT AWAY INSIDE THE SECRET VAULT FOR NOW.
BUT, SIR... SHOULDN'T BLUEPRINTS FOR SUCH A DANGEROUS DEMON TOOL BE DESTROYED RATHER THAN KEPT IN A VAULT?
NAIGUS.
WE READ YOU LOUD AND CLEAR.
WE'LL GO SEAL IT IN THE VAULT RIGHT AWAY.
LET'S GO.
......
SID. NAIGUS.

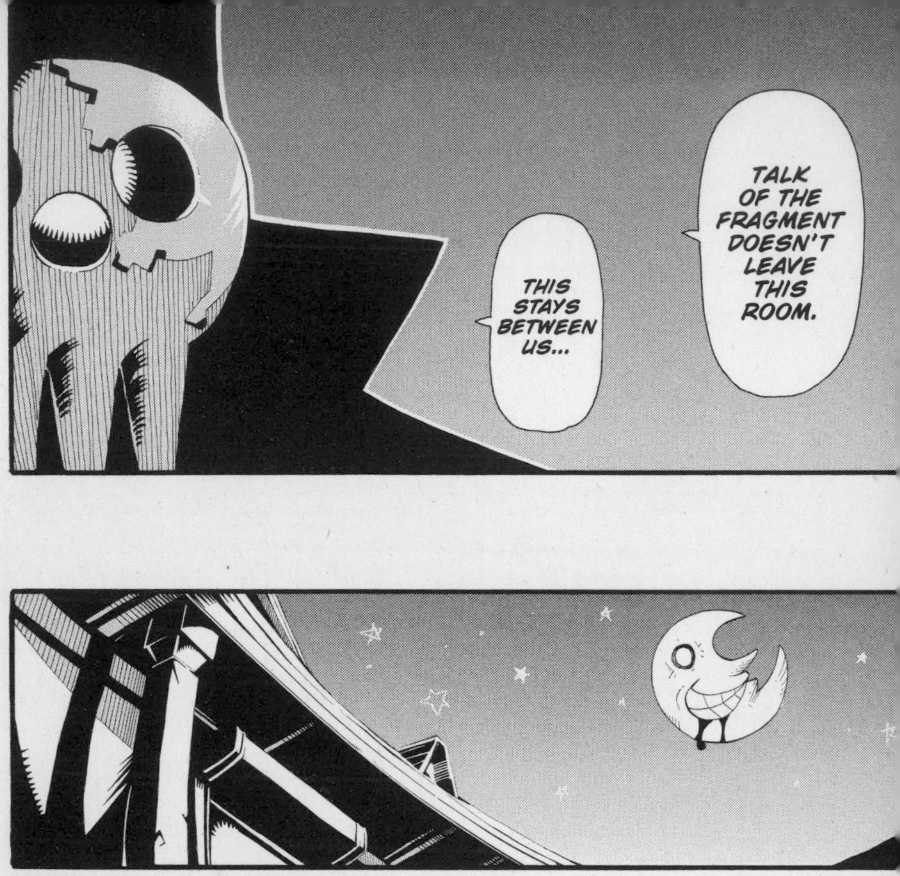
TALK OF THE FRAGMENT DOESN'T LEAVE THIS ROOM.
THIS STAYS BETWEEN US...

SFX: CHAA CHAA CHAKA CHA CHAA CHAA CHAKA CHA

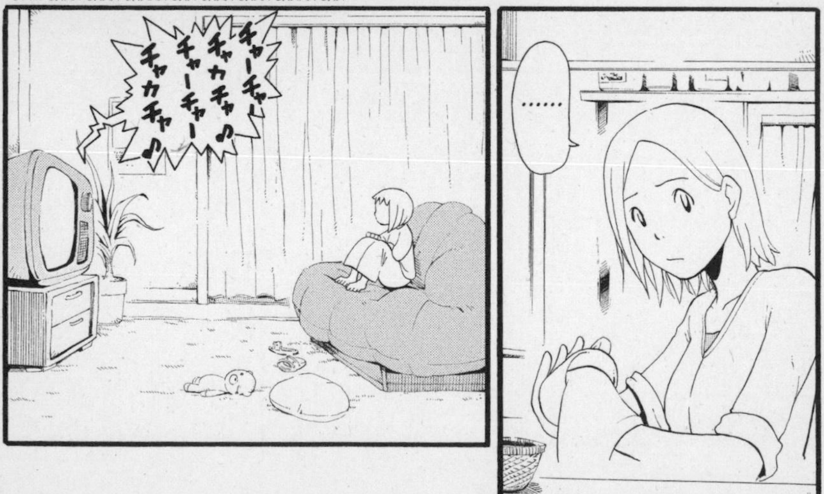
......
チャーチャーチャカチャ♪チャーチャーチャカチャ♪

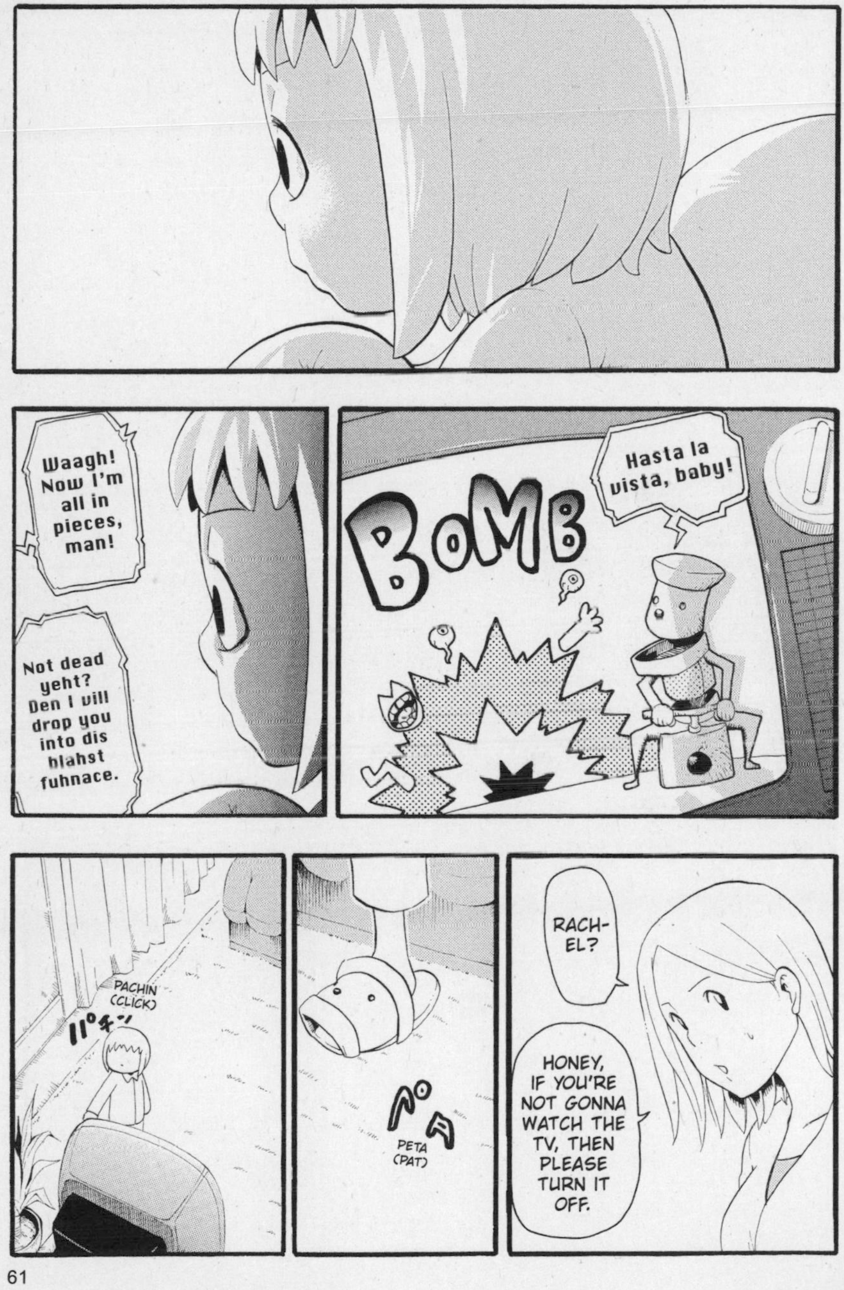
Hasta la vista, baby!
BOMB
Waagh! Now I'm all in pieces, man!
Not dead yeht? Den I vill drop you into dis blahst fuhnace.
RACH-EL?
HONEY, IF YOU'RE NOT GONNA WATCH THE TV, THEN PLEASE TURN IT OFF.
ペタ
PETA (PAT)
パチッ
PACHIN (CLICK)

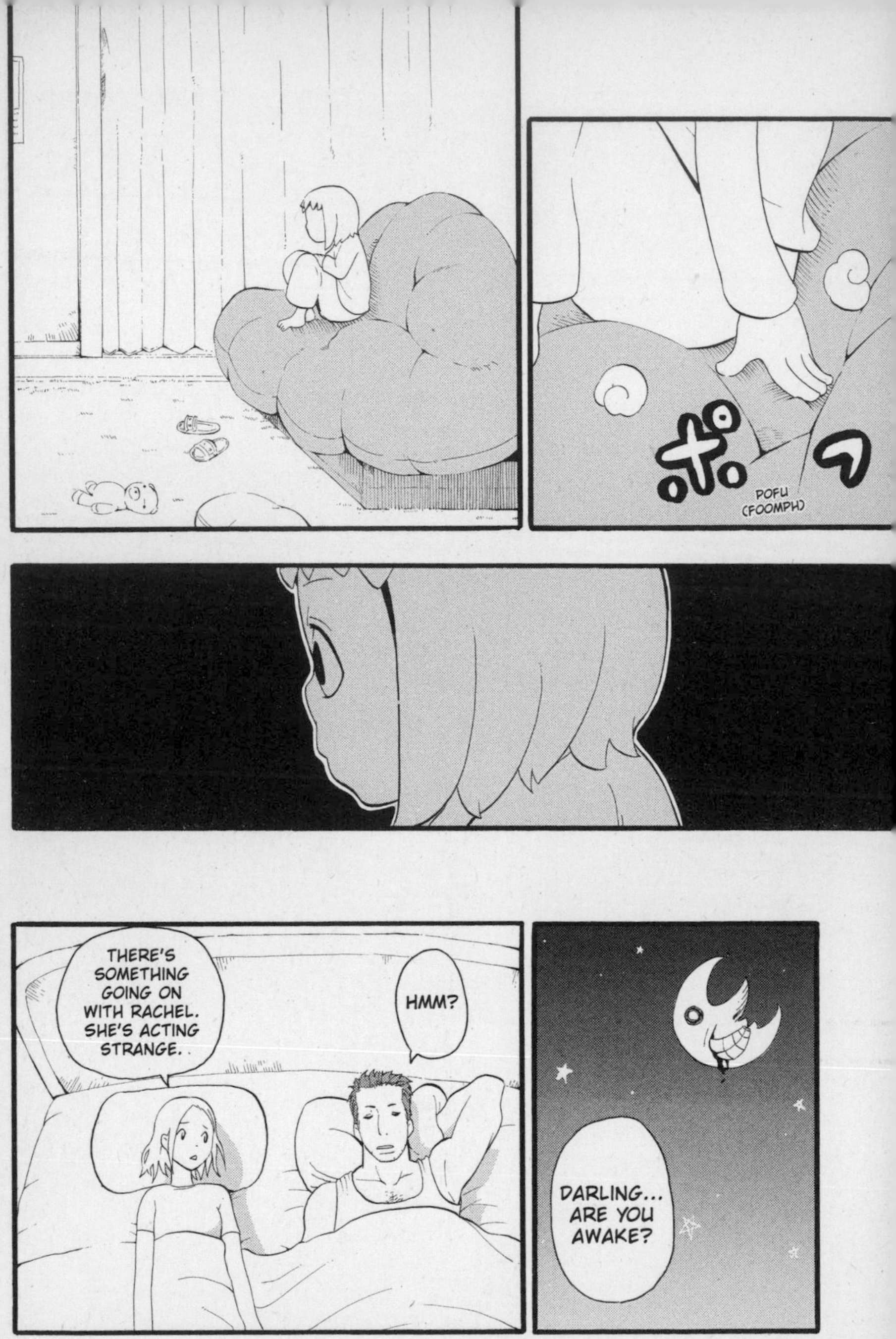
POFU
(FOOMPH)
DARLING... ARE YOU AWAKE?
HMM?
THERE'S SOMETHING GOING ON WITH RACHEL. SHE'S ACTING STRANGE.

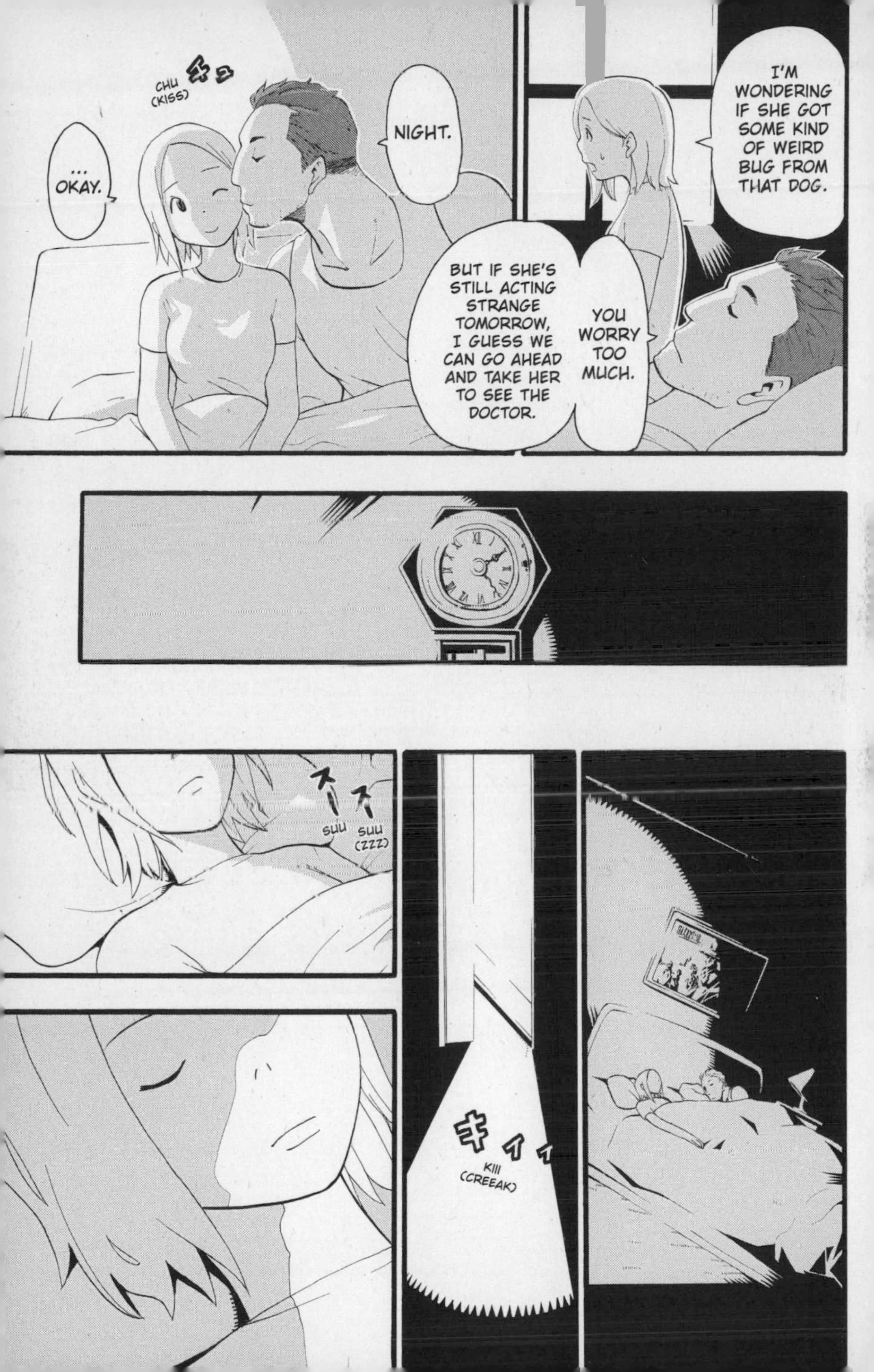
I'M WONDERING IF SHE GOT SOME KIND OF WEIRD BUG FROM THAT DOG.
YOU WORRY TOO MUCH.
BUT IF SHE'S STILL ACTING STRANGE TOMORROW, I GUESS WE CAN GO AHEAD AND TAKE HER TO SEE THE DOCTOR.
NIGHT.
CHU (KISS)
... OKAY.
KIII (CREEAK)
SUU SUU (ZZZ)

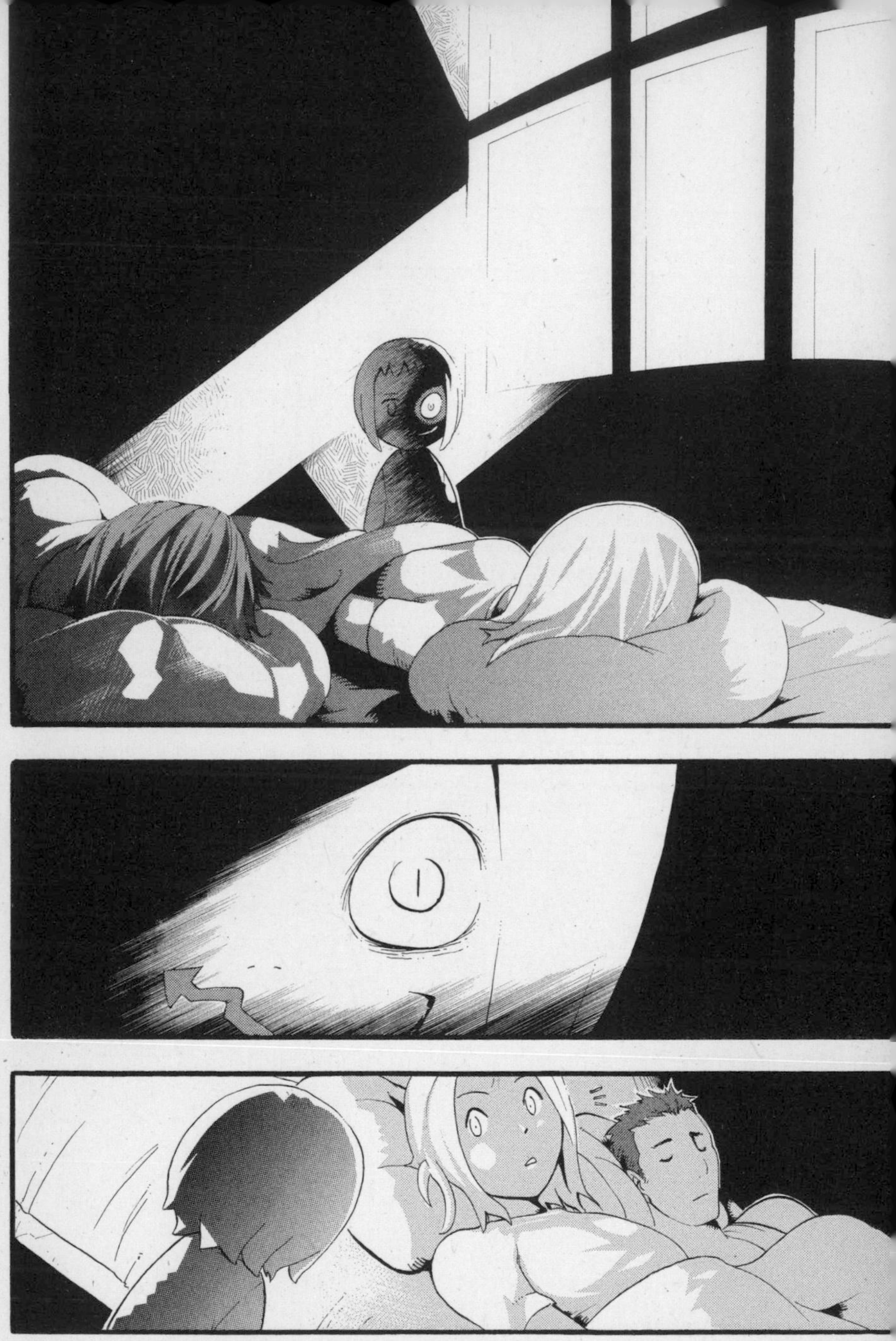

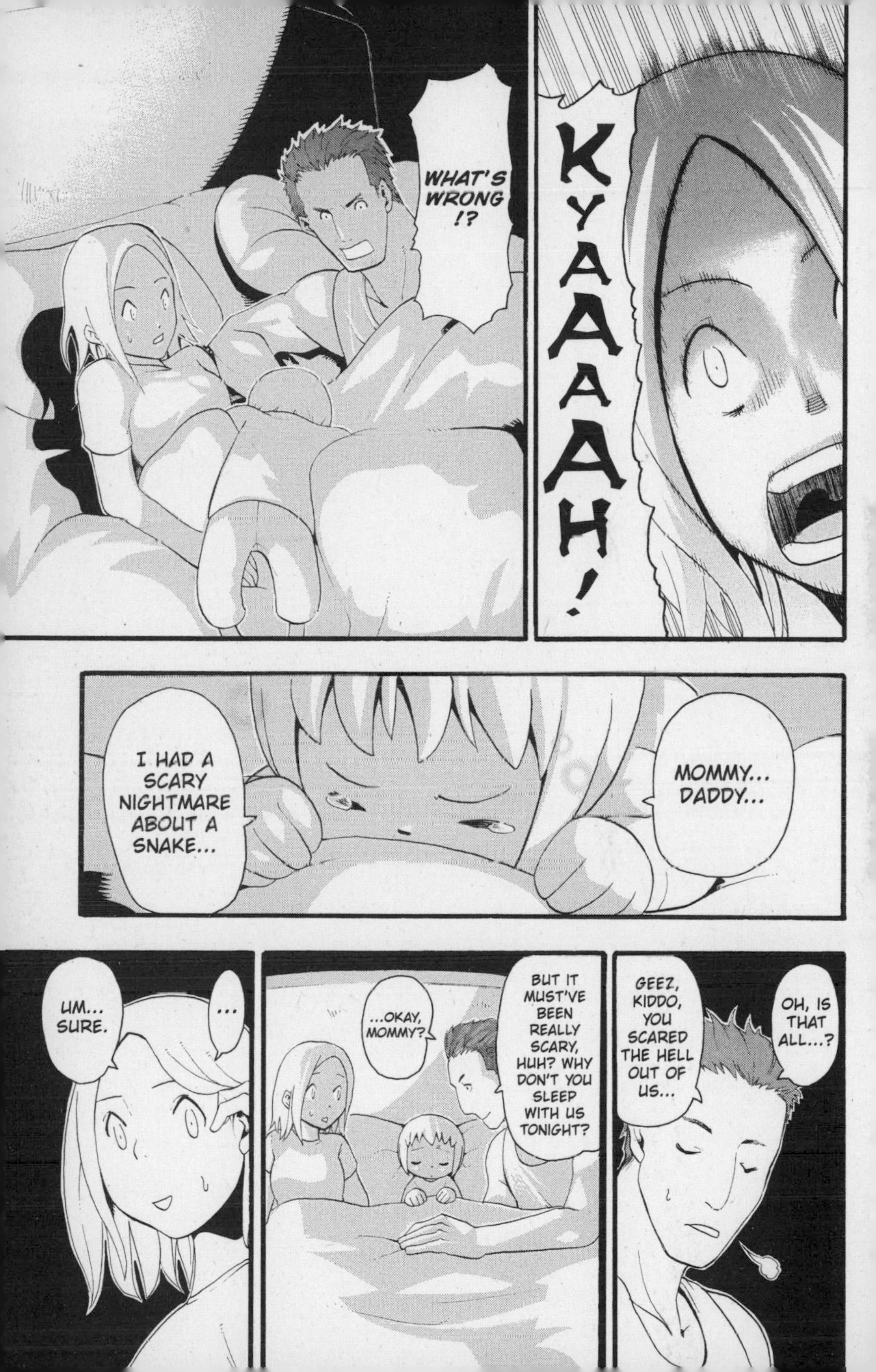
KYAAAAH!
WHAT'S WRONG !?
MOMMY... DADDY...
I HAD A SCARY NIGHTMARE ABOUT A SNAKE...
OH, IS THAT ALL...?
GEEZ, KIDDO, YOU SCARED THE HELL OUT OF US...
BUT IT MUST'VE BEEN REALLY SCARY, HUH? WHY DON'T YOU SLEEP WITH US TONIGHT?
...OKAY, MOMMY?
...
UM... SURE.

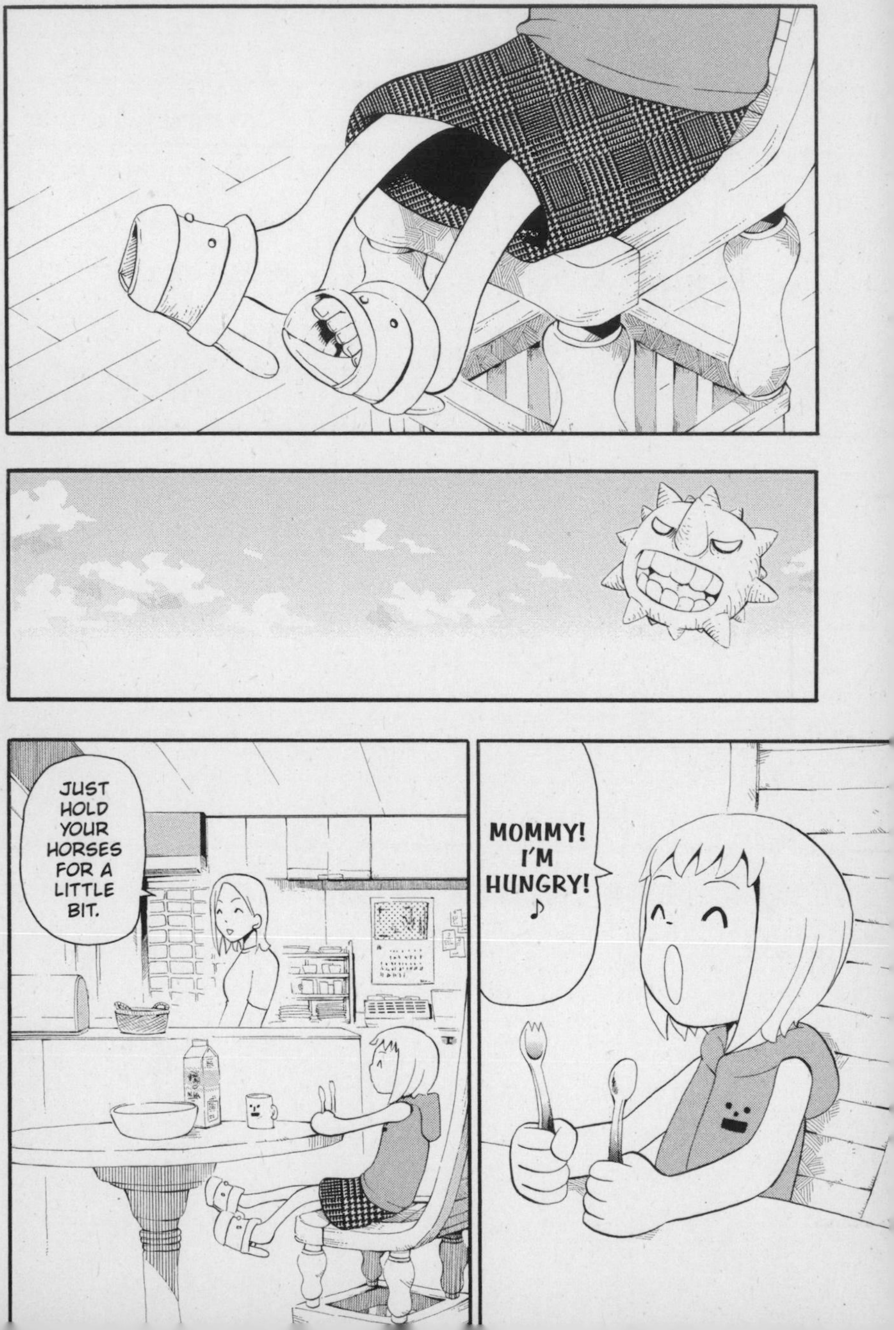
MOMMY! I'M HUNGRY! ♪
JUST HOLD YOUR HORSES FOR A LITTLE BIT.

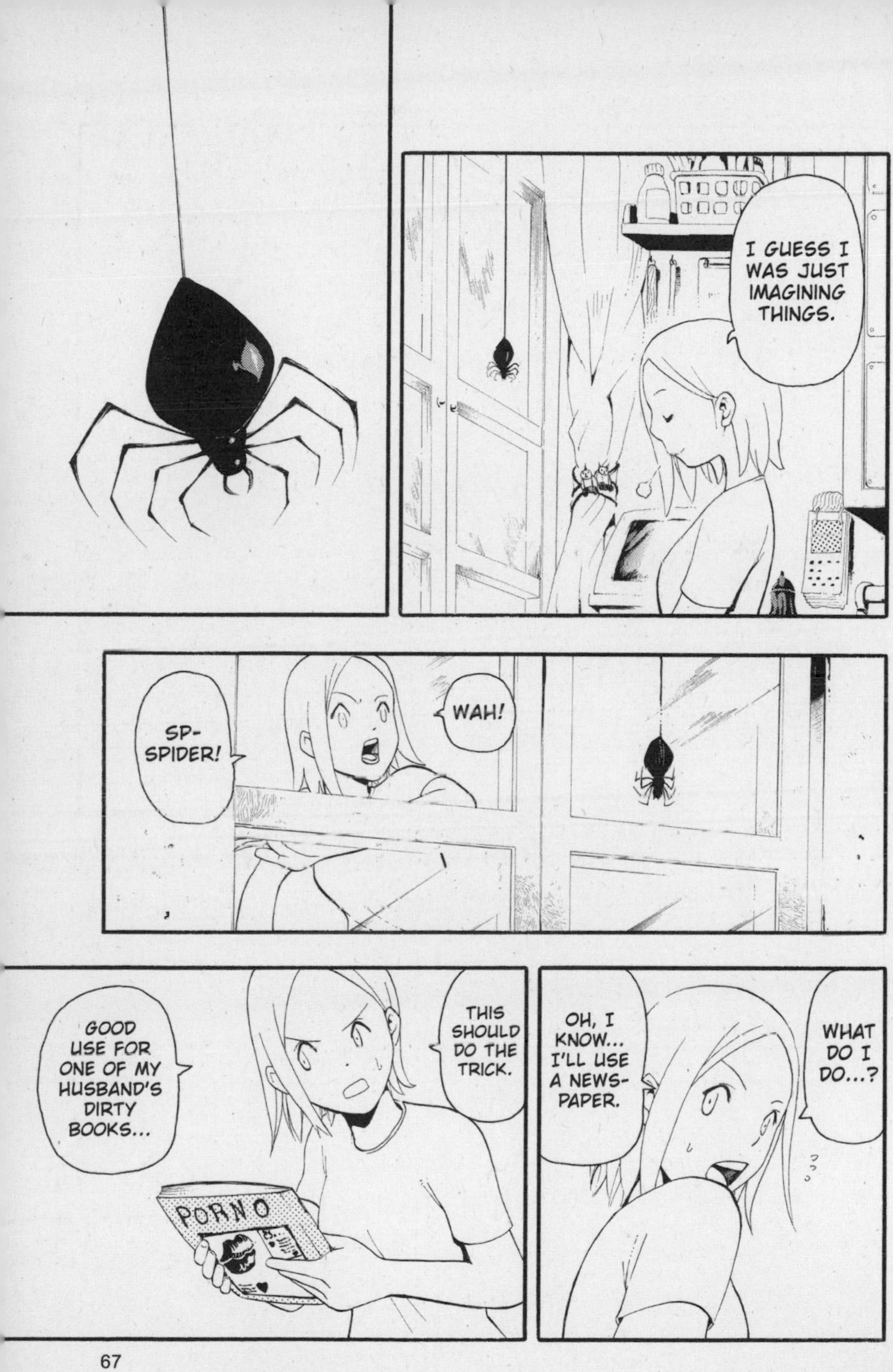
I GUESS I WAS JUST IMAGINING THINGS.
WAH!
SP-SPIDER!
WHAT DO I DO...?
OH, I KNOW... I'LL USE A NEWS-PAPER.
THIS SHOULD DO THE TRICK.
GOOD USE FOR ONE OF MY HUSBAND'S DIRTY BOOKS...
PORNO

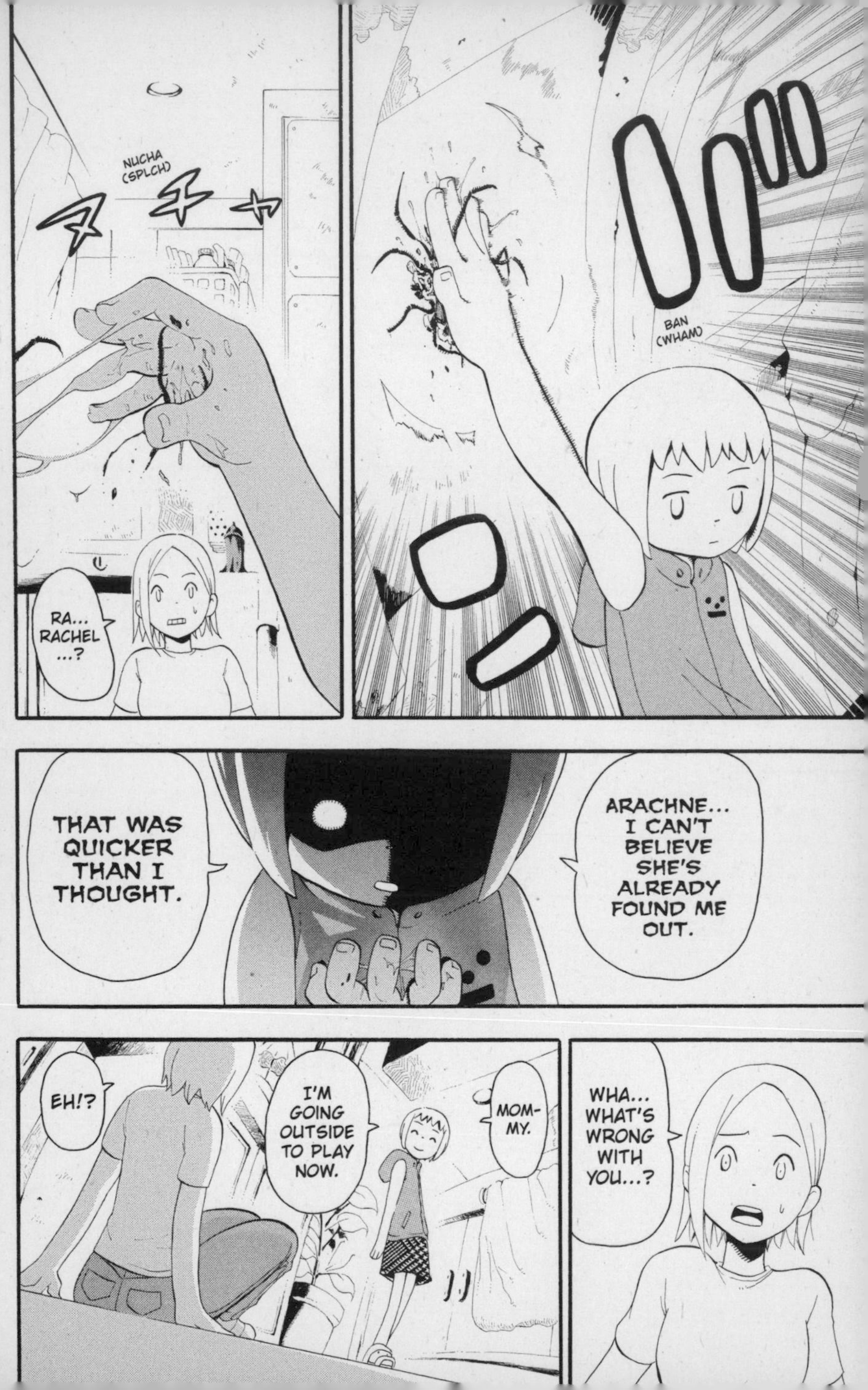
BAN
(WHAM)
NUCHA
(SPLCH)
RA... RACHEL ...?
ARACHNE... I CAN'T BELIEVE SHE'S ALREADY FOUND ME OUT.
THAT WAS QUICKER THAN I THOUGHT.
WHA... WHAT'S WRONG WITH YOU...?
MOM-MY.
I'M GOING OUTSIDE TO PLAY NOW.
EH!?

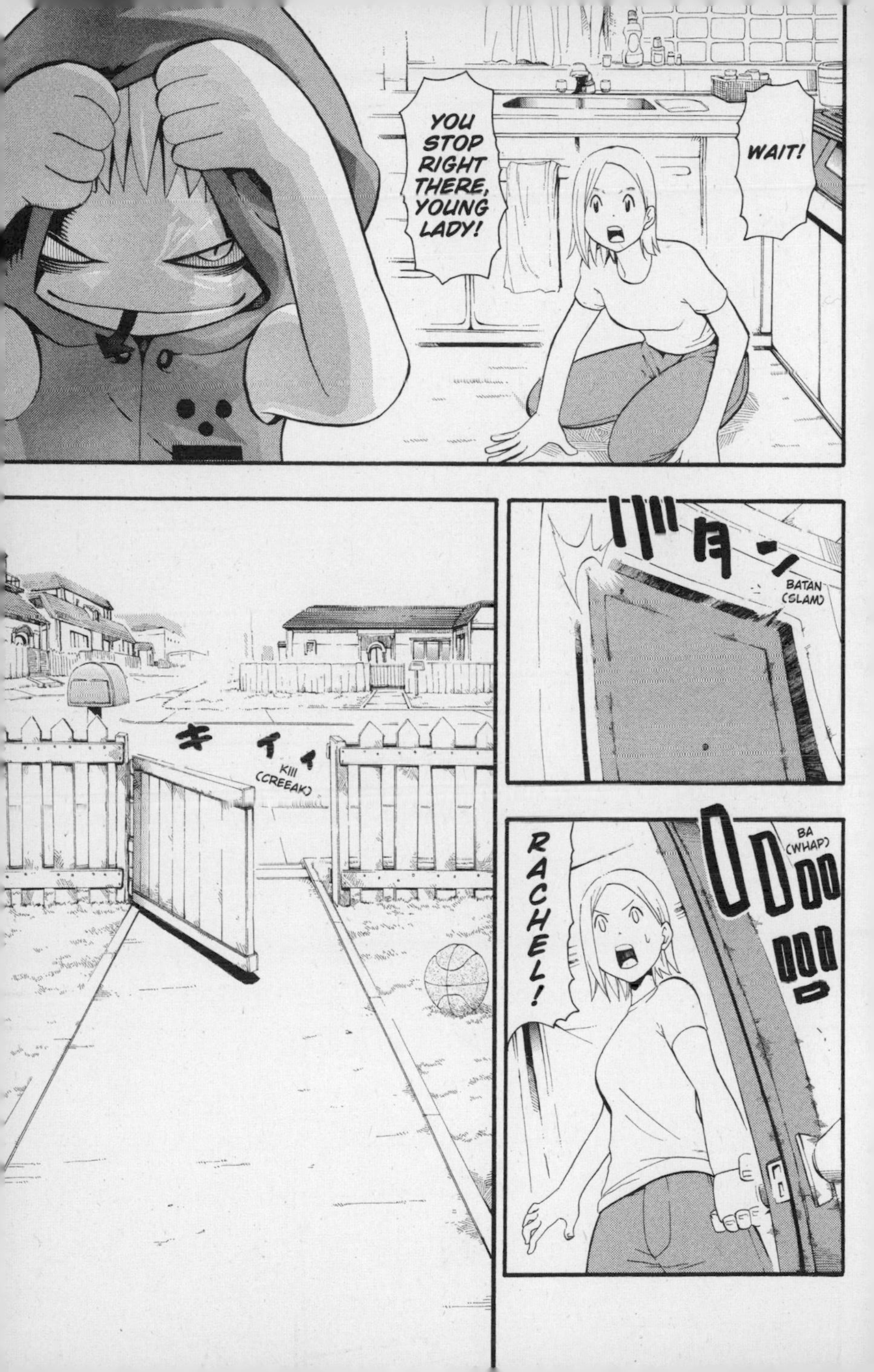

WAIT!
YOU STOP RIGHT THERE, YOUNG LADY!
バタン
BATAN (SLAM)
BA (WHAP)
RACHEL!
キイイ
KIII (CREEAK)

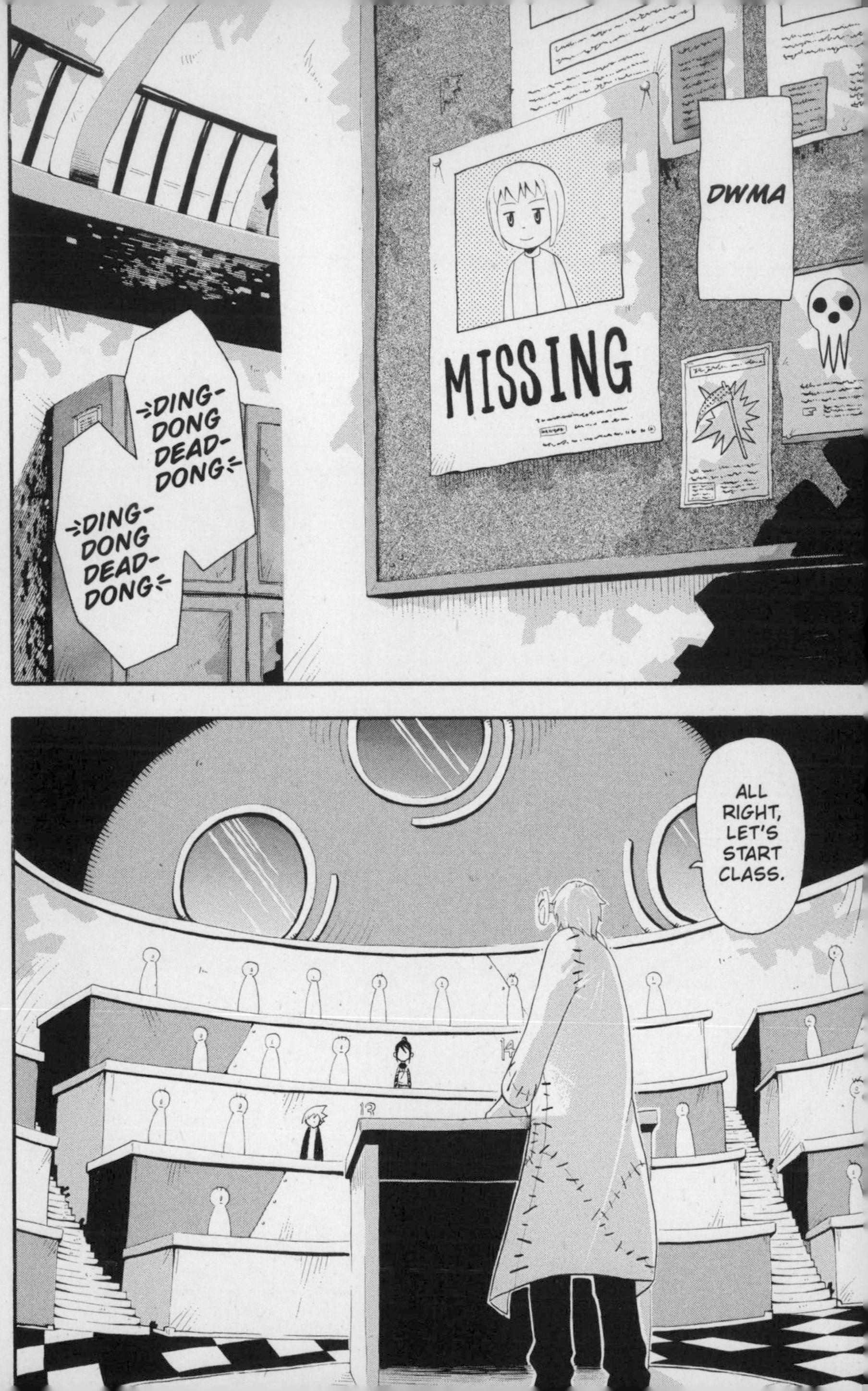
DWMA
MISSING
DING-DONG DEAD-DONG
DING-DONG DEAD-DONG
ALL RIGHT, LET'S START CLASS.

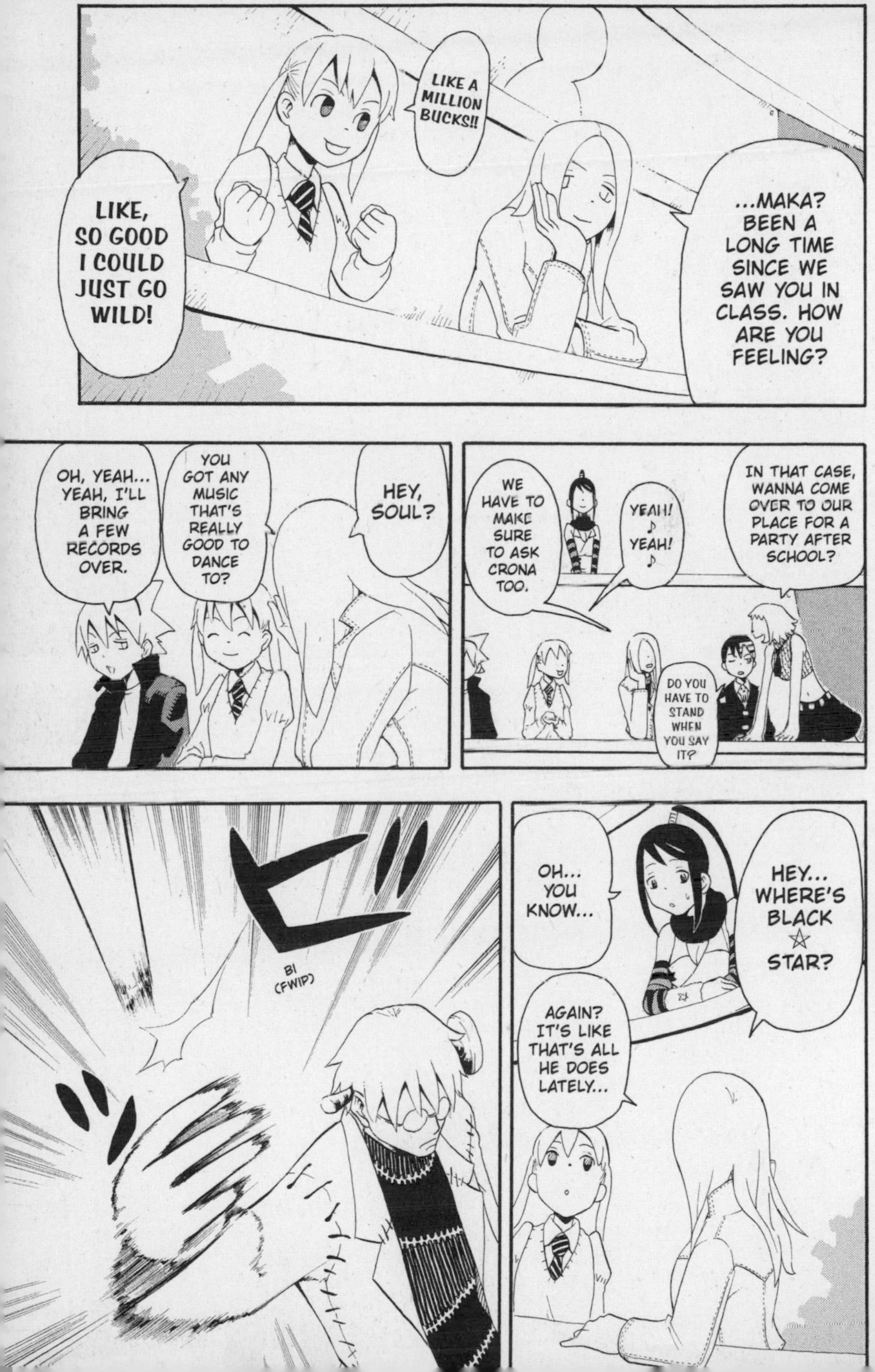
...MAKA? BEEN A LONG TIME SINCE WE SAW YOU IN CLASS. HOW ARE YOU FEELING?
LIKE A MILLION BUCKS!!
LIKE, SO GOOD I COULD JUST GO WILD!
IN THAT CASE, WANNA COME OVER TO OUR PLACE FOR A PARTY AFTER SCHOOL?
YEAH! ♪ YEAH! ♪
WE HAVE TO MAKE SURE TO ASK CRONA TOO.
DO YOU HAVE TO STAND WHEN YOU SAY IT?
HEY, SOUL?
YOU GOT ANY MUSIC THAT'S REALLY GOOD TO DANCE TO?
OH, YEAH... YEAH, I'LL BRING A FEW RECORDS OVER.
HEY... WHERE'S BLACK ☆ STAR?
OH... YOU KNOW...
AGAIN? IT'S LIKE THAT'S ALL HE DOES LATELY...
BI (FWIP)

...ME...!?

PUSHUU
(SSST)

NO TALKING IN CLASS.

...I WON'T MISS.

AND NEXT TIME...

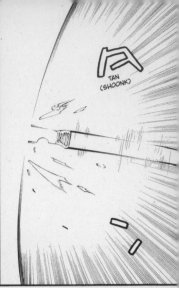

TAN
(SHOONK)

IT'S OKAY... IT'S OKAY...

HIRA
(WAVE)

HIRA

SORRYYYYY!

YO... SORRY I'M LATE.

GARARA
(SLIDE)

?

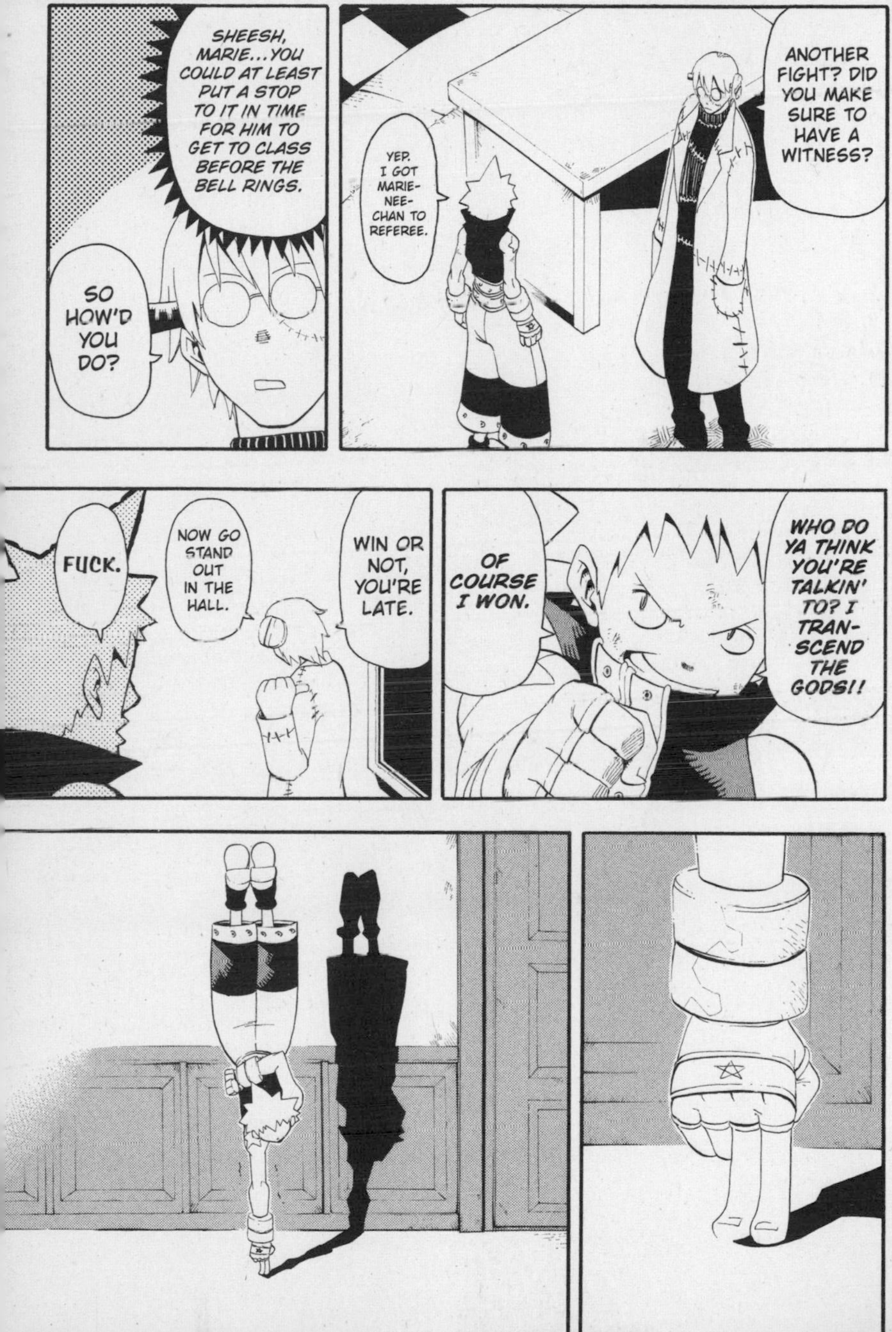
ANOTHER FIGHT? DID YOU MAKE SURE TO HAVE A WITNESS?
YEP. I GOT MARIE-NEE-CHAN TO REFEREE.
SHEESH, MARIE...YOU COULD AT LEAST PUT A STOP TO IT IN TIME FOR HIM TO GET TO CLASS BEFORE THE BELL RINGS.
SO HOW'D YOU DO?
WHO DO YA THINK YOU'RE TALKIN' TO? I TRAN-SCEND THE GODS!!
OF COURSE I WON.
WIN OR NOT, YOU'RE LATE.
NOW GO STAND OUT IN THE HALL.
FUCK.

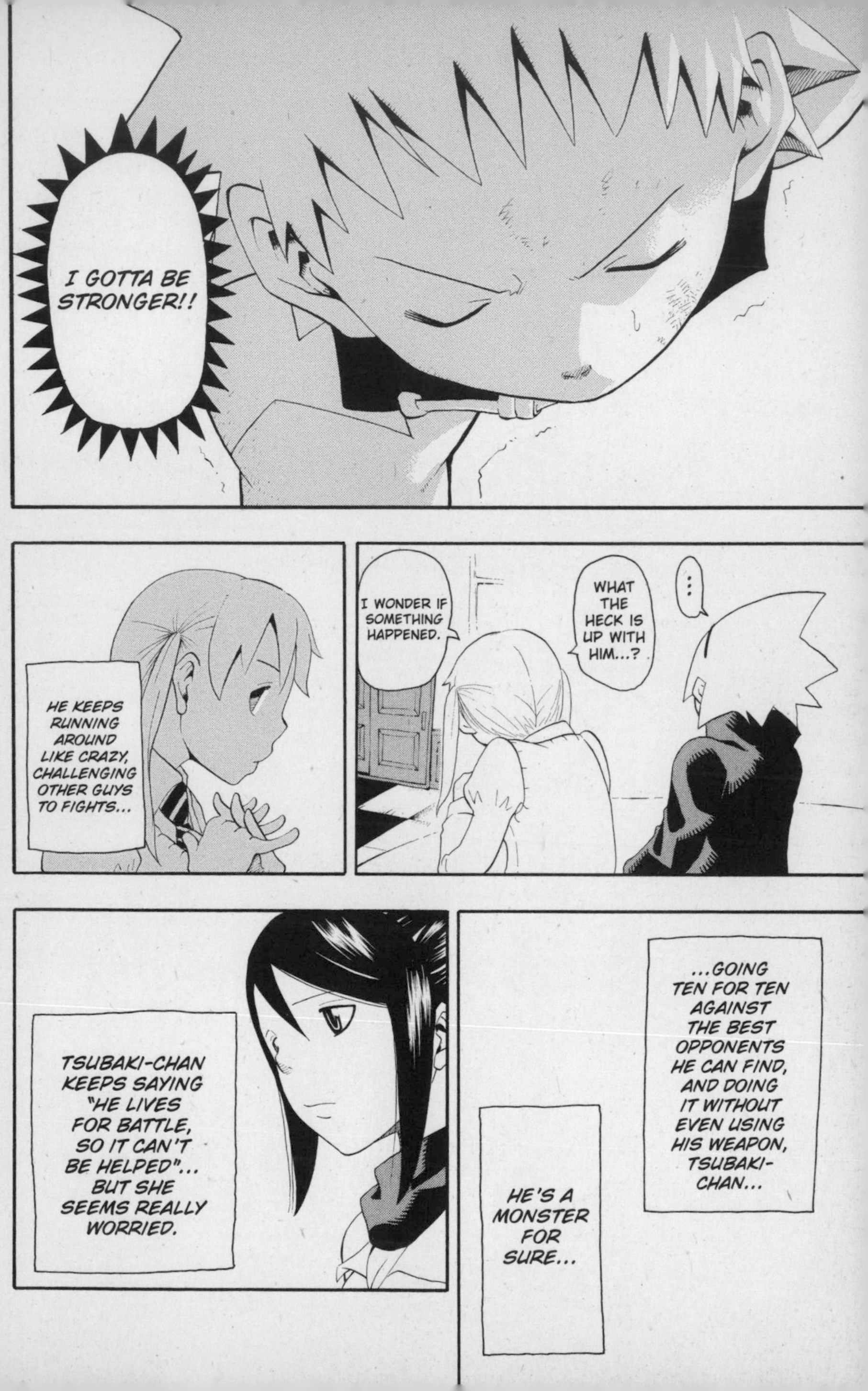
I GOTTA BE STRONGER!!
...
WHAT THE HECK IS UP WITH HIM...?
I WONDER IF SOMETHING HAPPENED.
HE KEEPS RUNNING AROUND LIKE CRAZY, CHALLENGING OTHER GUYS TO FIGHTS...
...GOING TEN FOR TEN AGAINST THE BEST OPPONENTS HE CAN FIND, AND DOING IT WITHOUT EVEN USING HIS WEAPON, TSUBAKI-CHAN...
HE'S A MONSTER FOR SURE...
TSUBAKI-CHAN KEEPS SAYING "HE LIVES FOR BATTLE, SO IT CAN'T BE HELPED"... BUT SHE SEEMS REALLY WORRIED.

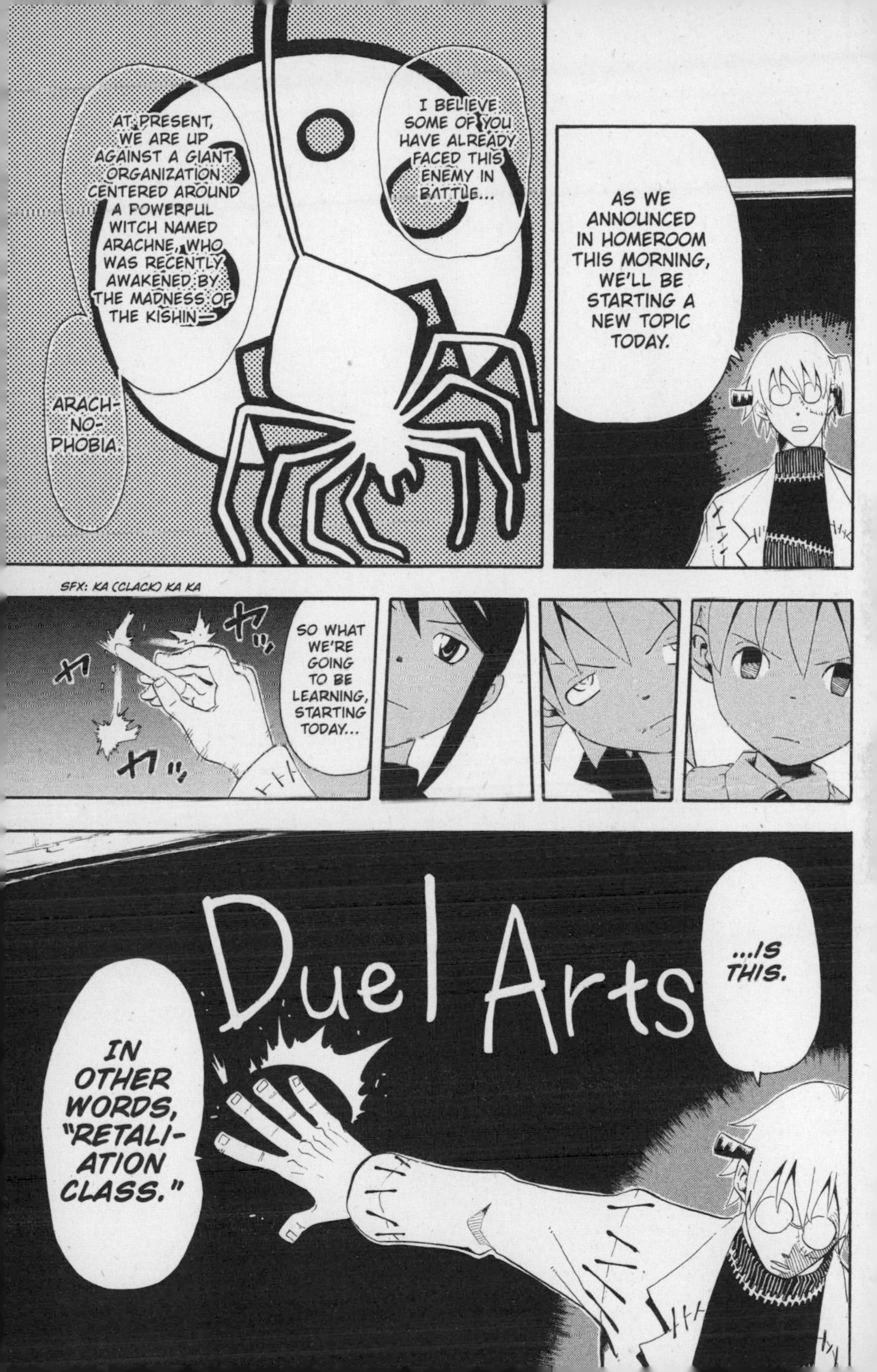
AS WE ANNOUNCED IN HOMEROOM THIS MORNING, WE'LL BE STARTING A NEW TOPIC TODAY.
I BELIEVE SOME OF YOU HAVE ALREADY FACED THIS ENEMY IN BATTLE...
AT PRESENT, WE ARE UP AGAINST A GIANT ORGANIZATION CENTERED AROUND A POWERFUL WITCH NAMED ARACHNE, WHO WAS RECENTLY AWAKENED BY THE MADNESS OF THE KISHIN—
ARACH-NO-PHOBIA.
SFX: KA (CLACK) KA KA
SO WHAT WE'RE GOING TO BE LEARNING, STARTING TODAY...
Duel Arts
...IS THIS.
IN OTHER WORDS, "RETALI-ATION CLASS."

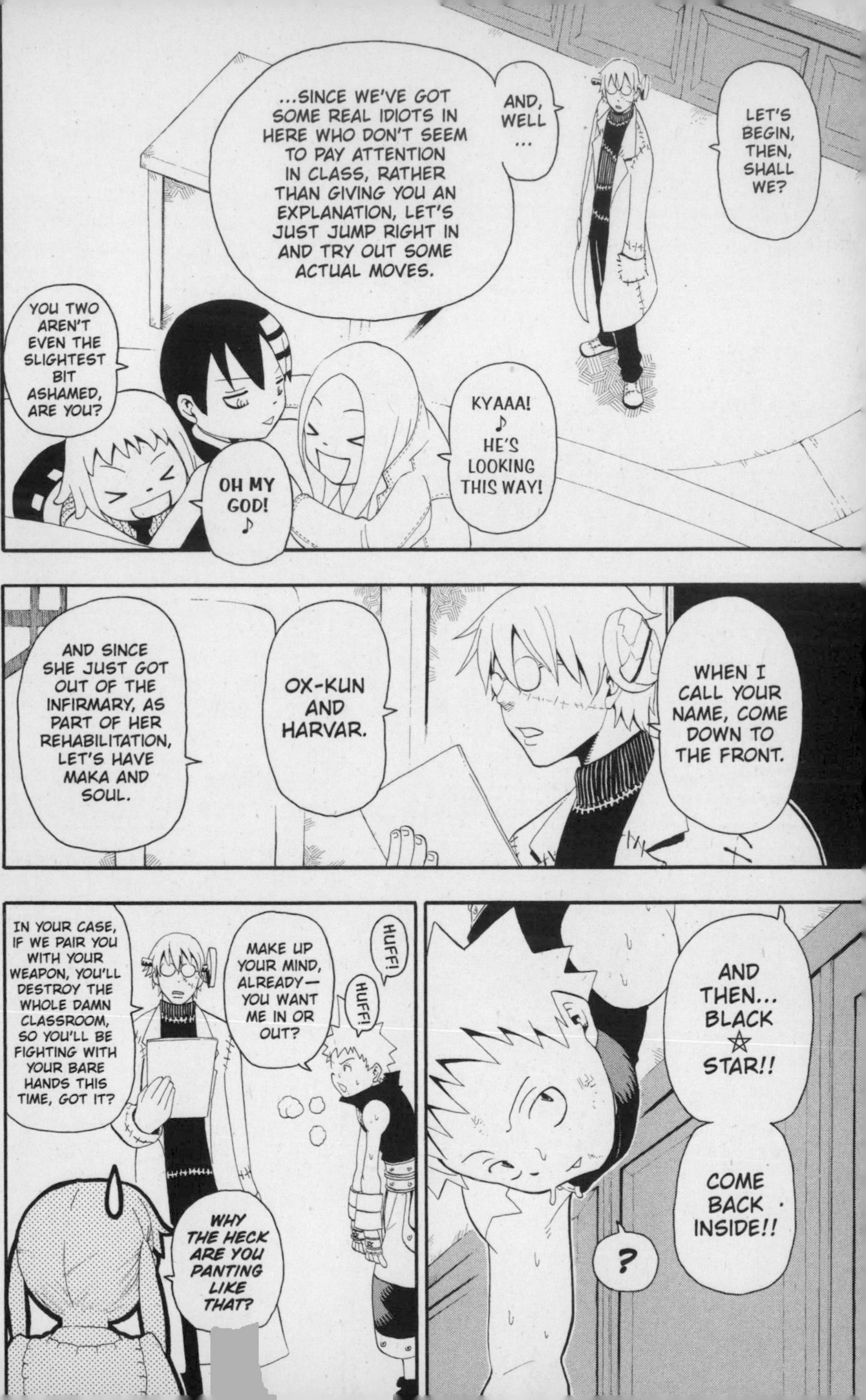
LET'S BEGIN, THEN, SHALL WE?
AND, WELL...
...SINCE WE'VE GOT SOME REAL IDIOTS IN HERE WHO DON'T SEEM TO PAY ATTENTION IN CLASS, RATHER THAN GIVING YOU AN EXPLANATION, LET'S JUST JUMP RIGHT IN AND TRY OUT SOME ACTUAL MOVES.
KYAAA! ♪ HE'S LOOKING THIS WAY!
OH MY GOD! ♪
YOU TWO AREN'T EVEN THE SLIGHTEST BIT ASHAMED, ARE YOU?
WHEN I CALL YOUR NAME, COME DOWN TO THE FRONT.
OX-KUN AND HARVAR.
AND SINCE SHE JUST GOT OUT OF THE INFIRMARY, AS PART OF HER REHABILITATION, LET'S HAVE MAKA AND SOUL.
AND THEN... BLACK ☆ STAR!!
COME BACK INSIDE!!
?
HUFF!
HUFF!
MAKE UP YOUR MIND, ALREADY— YOU WANT ME IN OR OUT?
IN YOUR CASE, IF WE PAIR YOU WITH YOUR WEAPON, YOU'LL DESTROY THE WHOLE DAMN CLASSROOM, SO YOU'LL BE FIGHTING WITH YOUR BARE HANDS THIS TIME, GOT IT?
WHY THE HECK ARE YOU PANTING LIKE THAT?

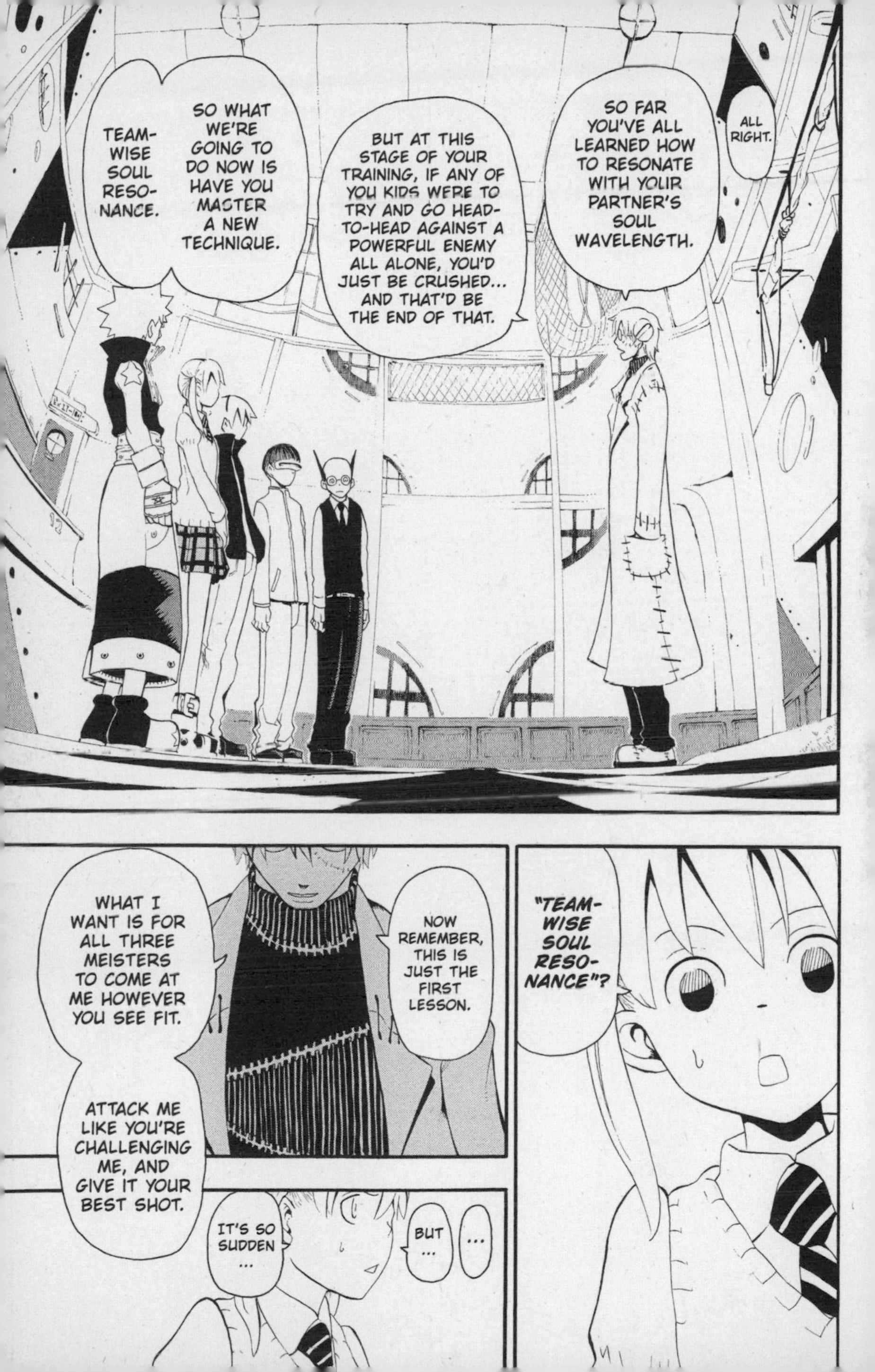
ALL RIGHT.
SO FAR YOU'VE ALL LEARNED HOW TO RESONATE WITH YOUR PARTNER'S SOUL WAVELENGTH.
BUT AT THIS STAGE OF YOUR TRAINING, IF ANY OF YOU KIDS WERE TO TRY AND GO HEAD-TO-HEAD AGAINST A POWERFUL ENEMY ALL ALONE, YOU'D JUST BE CRUSHED... AND THAT'D BE THE END OF THAT.
SO WHAT WE'RE GOING TO DO NOW IS HAVE YOU MASTER A NEW TECHNIQUE.
TEAM-WISE SOUL RESONANCE.
"TEAM-WISE SOUL RESONANCE"?
NOW REMEMBER, THIS IS JUST THE FIRST LESSON.
WHAT I WANT IS FOR ALL THREE MEISTERS TO COME AT ME HOWEVER YOU SEE FIT.
ATTACK ME LIKE YOU'RE CHALLENGING ME, AND GIVE IT YOUR BEST SHOT.
...
BUT ...
IT'S SO SUDDEN ...

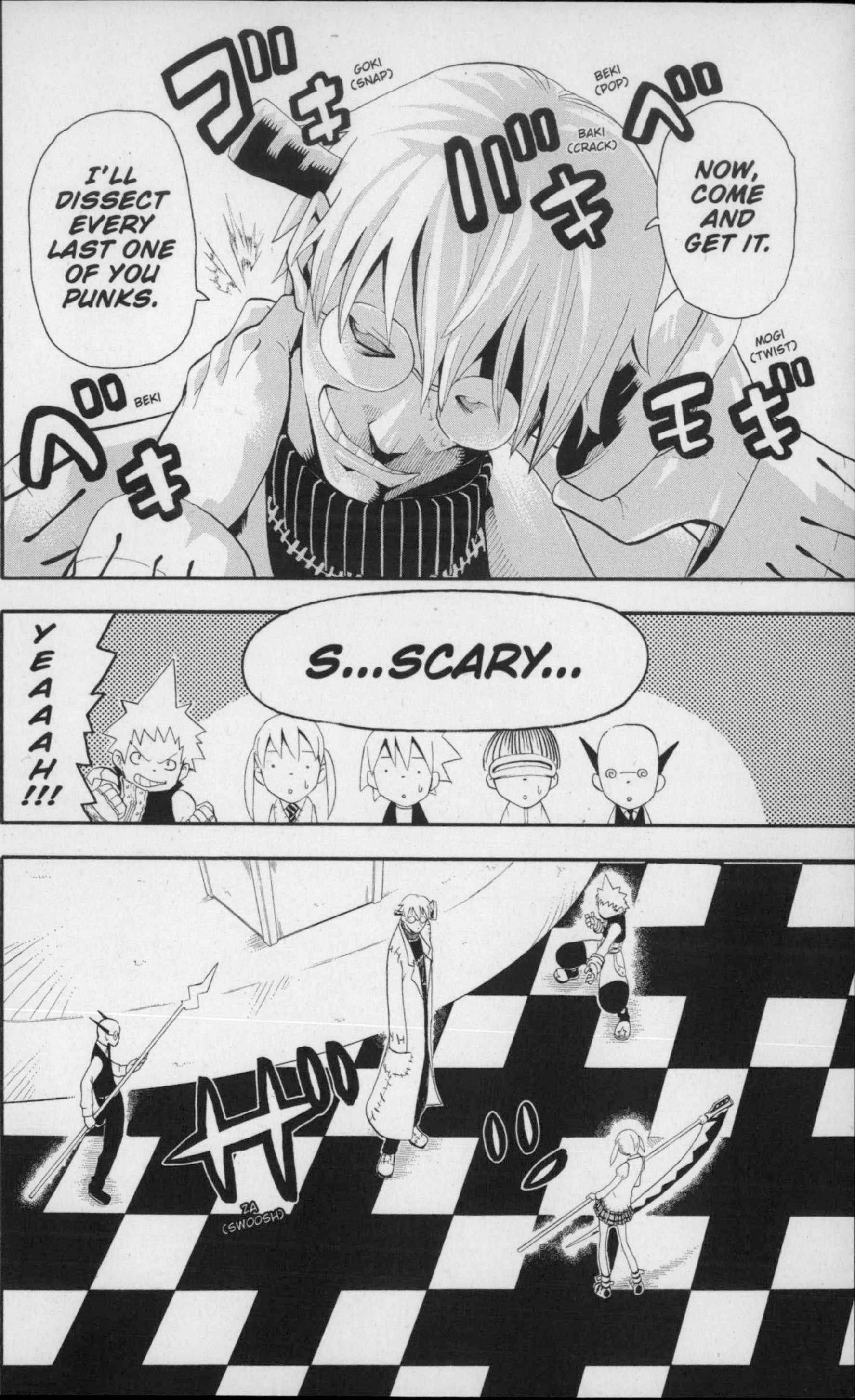
BEKI (POP)
NOW, COME AND GET IT.
BAKI (CRACK)
GOKI (SNAP)
I'LL DISSECT EVERY LAST ONE OF YOU PUNKS.
MOGI (TWIST)
BEKI
S...SCARY...
YEAAAAH!!!
ZA (SWOOSH)

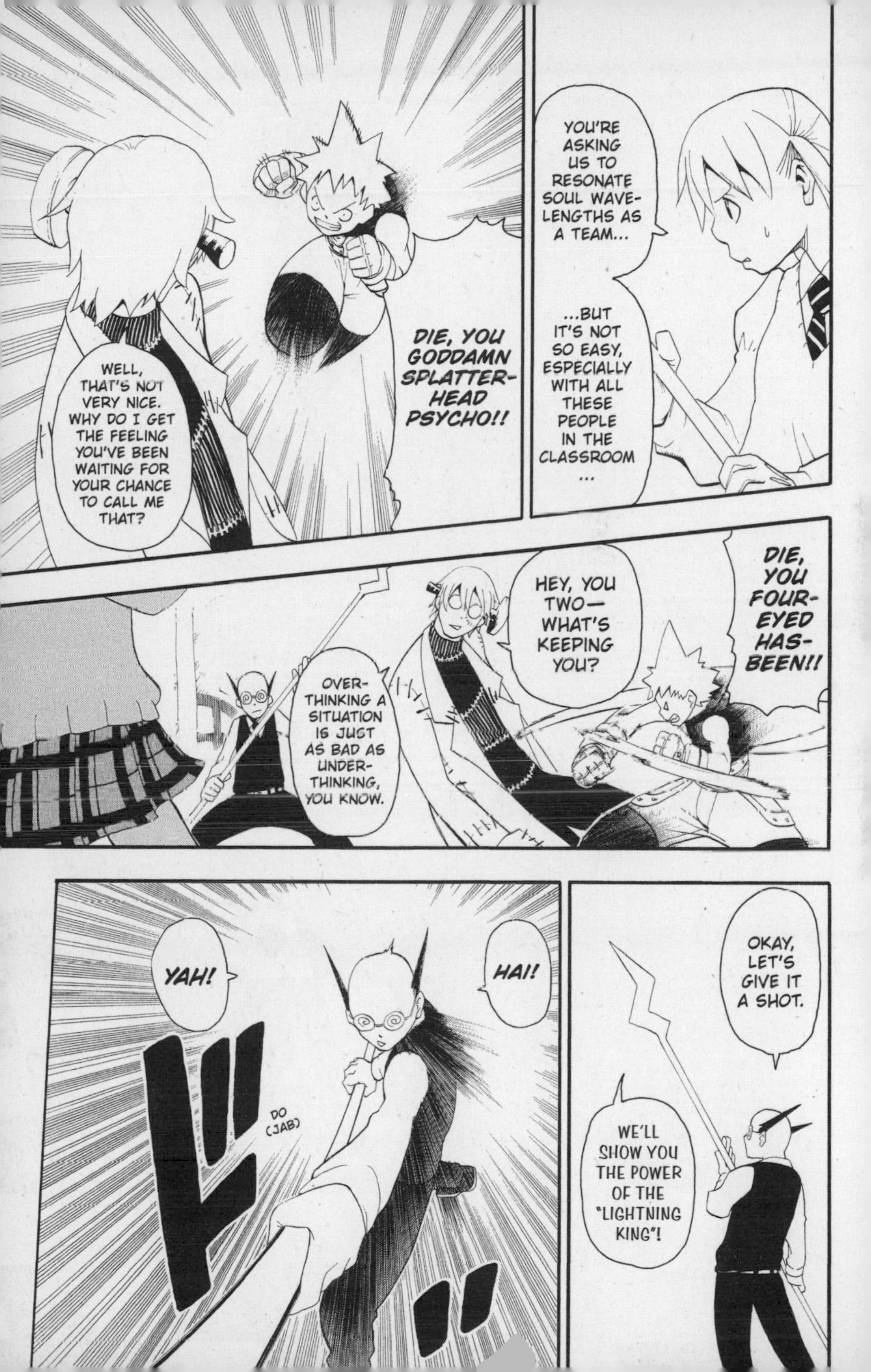

YOU'RE ASKING US TO RESONATE SOUL WAVE-LENGTHS AS A TEAM...
...BUT IT'S NOT SO EASY, ESPECIALLY WITH ALL THESE PEOPLE IN THE CLASSROOM...
DIE, YOU GODDAMN SPLATTER-HEAD PSYCHO!!
WELL, THAT'S NOT VERY NICE. WHY DO I GET THE FEELING YOU'VE BEEN WAITING FOR YOUR CHANCE TO CALL ME THAT?
DIE, YOU FOUR-EYED HAS-BEEN!!
HEY, YOU TWO—WHAT'S KEEPING YOU?
OVER-THINKING A SITUATION IS JUST AS BAD AS UNDER-THINKING, YOU KNOW.
OKAY, LET'S GIVE IT A SHOT.
WE'LL SHOW YOU THE POWER OF THE "LIGHTNING KING"!
HAI!
YAH!
DO (JAB)

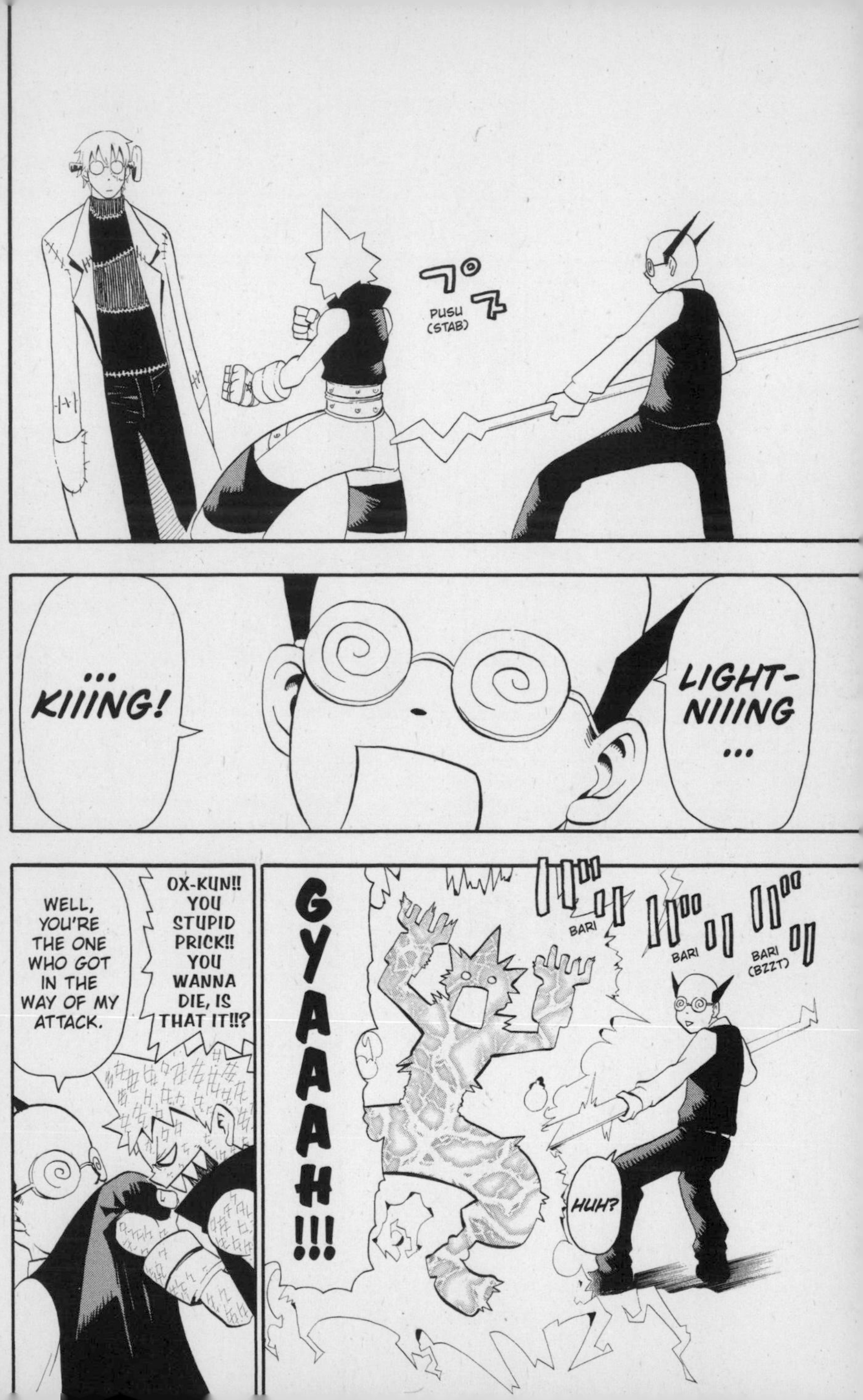
PUSU (STAB)
LIGHT-NIIING...
...KIIING!
BARI
BARI
BARI (BZZT)
GYAAAAH!!!
HUH?
OX-KUN!! YOU STUPID PRICK!! YOU WANNA DIE, IS THAT IT!!?
WELL, YOU'RE THE ONE WHO GOT IN THE WAY OF MY ATTACK.

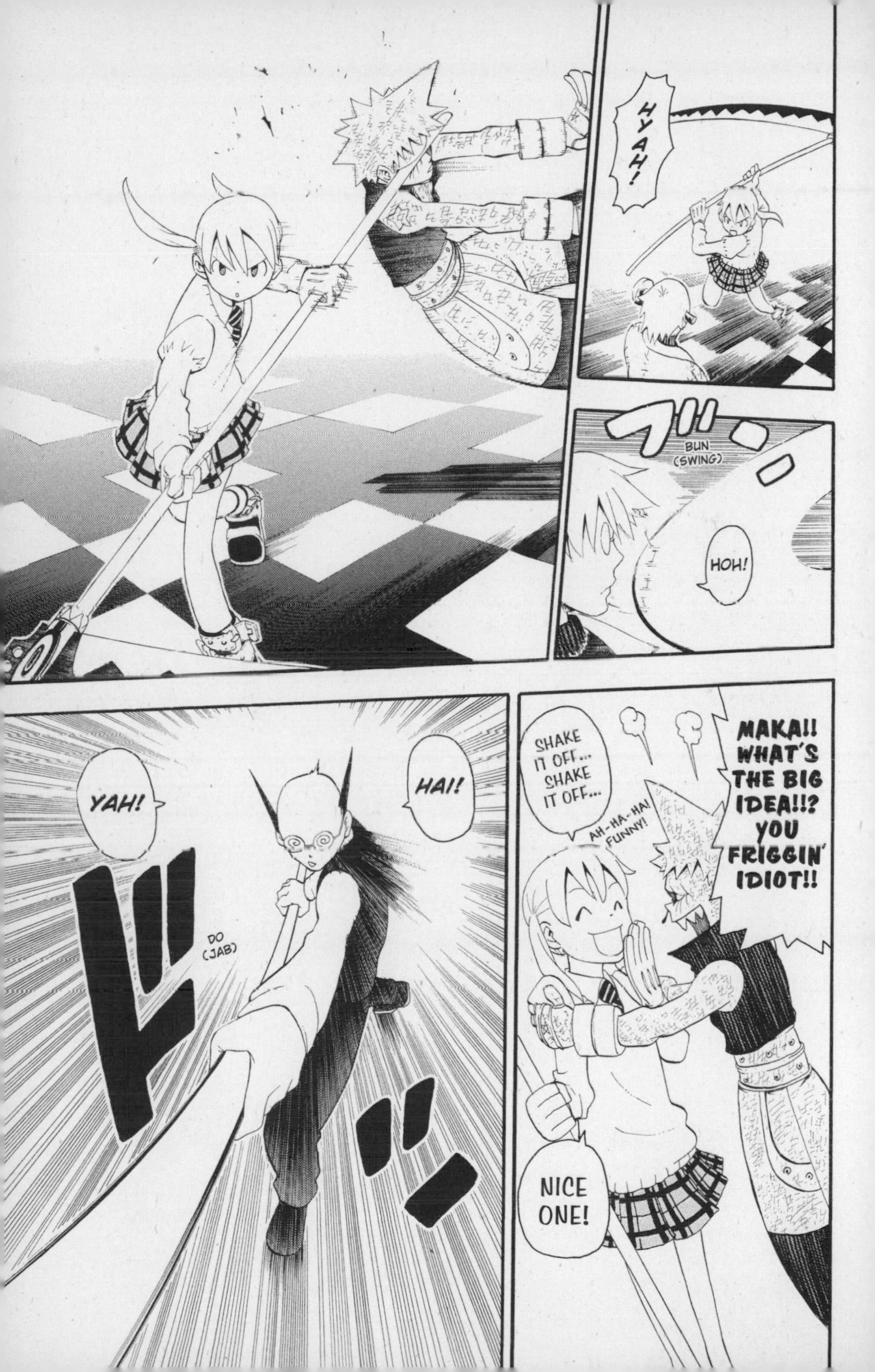
HYAH!
BUN (SWING)
HOH!
MAKA!! WHAT'S THE BIG IDEA!!? YOU FRIGGIN' IDIOT!!
SHAKE IT OFF... SHAKE IT OFF...
AH-HA-HA! FUNNY!
NICE ONE!
HAI!
YAH!
DO (JAB)

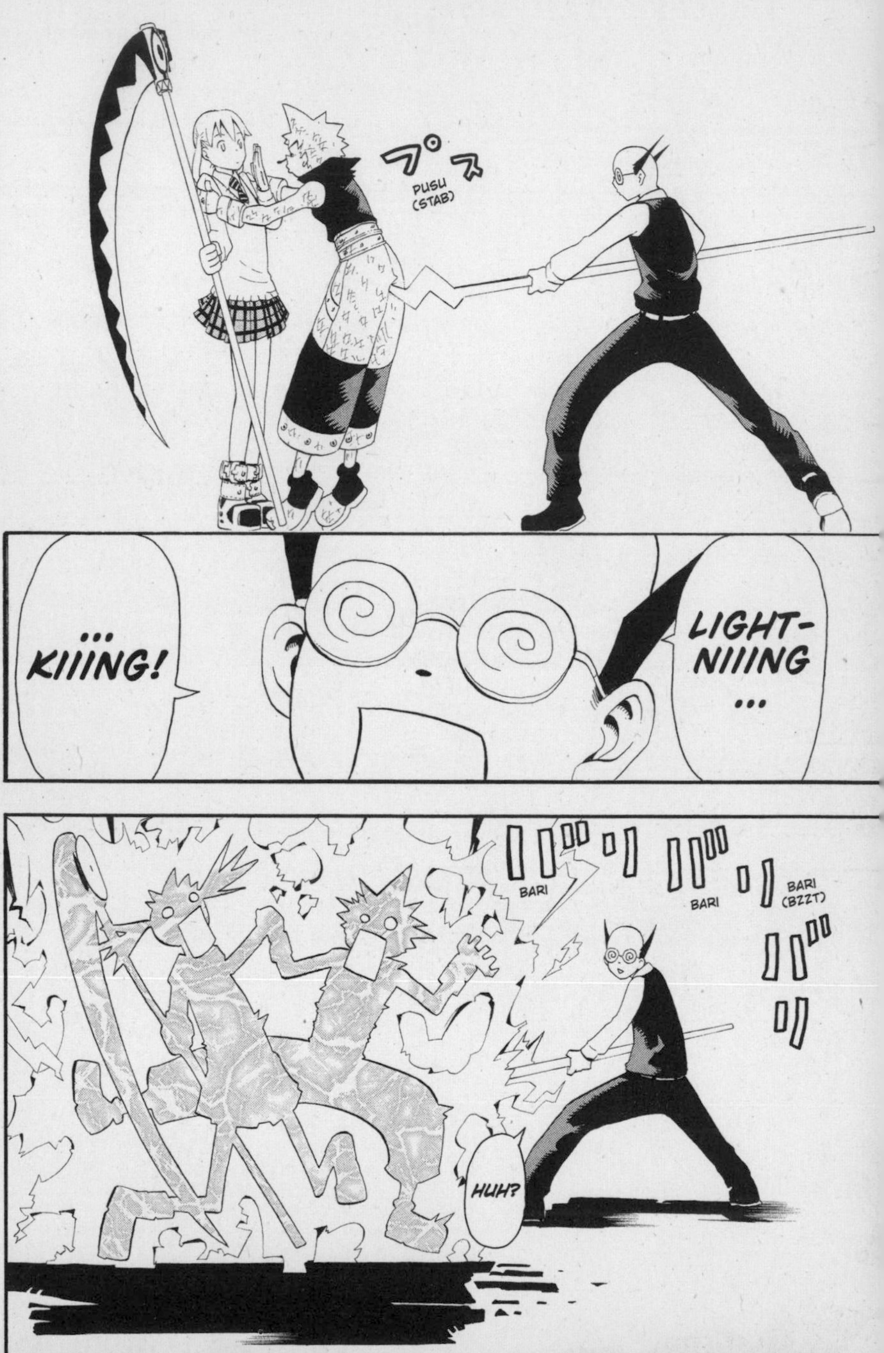
プス
PUSU
(STAB)
LIGHT-NIIING ...
... KIIING!
BARI
(BZZT)
BARI
BARI
HUH?

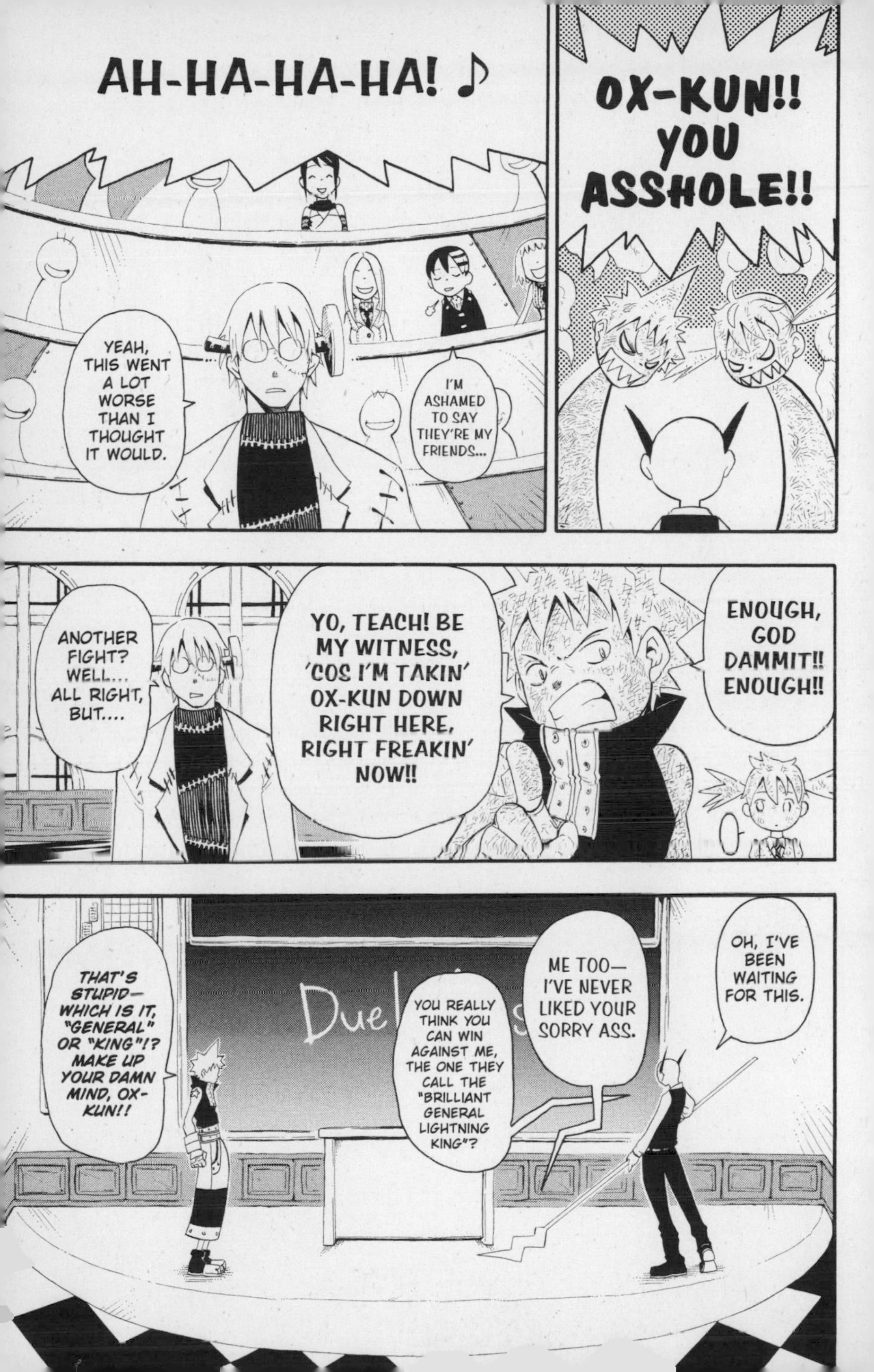
OX-KUN!! YOU ASSHOLE!!
AH-HA-HA-HA! ♪
I'M ASHAMED TO SAY THEY'RE MY FRIENDS...
YEAH, THIS WENT A LOT WORSE THAN I THOUGHT IT WOULD.
ENOUGH, GOD DAMMIT!! ENOUGH!!
YO, TEACH! BE MY WITNESS, 'COS I'M TAKIN' OX-KUN DOWN RIGHT HERE, RIGHT FREAKIN' NOW!!
ANOTHER FIGHT? WELL... ALL RIGHT, BUT....
OH, I'VE BEEN WAITING FOR THIS.
ME TOO— I'VE NEVER LIKED YOUR SORRY ASS.
YOU REALLY THINK YOU CAN WIN AGAINST ME, THE ONE THEY CALL THE "BRILLIANT GENERAL LIGHTNING KING"?
THAT'S STUPID— WHICH IS IT, "GENERAL" OR "KING"!? MAKE UP YOUR DAMN MIND, OX-KUN!!

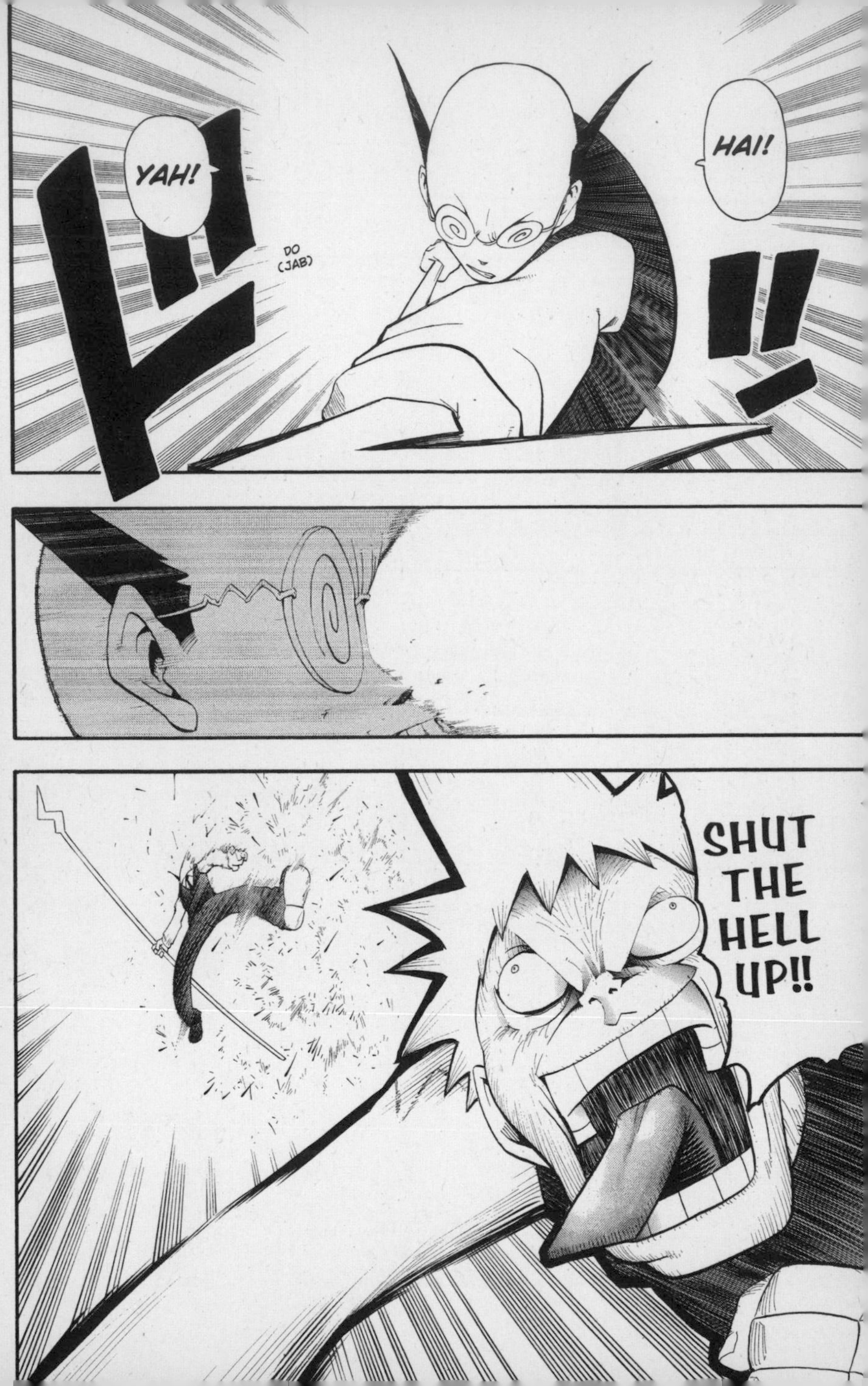
HAI!
YAH!
DO (JAB)
SHUT THE HELL UP!!

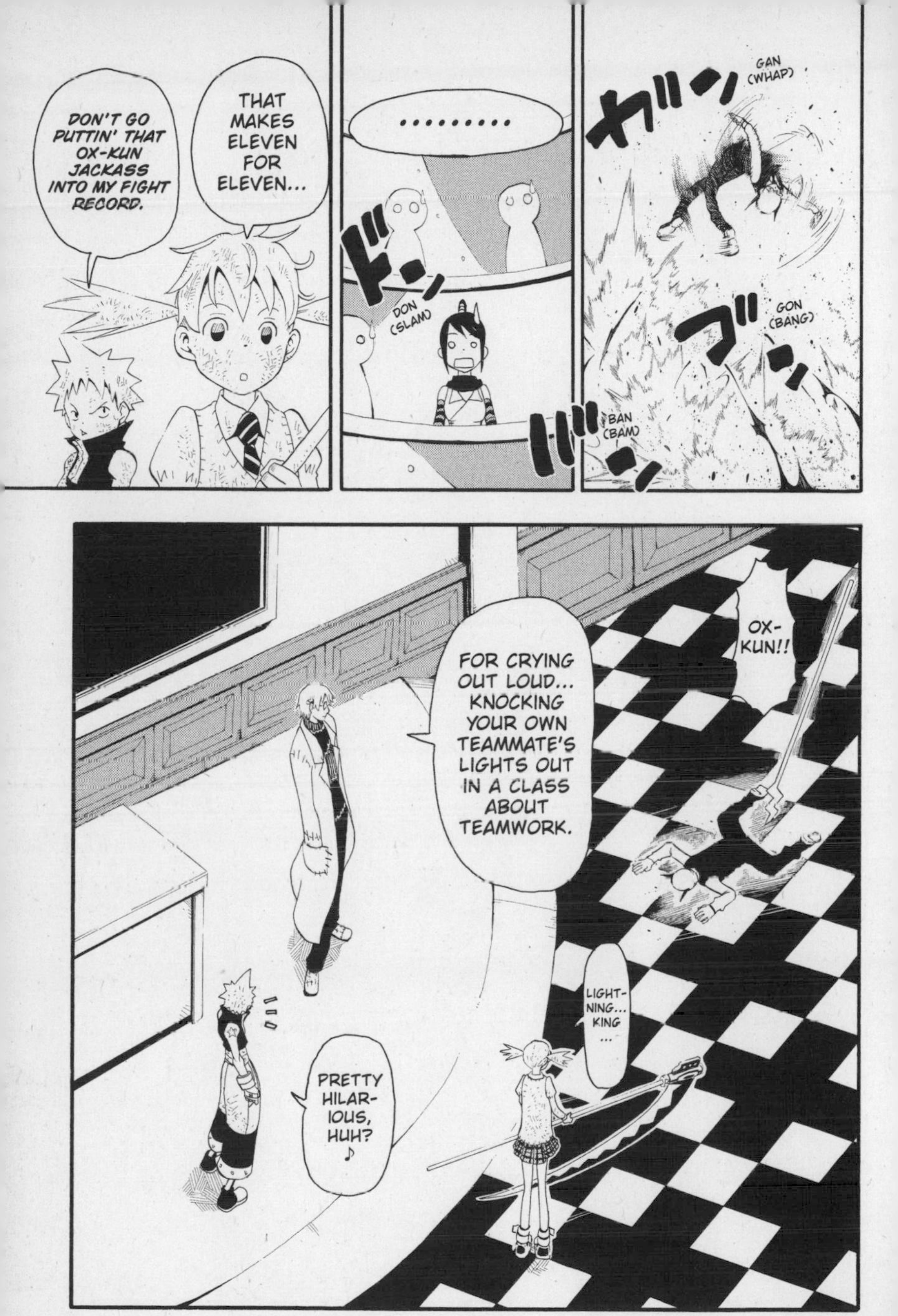
GAN (WHAP)
GON (BANG)
BAN (BAM)
DON (SLAM)
....
THAT MAKES ELEVEN FOR ELEVEN...
DON'T GO PUTTIN' THAT OX-KUN JACKASS INTO MY FIGHT RECORD.
OX-KUN!!
FOR CRYING OUT LOUD... KNOCKING YOUR OWN TEAMMATE'S LIGHTS OUT IN A CLASS ABOUT TEAMWORK.
LIGHTNING... KING...
PRETTY HILARIOUS, HUH? ♪

DWMA
UNDER-
GROUND

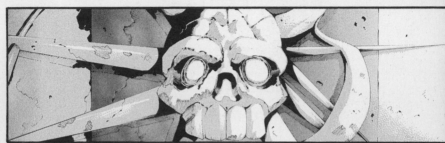

THE
SECRET
VAULT

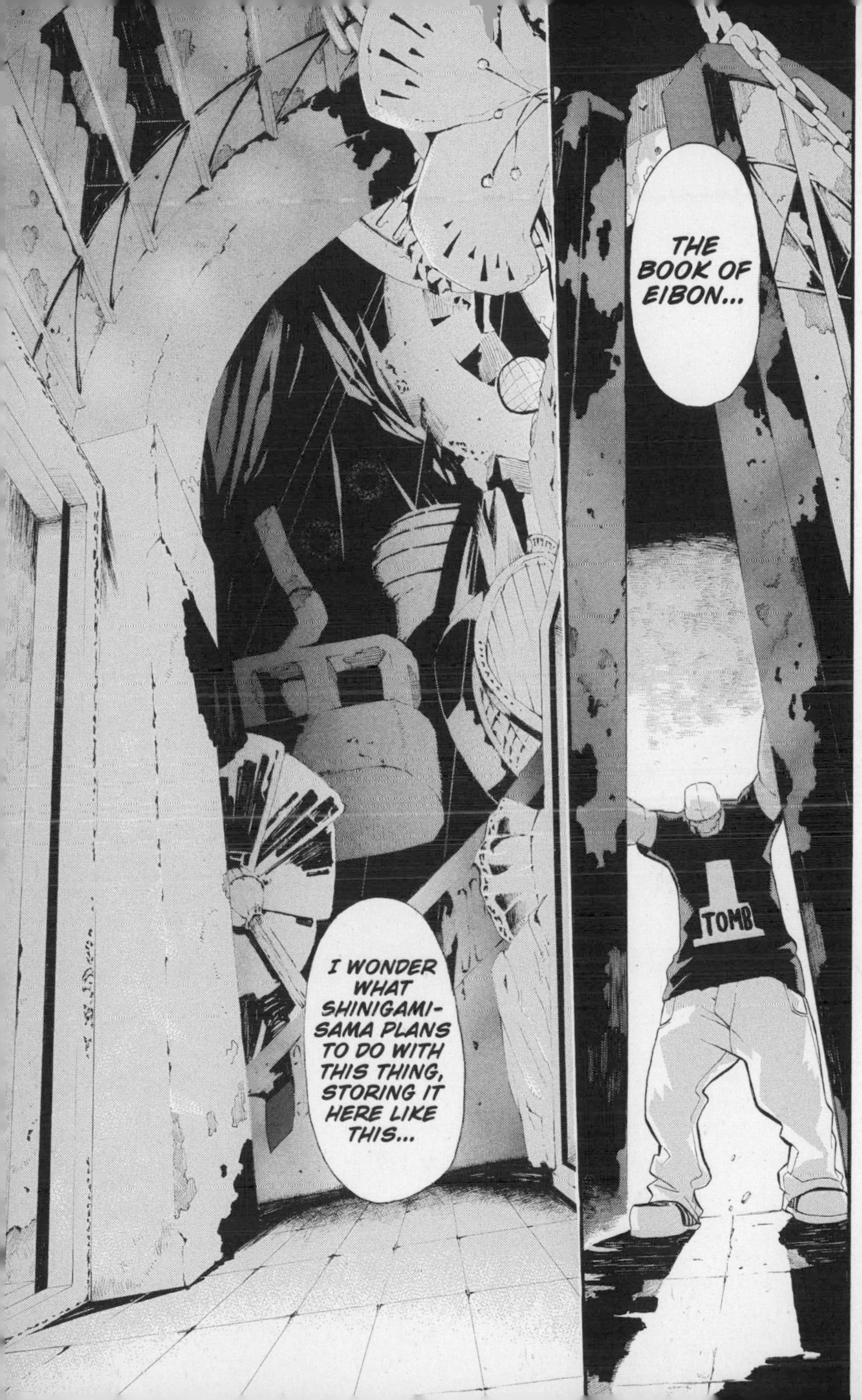
THE BOOK OF EIBON...
TOMB
I WONDER WHAT SHINIGAMI-SAMA PLANS TO DO WITH THIS THING, STORING IT HERE LIKE THIS...

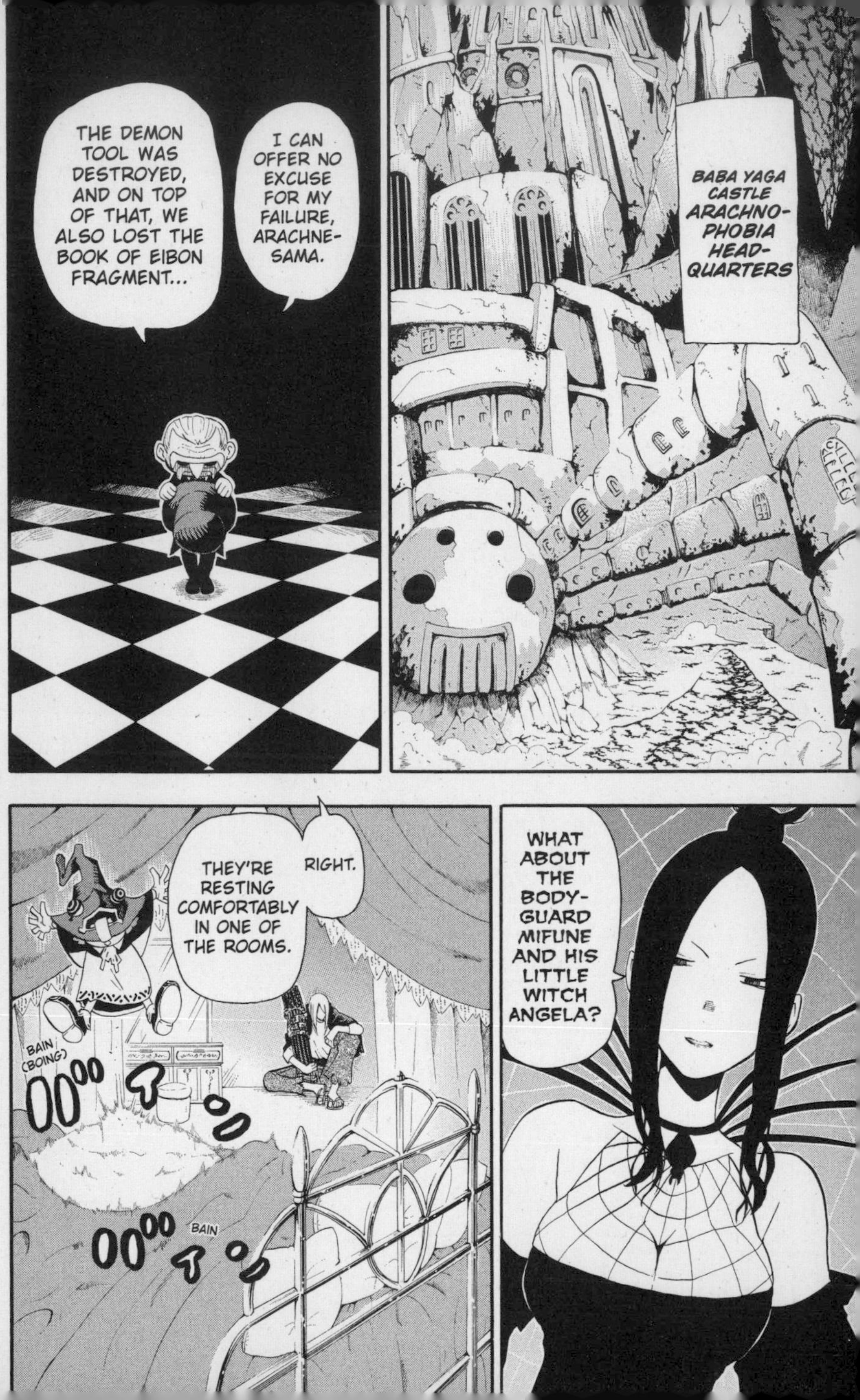
BABA YAGA CASTLE ARACHNOPHOBIA HEADQUARTERS
I CAN OFFER NO EXCUSE FOR MY FAILURE, ARACHNE-SAMA.
THE DEMON TOOL WAS DESTROYED, AND ON TOP OF THAT, WE ALSO LOST THE BOOK OF EIBON FRAGMENT...
WHAT ABOUT THE BODYGUARD MIFUNE AND HIS LITTLE WITCH ANGELA?
RIGHT.
THEY'RE RESTING COMFORTABLY IN ONE OF THE ROOMS.
BAIN (BOING)
BAIN

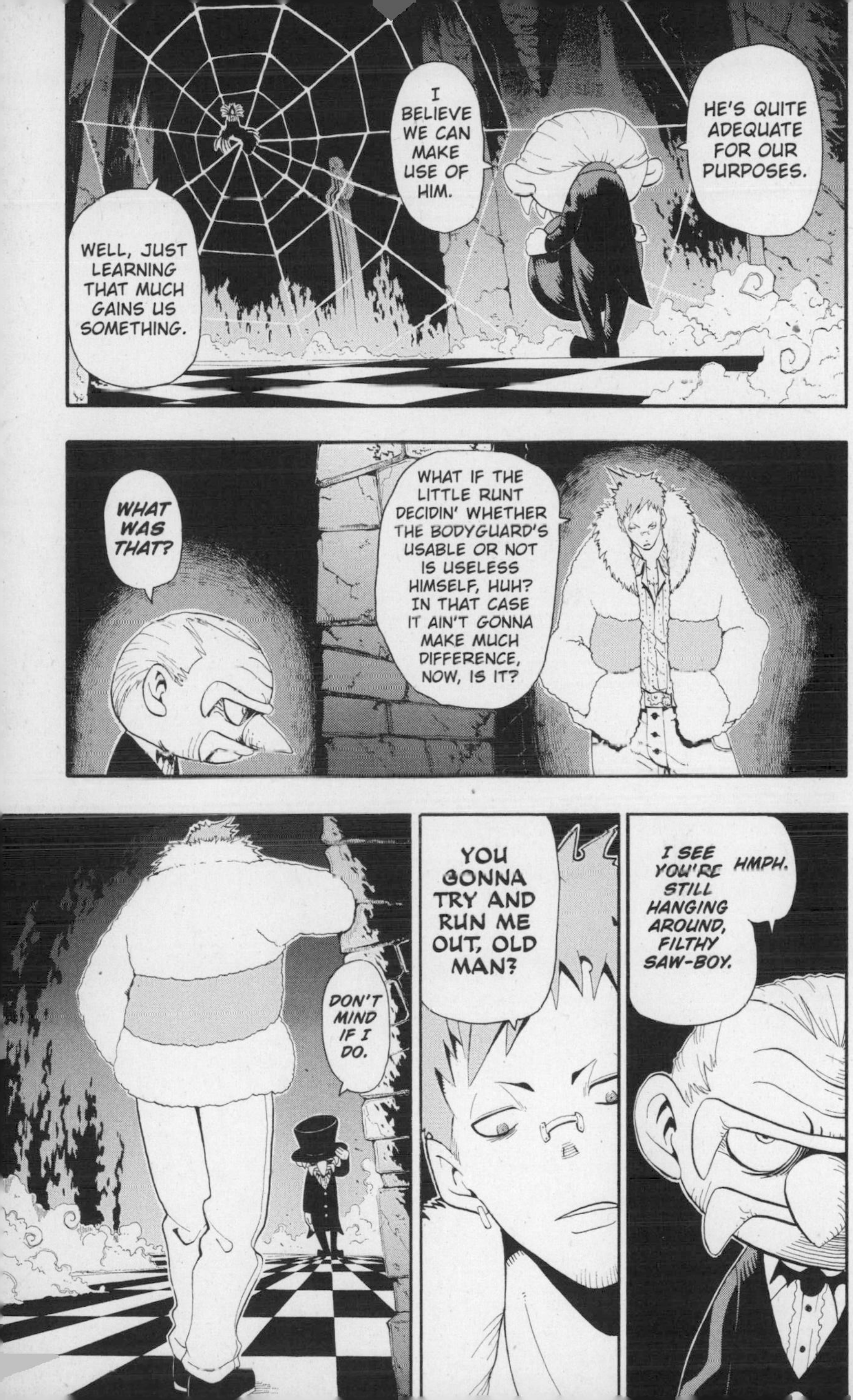
HE'S QUITE ADEQUATE FOR OUR PURPOSES.
I BELIEVE WE CAN MAKE USE OF HIM.
WELL, JUST LEARNING THAT MUCH GAINS US SOMETHING.
WHAT IF THE LITTLE RUNT DECIDIN' WHETHER THE BODYGUARD'S USABLE OR NOT IS USELESS HIMSELF, HUH? IN THAT CASE IT AIN'T GONNA MAKE MUCH DIFFERENCE, NOW, IS IT?
WHAT WAS THAT?
HMPH.
I SEE YOU'RE STILL HANGING AROUND, FILTHY SAW-BOY.
YOU GONNA TRY AND RUN ME OUT, OLD MAN?
DON'T MIND IF I DO.

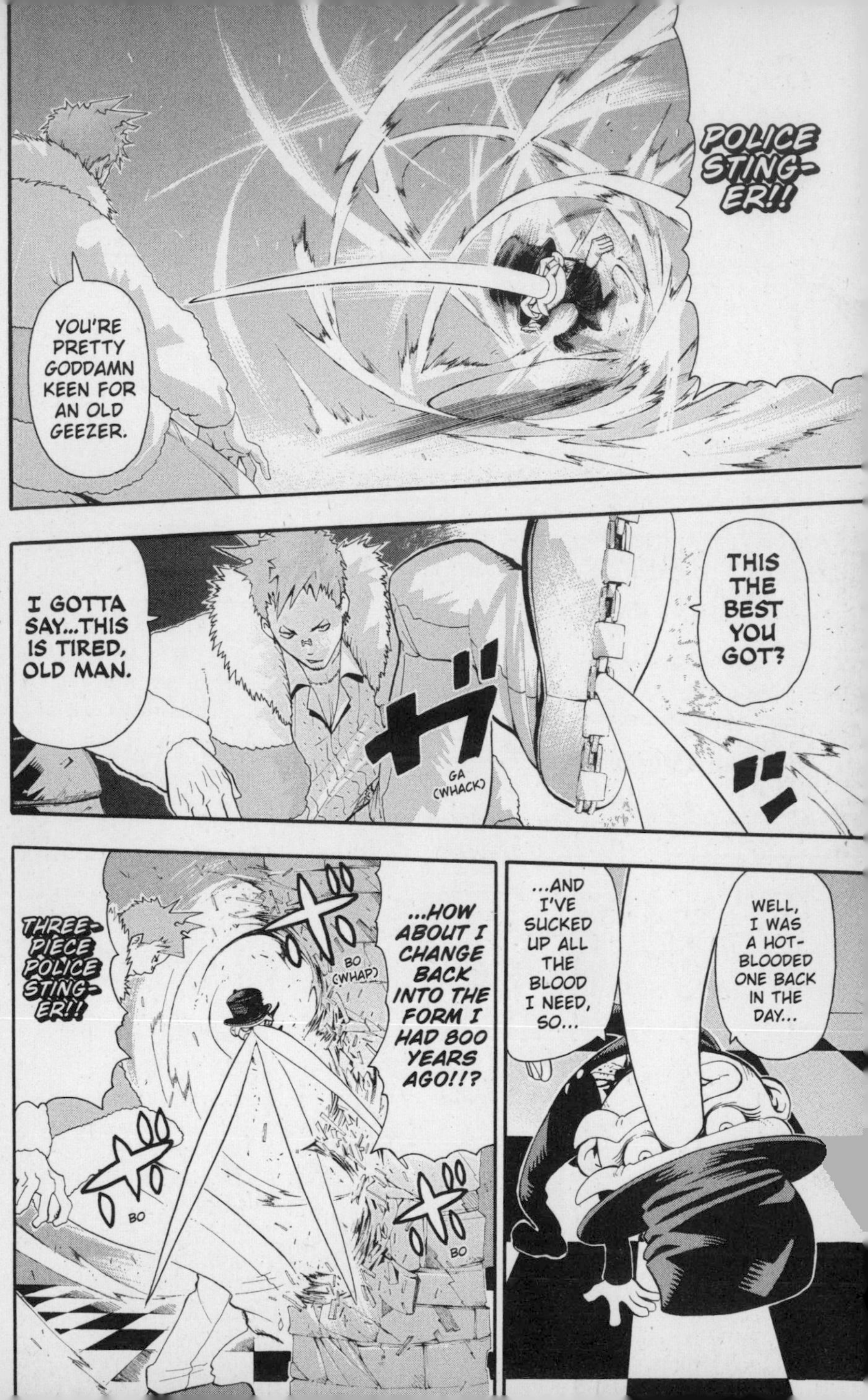
POLICE STINGER!!
YOU'RE PRETTY GODDAMN KEEN FOR AN OLD GEEZER.
THIS THE BEST YOU GOT?
GA (WHACK)
I GOTTA SAY...THIS IS TIRED, OLD MAN.
WELL, I WAS A HOT-BLOODED ONE BACK IN THE DAY...
...AND I'VE SUCKED UP ALL THE BLOOD I NEED, SO...
...HOW ABOUT I CHANGE BACK INTO THE FORM I HAD 800 YEARS AGO!!?
BO (WHAP)
THREE-PIECE POLICE STINGER!!
BO
BO

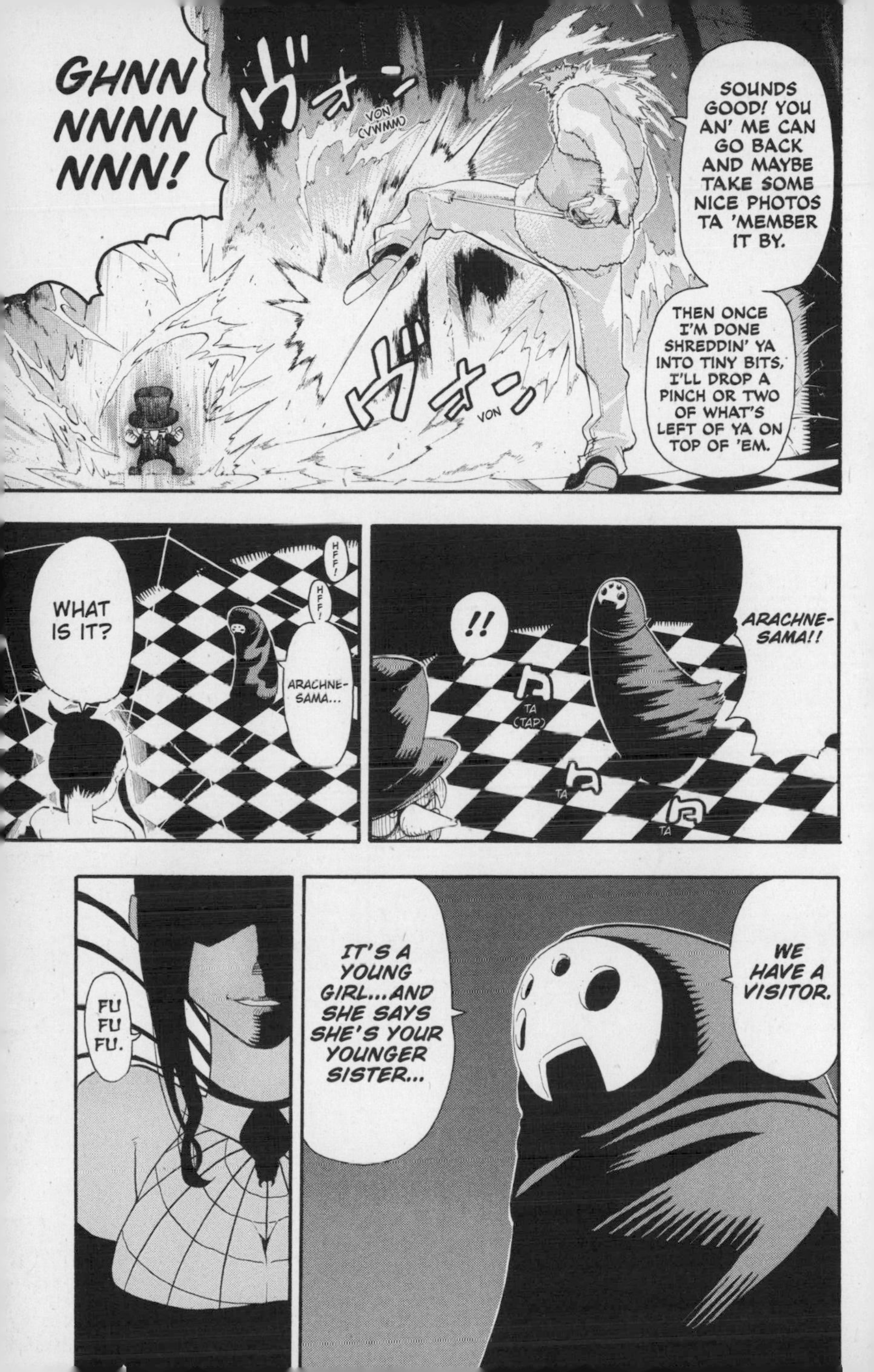
SOUNDS GOOD! YOU AN' ME CAN GO BACK AND MAYBE TAKE SOME NICE PHOTOS TA 'MEMBER IT BY.
THEN ONCE I'M DONE SHREDDIN' YA INTO TINY BITS, I'LL DROP A PINCH OR TWO OF WHAT'S LEFT OF YA ON TOP OF 'EM.
VON (VWMM)
VON
GHNN NNNN NNN!
ARACHNE-SAMA!!
!!
TA (TAP)
TA
TA
HFF!
HFF!
ARACHNE-SAMA...
WHAT IS IT?
WE HAVE A VISITOR.
IT'S A YOUNG GIRL...AND SHE SAYS SHE'S YOUR YOUNGER SISTER...
FU FU FU.

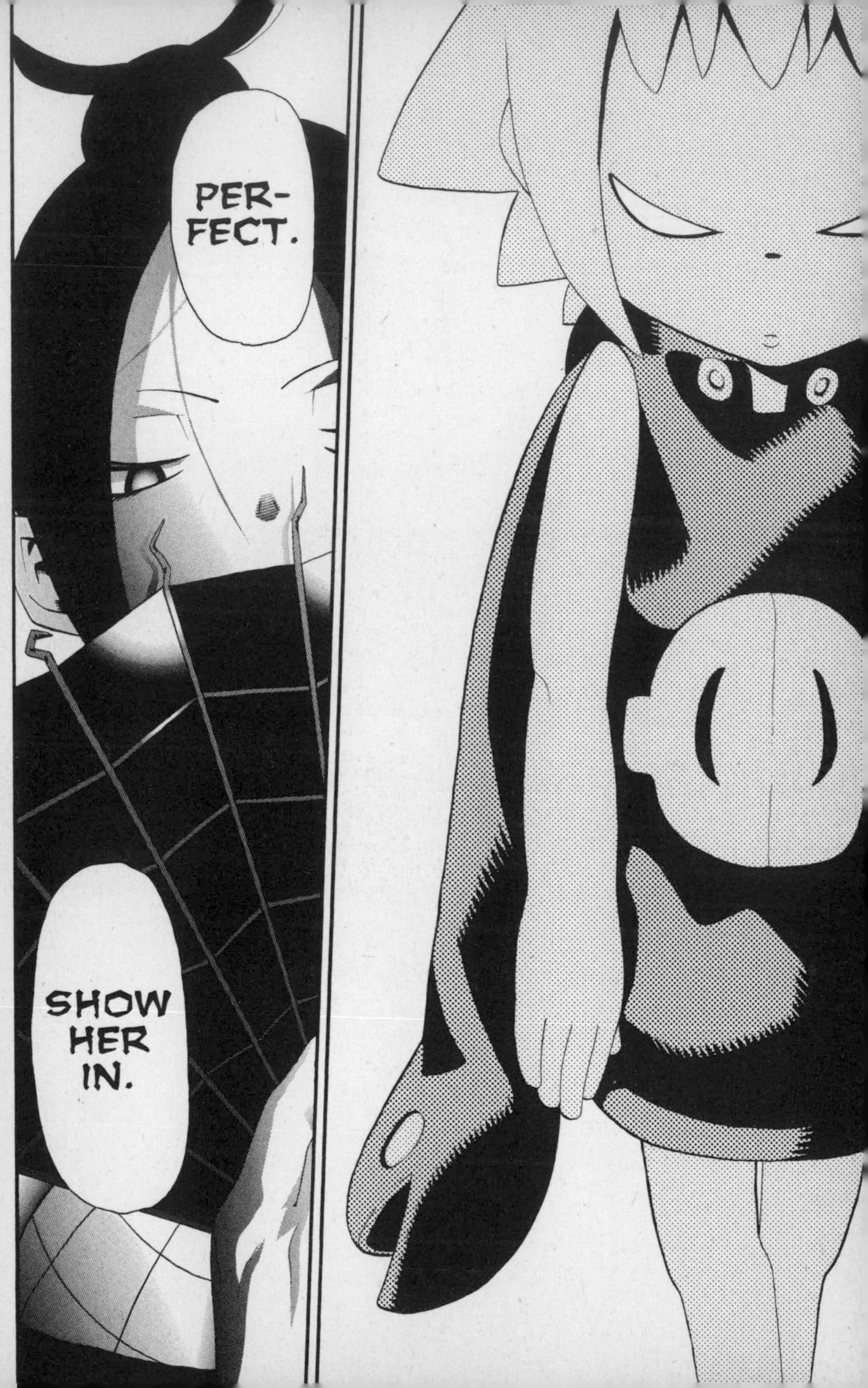
PER-FECT.
SHOW HER IN.

SOUL EATER

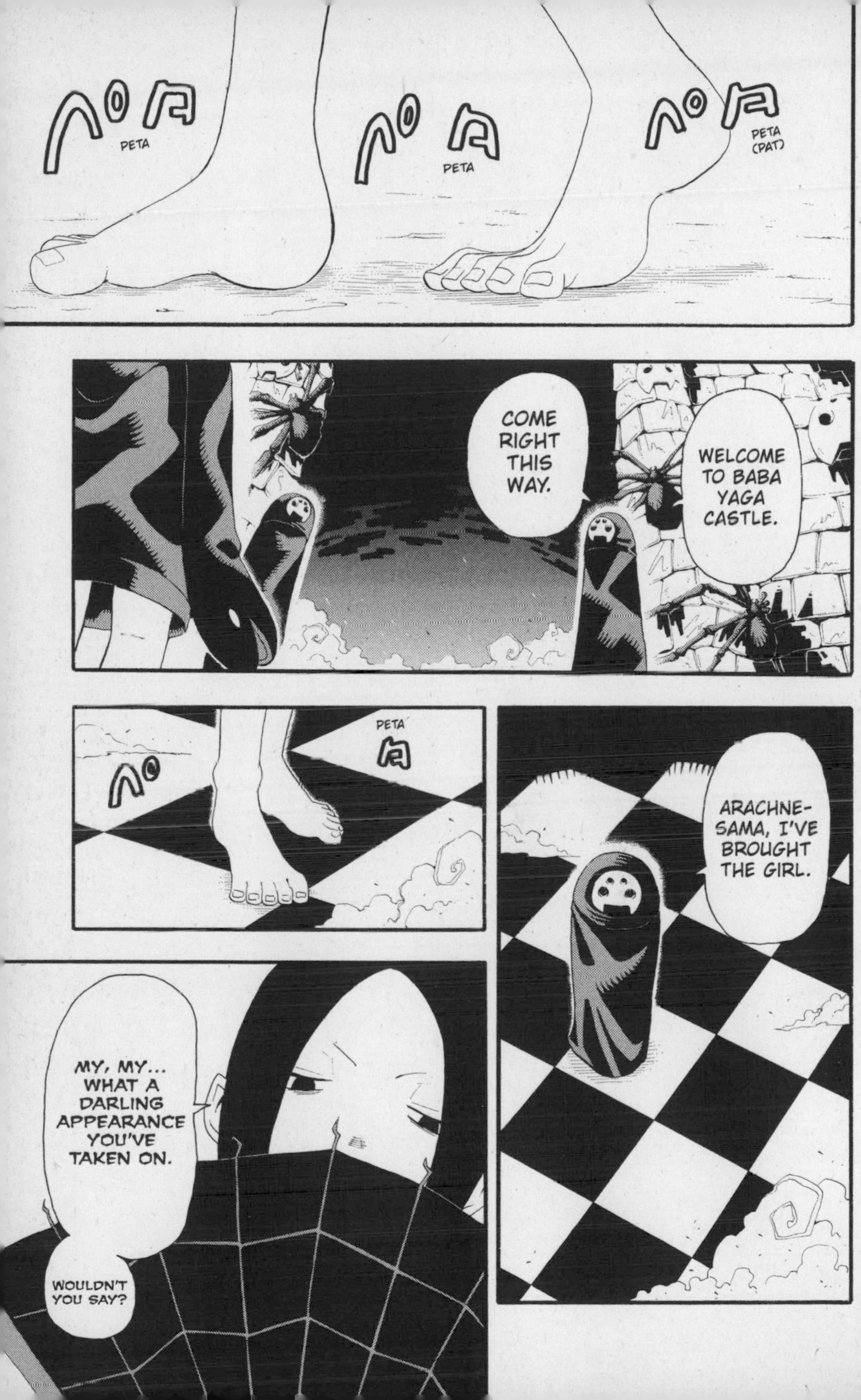
PETA (PAT)
PETA
PETA
WELCOME TO BABA YAGA CASTLE.
COME RIGHT THIS WAY.
ARACHNE-SAMA, I'VE BROUGHT THE GIRL.
PETA
MY, MY... WHAT A DARLING APPEARANCE YOU'VE TAKEN ON.
WOULDN'T YOU SAY?

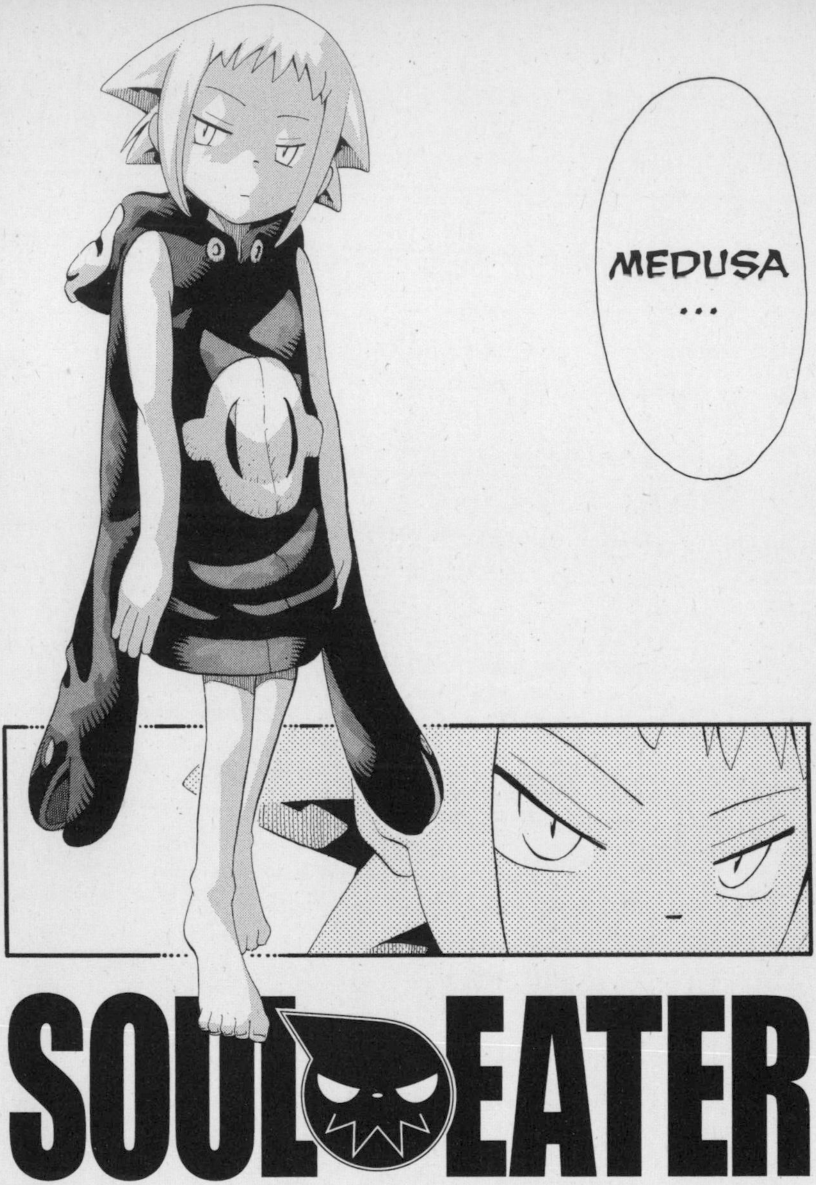
MEDUSA
...

SOUL EATER

CHAPTER 30: THE REUNION EXPRESS (PART 1)

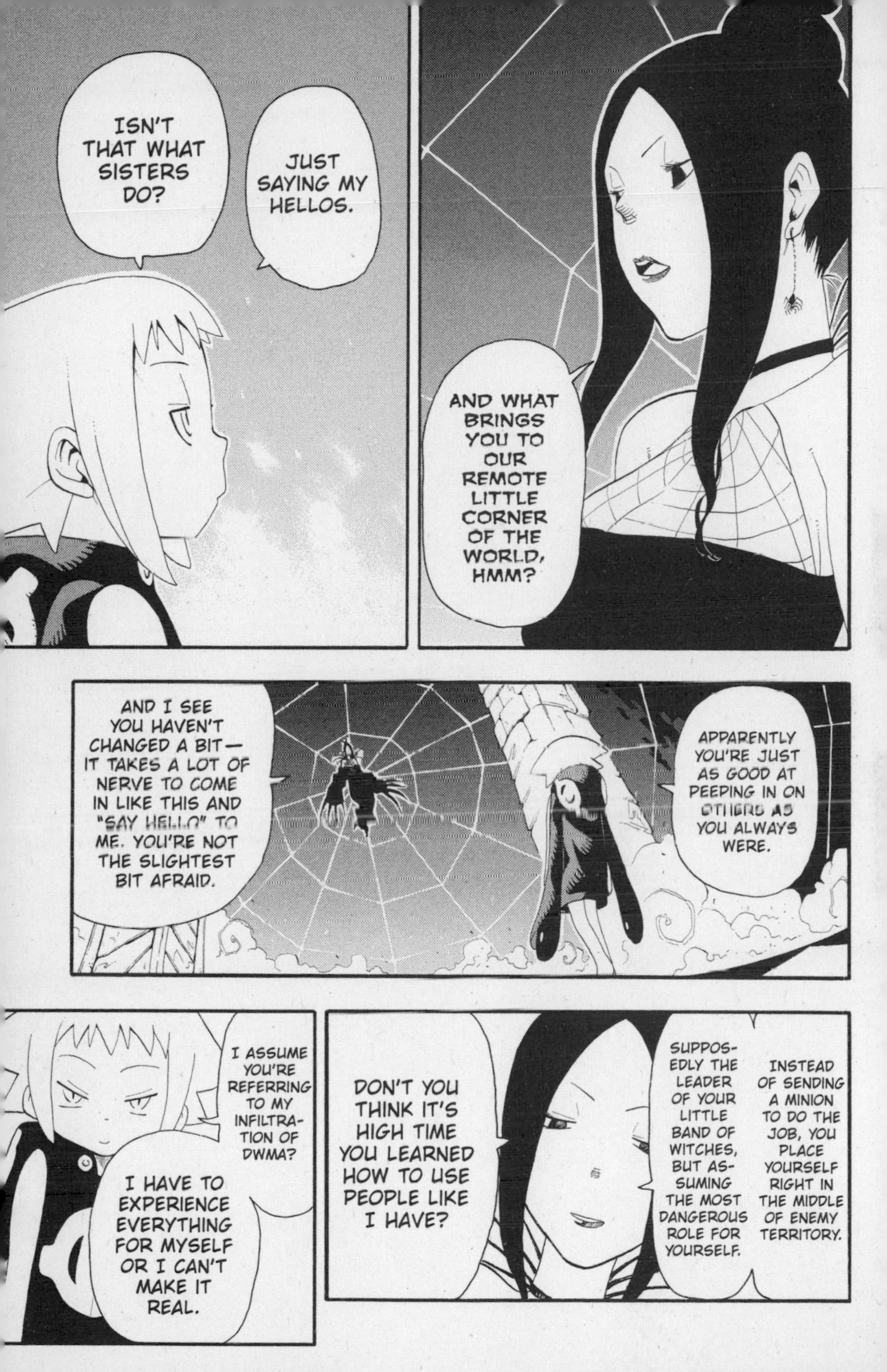
AND WHAT BRINGS YOU TO OUR REMOTE LITTLE CORNER OF THE WORLD, HMM?
JUST SAYING MY HELLOS.
ISN'T THAT WHAT SISTERS DO?
APPARENTLY YOU'RE JUST AS GOOD AT PEEPING IN ON OTHERS AS YOU ALWAYS WERE.
AND I SEE YOU HAVEN'T CHANGED A BIT— IT TAKES A LOT OF NERVE TO COME IN LIKE THIS AND "SAY HELLO" TO ME. YOU'RE NOT THE SLIGHTEST BIT AFRAID.
INSTEAD OF SENDING A MINION TO DO THE JOB, YOU PLACE YOURSELF RIGHT IN THE MIDDLE OF ENEMY TERRITORY.
SUPPOSEDLY THE LEADER OF YOUR LITTLE BAND OF WITCHES, BUT ASSUMING THE MOST DANGEROUS ROLE FOR YOURSELF.
DON'T YOU THINK IT'S HIGH TIME YOU LEARNED HOW TO USE PEOPLE LIKE I HAVE?
I ASSUME YOU'RE REFERRING TO MY INFILTRATION OF DWMA?
I HAVE TO EXPERIENCE EVERYTHING FOR MYSELF OR I CAN'T MAKE IT REAL.

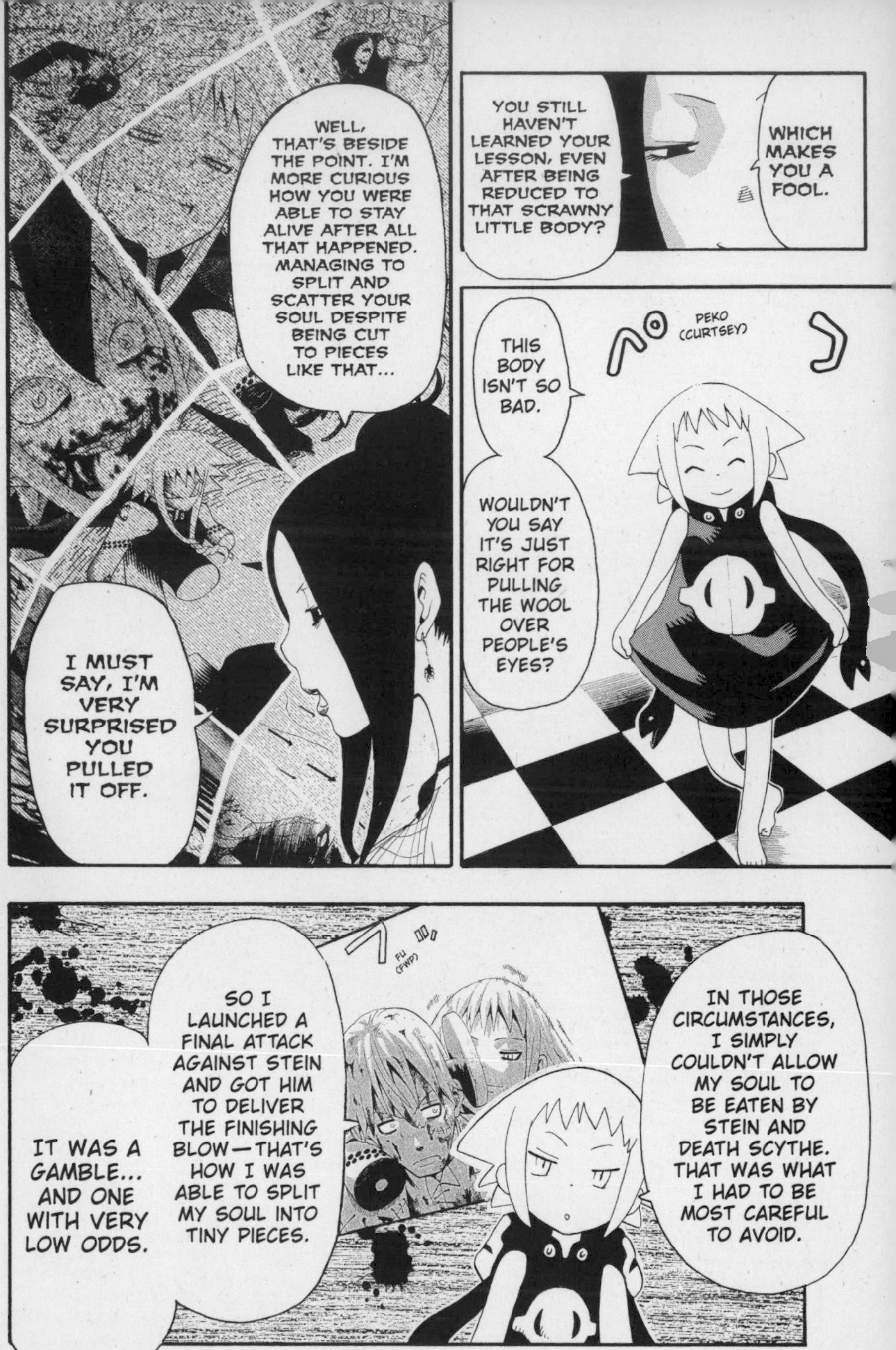
WHICH MAKES YOU A FOOL.
YOU STILL HAVEN'T LEARNED YOUR LESSON, EVEN AFTER BEING REDUCED TO THAT SCRAWNY LITTLE BODY?
PEKO (CURTSEY)
THIS BODY ISN'T SO BAD.
WOULDN'T YOU SAY IT'S JUST RIGHT FOR PULLING THE WOOL OVER PEOPLE'S EYES?
WELL, THAT'S BESIDE THE POINT. I'M MORE CURIOUS HOW YOU WERE ABLE TO STAY ALIVE AFTER ALL THAT HAPPENED. MANAGING TO SPLIT AND SCATTER YOUR SOUL DESPITE BEING CUT TO PIECES LIKE THAT...
I MUST SAY, I'M VERY SURPRISED YOU PULLED IT OFF.
IN THOSE CIRCUMSTANCES, I SIMPLY COULDN'T ALLOW MY SOUL TO BE EATEN BY STEIN AND DEATH SCYTHE. THAT WAS WHAT I HAD TO BE MOST CAREFUL TO AVOID.
FU (PWP)
SO I LAUNCHED A FINAL ATTACK AGAINST STEIN AND GOT HIM TO DELIVER THE FINISHING BLOW—THAT'S HOW I WAS ABLE TO SPLIT MY SOUL INTO TINY PIECES.
IT WAS A GAMBLE... AND ONE WITH VERY LOW ODDS.

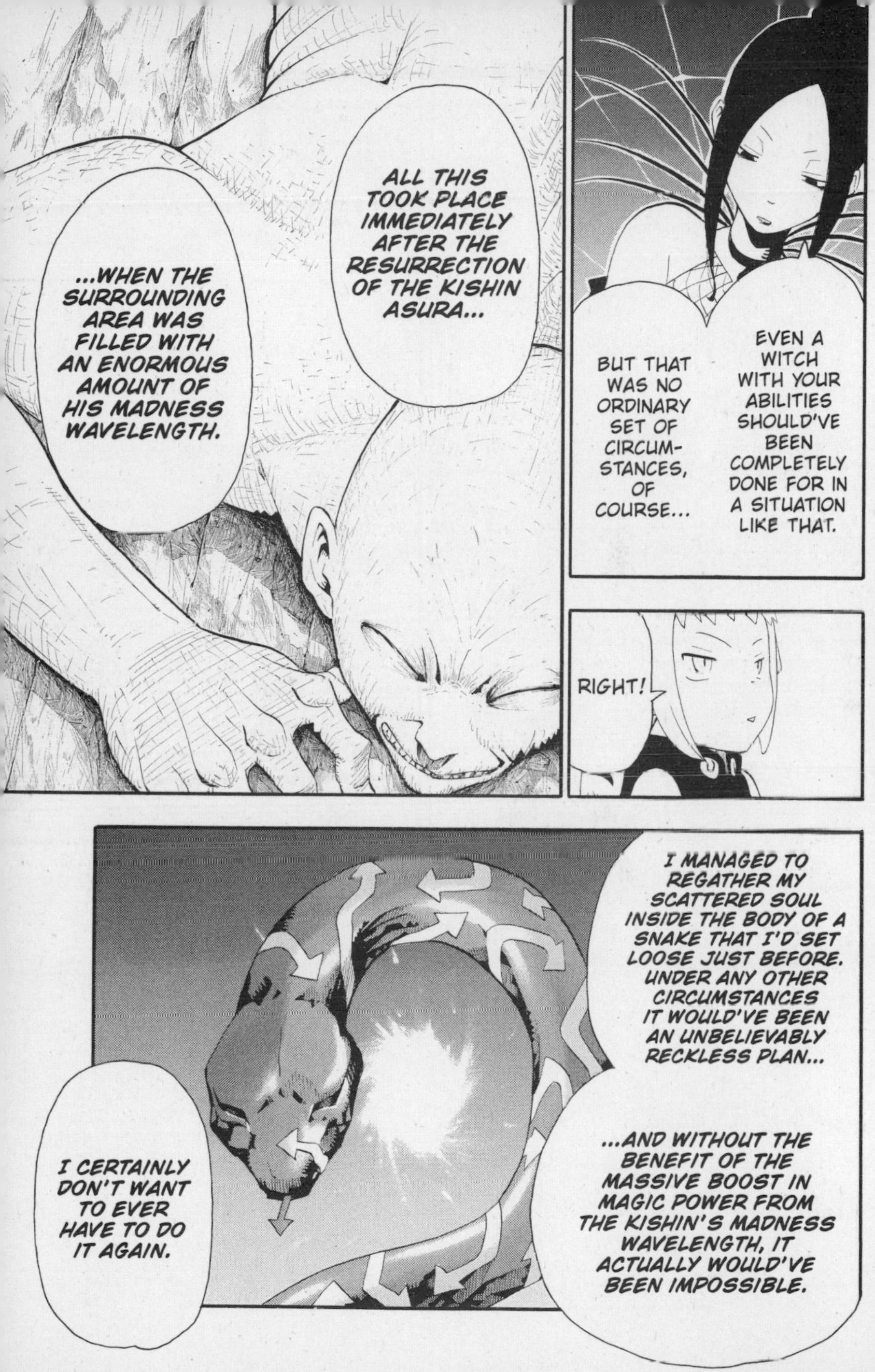
EVEN A WITCH WITH YOUR ABILITIES SHOULD'VE BEEN COMPLETELY DONE FOR IN A SITUATION LIKE THAT.
BUT THAT WAS NO ORDINARY SET OF CIRCUM-STANCES, OF COURSE...
RIGHT!
ALL THIS TOOK PLACE IMMEDIATELY AFTER THE RESURRECTION OF THE KISHIN ASURA...
...WHEN THE SURROUNDING AREA WAS FILLED WITH AN ENORMOUS AMOUNT OF HIS MADNESS WAVELENGTH.
I MANAGED TO REGATHER MY SCATTERED SOUL INSIDE THE BODY OF A SNAKE THAT I'D SET LOOSE JUST BEFORE. UNDER ANY OTHER CIRCUMSTANCES IT WOULD'VE BEEN AN UNBELIEVABLY RECKLESS PLAN...
...AND WITHOUT THE BENEFIT OF THE MASSIVE BOOST IN MAGIC POWER FROM THE KISHIN'S MADNESS WAVELENGTH, IT ACTUALLY WOULD'VE BEEN IMPOSSIBLE.
I CERTAINLY DON'T WANT TO EVER HAVE TO DO IT AGAIN.

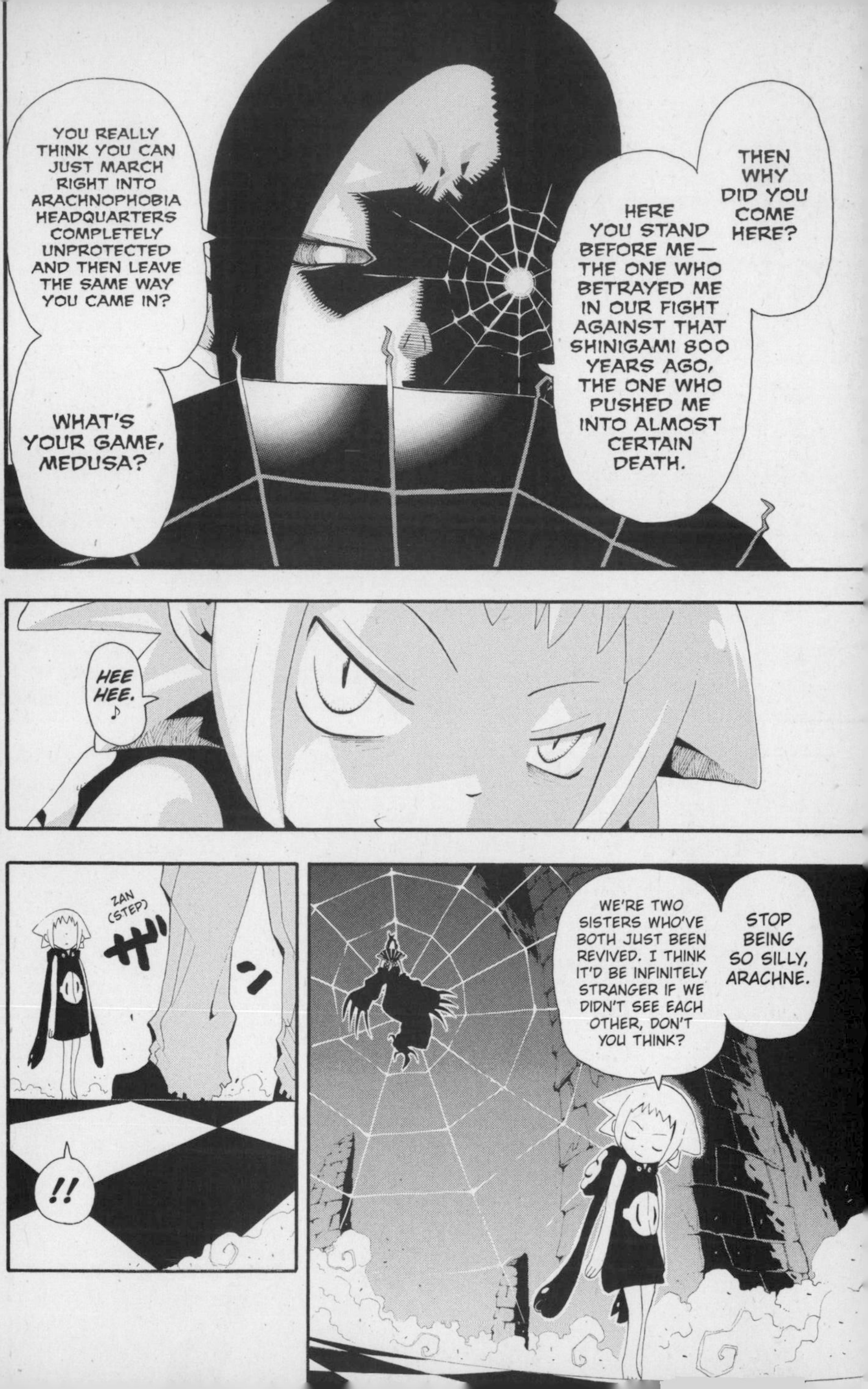
THEN WHY DID YOU COME HERE?
HERE YOU STAND BEFORE ME—THE ONE WHO BETRAYED ME IN OUR FIGHT AGAINST THAT SHINIGAMI 800 YEARS AGO, THE ONE WHO PUSHED ME INTO ALMOST CERTAIN DEATH.
YOU REALLY THINK YOU CAN JUST MARCH RIGHT INTO ARACHNOPHOBIA HEADQUARTERS COMPLETELY UNPROTECTED AND THEN LEAVE THE SAME WAY YOU CAME IN?
WHAT'S YOUR GAME, MEDUSA?
HEE HEE. ♪
STOP BEING SO SILLY, ARACHNE.
WE'RE TWO SISTERS WHO'VE BOTH JUST BEEN REVIVED. I THINK IT'D BE INFINITELY STRANGER IF WE DIDN'T SEE EACH OTHER, DON'T YOU THINK?
ZAN (STEP)
!!

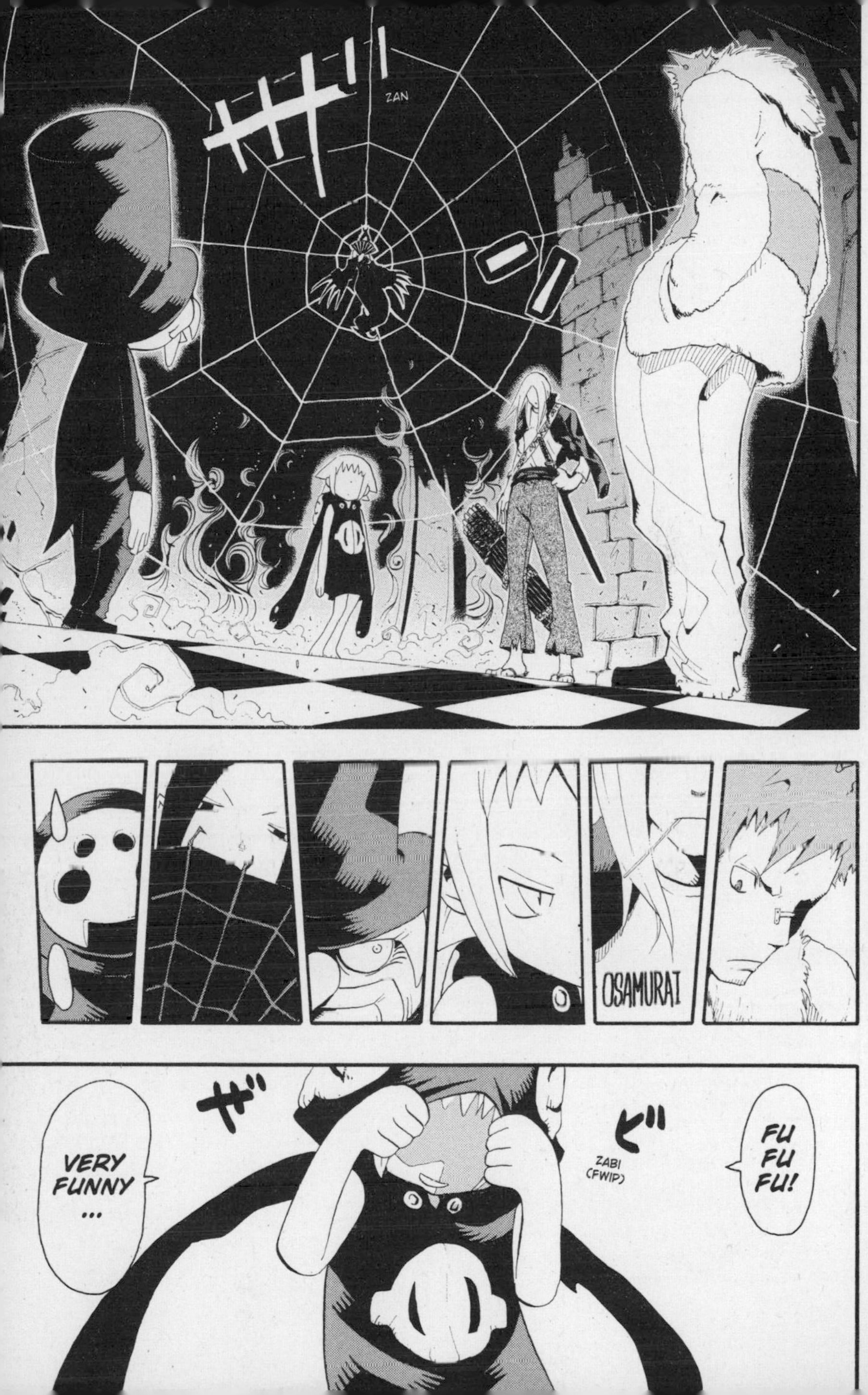
ZAN
OSAMURAI
FU FU FU!
ZABI (FWIP)
VERY FUNNY ...

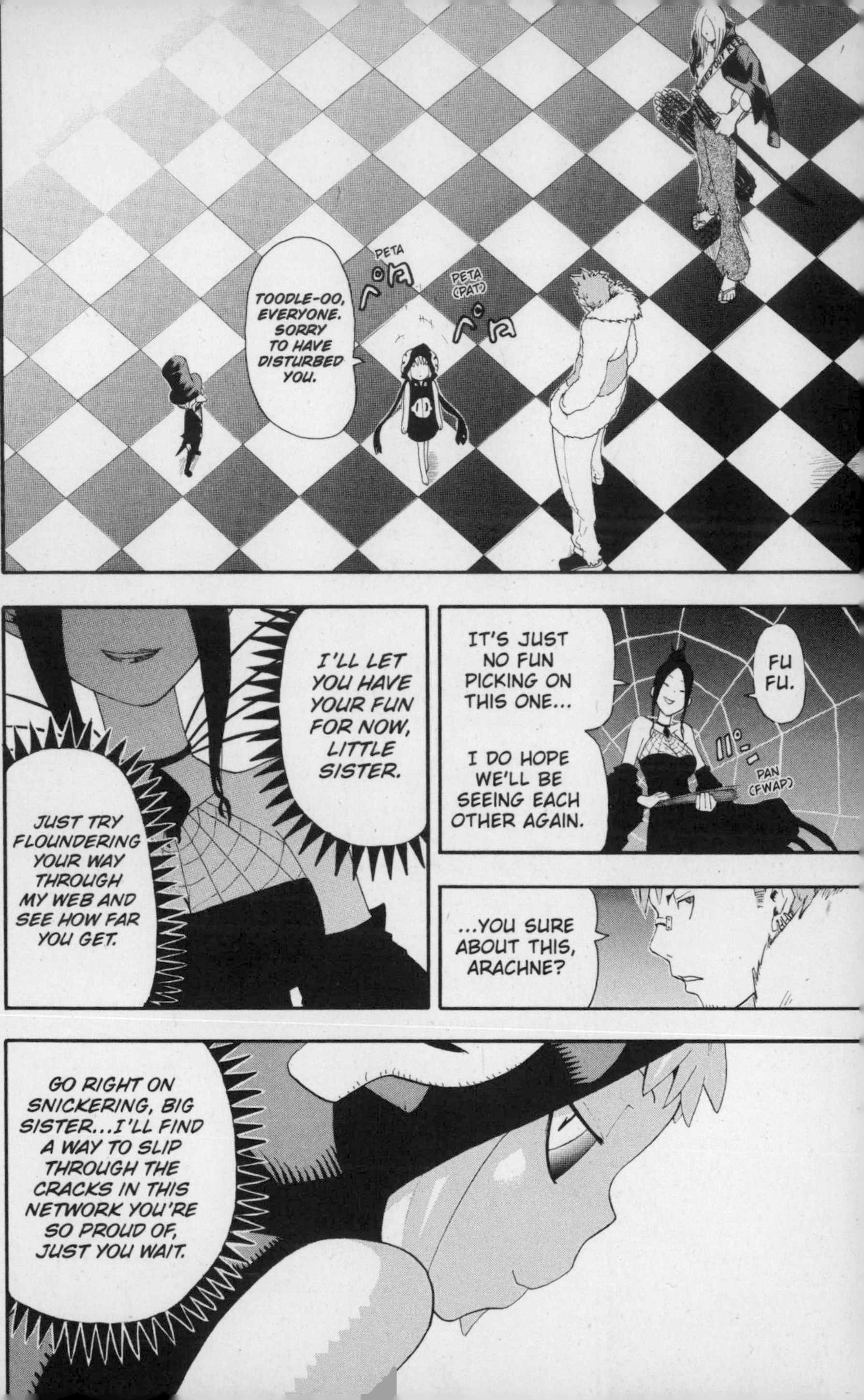
PETA
(PAT)
PETA
TOODLE-OO, EVERYONE. SORRY TO HAVE DISTURBED YOU.
FU FU.
IT'S JUST NO FUN PICKING ON THIS ONE...
I DO HOPE WE'LL BE SEEING EACH OTHER AGAIN.
PAN
(FWAP)
...YOU SURE ABOUT THIS, ARACHNE?
I'LL LET YOU HAVE YOUR FUN FOR NOW, LITTLE SISTER.
JUST TRY FLOUNDERING YOUR WAY THROUGH MY WEB AND SEE HOW FAR YOU GET.
GO RIGHT ON SNICKERING, BIG SISTER...I'LL FIND A WAY TO SLIP THROUGH THE CRACKS IN THIS NETWORK YOU'RE SO PROUD OF, JUST YOU WAIT.

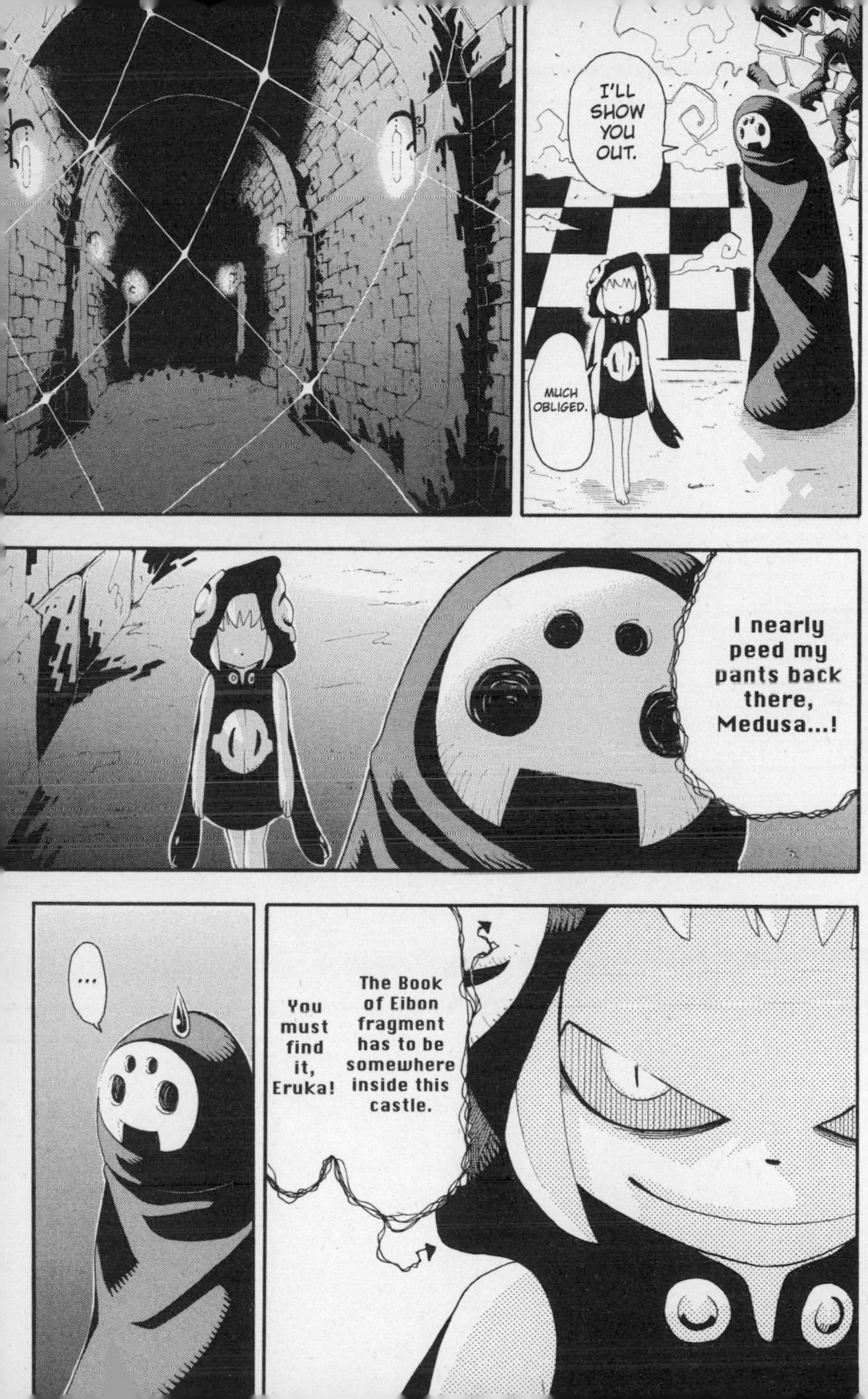
I'LL SHOW YOU OUT.
MUCH OBLIGED.
I nearly peed my pants back there, Medusa...!
The Book of Eibon fragment has to be somewhere inside this castle.
You must find it, Eruka!
...

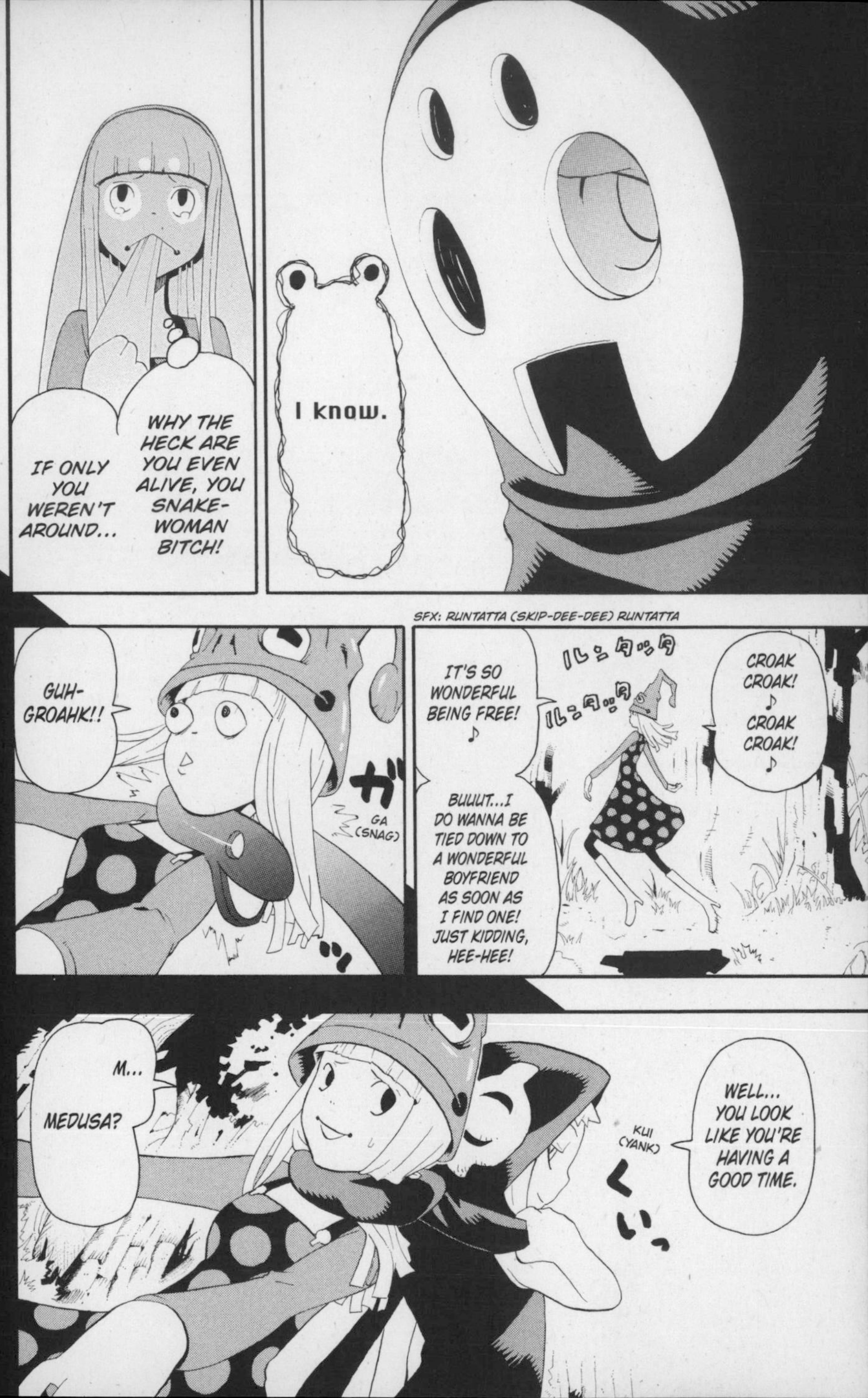
I know.
WHY THE HECK ARE YOU EVEN ALIVE, YOU SNAKE-WOMAN BITCH!
IF ONLY YOU WEREN'T AROUND...
SFX: RUNTATTA (SKIP-DEE-DEE) RUNTATTA
CROAK CROAK! ♪ CROAK CROAK! ♪
IT'S SO WONDERFUL BEING FREE! ♪
BUUUT...I DO WANNA BE TIED DOWN TO A WONDERFUL BOYFRIEND AS SOON AS I FIND ONE! JUST KIDDING, HEE-HEE!
GA (SNAG)
GUH-GROAHK!!
WELL... YOU LOOK LIKE YOU'RE HAVING A GOOD TIME.
KUI (YANK)
M...
MEDUSA?

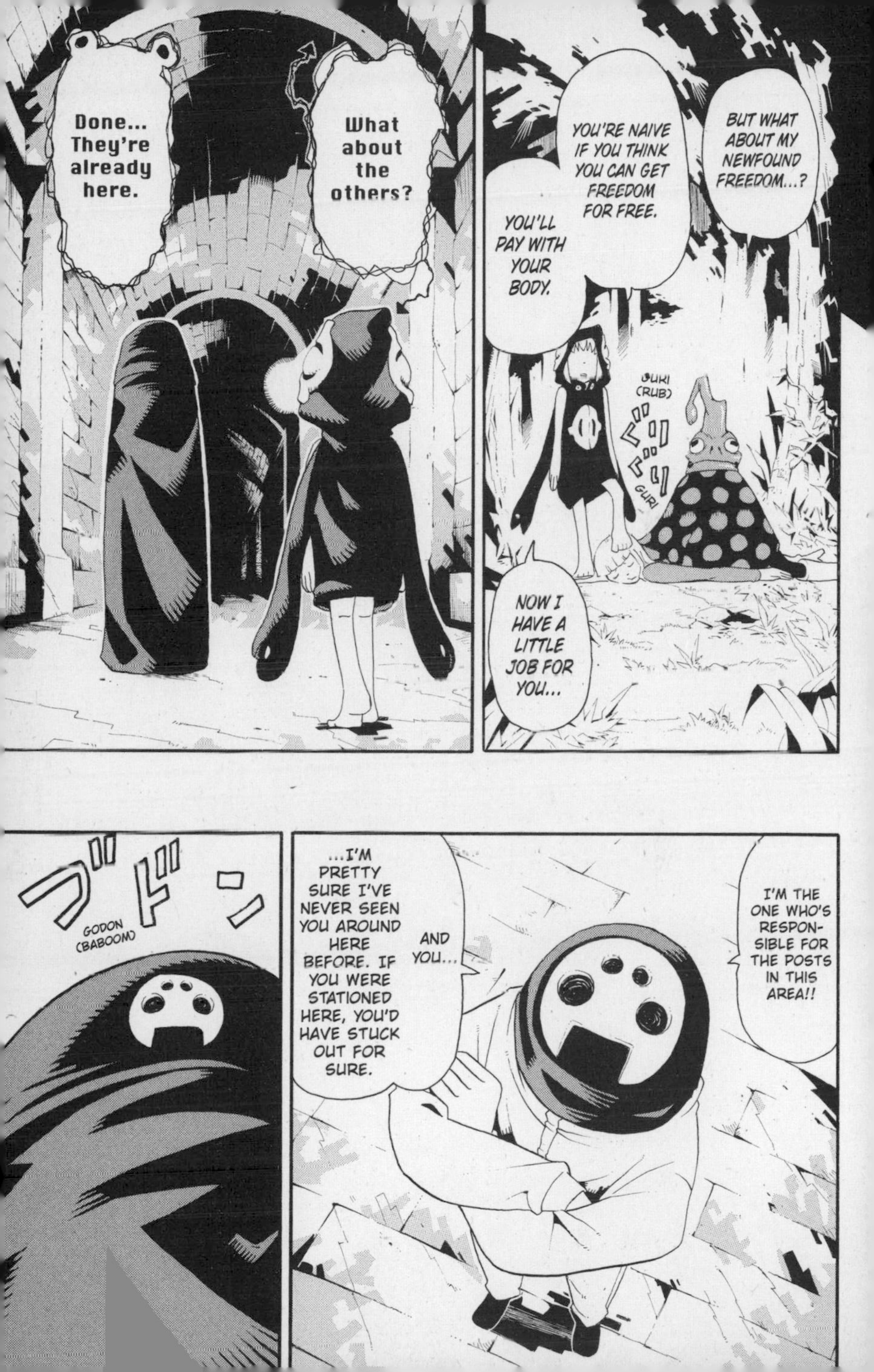
BUT WHAT ABOUT MY NEWFOUND FREEDOM...?
YOU'RE NAIVE IF YOU THINK YOU CAN GET FREEDOM FOR FREE.
YOU'LL PAY WITH YOUR BODY.
GURI (RUB)
GURI
NOW I HAVE A LITTLE JOB FOR YOU...
What about the others?
Done... They're already here.
I'M THE ONE WHO'S RESPON-SIBLE FOR THE POSTS IN THIS AREA!!
AND YOU...
...I'M PRETTY SURE I'VE NEVER SEEN YOU AROUND HERE BEFORE. IF YOU WERE STATIONED HERE, YOU'D HAVE STUCK OUT FOR SURE.
GODON (BABOOM)

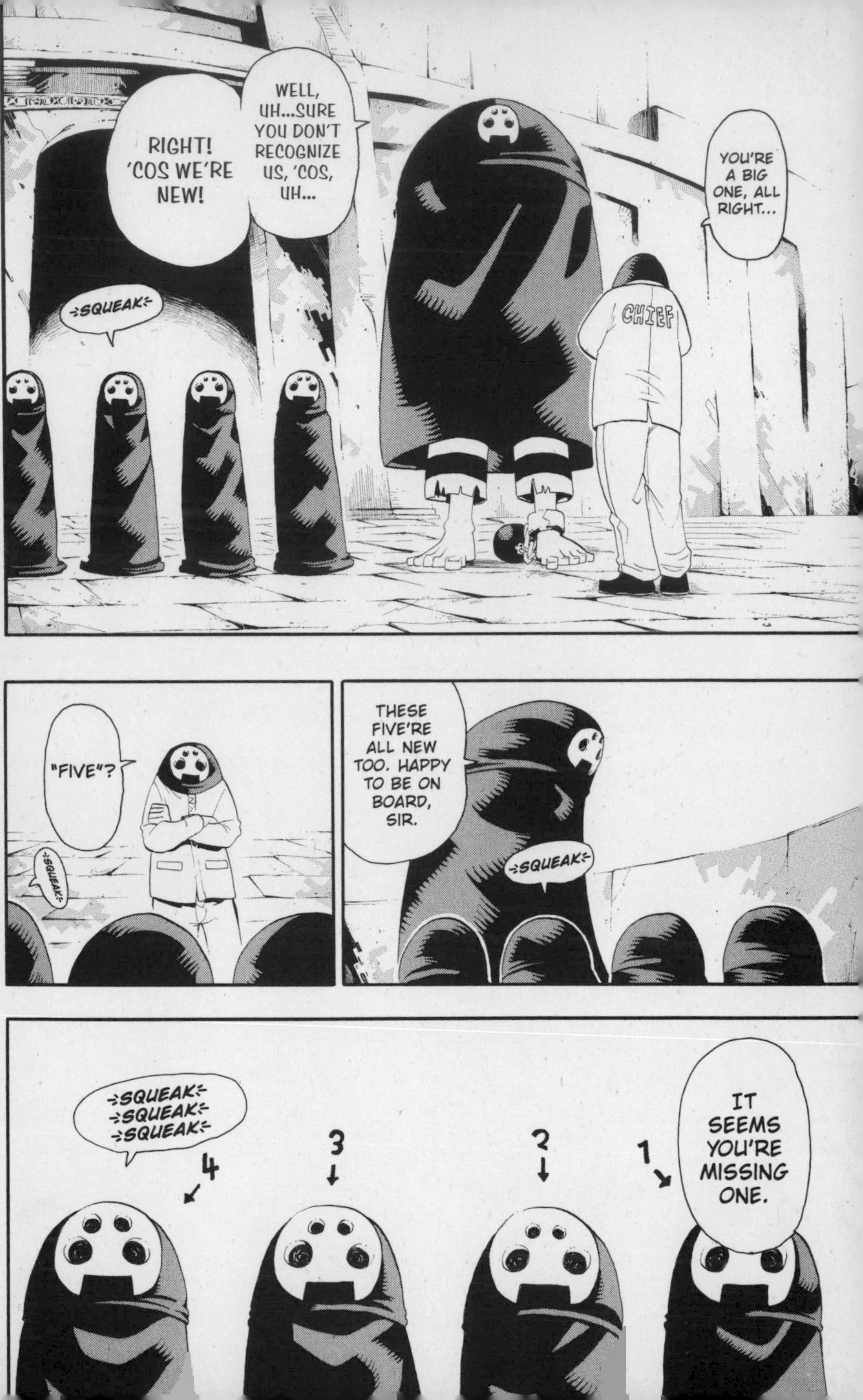
YOU'RE A BIG ONE, ALL RIGHT...
WELL, UH...SURE YOU DON'T RECOGNIZE US, 'COS, UH...
RIGHT! 'COS WE'RE NEW!
SQUEAK
CHIEF
THESE FIVE'RE ALL NEW TOO. HAPPY TO BE ON BOARD, SIR.
SQUEAK
"FIVE"?
SQUEAK
IT SEEMS YOU'RE MISSING ONE.
1
2
3
4
SQUEAK
SQUEAK
SQUEAK

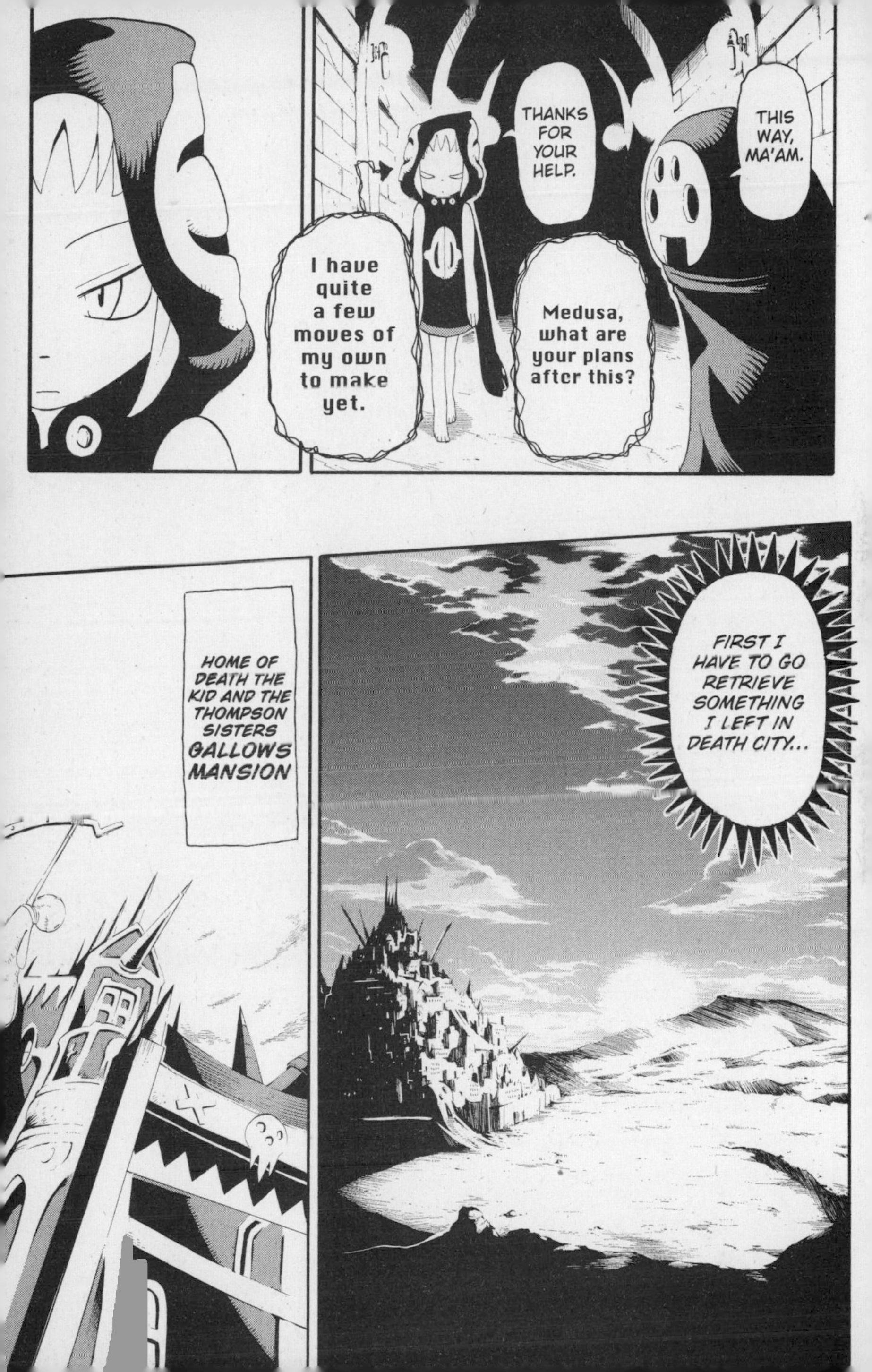
THIS WAY, MA'AM.
THANKS FOR YOUR HELP.
Medusa, what are your plans after this?
I have quite a few moves of my own to make yet.
FIRST I HAVE TO GO RETRIEVE SOMETHING I LEFT IN DEATH CITY...
HOME OF DEATH THE KID AND THE THOMPSON SISTERS GALLOWS MANSION

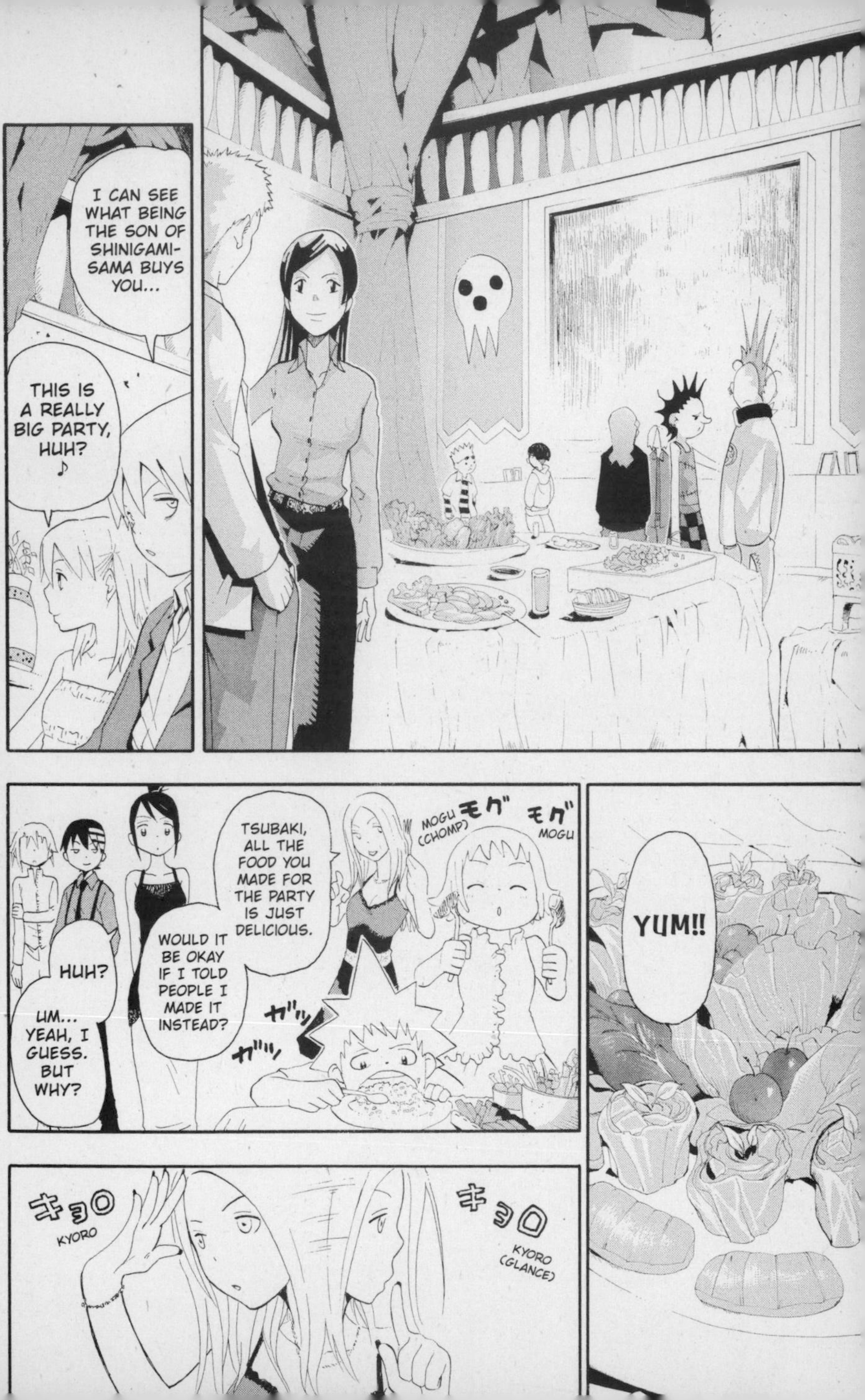
I CAN SEE WHAT BEING THE SON OF SHINIGAMI-SAMA BUYS YOU...
THIS IS A REALLY BIG PARTY, HUH? ♪
YUM!!
モグ MOGU
モグ MOGU (CHOMP)
TSUBAKI, ALL THE FOOD YOU MADE FOR THE PARTY IS JUST DELICIOUS.
WOULD IT BE OKAY IF I TOLD PEOPLE I MADE IT INSTEAD?
HUH?
UM... YEAH, I GUESS. BUT WHY?
ガツ
ガツ
キョロ
KYORO (GLANCE)
キョロ
KYORO

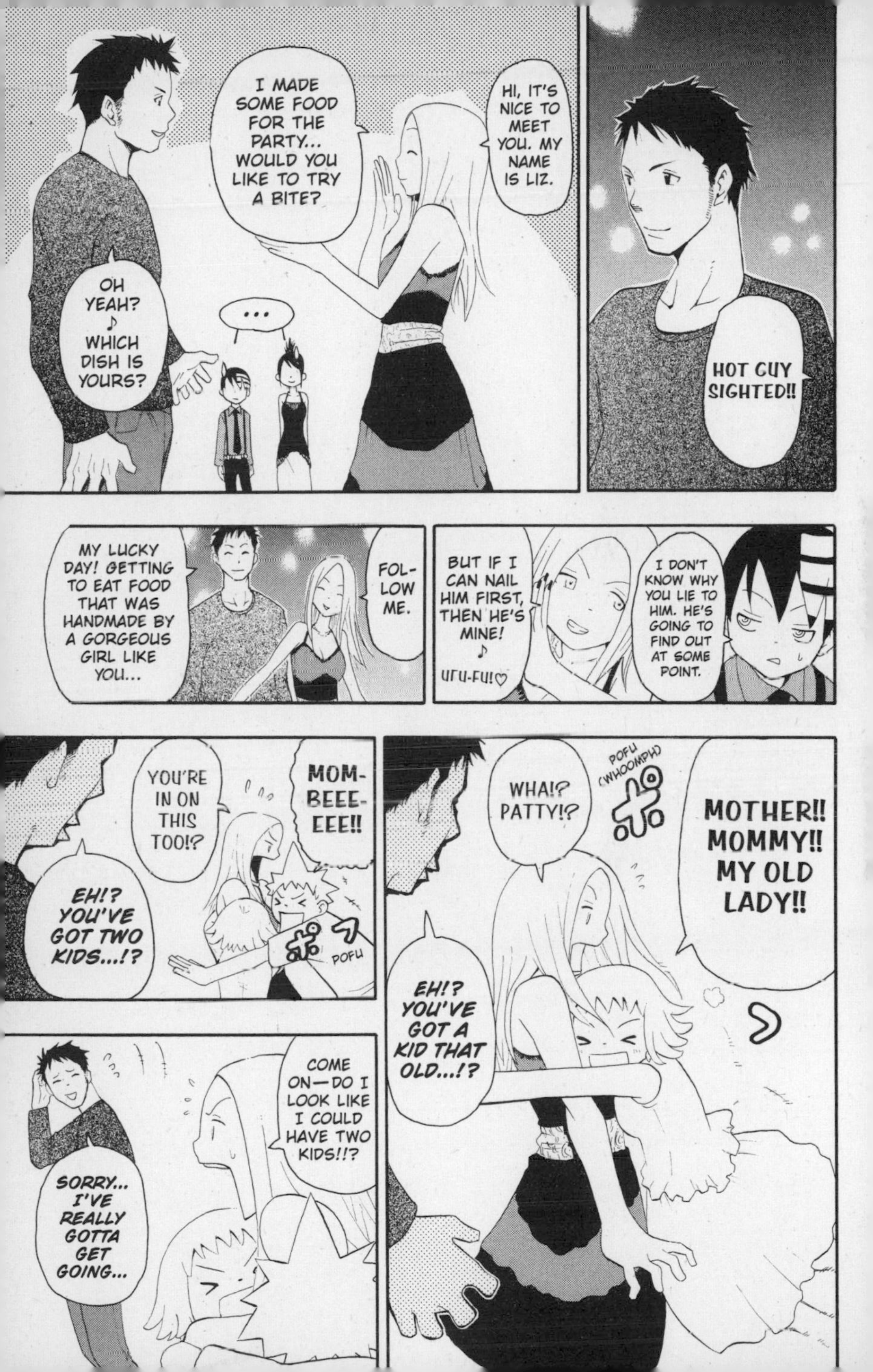
HOT GUY SIGHTED!!
HI, IT'S NICE TO MEET YOU. MY NAME IS LIZ.
I MADE SOME FOOD FOR THE PARTY... WOULD YOU LIKE TO TRY A BITE?
...
OH YEAH? ♪ WHICH DISH IS YOURS?
I DON'T KNOW WHY YOU LIE TO HIM. HE'S GOING TO FIND OUT AT SOME POINT.
BUT IF I CAN NAIL HIM FIRST, THEN HE'S MINE! ♪
UFU-FU!♡
FOL-LOW ME.
MY LUCKY DAY! GETTING TO EAT FOOD THAT WAS HANDMADE BY A GORGEOUS GIRL LIKE YOU...
MOTHER!! MOMMY!! MY OLD LADY!!
POFU (WHOOMPH)
WHA!? PATTY!?
EH!? YOU'VE GOT A KID THAT OLD...!?
MOM-BEEE-EEE!!
YOU'RE IN ON THIS TOO!?
POFU
EH!? YOU'VE GOT TWO KIDS...!?
COME ON—DO I LOOK LIKE I COULD HAVE TWO KIDS!!?
SORRY... I'VE REALLY GOTTA GET GOING...

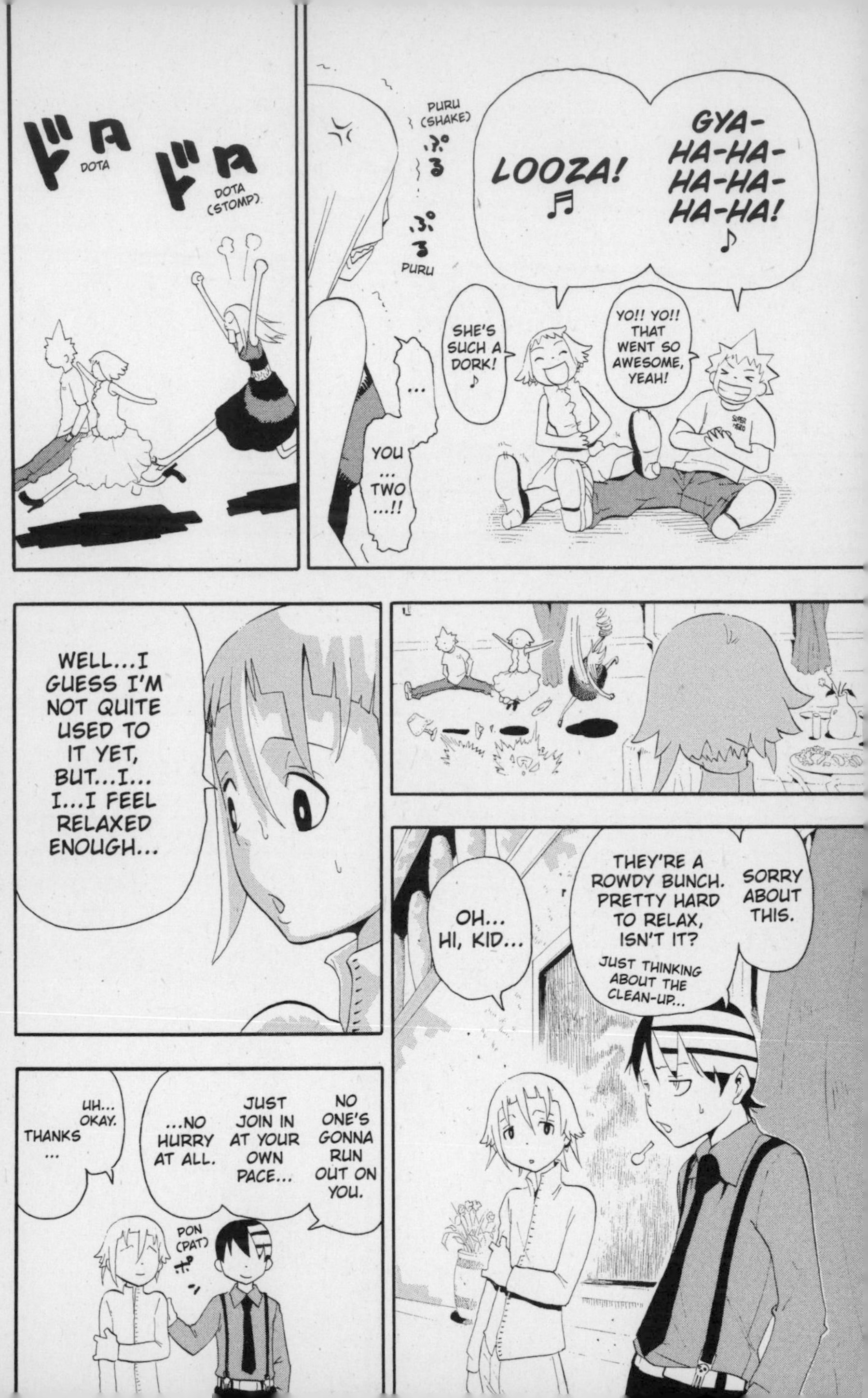
GYA-HA-HA-HA-HA-HA-HA! ♪
LOOZA! ♬
YO!! YO!! THAT WENT SO AWESOME, YEAH!
SHE'S SUCH A DORK! ♪
ぷる PURU (SHAKE)
ぷる PURU
...
YOU ... TWO ...!!
ドタ DOTA (STOMP)
ドタ DOTA
SORRY ABOUT THIS.
THEY'RE A ROWDY BUNCH. PRETTY HARD TO RELAX, ISN'T IT?
JUST THINKING ABOUT THE CLEAN-UP...
OH... HI, KID...
WELL...I GUESS I'M NOT QUITE USED TO IT YET, BUT...I... I...I FEEL RELAXED ENOUGH...
NO ONE'S GONNA RUN OUT ON YOU.
JUST JOIN IN AT YOUR OWN PACE...
...NO HURRY AT ALL.
PON (PAT)
UH... OKAY.
THANKS ...

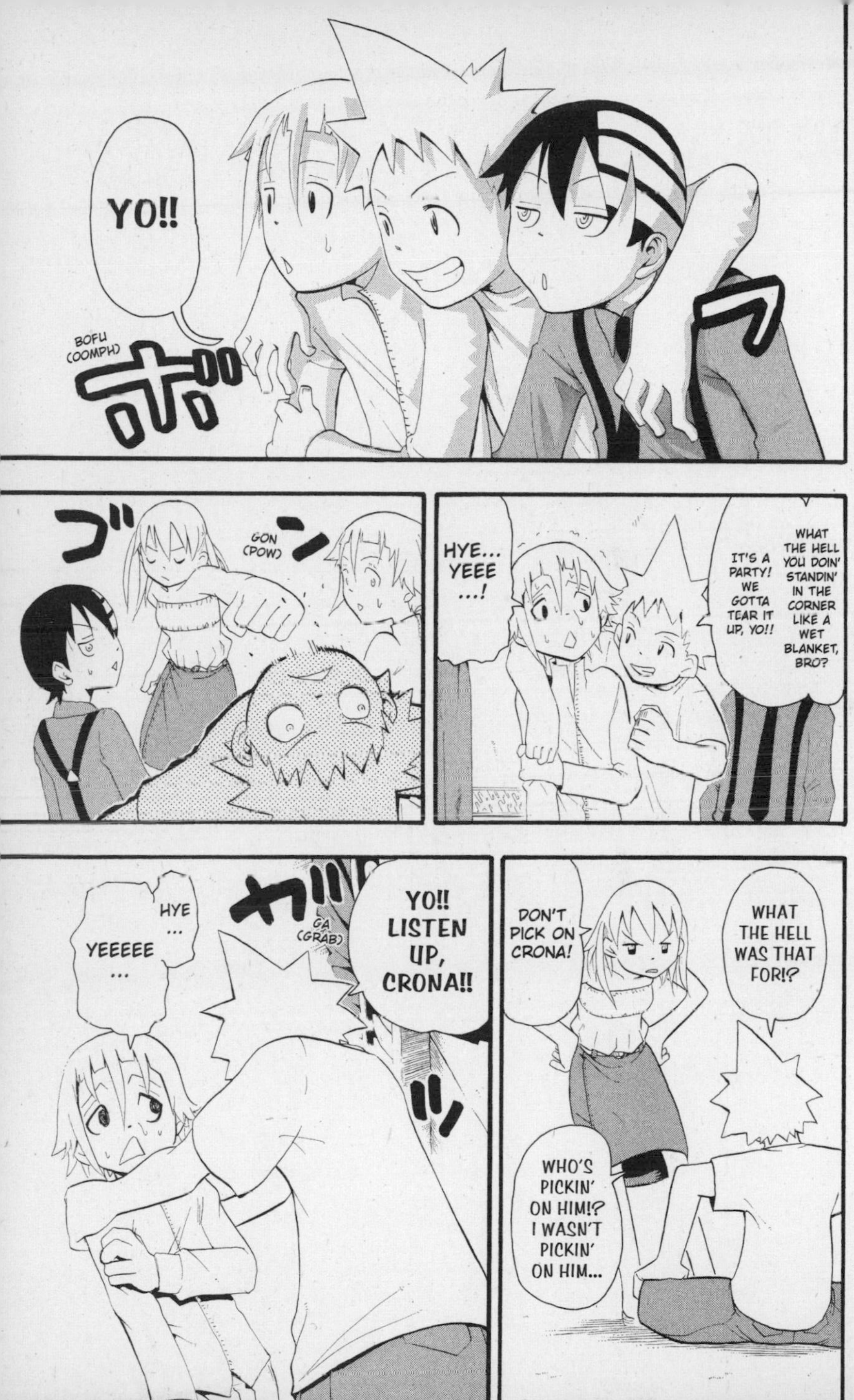
YO!!
BOFU (COOMPH)
WHAT THE HELL YOU DOIN' STANDIN' IN THE CORNER LIKE A WET BLANKET, BRO?
IT'S A PARTY! WE GOTTA TEAR IT UP, YO!!
HYE... YEEE ...!
GON (POW)
WHAT THE HELL WAS THAT FOR!?
DON'T PICK ON CRONA!
WHO'S PICKIN' ON HIM!? I WASN'T PICKIN' ON HIM...
YO!! LISTEN UP, CRONA!!
GA (GRAB)
HYE ... YEEEEE ...

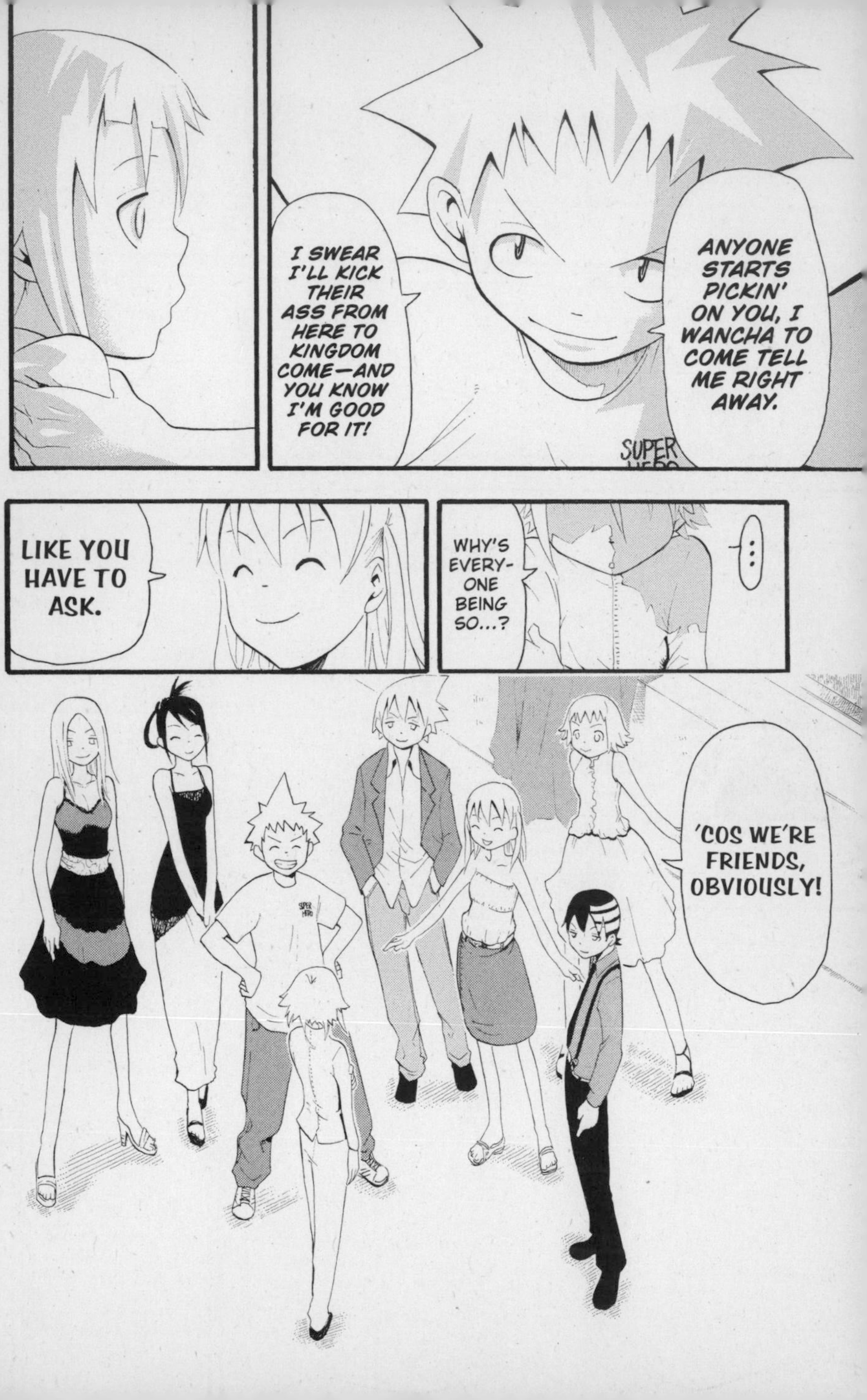
ANYONE STARTS PICKIN' ON YOU, I WANCHA TO COME TELL ME RIGHT AWAY.
I SWEAR I'LL KICK THEIR ASS FROM HERE TO KINGDOM COME—AND YOU KNOW I'M GOOD FOR IT!
SUPER
...
WHY'S EVERY-ONE BEING SO...?
LIKE YOU HAVE TO ASK.
'COS WE'RE FRIENDS, OBVIOUSLY!

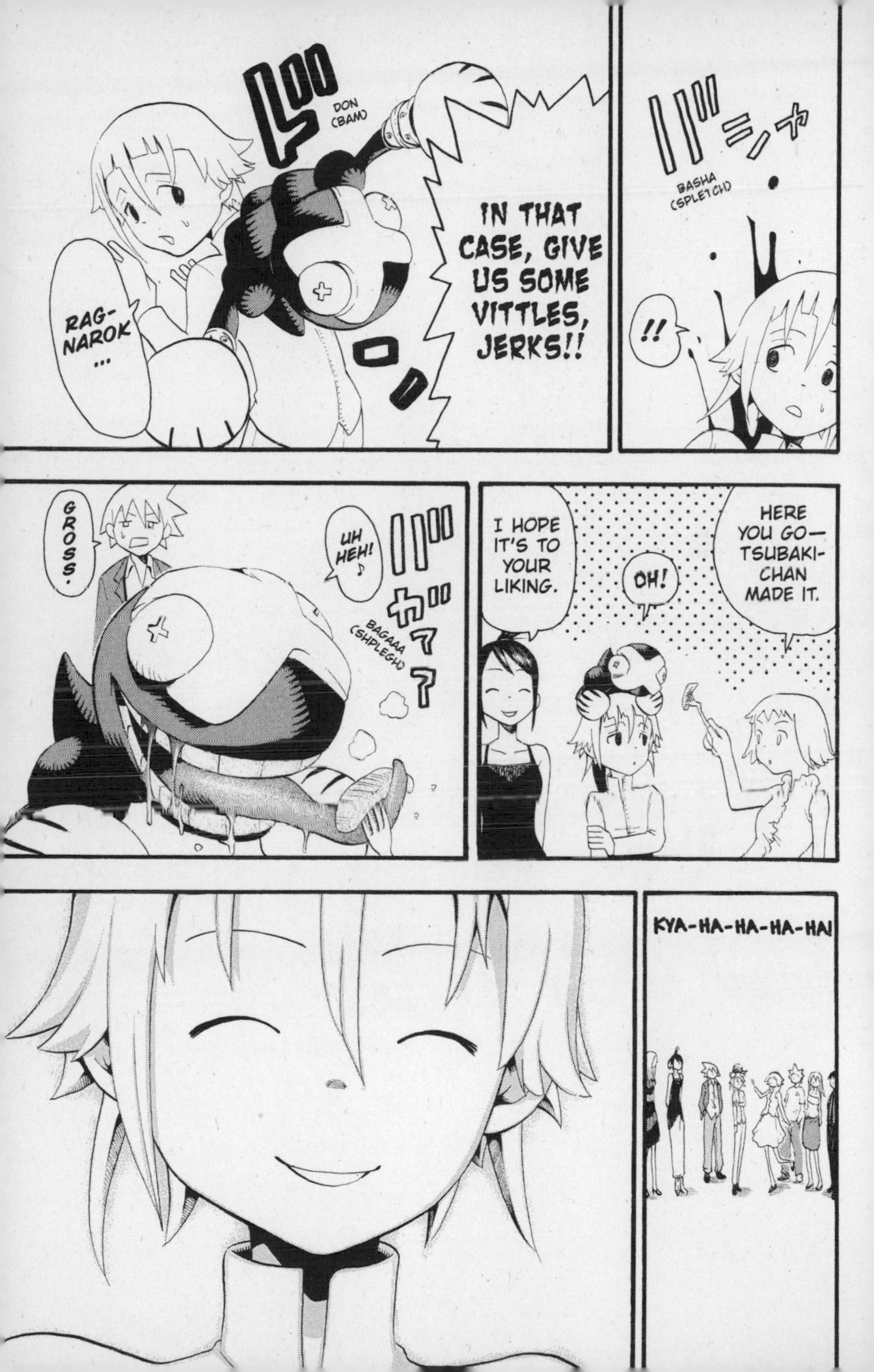
BASHA (SPLETCH)
!!
DON (BAM)
IN THAT CASE, GIVE US SOME VITTLES, JERKS!!
RAG-NAROK ...
HERE YOU GO—TSUBAKI-CHAN MADE IT.
OH!
I HOPE IT'S TO YOUR LIKING.
UH HEH! ♪
BAGAAA (SHPLEGH)
GROSS.
KYA-HA-HA-HA-HA!

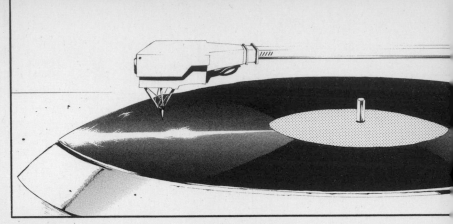

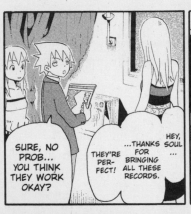

ストン
SUTON (SLIP)
HEY, SOUL...
...THANKS FOR BRINGING ALL THESE RECORDS.
THEY'RE PERFECT!
SURE, NO PROB... YOU THINK THEY WORK OKAY?
YOU SAID YOU WANTED SOMETHIN' WITH A GOOD BEAT, SO I BROUGHT A BUNCH OF FUNK AND STUFF, BUT...
OH YEAH?
...IT DOESN'T REALLY GO WITH THE FEEL OF THE ROOM...
!!
I KNOW— YOU SHOULD PLAY THE PIANO!
THEY'VE GOT ONE RIGHT HERE.
WHAT, YOU MEAN... NOW?
IT'S BEEN SO LONG... I WANNA HEAR YOU PLAY AGAIN.

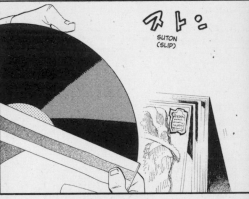

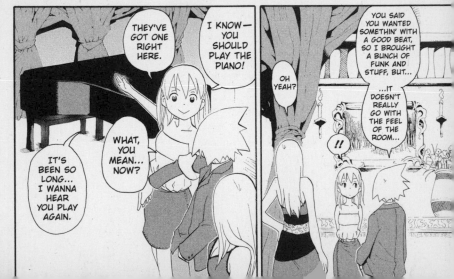

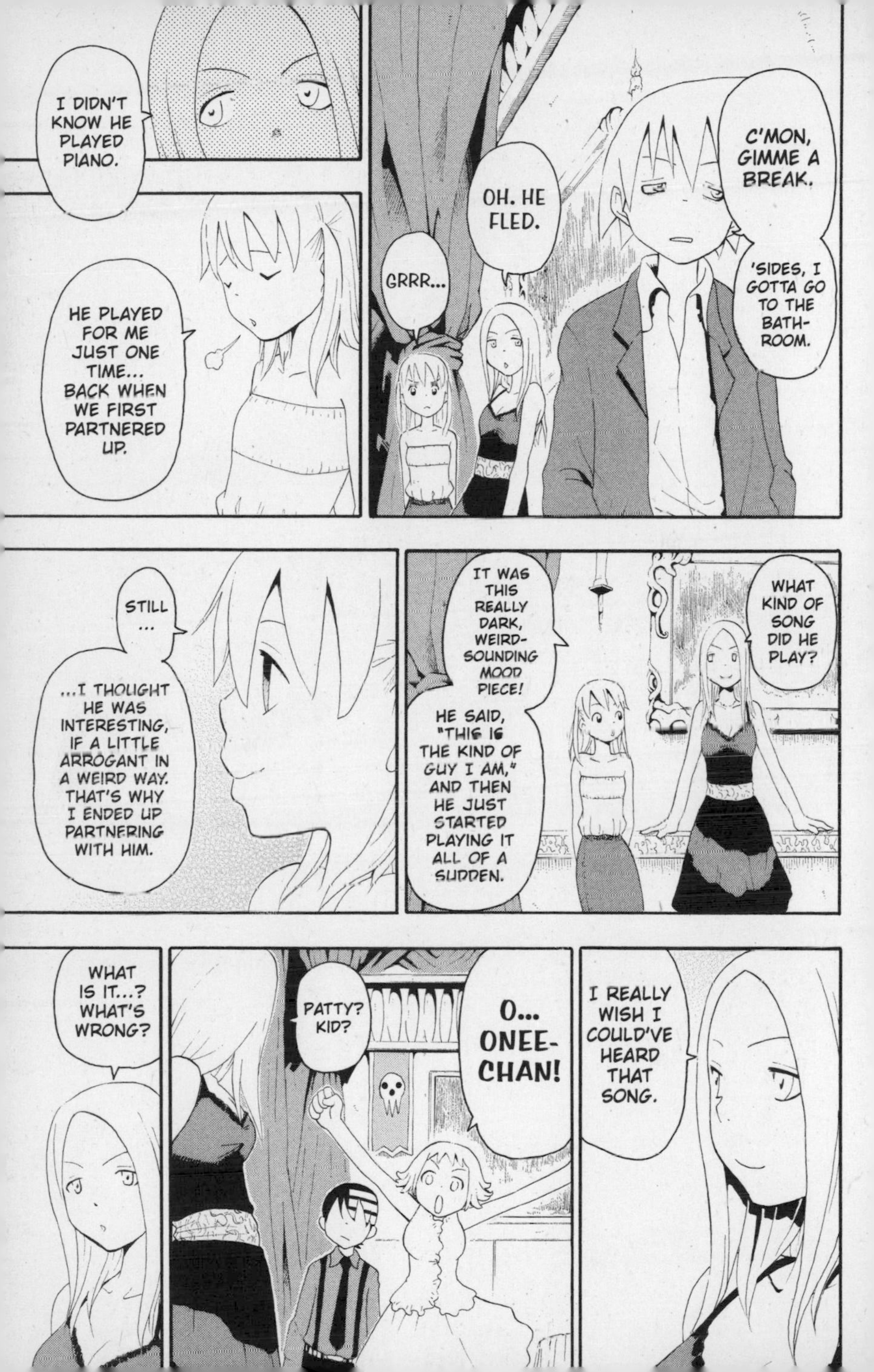
C'MON, GIMME A BREAK.
'SIDES, I GOTTA GO TO THE BATH-ROOM.
OH. HE FLED.
GRRR...
I DIDN'T KNOW HE PLAYED PIANO.
HE PLAYED FOR ME JUST ONE TIME... BACK WHEN WE FIRST PARTNERED UP.
WHAT KIND OF SONG DID HE PLAY?
IT WAS THIS REALLY DARK, WEIRD-SOUNDING MOOD PIECE!
HE SAID, "THIS IS THE KIND OF GUY I AM," AND THEN HE JUST STARTED PLAYING IT ALL OF A SUDDEN.
STILL...
...I THOUGHT HE WAS INTERESTING, IF A LITTLE ARROGANT IN A WEIRD WAY. THAT'S WHY I ENDED UP PARTNERING WITH HIM.
I REALLY WISH I COULD'VE HEARD THAT SONG.
O... ONEE-CHAN!
PATTY? KID?
WHAT IS IT...? WHAT'S WRONG?

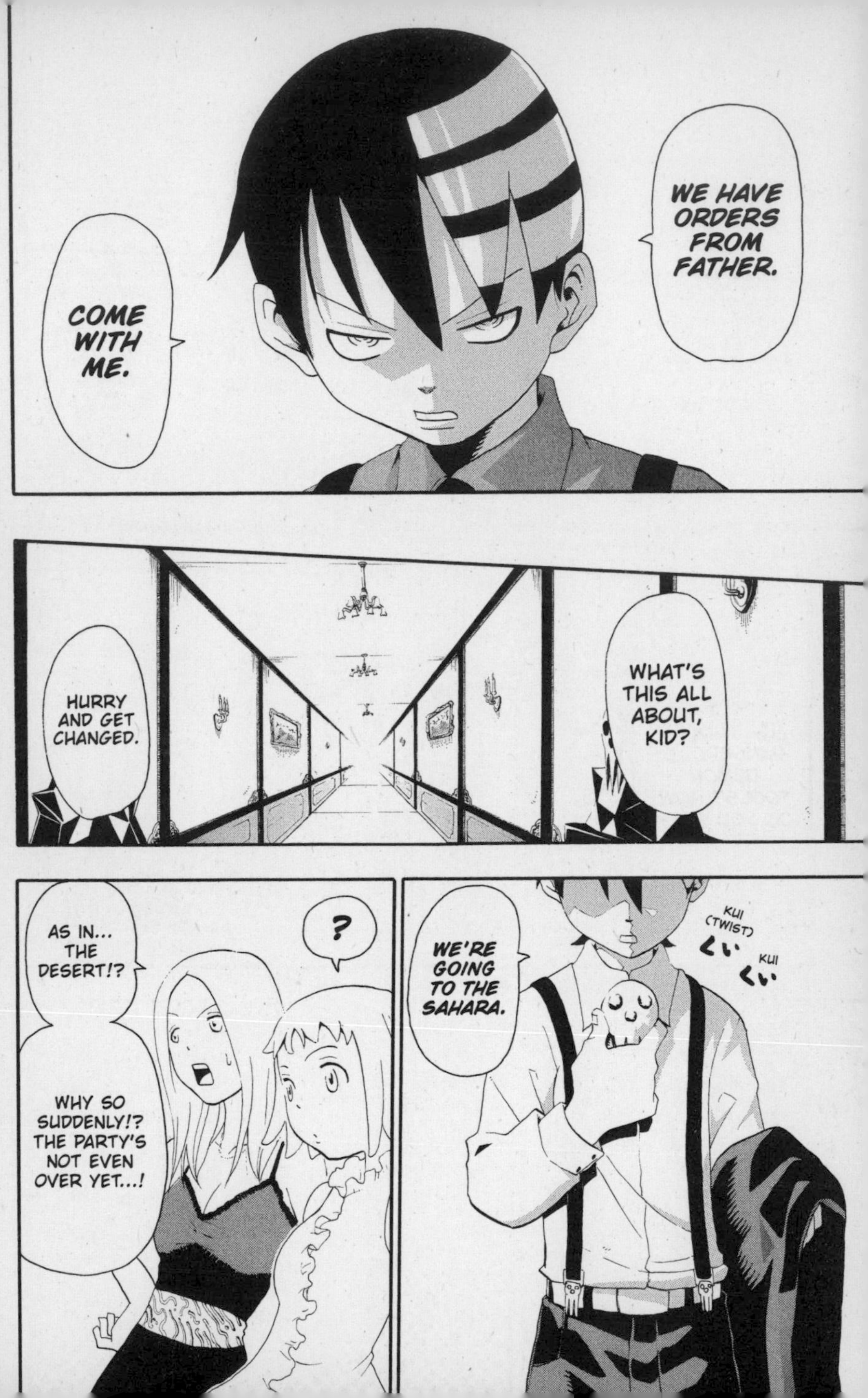

WE HAVE ORDERS FROM FATHER.
COME WITH ME.
WHAT'S THIS ALL ABOUT, KID?
HURRY AND GET CHANGED.
KUI (TWIST) くい
KUI くい
WE'RE GOING TO THE SAHARA.
?
AS IN... THE DESERT!?
WHY SO SUDDENLY!? THE PARTY'S NOT EVEN OVER YET...!

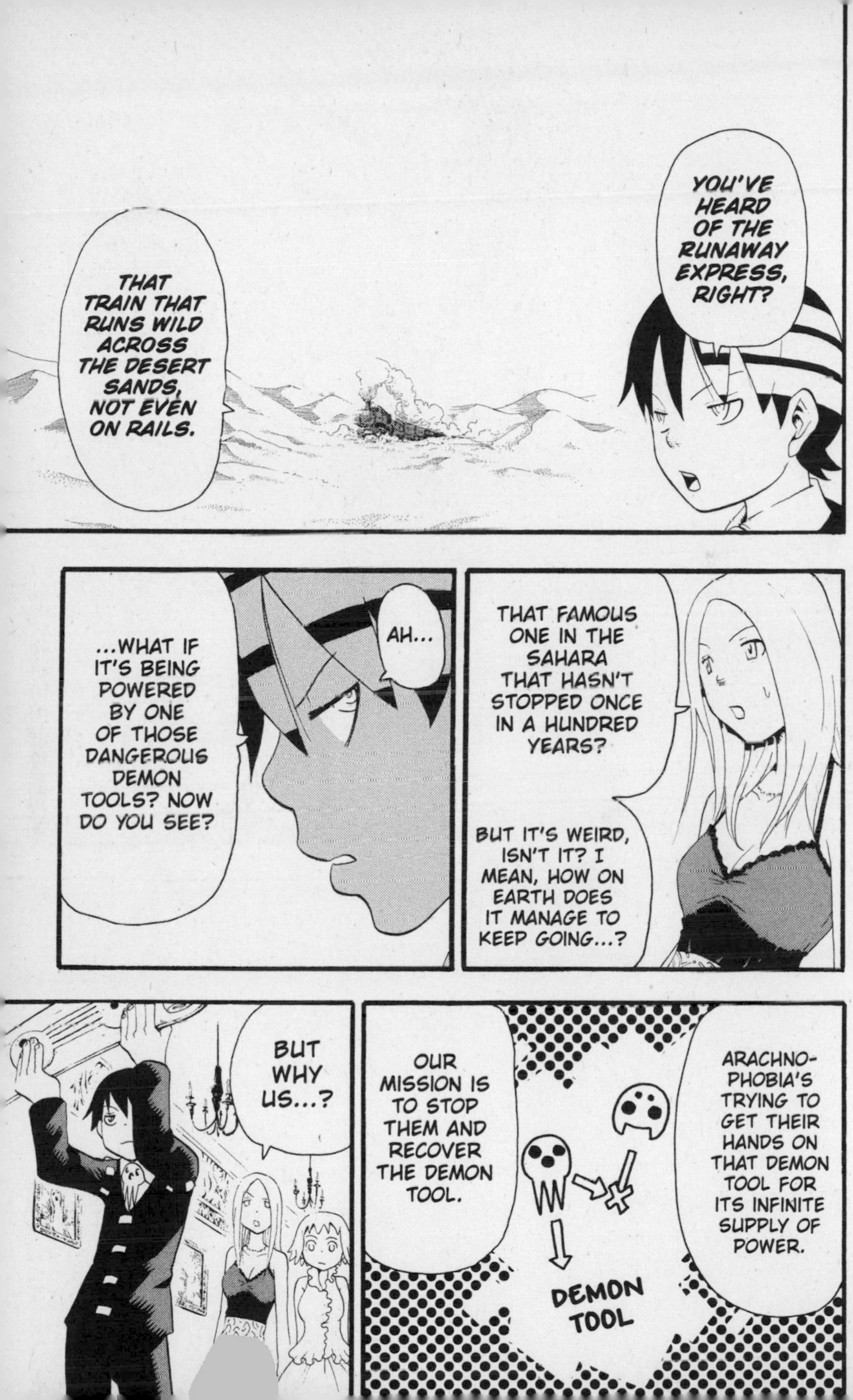
YOU'VE HEARD OF THE RUNAWAY EXPRESS, RIGHT?
THAT TRAIN THAT RUNS WILD ACROSS THE DESERT SANDS, NOT EVEN ON RAILS.
THAT FAMOUS ONE IN THE SAHARA THAT HASN'T STOPPED ONCE IN A HUNDRED YEARS?
BUT IT'S WEIRD, ISN'T IT? I MEAN, HOW ON EARTH DOES IT MANAGE TO KEEP GOING...?
AH...
...WHAT IF IT'S BEING POWERED BY ONE OF THOSE DANGEROUS DEMON TOOLS? NOW DO YOU SEE?
ARACHNO-PHOBIA'S TRYING TO GET THEIR HANDS ON THAT DEMON TOOL FOR ITS INFINITE SUPPLY OF POWER.
OUR MISSION IS TO STOP THEM AND RECOVER THE DEMON TOOL.
DEMON TOOL
BUT WHY US...?

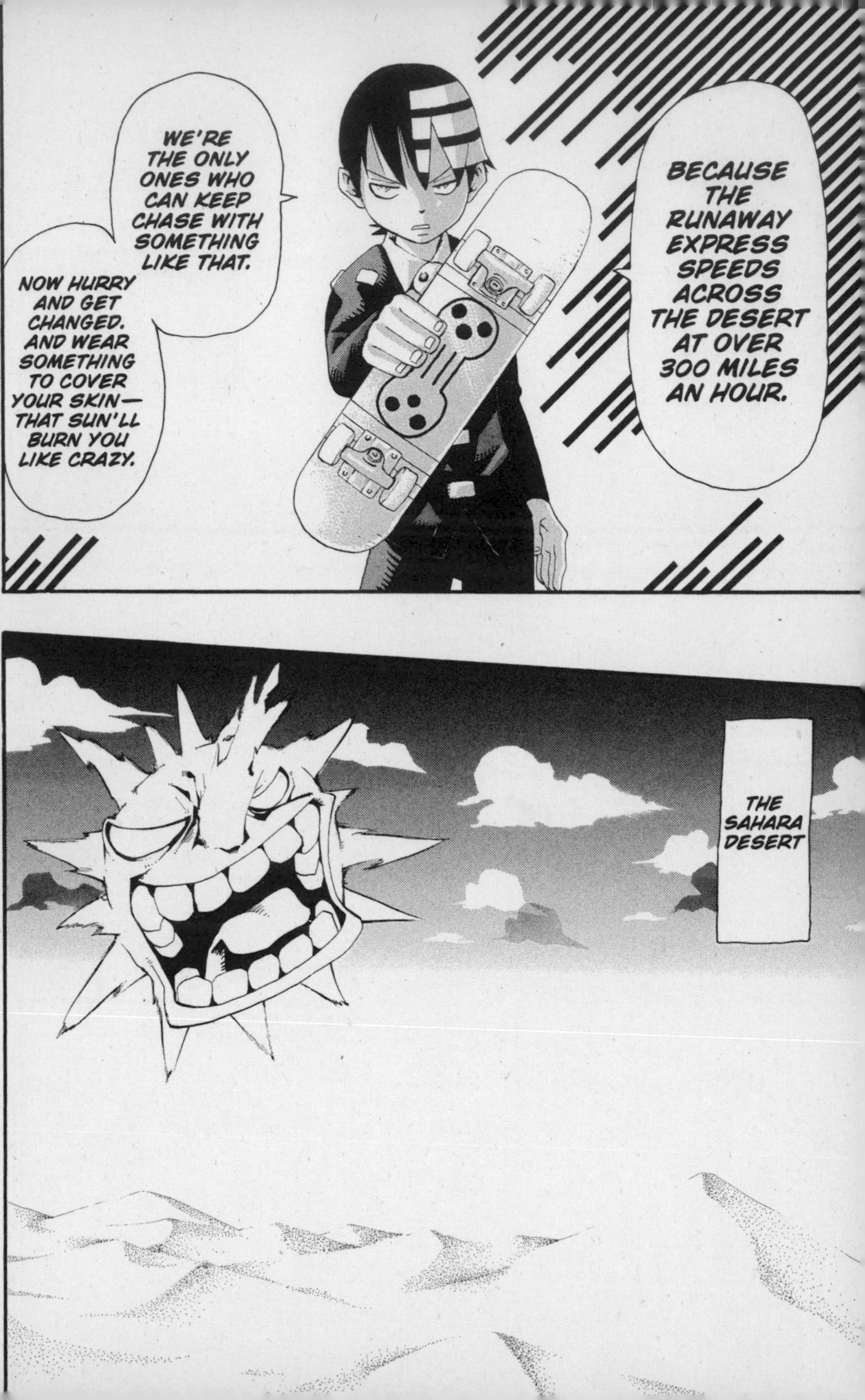
BECAUSE THE RUNAWAY EXPRESS SPEEDS ACROSS THE DESERT AT OVER 300 MILES AN HOUR.
WE'RE THE ONLY ONES WHO CAN KEEP CHASE WITH SOMETHING LIKE THAT.
NOW HURRY AND GET CHANGED. AND WEAR SOMETHING TO COVER YOUR SKIN—THAT SUN'LL BURN YOU LIKE CRAZY.
THE SAHARA DESERT

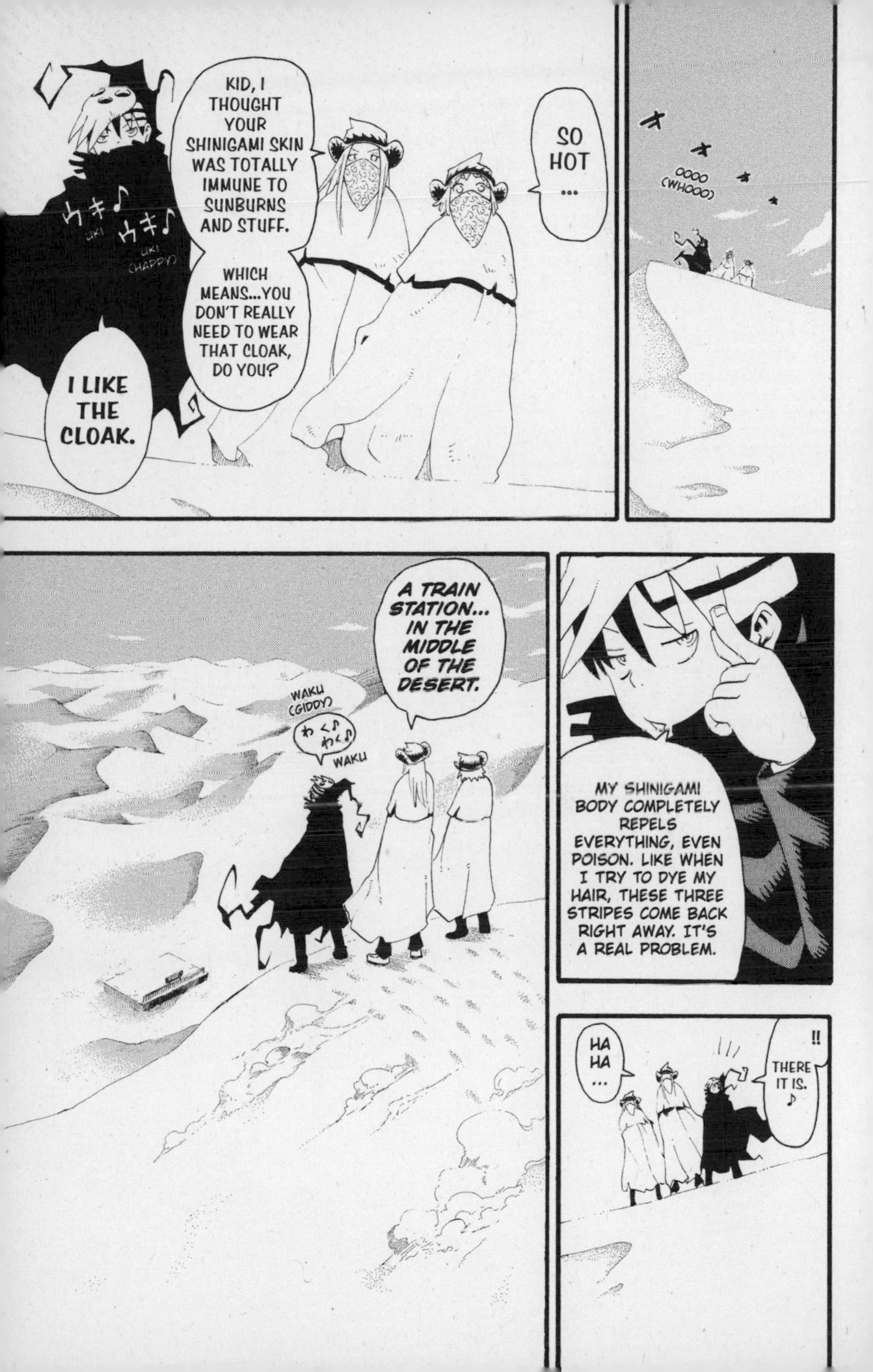

OOOO (WHOOO)
SO HOT ...
KID, I THOUGHT YOUR SHINIGAMI SKIN WAS TOTALLY IMMUNE TO SUNBURNS AND STUFF.
WHICH MEANS...YOU DON'T REALLY NEED TO WEAR THAT CLOAK, DO YOU?
ウキ♪ ウキ♪
UKI UKI (HAPPY)
I LIKE THE CLOAK.
MY SHINIGAMI BODY COMPLETELY REPELS EVERYTHING, EVEN POISON. LIKE WHEN I TRY TO DYE MY HAIR, THESE THREE STRIPES COME BACK RIGHT AWAY. IT'S A REAL PROBLEM.
!! THERE IT IS. ♪
HA HA ...
A TRAIN STATION... IN THE MIDDLE OF THE DESERT.
わく♪ わく♪
WAKU (GIDDY) WAKU

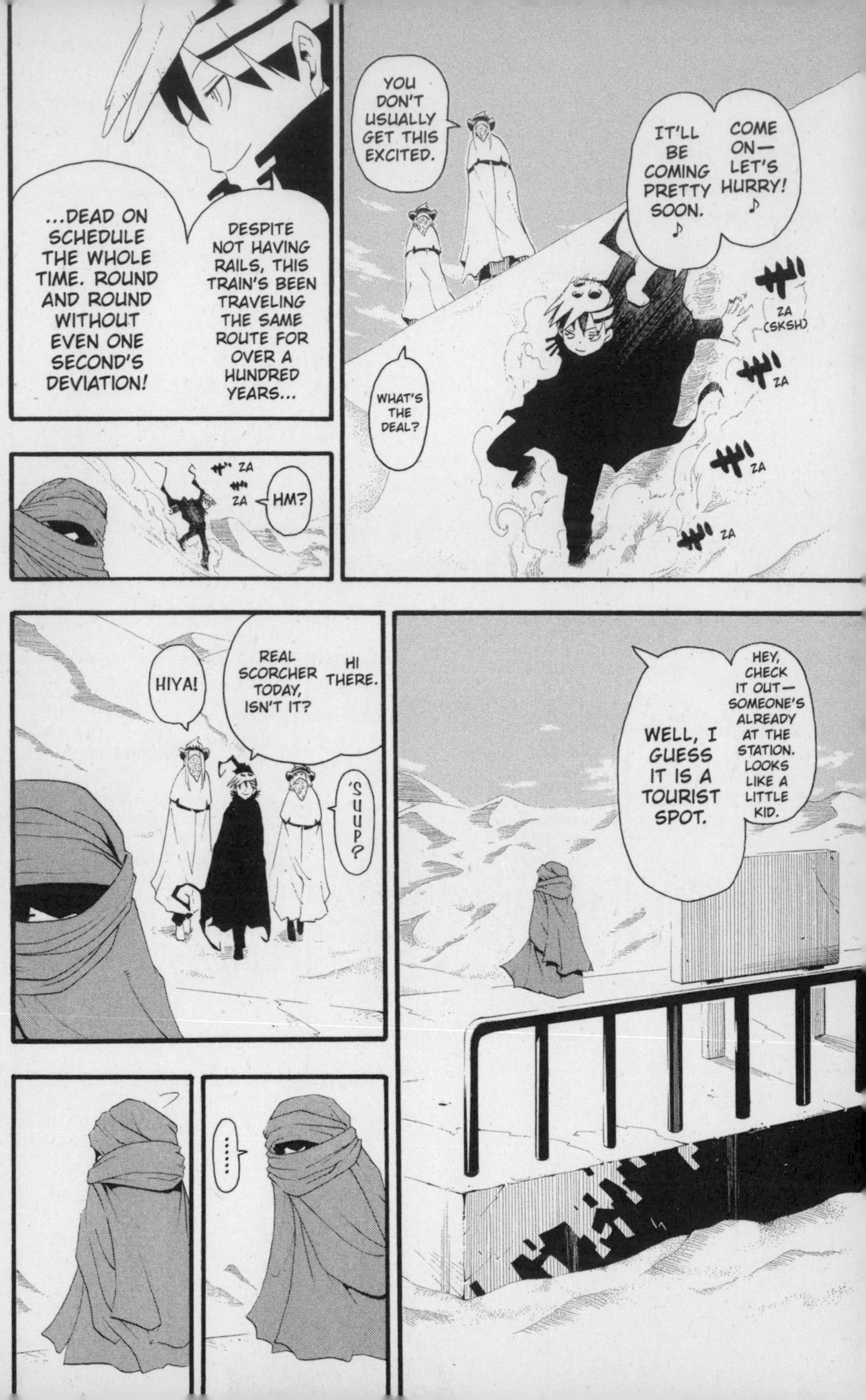
COME ON— LET'S HURRY! ♪
IT'LL BE COMING PRETTY SOON. ♪
YOU DON'T USUALLY GET THIS EXCITED.
WHAT'S THE DEAL?
ZA (SKSH)
ZA
ZA
ZA
DESPITE NOT HAVING RAILS, THIS TRAIN'S BEEN TRAVELING THE SAME ROUTE FOR OVER A HUNDRED YEARS...
...DEAD ON SCHEDULE THE WHOLE TIME. ROUND AND ROUND WITHOUT EVEN ONE SECOND'S DEVIATION!
ZA
ZA
HM?
HEY, CHECK IT OUT— SOMEONE'S ALREADY AT THE STATION. LOOKS LIKE A LITTLE KID.
WELL, I GUESS IT IS A TOURIST SPOT.
HI THERE.
REAL SCORCHER TODAY, ISN'T IT?
HIYA!
'SUUP?
......

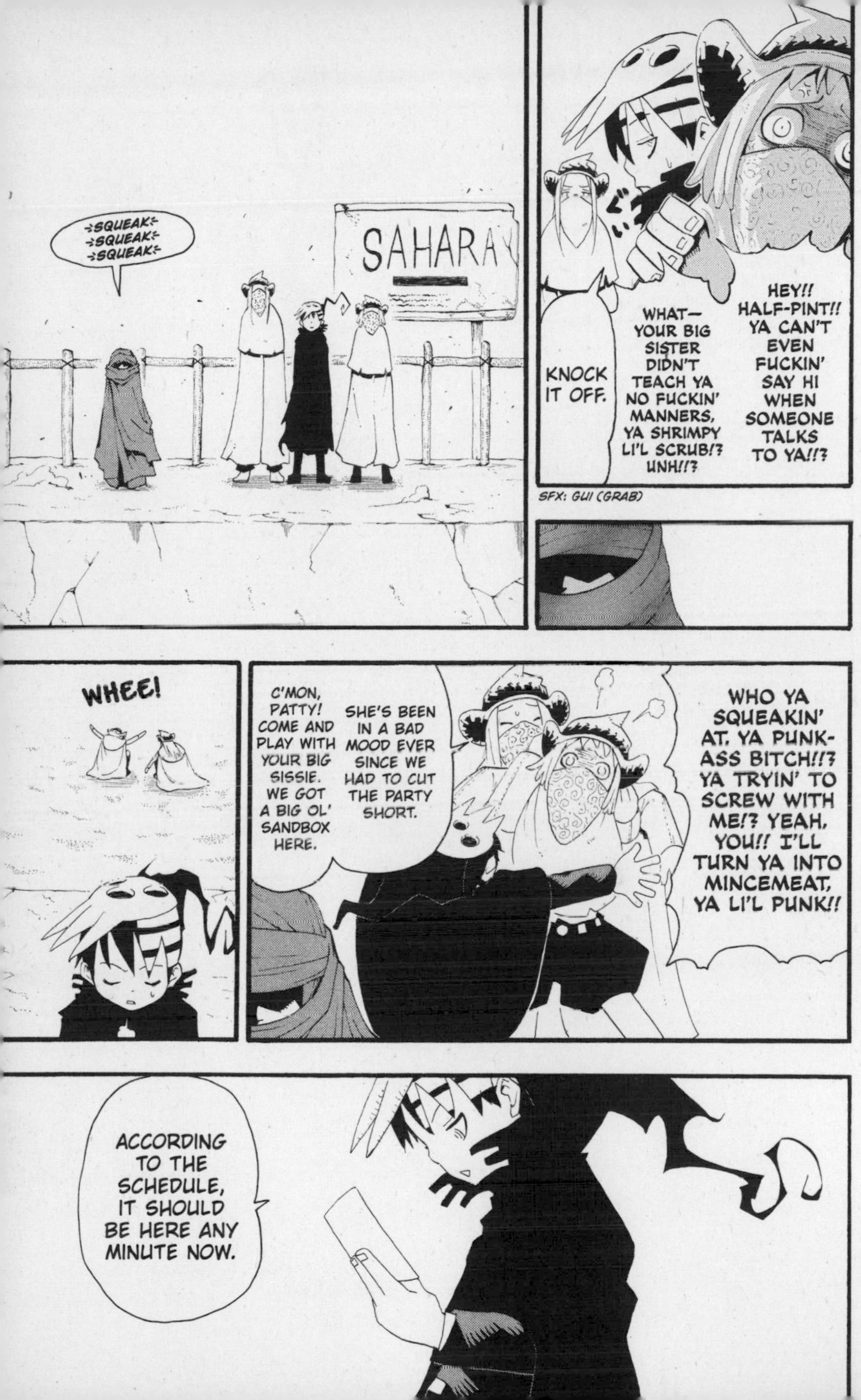
HEY!! HALF-PINT!! YA CAN'T EVEN FUCKIN' SAY HI WHEN SOMEONE TALKS TO YA!!?
WHAT— YOUR BIG SISTER DIDN'T TEACH YA NO FUCKIN' MANNERS, YA SHRIMPY LI'L SCRUB!? UNH!!?
KNOCK IT OFF.
SFX: GUI (GRAB)
SAHARA
-SQUEAK- -SQUEAK- -SQUEAK-
WHO YA SQUEAKIN' AT, YA PUNK-ASS BITCH!!? YA TRYIN' TO SCREW WITH ME!? YEAH, YOU!! I'LL TURN YA INTO MINCEMEAT, YA LI'L PUNK!!
SHE'S BEEN IN A BAD MOOD EVER SINCE WE HAD TO CUT THE PARTY SHORT.
C'MON, PATTY! COME AND PLAY WITH YOUR BIG SISSIE. WE GOT A BIG OL' SANDBOX HERE.
WHEE!
ACCORDING TO THE SCHEDULE, IT SHOULD BE HERE ANY MINUTE NOW.

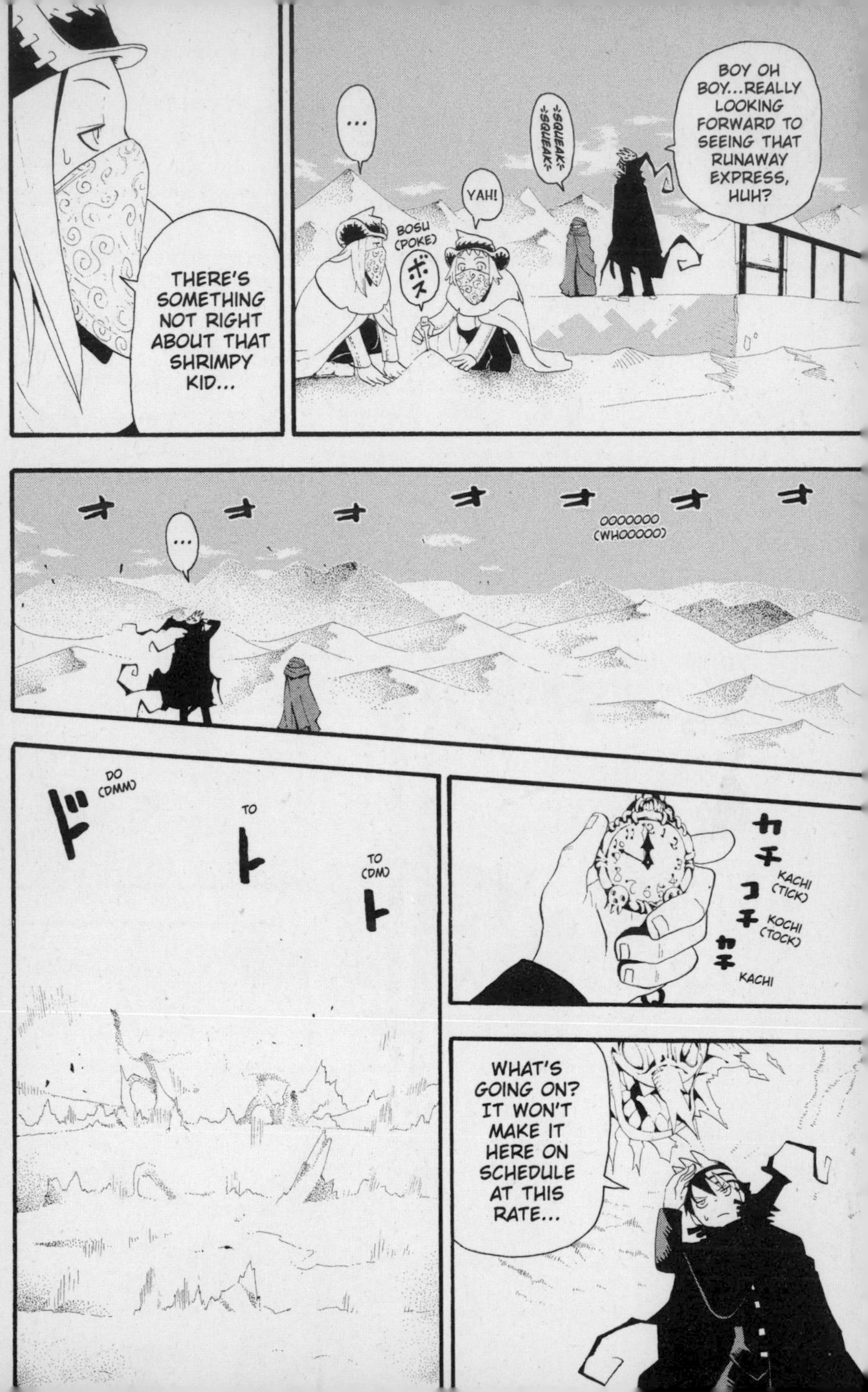
BOY OH BOY...REALLY LOOKING FORWARD TO SEEING THAT RUNAWAY EXPRESS, HUH?
-SQUEAK- -SQUEAK-
YAH!
ボス
BOSU (POKE)
...
THERE'S SOMETHING NOT RIGHT ABOUT THAT SHRIMPY KID...
オ オ オ オ オ オ オ
OOOOOOO (WHOOOOO)
...
カチ
KACHI (TICK)
コチ
KOCHI (TOCK)
カチ
KACHI
WHAT'S GOING ON? IT WON'T MAKE IT HERE ON SCHEDULE AT THIS RATE...
ド
DO (DMM)
ト
TO
ト
TO (DM)

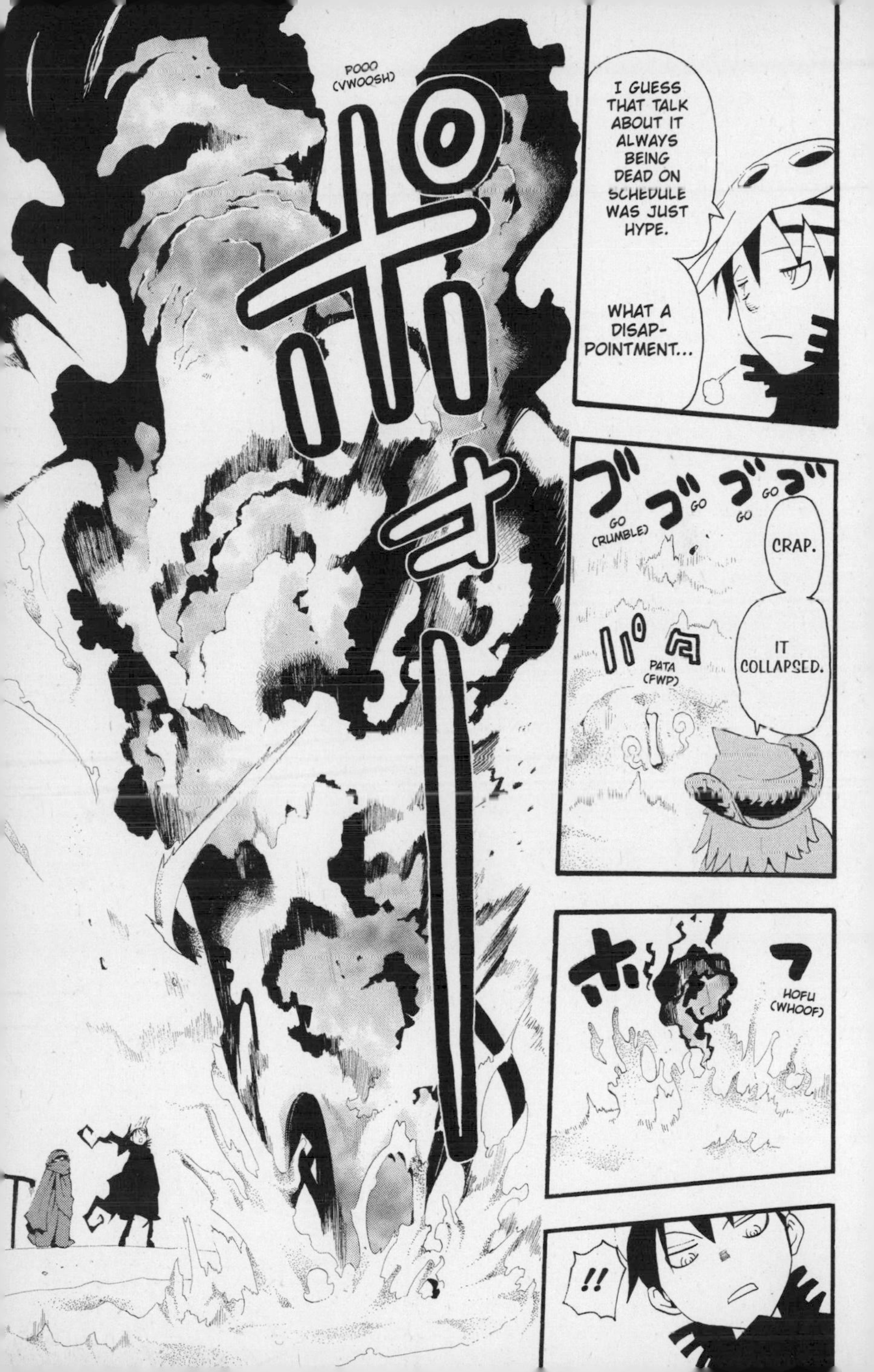
I GUESS THAT TALK ABOUT IT ALWAYS BEING DEAD ON SCHEDULE WAS JUST HYPE.
WHAT A DISAP-POINTMENT...
GO (RUMBLE) GO GO
CRAP.
IT COLLAPSED.
PATA (FWP)
HOFU (WHOOF)
!!
POOO (VWOOSH)

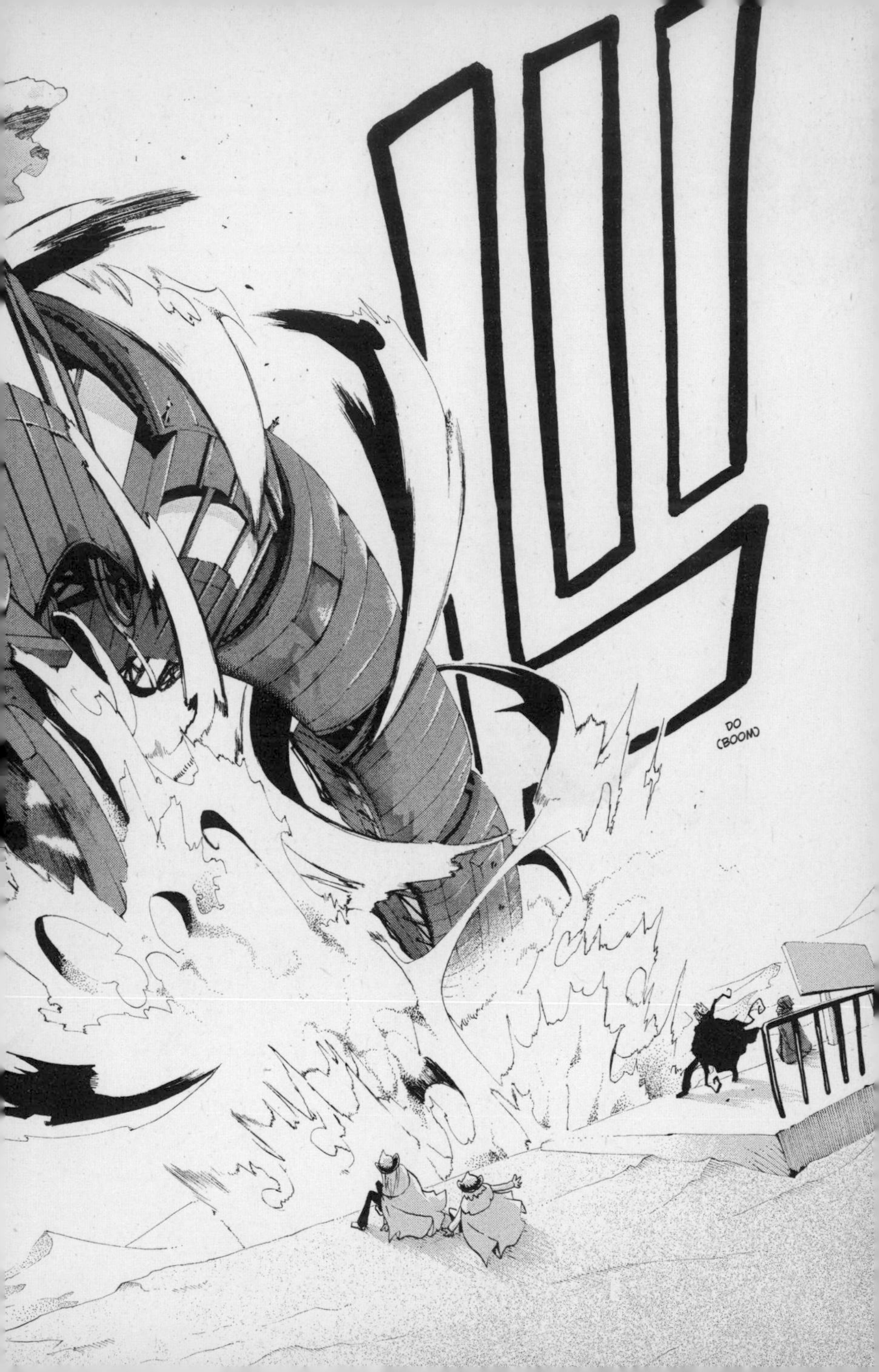
DO
(BOOM)

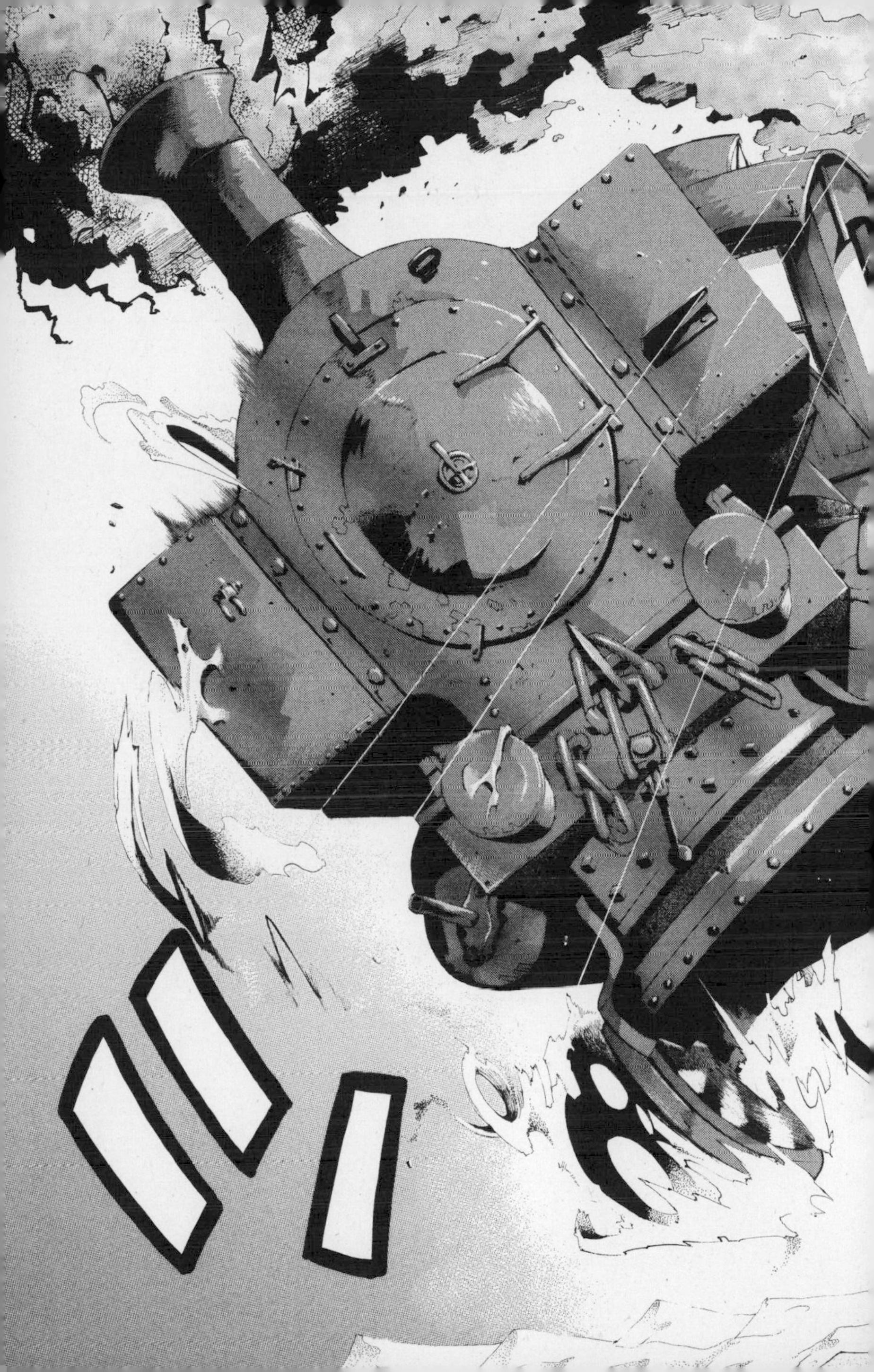

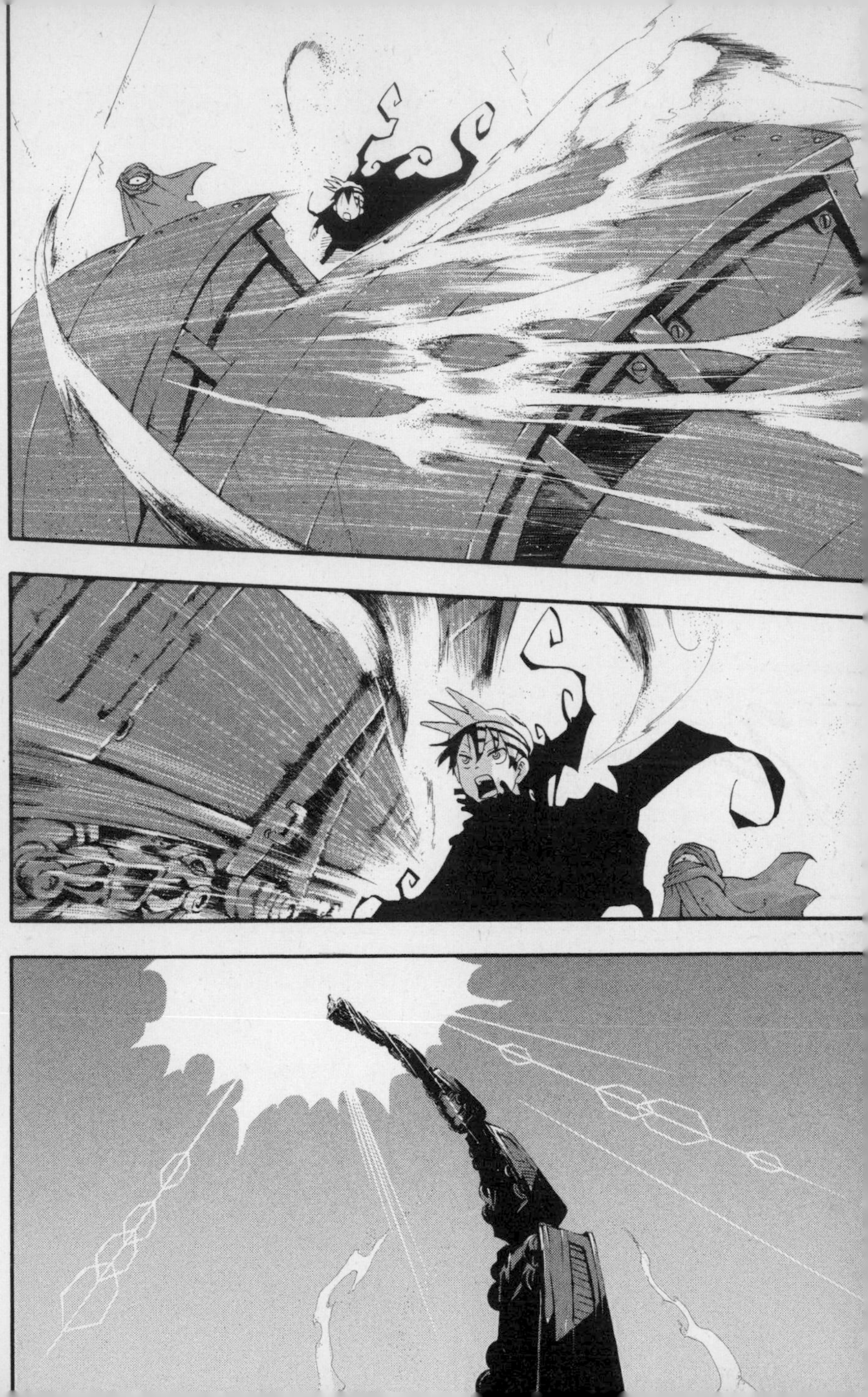

DOZAN
(KABOOM)

BUOOOOOO
(BLAAAST)

WHOA!

AWE-
SOME!!

OOH!!

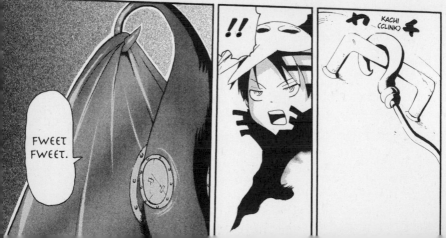

FWEET
FWEET.

!!

KACHI
(CLINK)

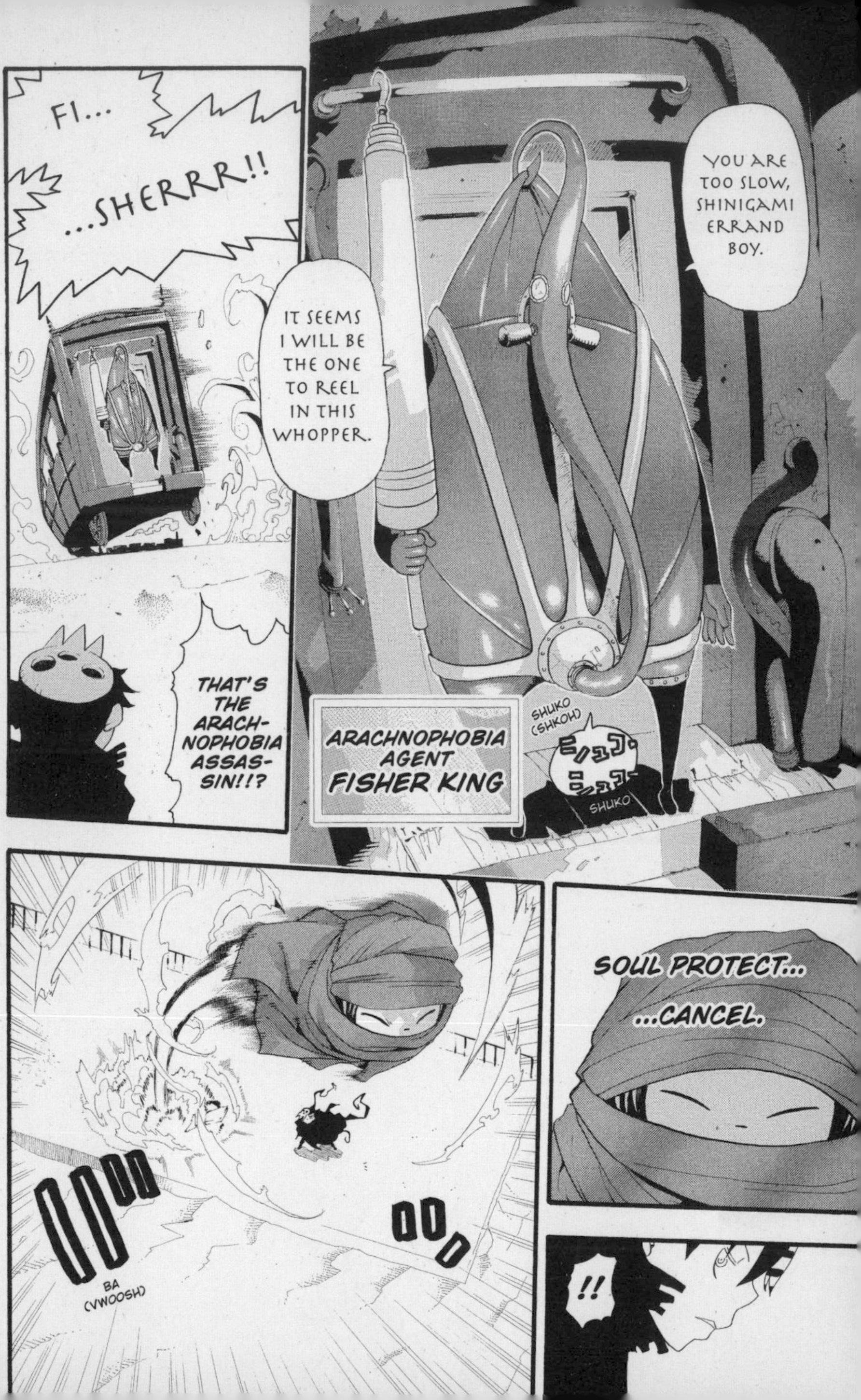
YOU ARE TOO SLOW, SHINIGAMI ERRAND BOY.
IT SEEMS I WILL BE THE ONE TO REEL IN THIS WHOPPER.
SHUKO (SHKOH)
SHUKO
ARACHNOPHOBIA AGENT FISHER KING
FI...
...SHERRR!!
THAT'S THE ARACHNOPHOBIA ASSASSIN!!?
SOUL PROTECT...
...CANCEL.
!!
BA (VWOOSH)

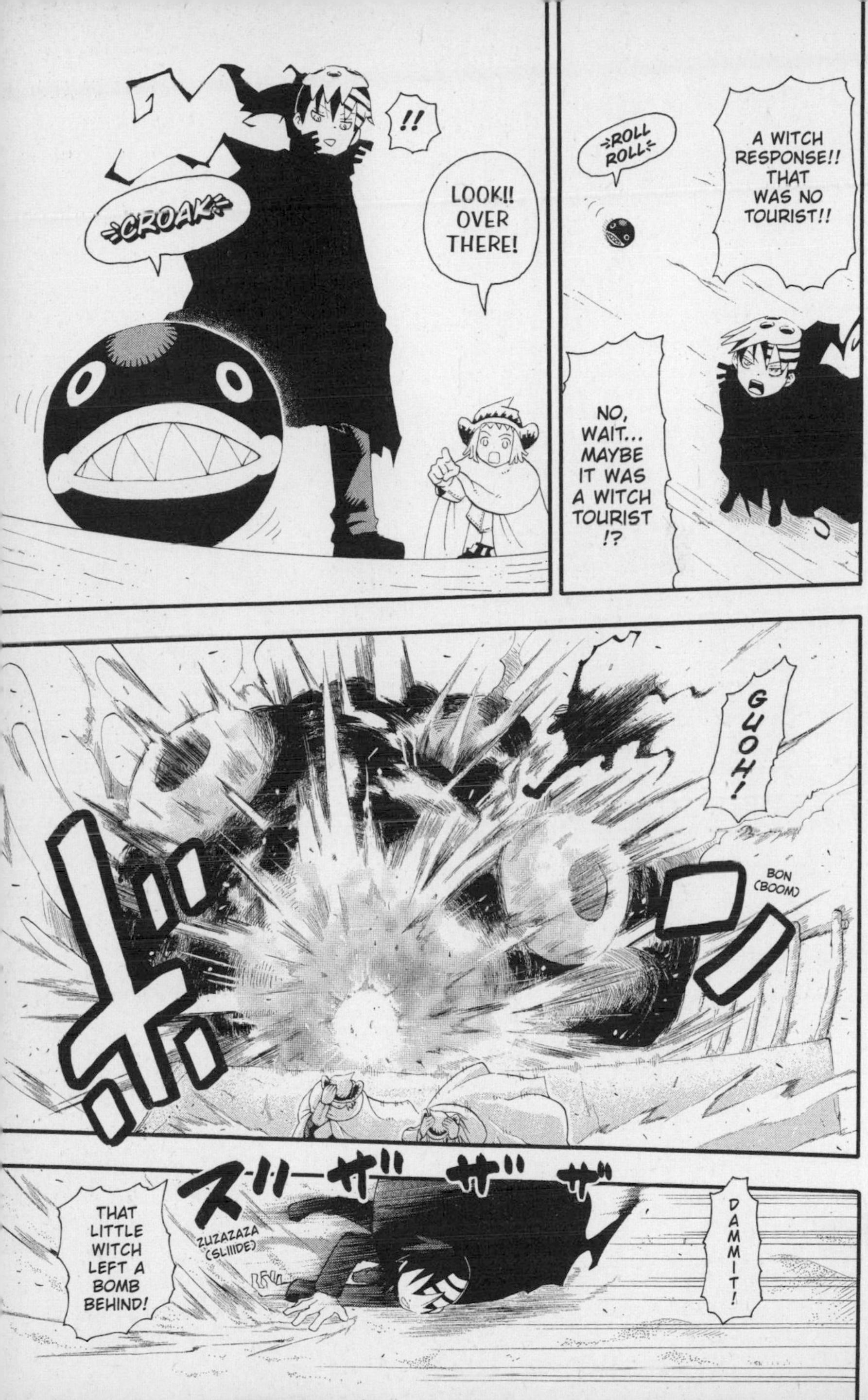
A WITCH RESPONSE!! THAT WAS NO TOURIST!!
ROLL ROLL
NO, WAIT... MAYBE IT WAS A WITCH TOURIST !?
!!
LOOK!! OVER THERE!
CROAK
GUOH!
BON (BOOM)
ドン
DAMMIT!
ズザザザ
ZUZAZAZA (SLIIIDE)
THAT LITTLE WITCH LEFT A BOMB BEHIND!

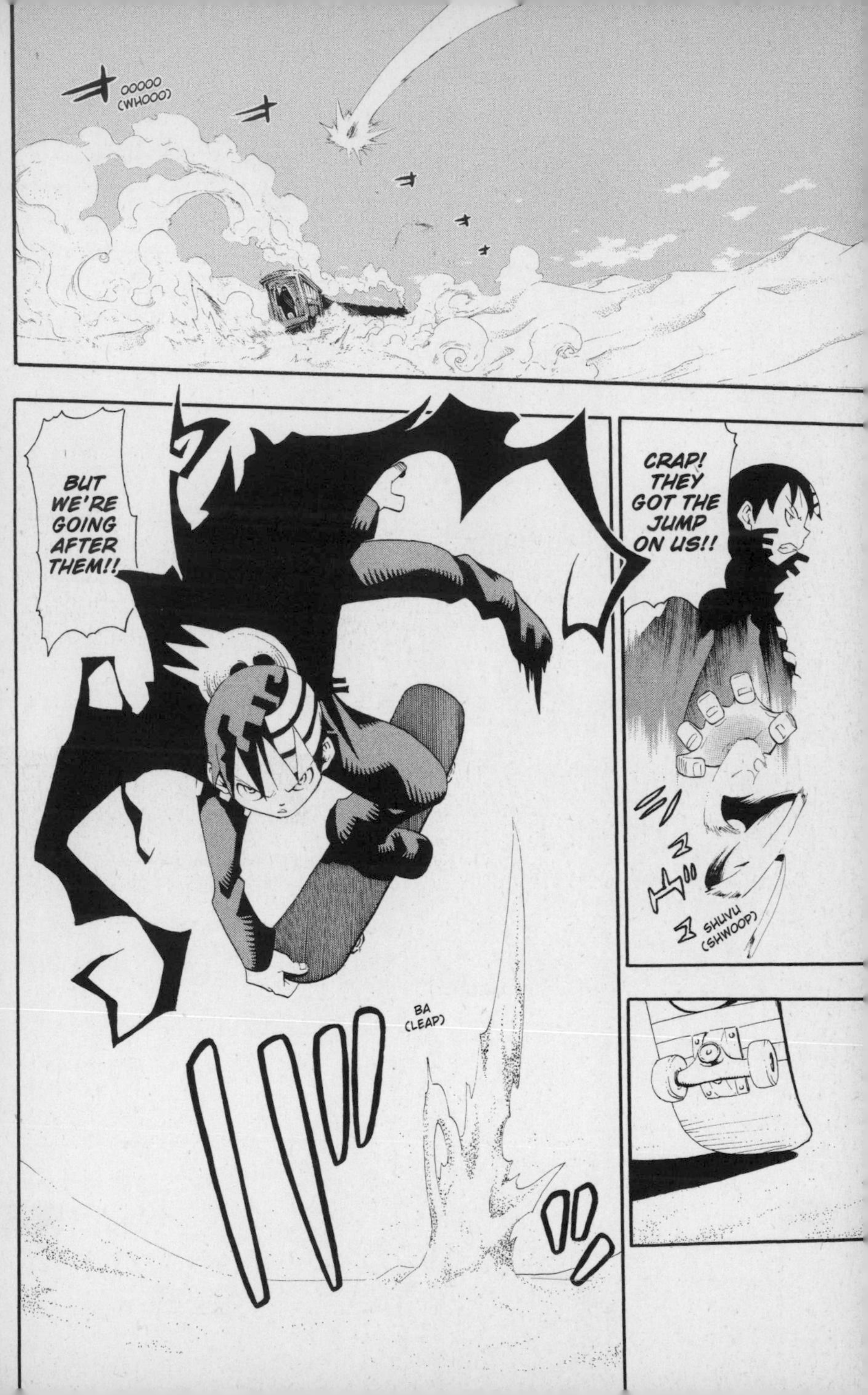
OOOOO
(WHOOO)
CRAP! THEY GOT THE JUMP ON US!!
SHUVU
(SHWOOP)
BUT WE'RE GOING AFTER THEM!!
BA
(LEAP)

SOUL EATER

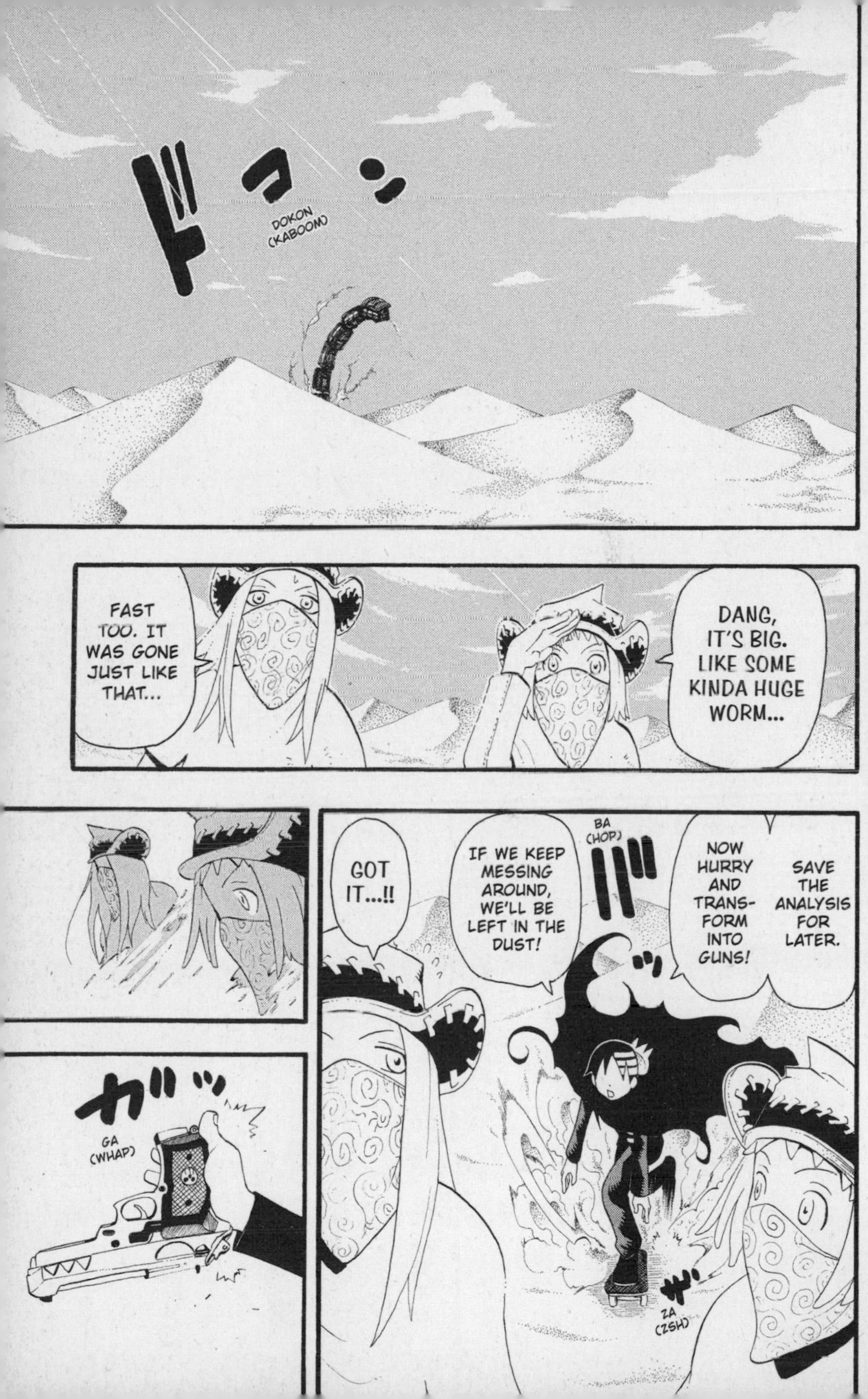
DOKON (KABOOM)
DANG, IT'S BIG. LIKE SOME KINDA HUGE WORM...
FAST TOO. IT WAS GONE JUST LIKE THAT...
SAVE THE ANALYSIS FOR LATER.
NOW HURRY AND TRANS-FORM INTO GUNS!
BA (HOP)
IF WE KEEP MESSING AROUND, WE'LL BE LEFT IN THE DUST!
GOT IT...!!
ZA (ZSH)
GA (WHAP)

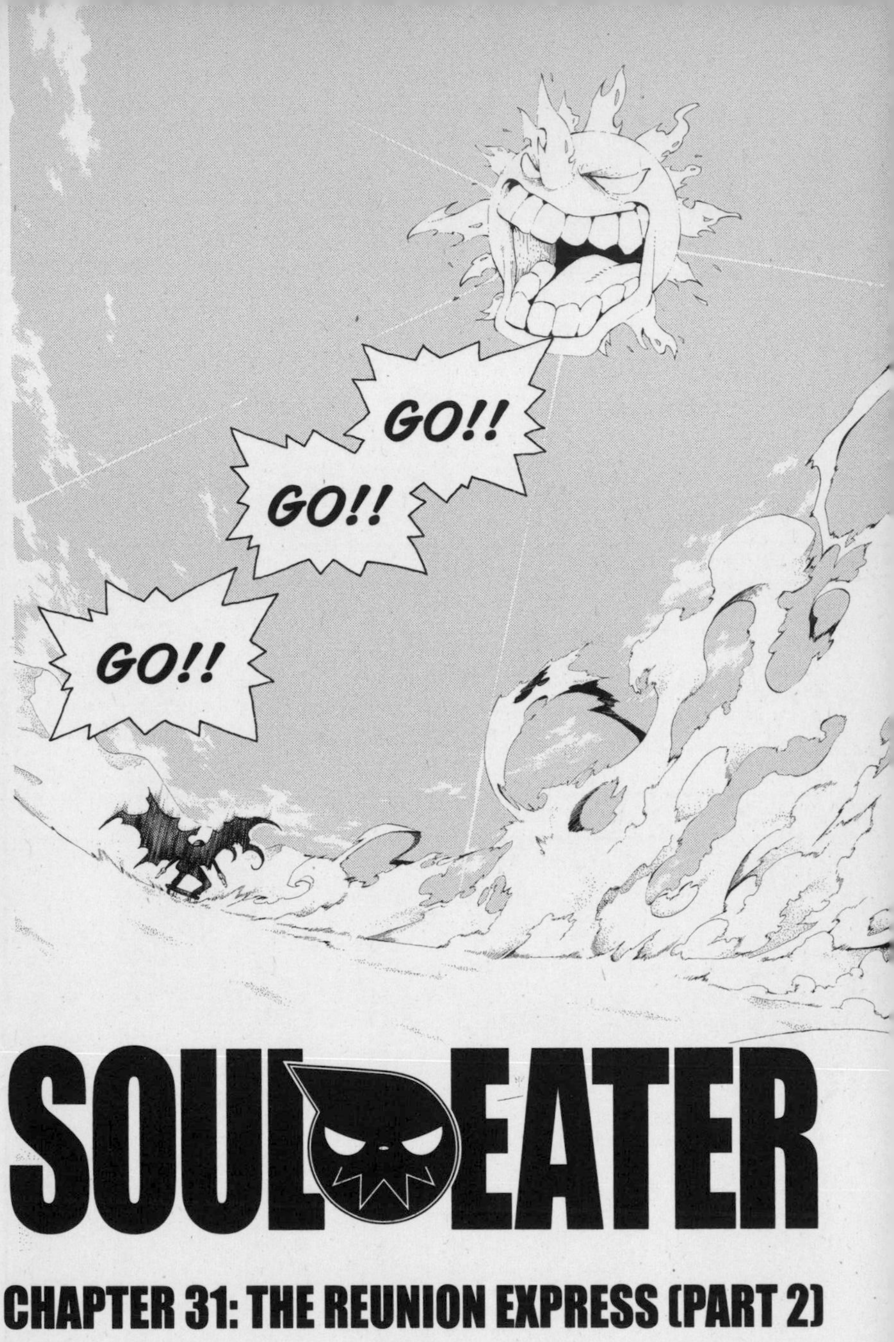
GO!!
GO!!
GO!!

SOUL EATER

CHAPTER 31: THE REUNION EXPRESS (PART 2)

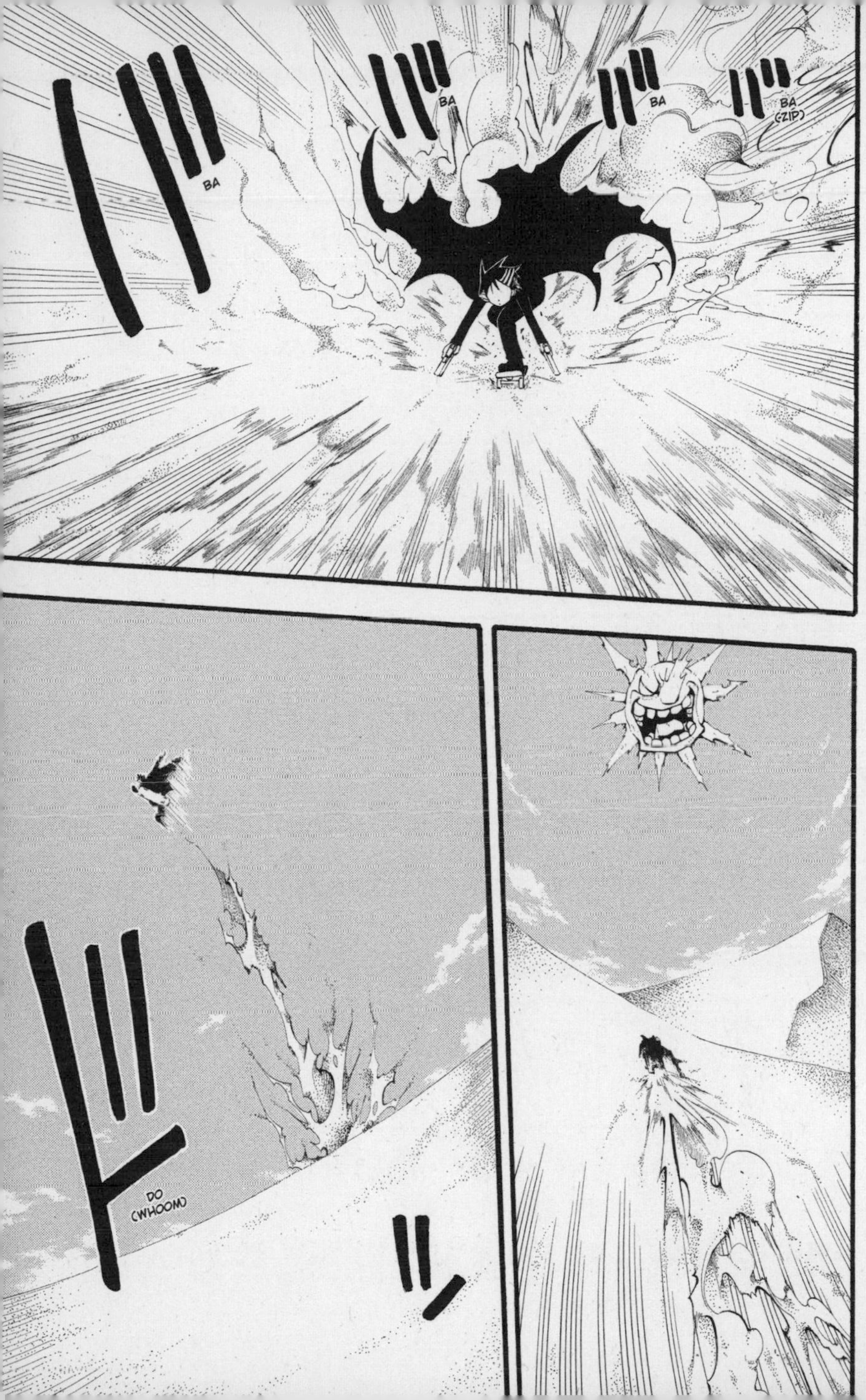
BA (ZIP)
BA
BA
BA
DO (WHOOM)

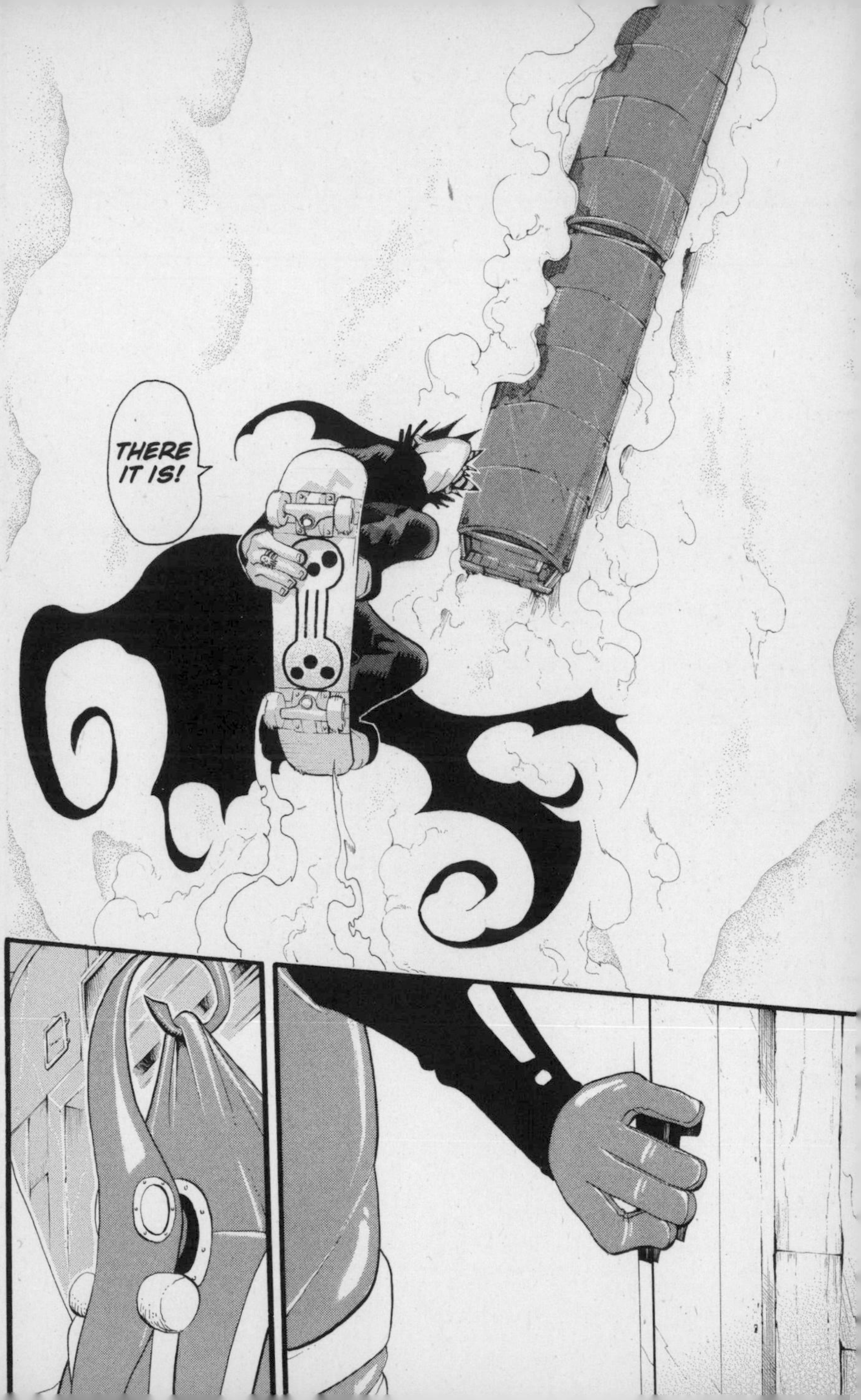
THERE IT IS!

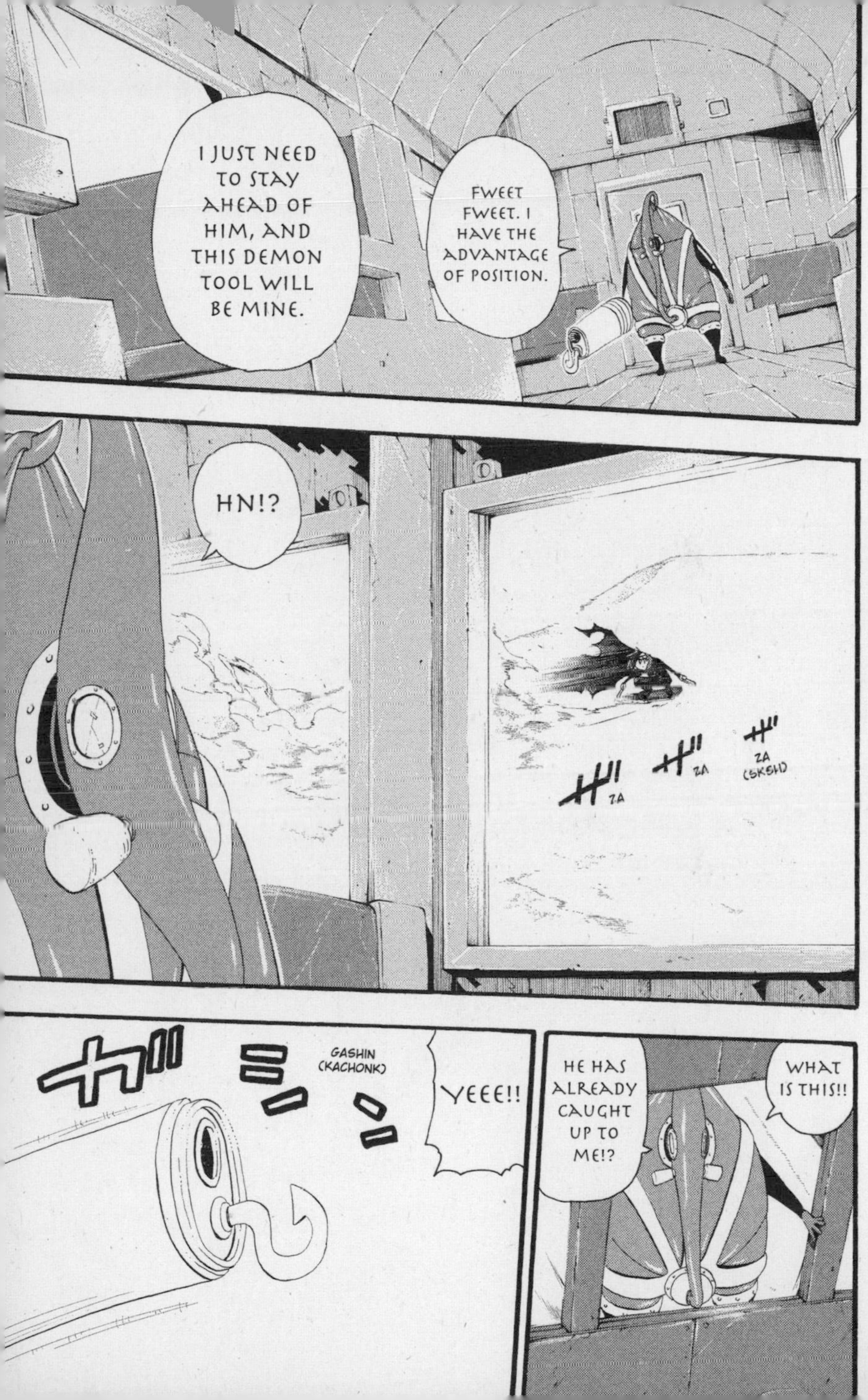
FWEET FWEET. I HAVE THE ADVANTAGE OF POSITION.
I JUST NEED TO STAY AHEAD OF HIM, AND THIS DEMON TOOL WILL BE MINE.
ZA (SKSH)
ZA
ZA
HN!?
WHAT IS THIS!!
HE HAS ALREADY CAUGHT UP TO ME!?
YEEE!!
GASHIN (KACHONK)

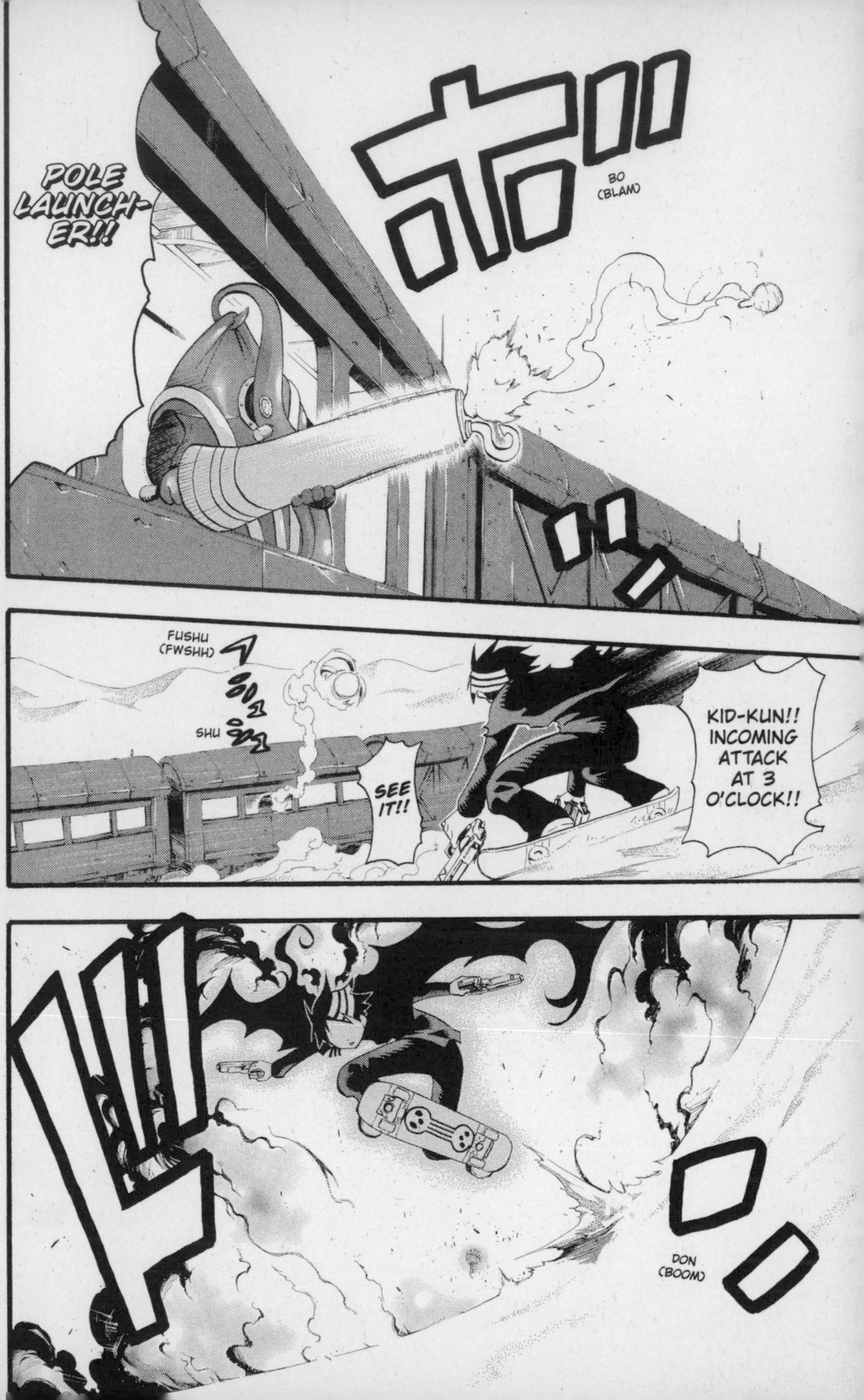
BO (BLAM)
POLE LAUNCHER!!
KID-KUN!! INCOMING ATTACK AT 3 O'CLOCK!!
SEE IT!!
FUSHU (FWSHH)
SHU
DON (BOOM)

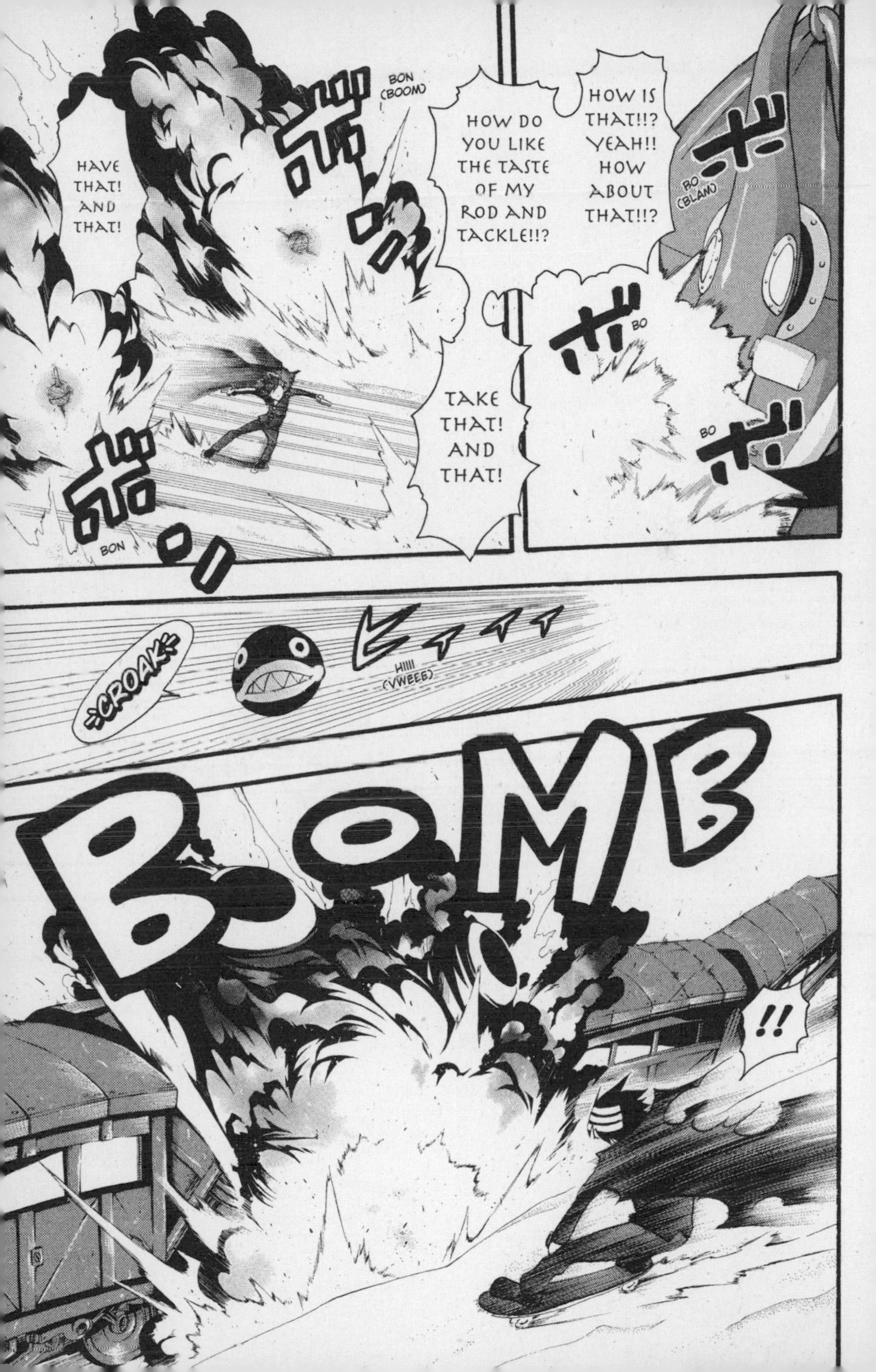
HOW IS THAT!!? YEAH!! HOW ABOUT THAT!!?
BO (BLAM)
BO
BO
HOW DO YOU LIKE THE TASTE OF MY ROD AND TACKLE!!?
BON (BOOM)
HAVE THAT! AND THAT!
TAKE THAT! AND THAT!
BON
HIIII (VWEEE)
CROAK
BOMB
!!

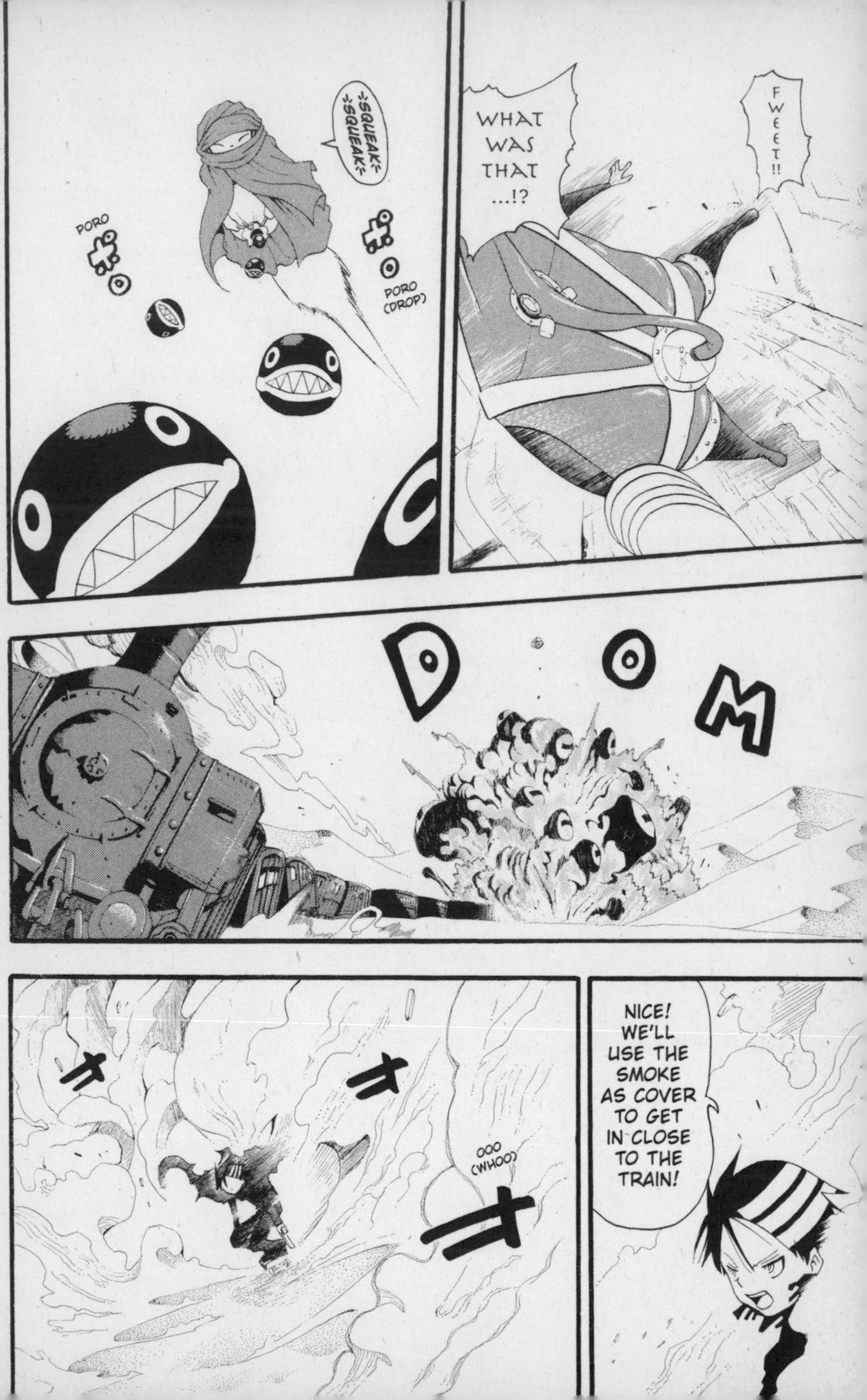
FWEET!!
WHAT WAS THAT ...!?
SQUEAK SQUEAK
PORO
PORO (DROP)
DOM
NICE! WE'LL USE THE SMOKE AS COVER TO GET IN CLOSE TO THE TRAIN!
OOO (WHOO)

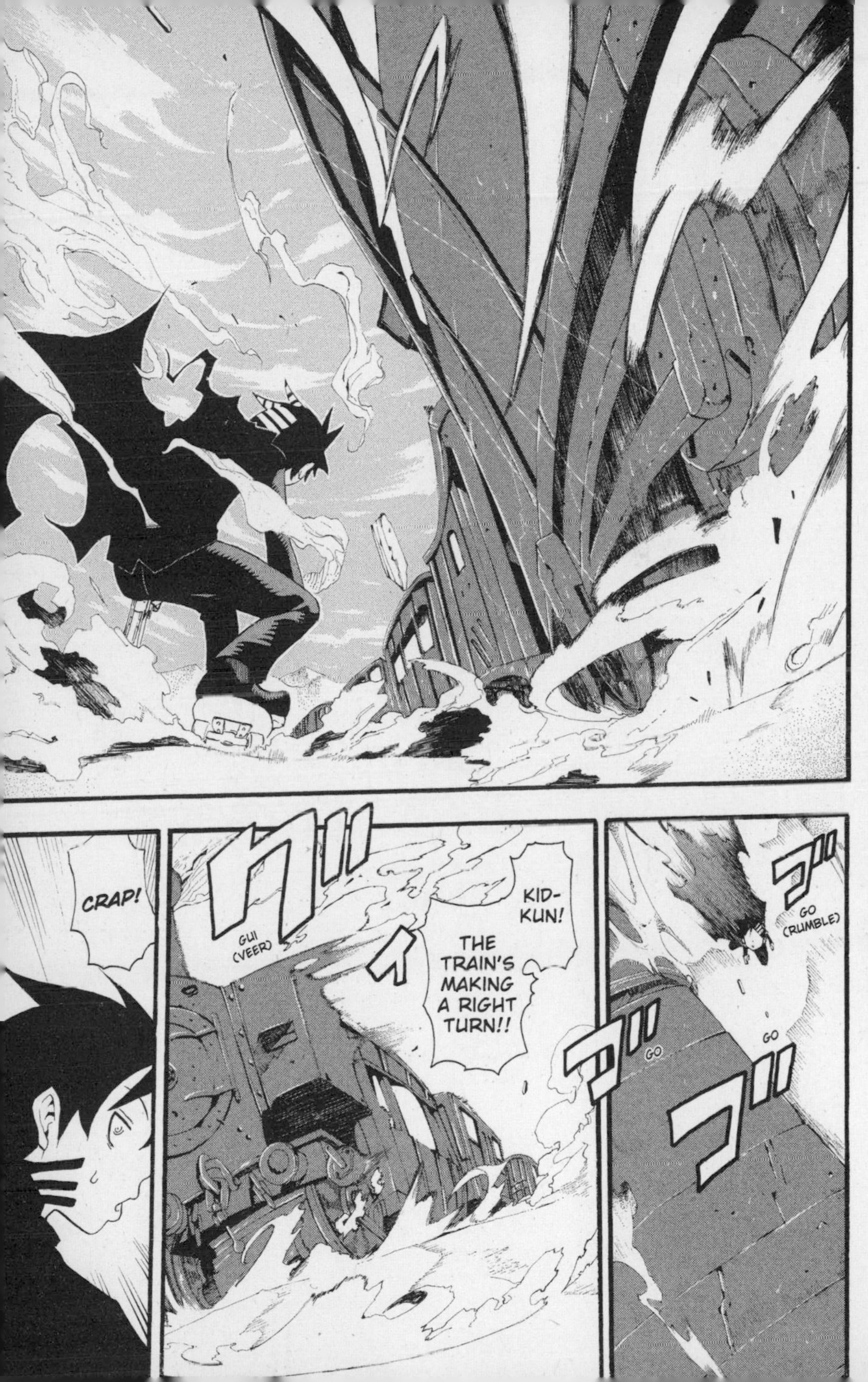
GO (RUMBLE)
GO
GO
KID-KUN!
THE TRAIN'S MAKING A RIGHT TURN!!
GUI (VEER)
CRAP!

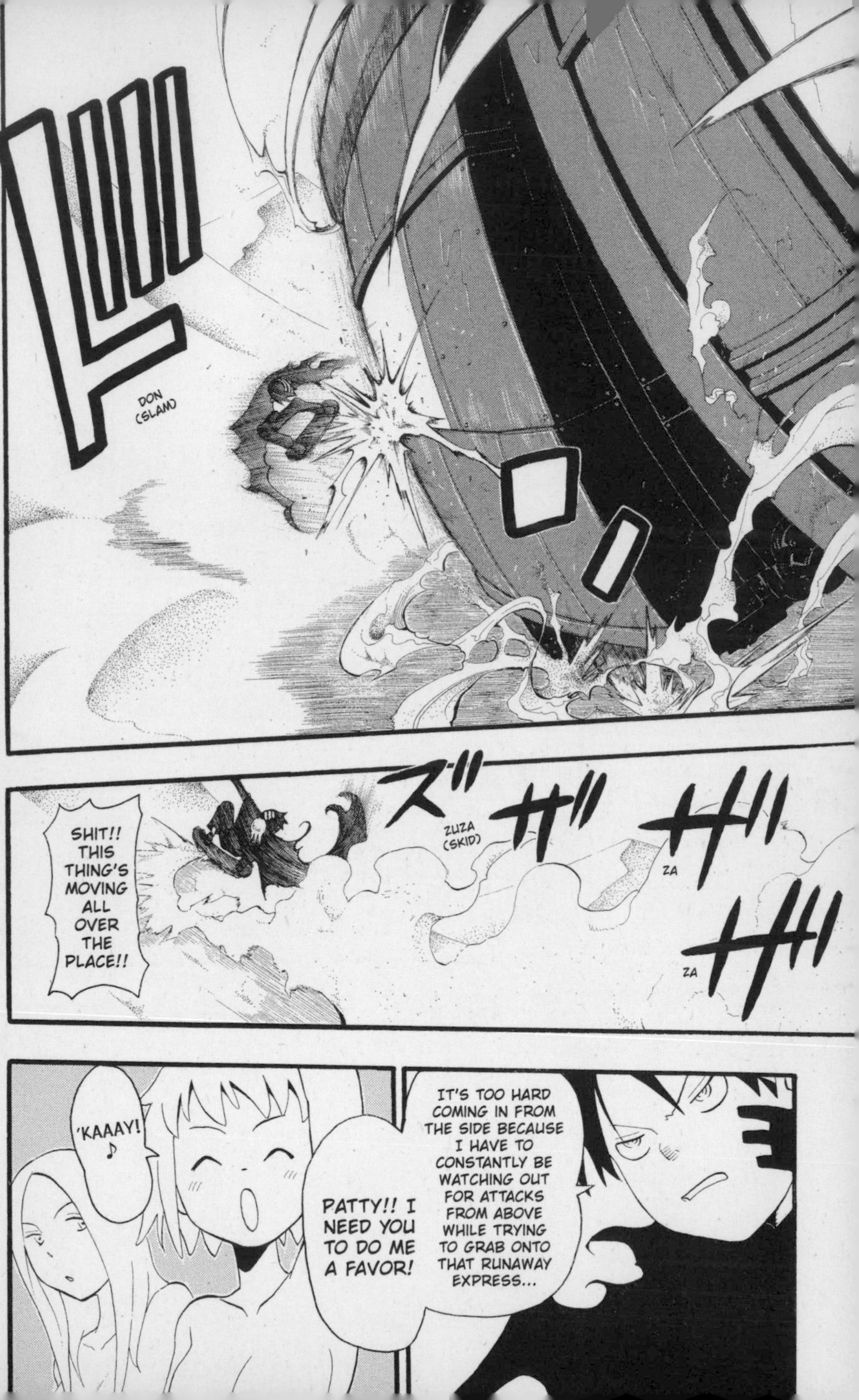
DON (SLAM)
ZUZA (SKID)
ZA
ZA
SHIT!! THIS THING'S MOVING ALL OVER THE PLACE!!
IT'S TOO HARD COMING IN FROM THE SIDE BECAUSE I HAVE TO CONSTANTLY BE WATCHING OUT FOR ATTACKS FROM ABOVE WHILE TRYING TO GRAB ONTO THAT RUNAWAY EXPRESS...
PATTY!! I NEED YOU TO DO ME A FAVOR!
'KAAAY! ♪

SO...YOU JUST WANT ME TO SHOOT THE BAD GUY, THEN?

I'M COUNT-ING ON YOU.

CHA (CHAK)

GACHA (KACHAK)

DAN (BLAM)

DAN

DAN

WHOA!!

DIE, YOU FAT BATHTUB!! COME OUTTA THERE!!

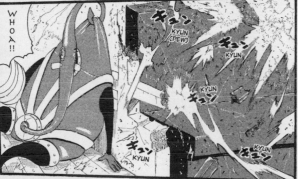

KYUN (PEW)

KYUN

KYUN

KYUN

KYUN

KYUN

TIME TO DIE, POLE MAN!!

THERE HE IS!!

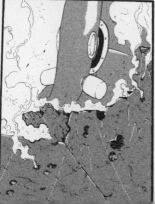

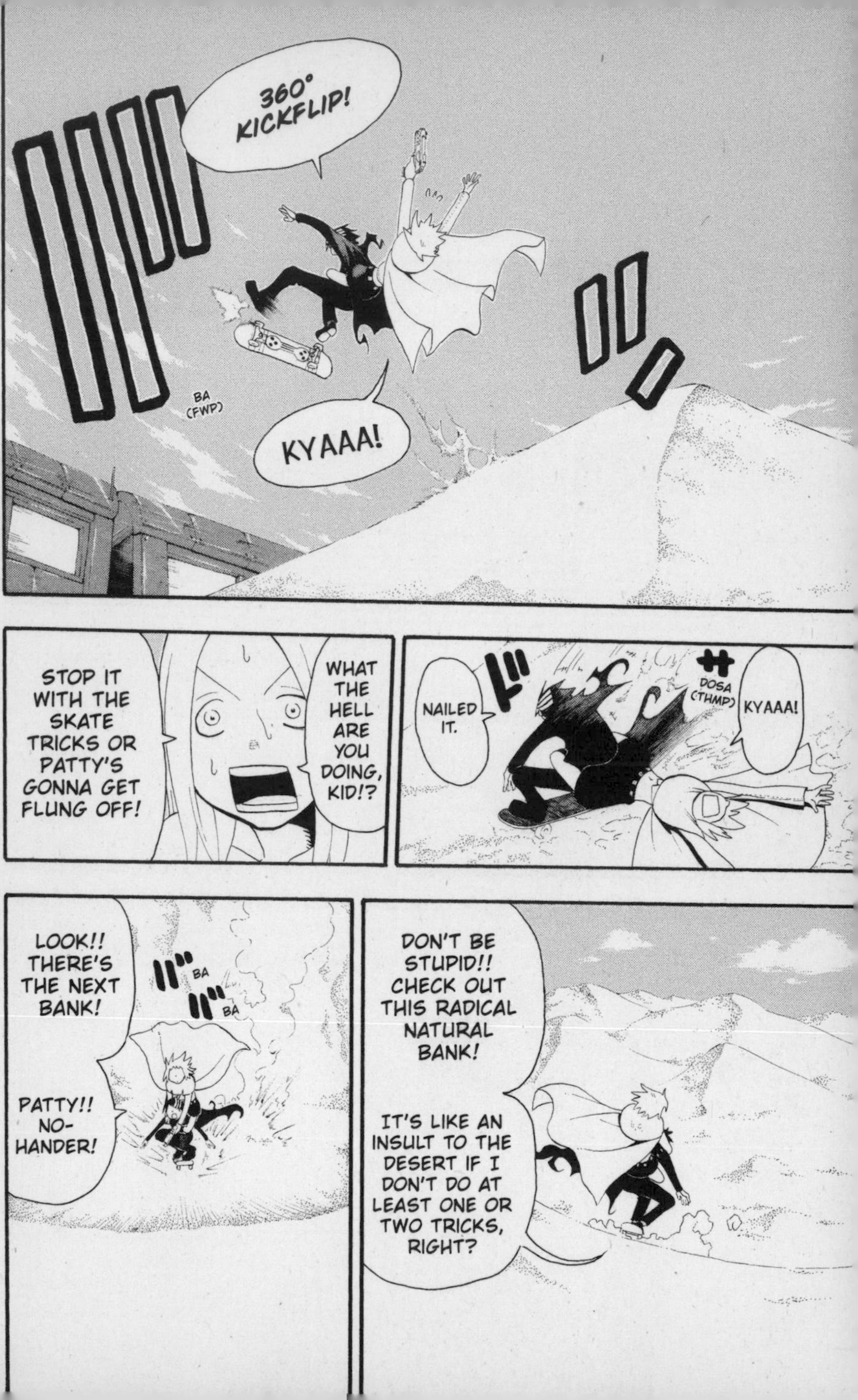
360° KICKFLIP!
BA (FWP)
KYAAA!
KYAAA!
DOSA (THMP)
NAILED IT.
WHAT THE HELL ARE YOU DOING, KID!?
STOP IT WITH THE SKATE TRICKS OR PATTY'S GONNA GET FLUNG OFF!
DON'T BE STUPID!! CHECK OUT THIS RADICAL NATURAL BANK!
IT'S LIKE AN INSULT TO THE DESERT IF I DON'T DO AT LEAST ONE OR TWO TRICKS, RIGHT?
LOOK!! THERE'S THE NEXT BANK!
BA
BA
PATTY!! NO-HANDER!

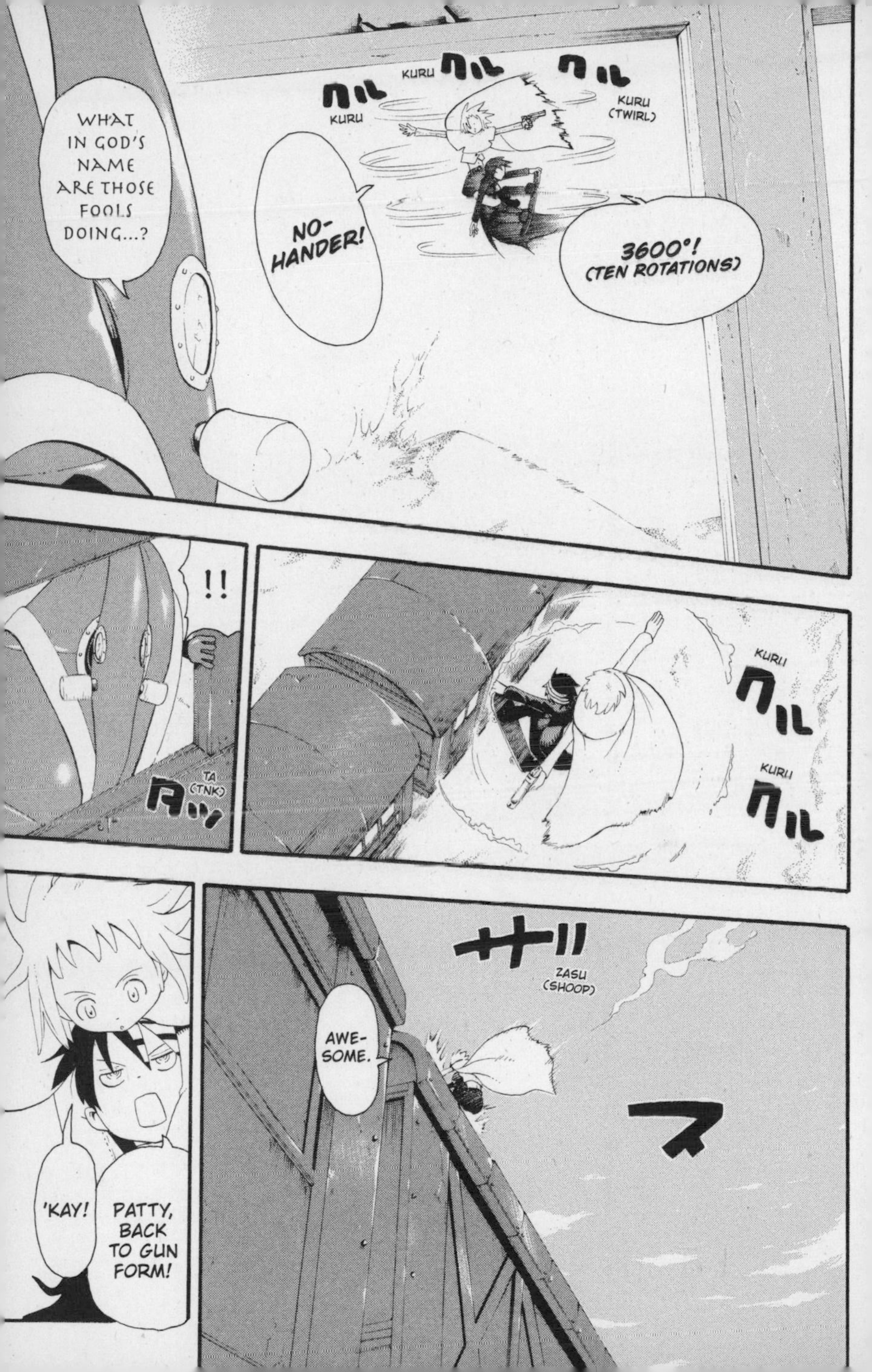

KURU (TWIRL)
KURU
KURU
3600°! (TEN ROTATIONS)
NO-HANDER!
WHAT IN GOD'S NAME ARE THOSE FOOLS DOING...?
KURU
KURU
!!
TA (TNK)
ZASU (SHOOP)
AWE-SOME.
PATTY, BACK TO GUN FORM!
'KAY!

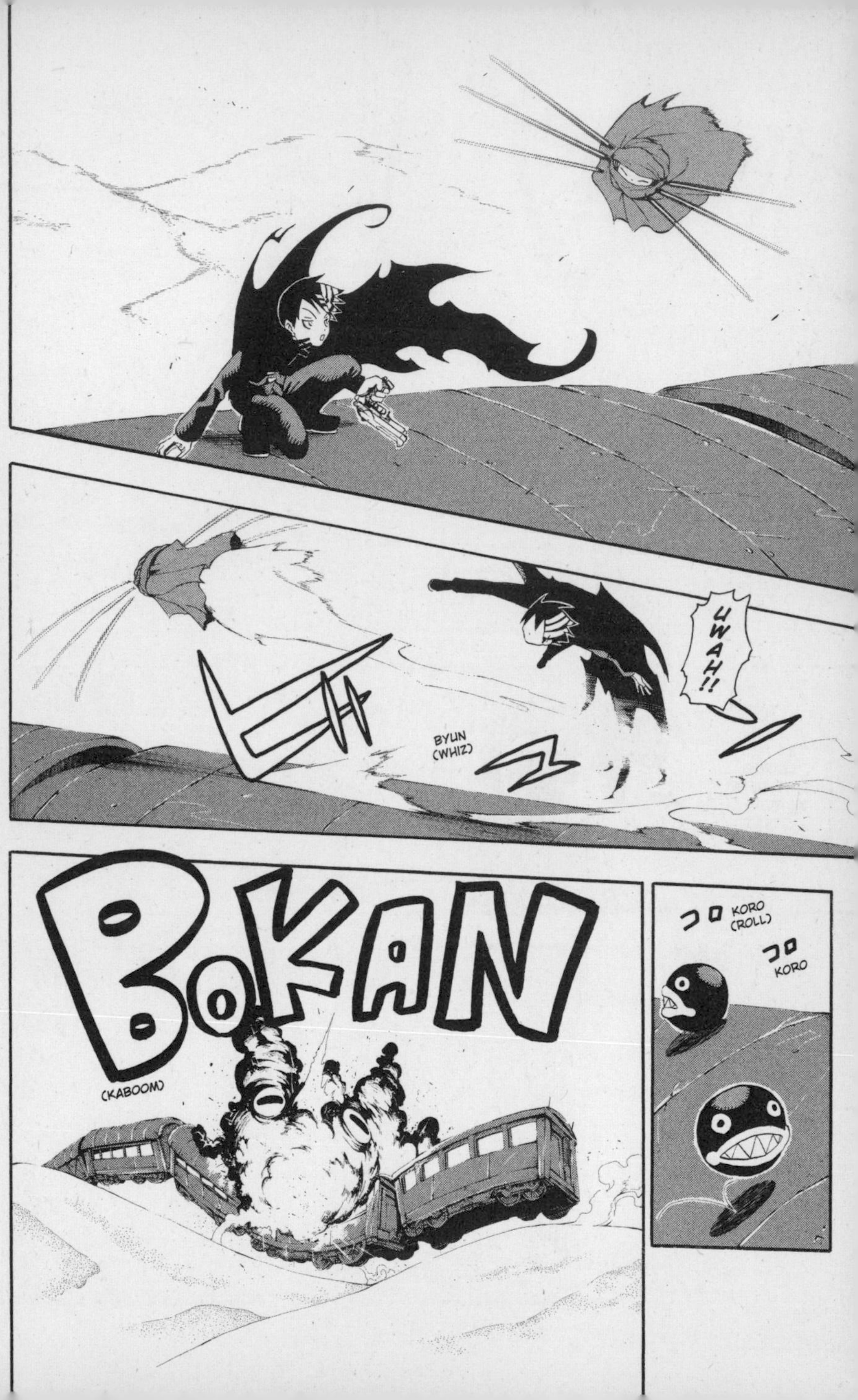
UWAH!!
BYUN
(WHIZ)
コロ KORO
(ROLL)
コロ
KORO
BOKAN
(KABOOM)

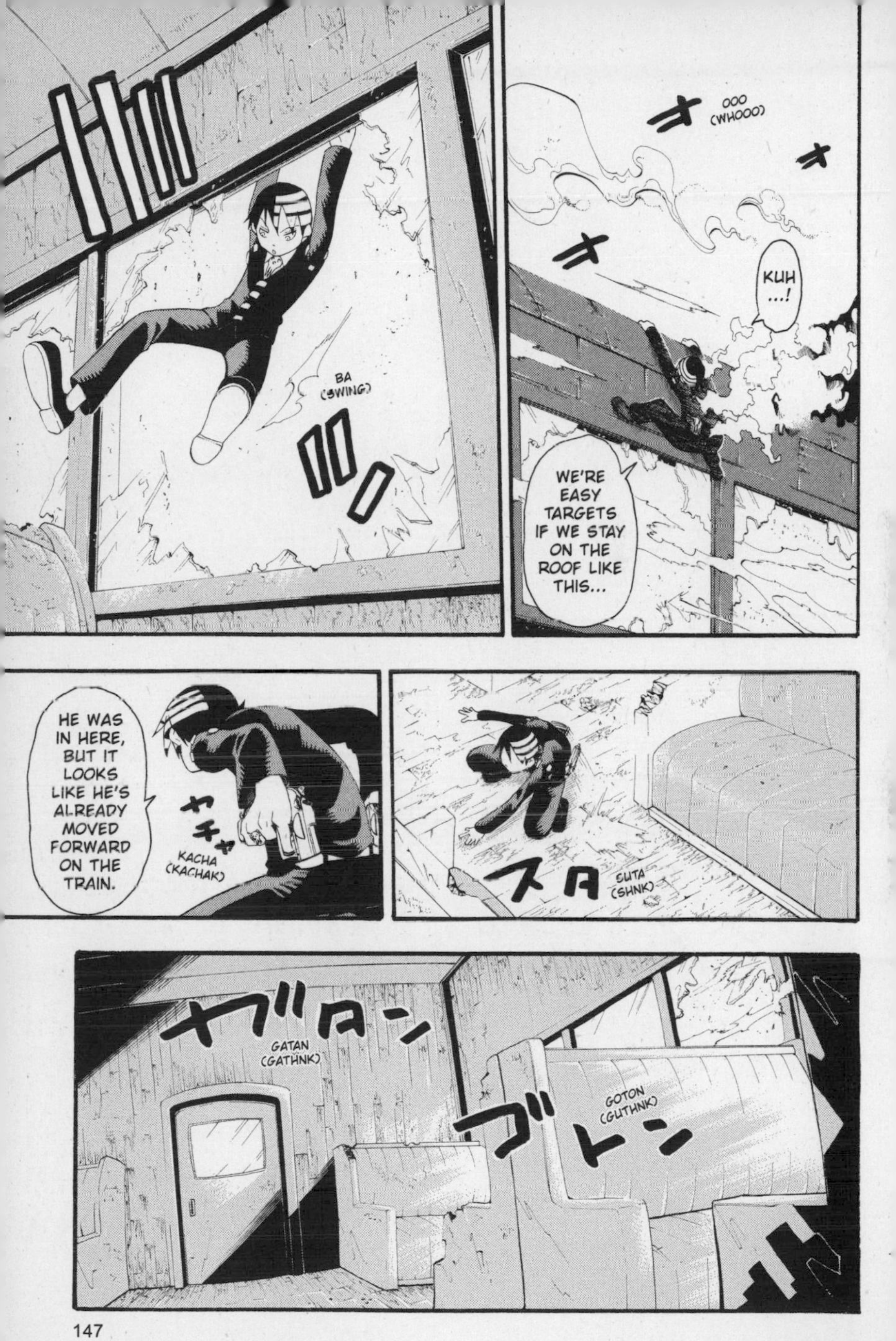
OOO
(WHOOO)
KUH ...!
WE'RE EASY TARGETS IF WE STAY ON THE ROOF LIKE THIS...
BA
(SWING)
SUTA
(SHNK)
HE WAS IN HERE, BUT IT LOOKS LIKE HE'S ALREADY MOVED FORWARD ON THE TRAIN.
KACHA
(KACHAK)
GATAN
(GATHNK)
GOTON
(GUTHNK)

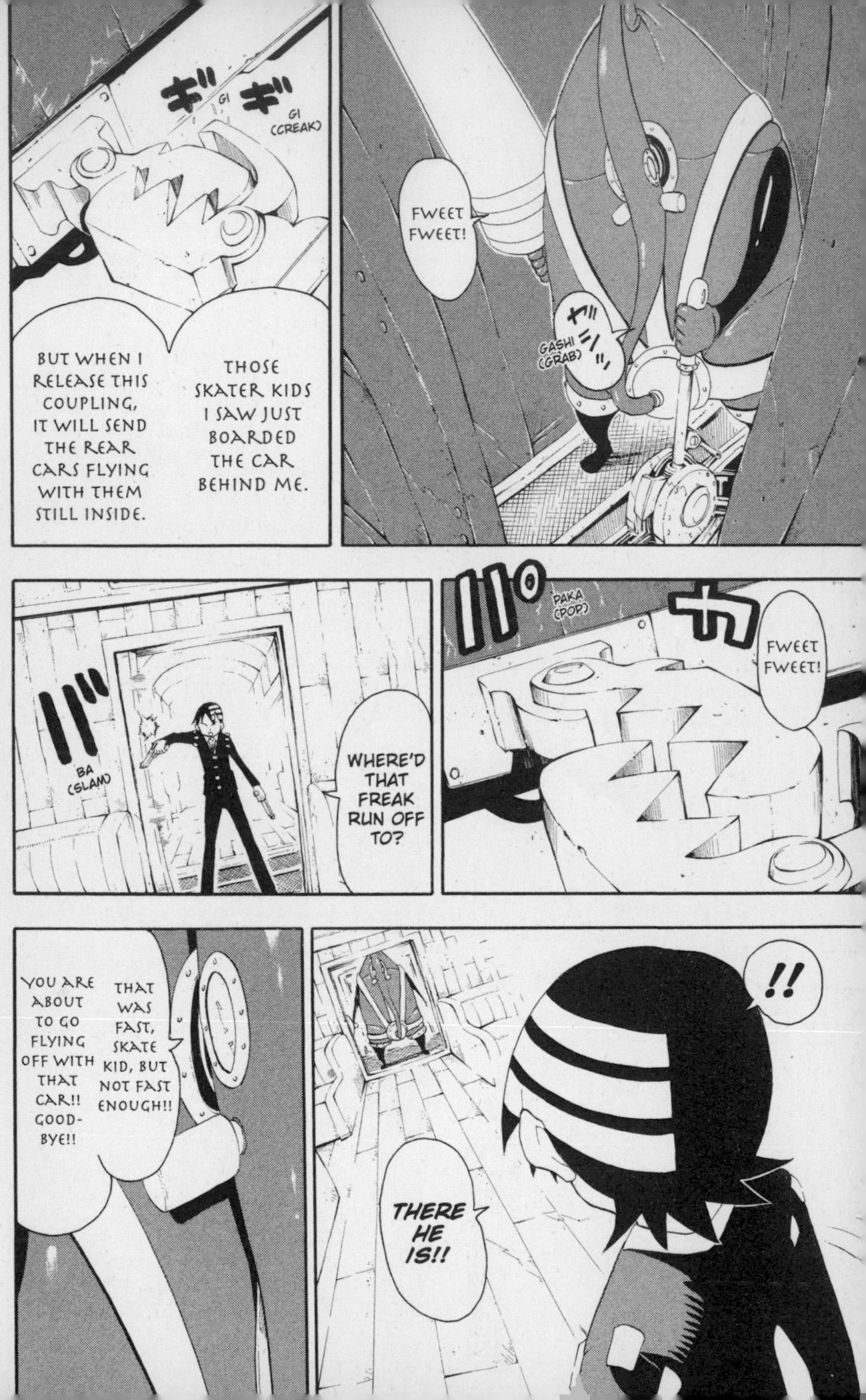
FWEET FWEET!
GASHI (GRAB)
GI GI (CREAK)
THOSE SKATER KIDS I SAW JUST BOARDED THE CAR BEHIND ME.
BUT WHEN I RELEASE THIS COUPLING, IT WILL SEND THE REAR CARS FLYING WITH THEM STILL INSIDE.
PAKA (POP)
FWEET FWEET!
WHERE'D THAT FREAK RUN OFF TO?
BA (SLAM)
!!
THERE HE IS!!
THAT WAS FAST, SKATE KID, BUT NOT FAST ENOUGH!!
YOU ARE ABOUT TO GO FLYING OFF WITH THAT CAR!! GOOD-BYE!!

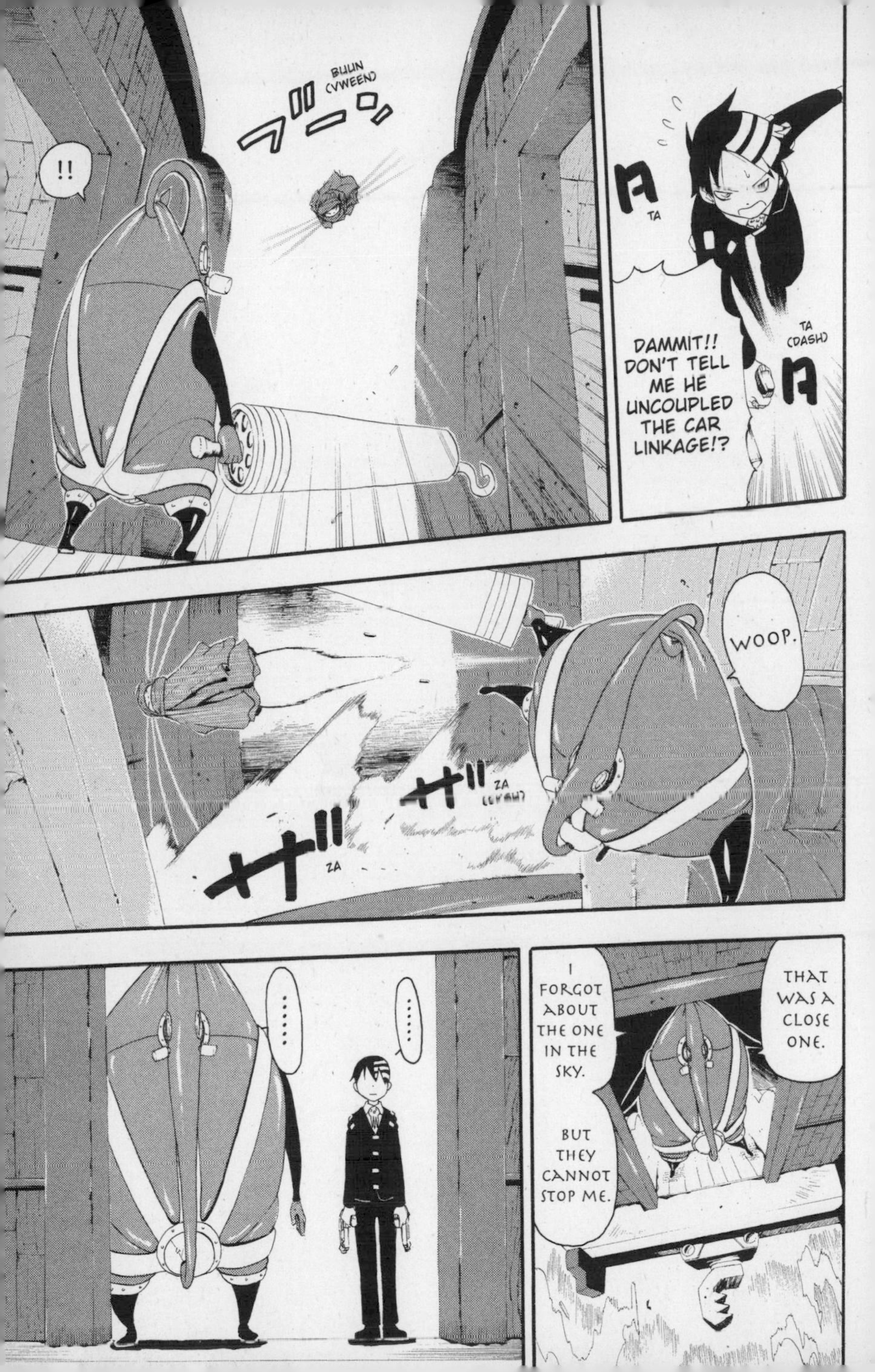

TA
TA (DASH)
DAMMIT!! DON'T TELL ME HE UNCOUPLED THE CAR LINKAGE!?
BUUN (VWEEN)
!!
WOOP.
ZA
ZA
THAT WAS A CLOSE ONE.
I FORGOT ABOUT THE ONE IN THE SKY.
BUT THEY CANNOT STOP ME.
......
......

OH NO!! I PANICKED AND ACCIDENTALLY JUMPED BACKWARD ONTO THE WRONG CAR!

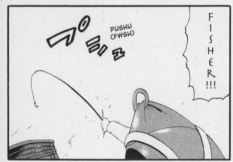

PUSHU (FWSH)

FISHER!!!

THIS GUY IS AN IDIOT.

YEEE!!

IDIOT CITY.

IDIOT.

COMPLETE IDIOT.

PYUU (WHEEW)

GOODBYE.

KAN (CLANK)

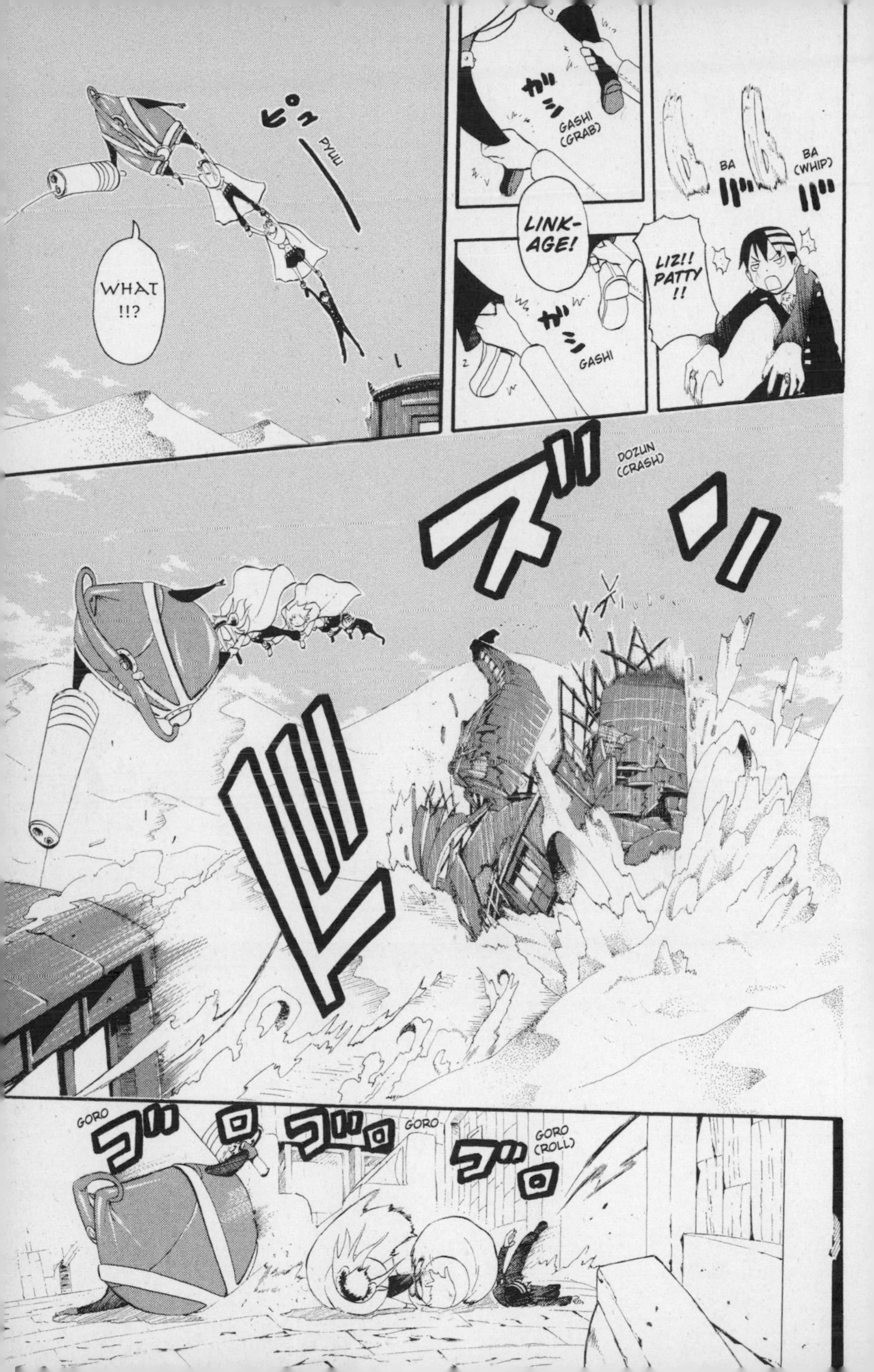
バッ
BA
バッ
BA (WHIP)
LIZ!! PATTY!!
ガシッ
GASHI (GRAB)
LINK-AGE!
ガシッ
GASHI
ピュー
PYUU
WHAT!!?
ズドンッ
DOZUN (CRASH)
ゴロ
GORO (ROLL)
ゴロ
GORO
ゴロ
GORO

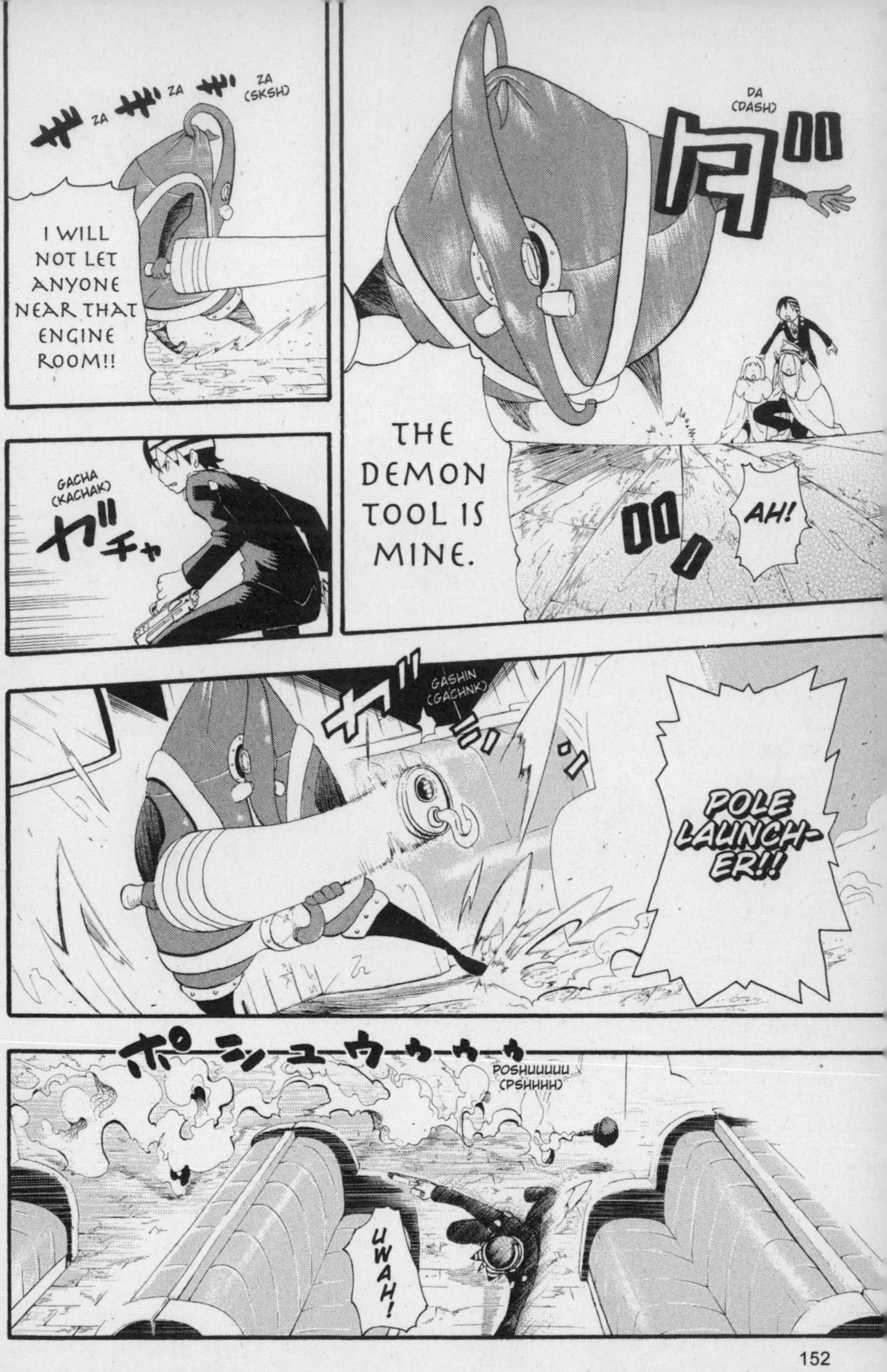

DA (DASH)
THE DEMON TOOL IS MINE.
AH!
ZA ZA ZA (SKSH)
I WILL NOT LET ANYONE NEAR THAT ENGINE ROOM!!
GACHA (KACHAK)
GASHIN (GACHNK)
POLE LAUNCHER!!
POSHUUUUU (PSHHHH)
UWAH!

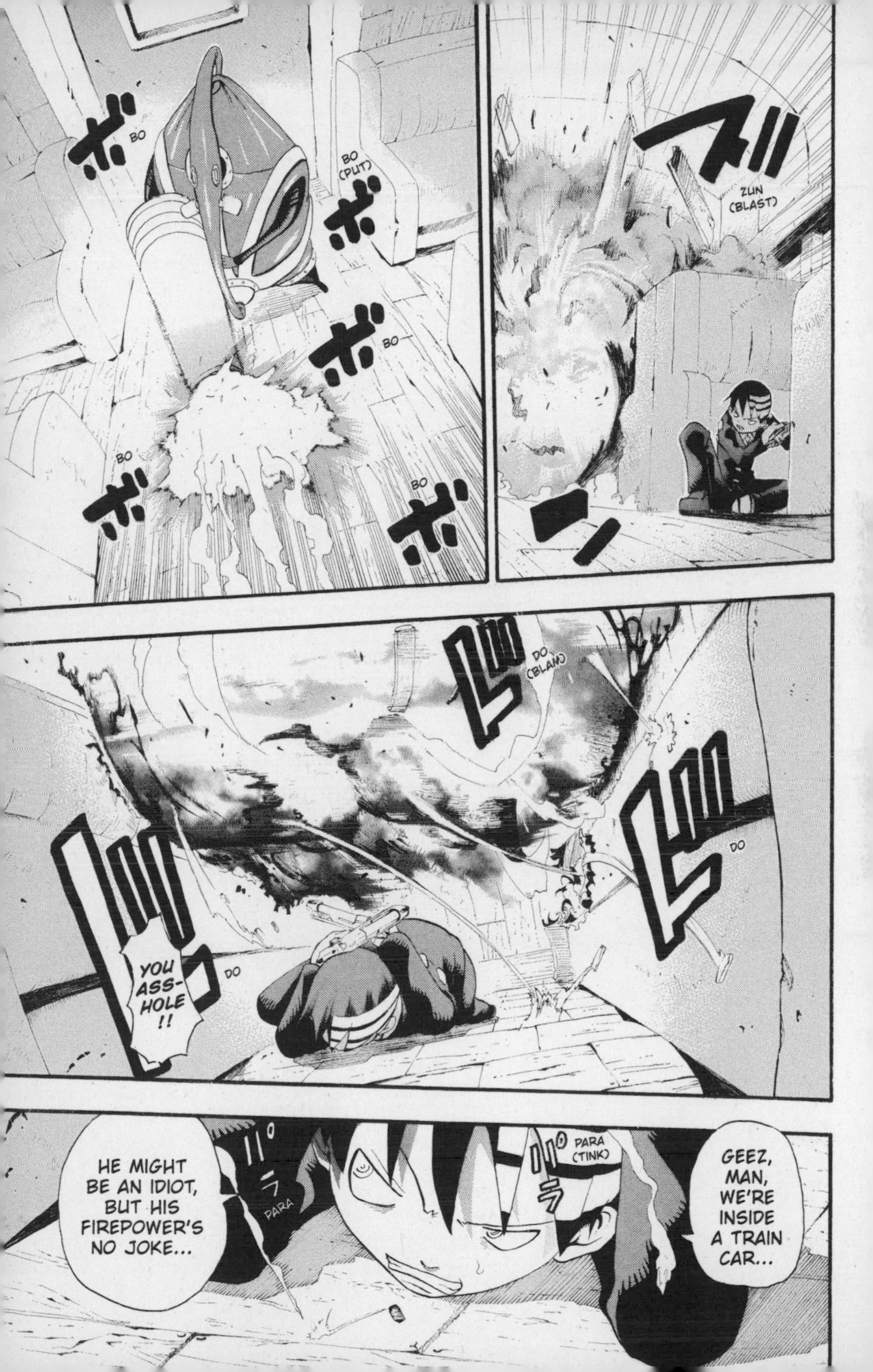

ズン
ZUN (BLAST)
ボ
BO
ボ
BO (PUT)
ボ
BO
ボ
BO
ボ
BO
ド
DO (BLAM)
ド
DO
YOU ASSHOLE!!
ド
DO
GEEZ, MAN, WE'RE INSIDE A TRAIN CAR...
パラ
PARA (TINK)
パラ
PARA
HE MIGHT BE AN IDIOT, BUT HIS FIREPOWER'S NO JOKE...

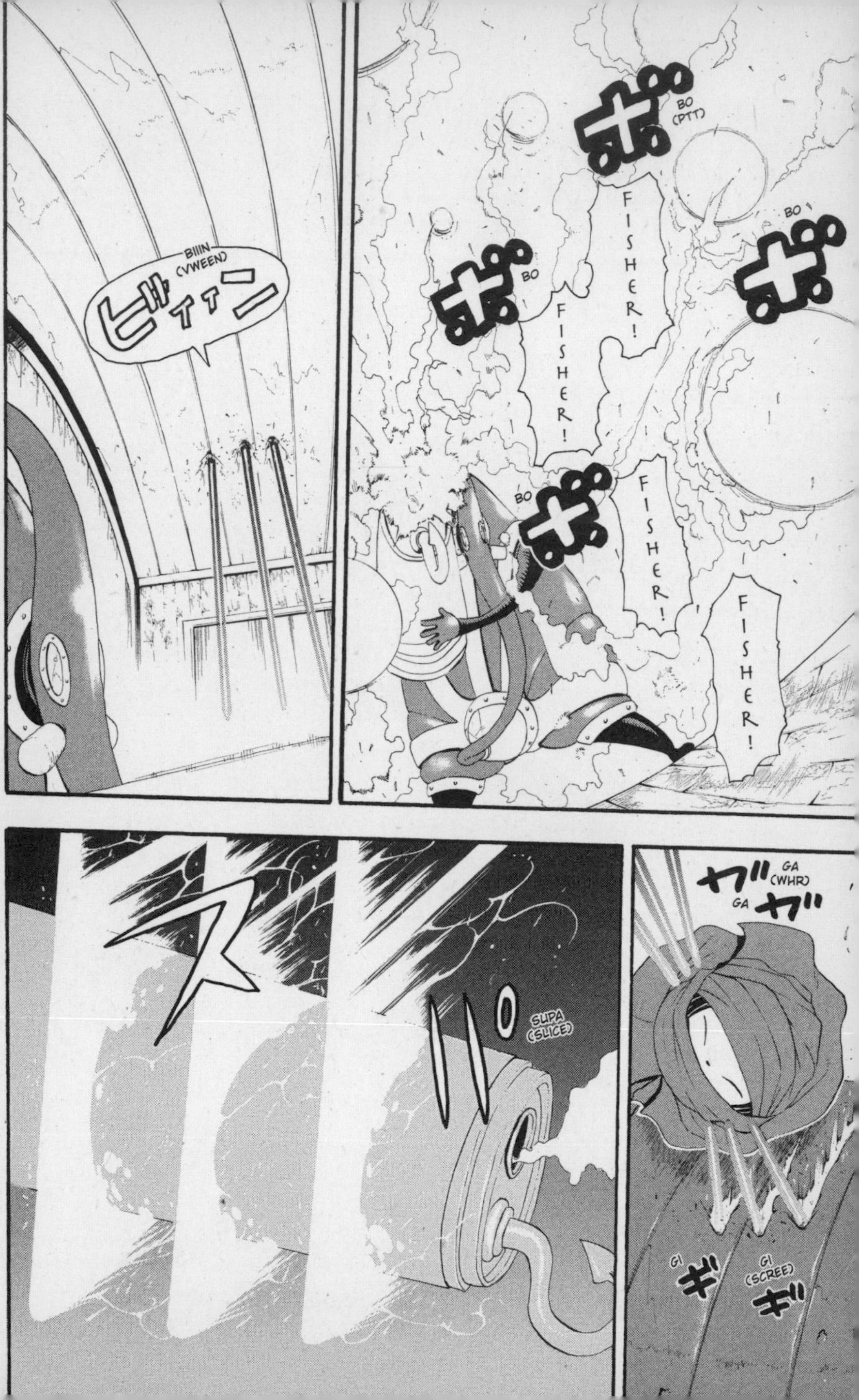
BO (PTT)
BO
FISHER!
FISHER!
FISHER!
FISHER!
BO
BO
BIIIN (VWEEN)
GA (WHR)
GA
GI
GI (SCREE)
SUPA (SLICE)

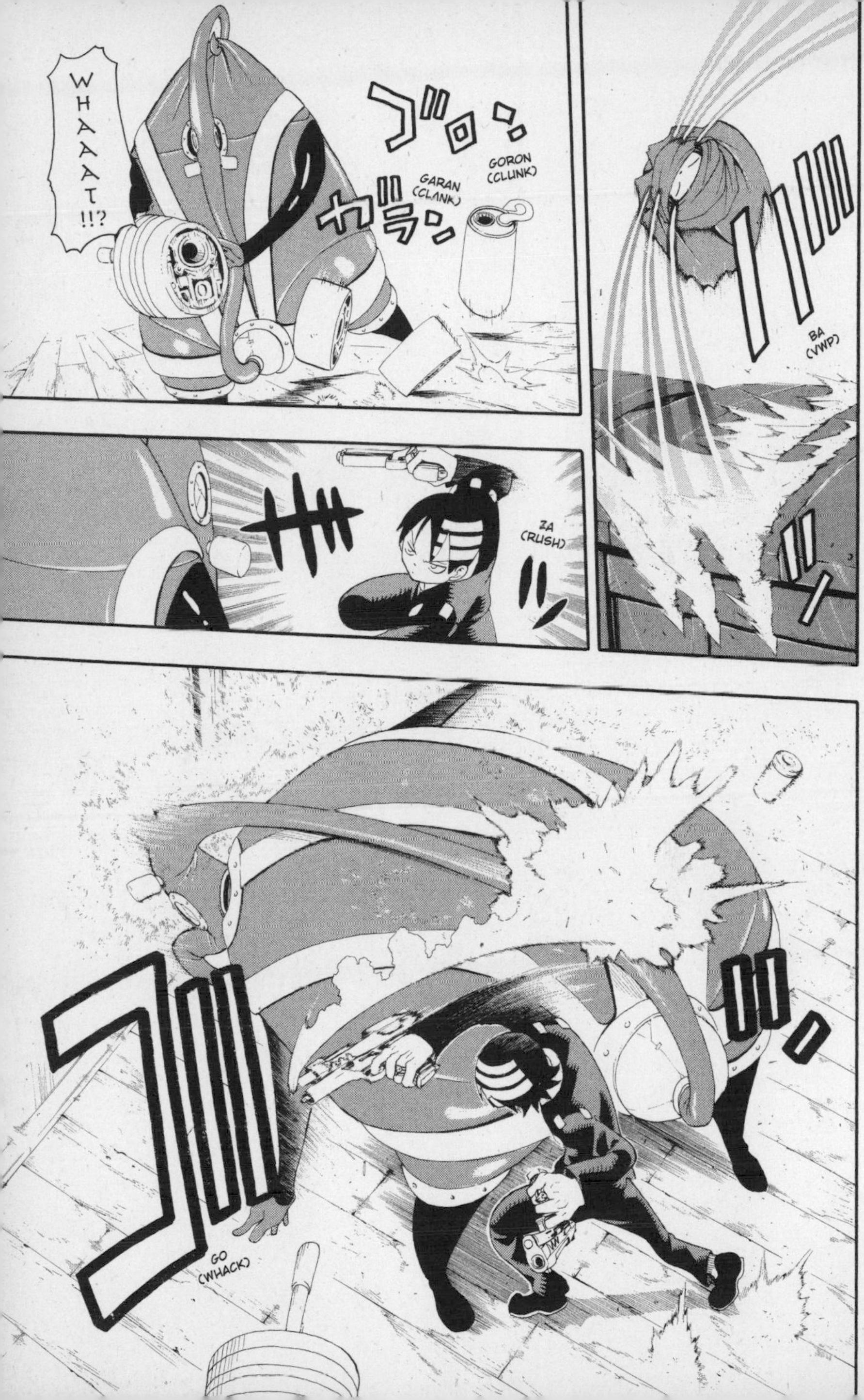
BA
(VWP)
GORON
(CLUNK)
GARAN
(CLANK)
WHAAAT!!?
ZA
(RUSH)
GO
(WHACK)

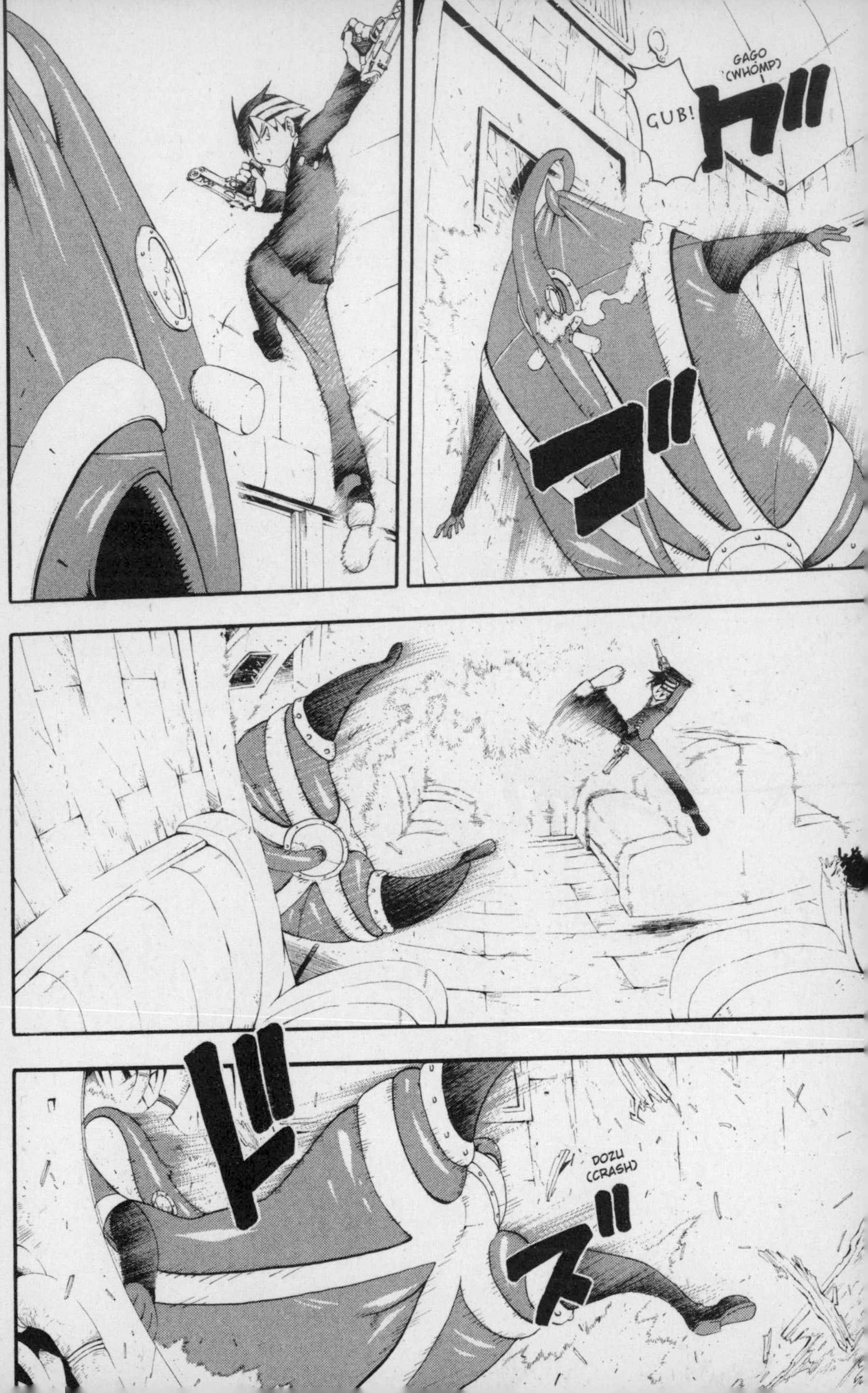
GAGO (WHOMP)
ガ
GUB!
ゴ
ド
DOZU (CRASH)
ズ

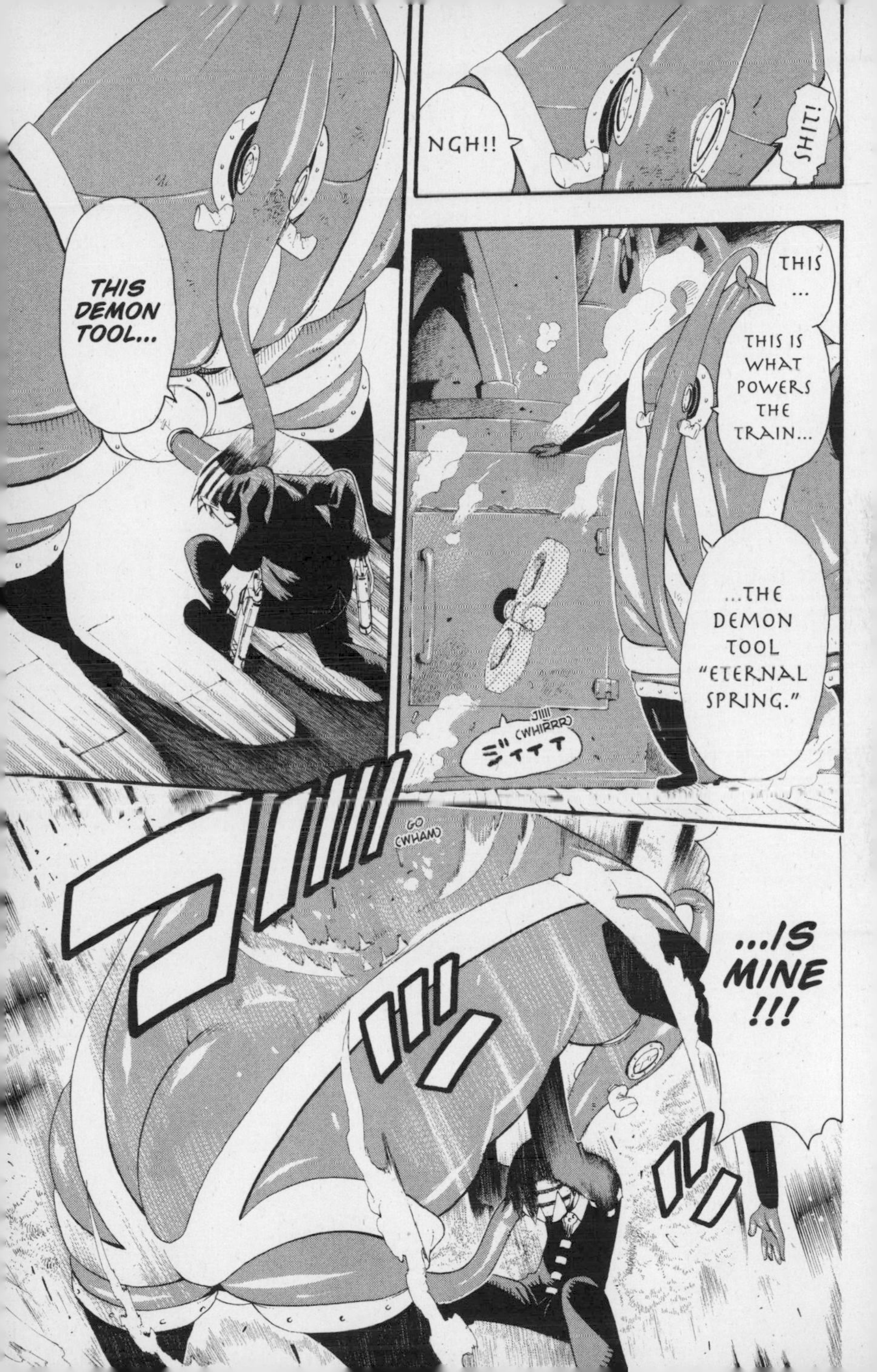
SHIT!
NGH!!
THIS ...
THIS IS WHAT POWERS THE TRAIN...
...THE DEMON TOOL "ETERNAL SPRING."
JIIII (WHIRRR)
THIS DEMON TOOL...
...IS MINE !!!
GO (WHAM)

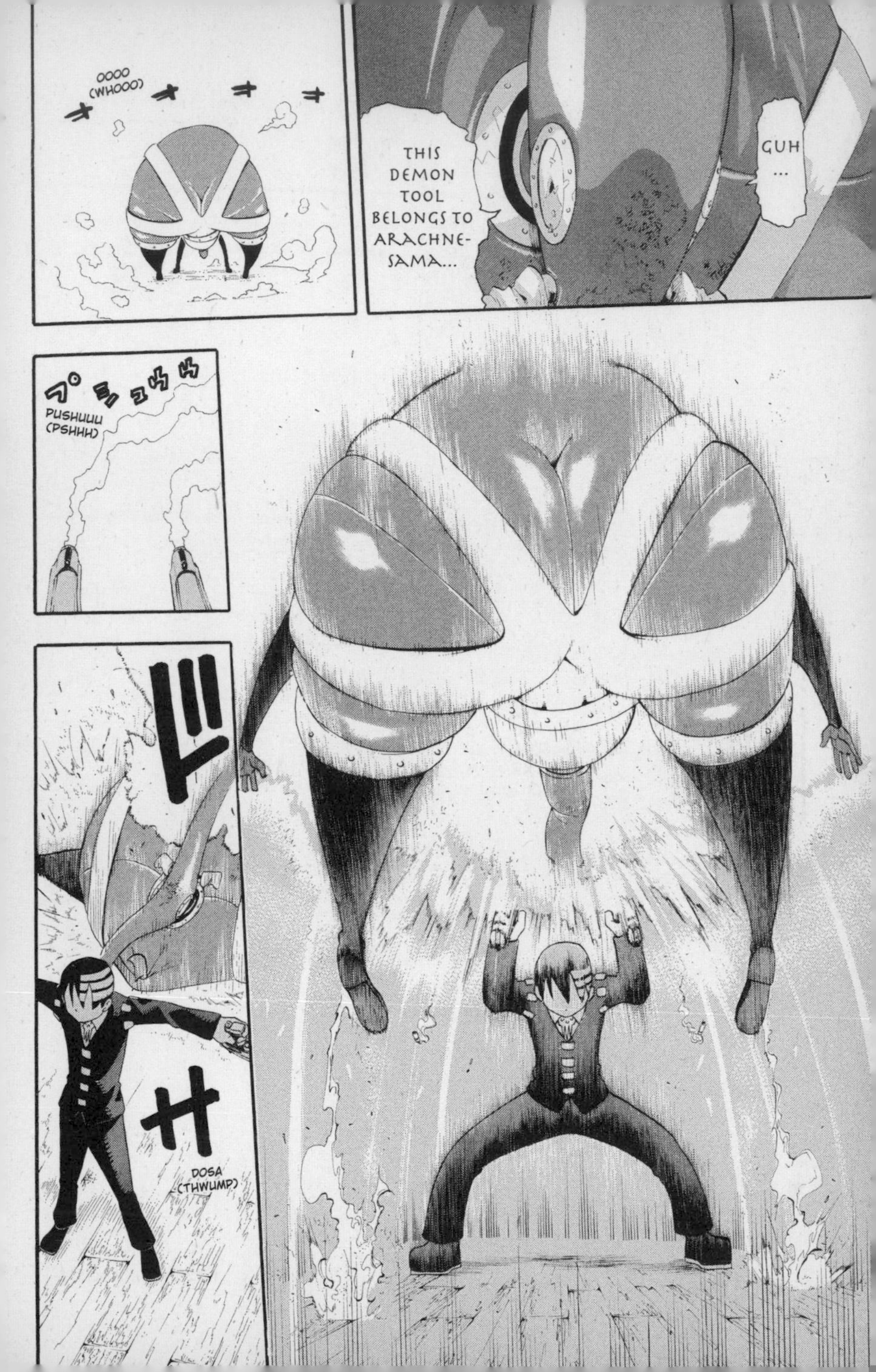
GUH ...
THIS DEMON TOOL BELONGS TO ARACHNE-SAMA...
オ オ オ オ
OOOO (WHOOO)
プシュウウ
PUSHUUU (PSHHH)
ドサッ
DOSA (THWUMP)

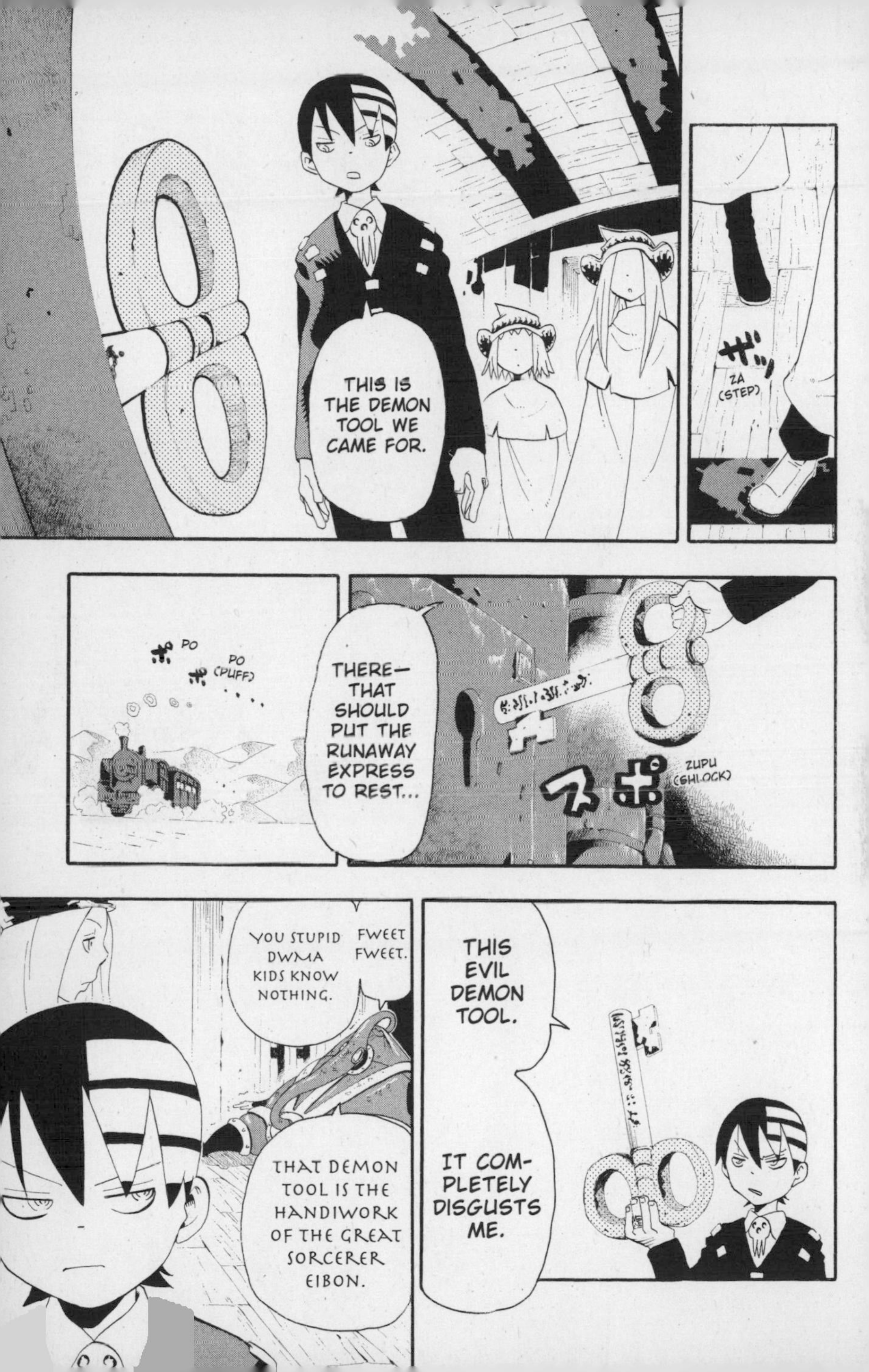
ザッ
ZA (STEP)
THIS IS THE DEMON TOOL WE CAME FOR.
ズポ
ZUPU (SHLOCK)
THERE— THAT SHOULD PUT THE RUNAWAY EXPRESS TO REST...
ポ PO
ポ PO (PUFF)
THIS EVIL DEMON TOOL.
IT COMPLETELY DISGUSTS ME.
FWEET FWEET.
YOU STUPID DWMA KIDS KNOW NOTHING.
THAT DEMON TOOL IS THE HANDIWORK OF THE GREAT SORCERER EIBON.

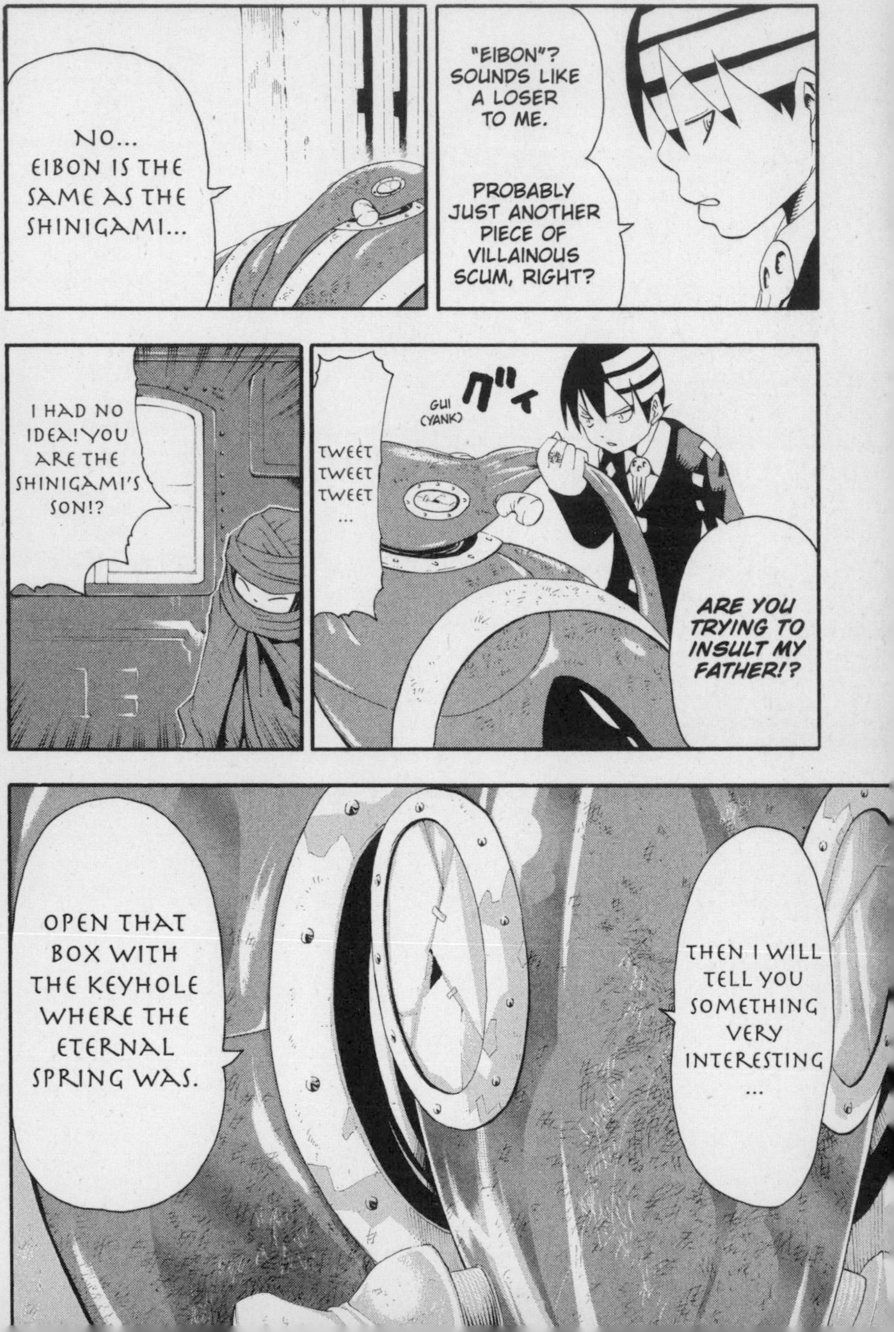
"EIBON"? SOUNDS LIKE A LOSER TO ME.
PROBABLY JUST ANOTHER PIECE OF VILLAINOUS SCUM, RIGHT?
NO... EIBON IS THE SAME AS THE SHINIGAMI...
GUI (YANK)
TWEET TWEET TWEET ...
ARE YOU TRYING TO INSULT MY FATHER!?
I HAD NO IDEA! YOU ARE THE SHINIGAMI'S SON!?
THEN I WILL TELL YOU SOMETHING VERY INTERESTING ...
OPEN THAT BOX WITH THE KEYHOLE WHERE THE ETERNAL SPRING WAS.

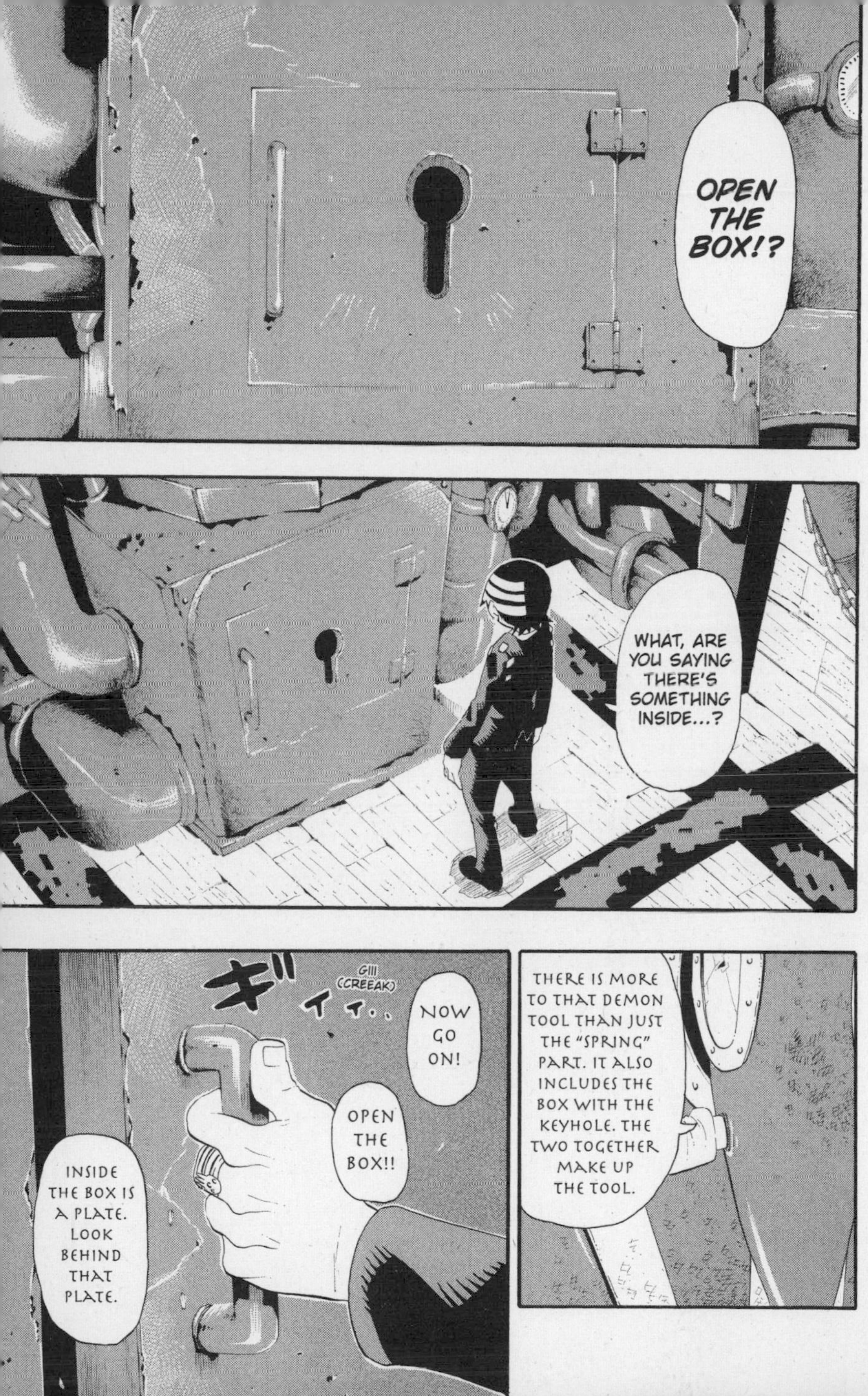
OPEN THE BOX!?
WHAT, ARE YOU SAYING THERE'S SOMETHING INSIDE...?
THERE IS MORE TO THAT DEMON TOOL THAN JUST THE "SPRING" PART. IT ALSO INCLUDES THE BOX WITH THE KEYHOLE. THE TWO TOGETHER MAKE UP THE TOOL.
NOW GO ON!
OPEN THE BOX!!
GIII (CREEAK)
ギィィ..
INSIDE THE BOX IS A PLATE. LOOK BEHIND THAT PLATE.

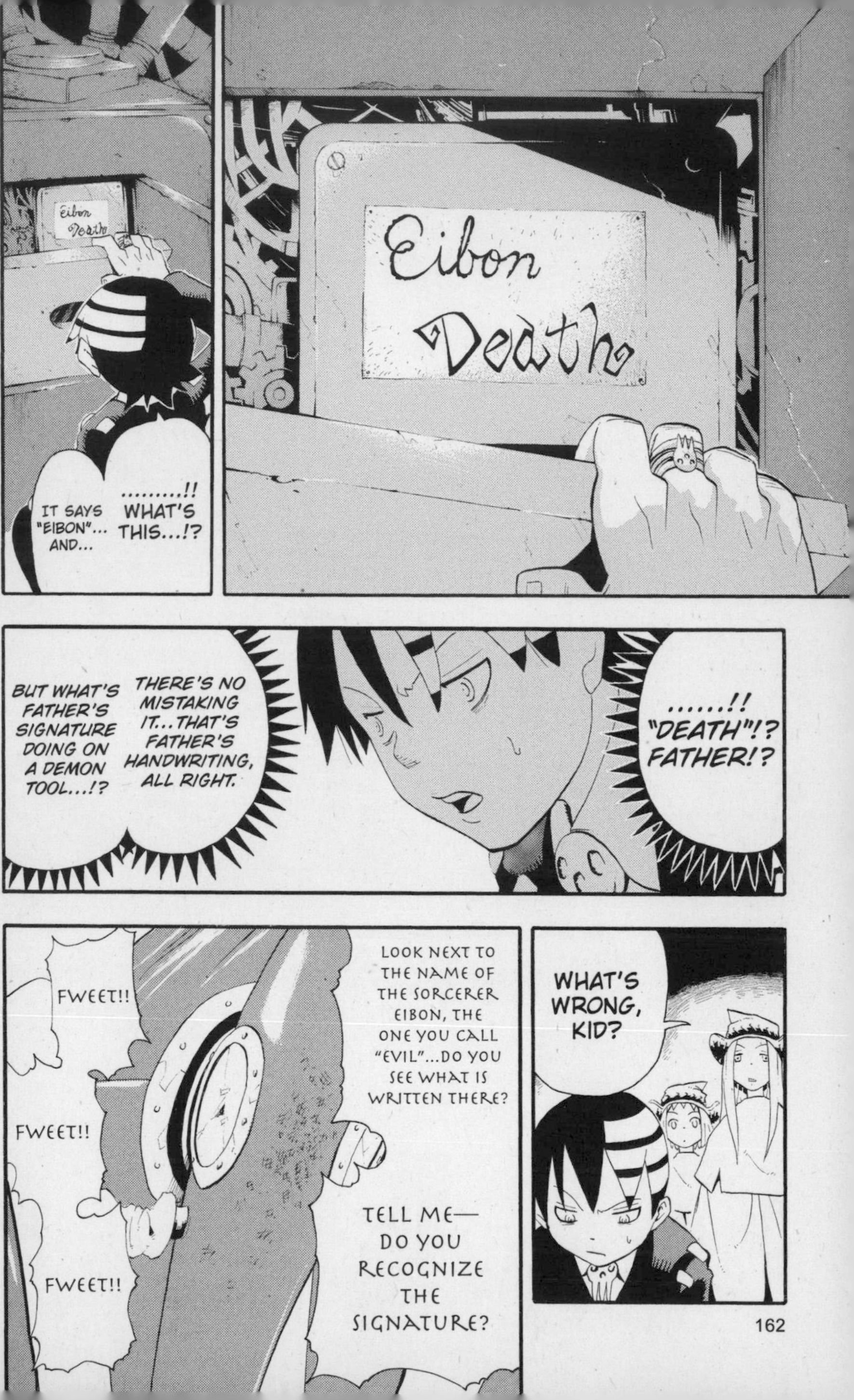
Eibon Death
.........!! WHAT'S THIS...!?
IT SAYS "EIBON"... AND...
......!! "DEATH"!? FATHER!?
THERE'S NO MISTAKING IT...THAT'S FATHER'S HANDWRITING, ALL RIGHT.
BUT WHAT'S FATHER'S SIGNATURE DOING ON A DEMON TOOL...!?
WHAT'S WRONG, KID?
LOOK NEXT TO THE NAME OF THE SORCERER EIBON, THE ONE YOU CALL "EVIL"...DO YOU SEE WHAT IS WRITTEN THERE?
TELL ME— DO YOU RECOGNIZE THE SIGNATURE?
FWEET!!
FWEET!!
FWEET!!

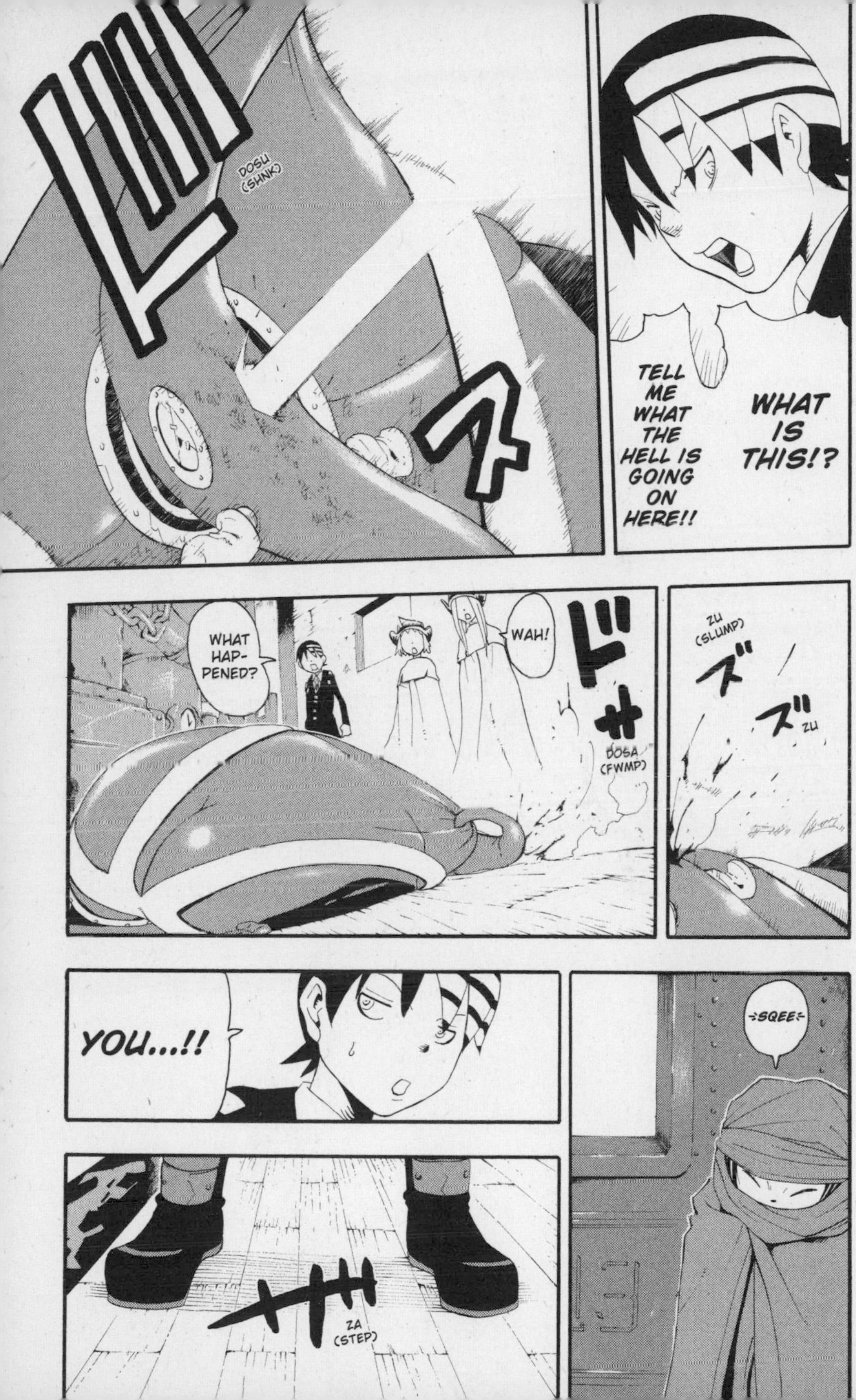
WHAT IS THIS!?
TELL ME WHAT THE HELL IS GOING ON HERE!!
DOSU (SHNK)
ZU (SLUMP)
ZU
WAH!
WHAT HAP-PENED?
DOSA (FWMP)
SQEE
YOU...!!
ZA (STEP)

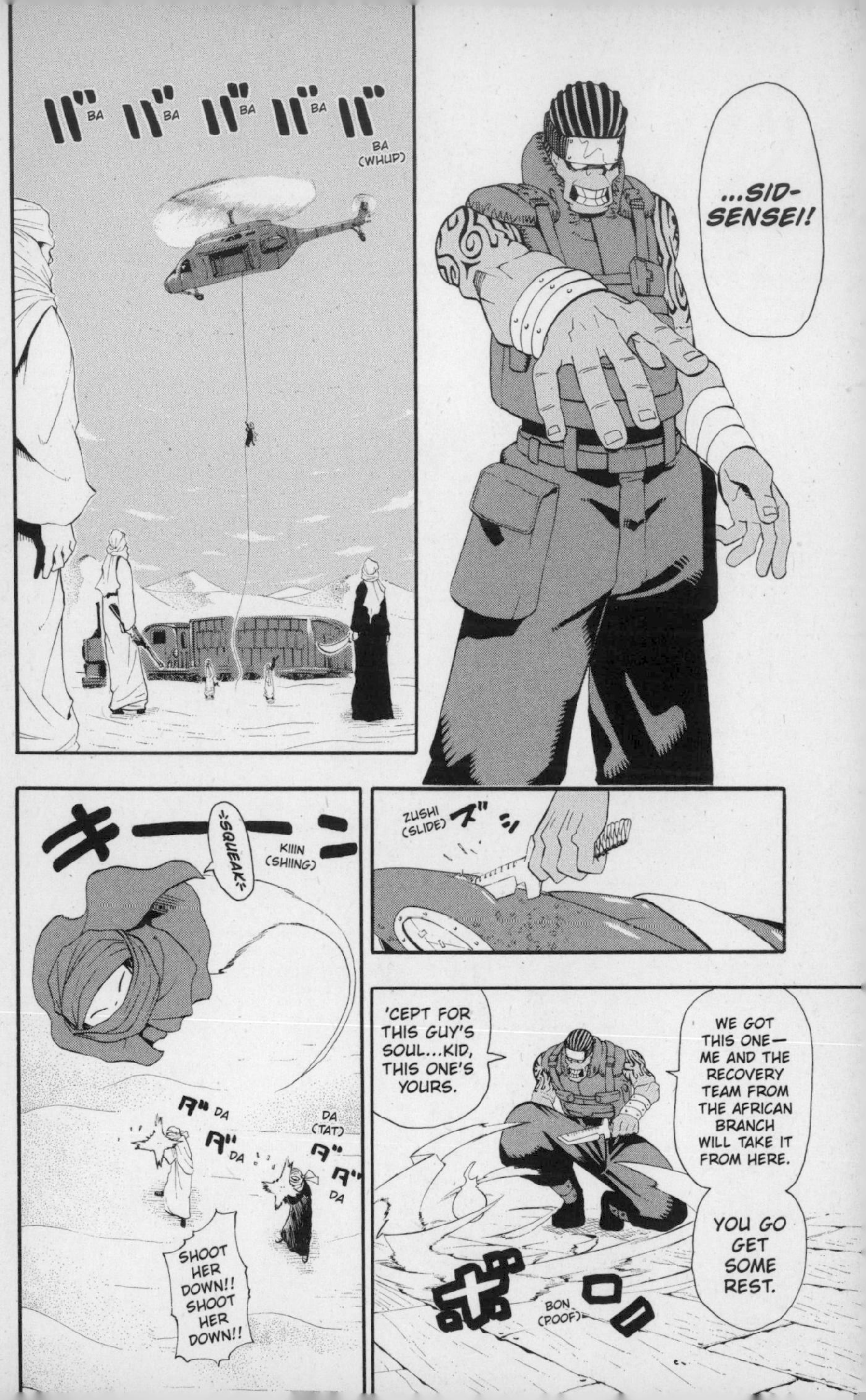

...SID-SENSEI!
BA BA BA BA BA (WHUP)
ZUSHI (SLIDE)
WE GOT THIS ONE—ME AND THE RECOVERY TEAM FROM THE AFRICAN BRANCH WILL TAKE IT FROM HERE.
'CEPT FOR THIS GUY'S SOUL...KID, THIS ONE'S YOURS.
YOU GO GET SOME REST.
BON (POOF)
KIIIN (SHIING)
SQUEAK
DA DA DA DA (TAT)
SHOOT HER DOWN!! SHOOT HER DOWN!!

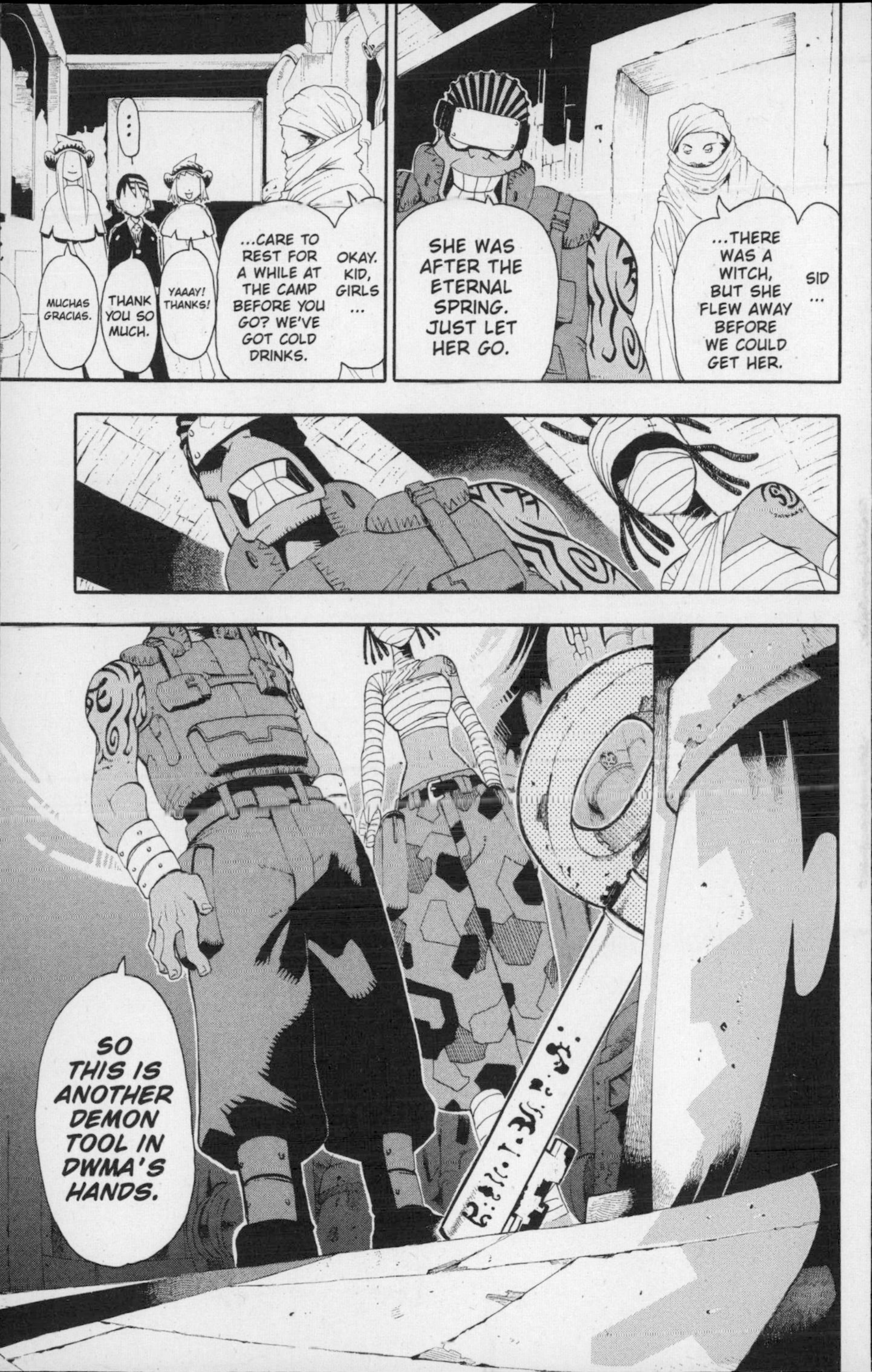
SID ...
...THERE WAS A WITCH, BUT SHE FLEW AWAY BEFORE WE COULD GET HER.
SHE WAS AFTER THE ETERNAL SPRING. JUST LET HER GO.
OKAY. KID, GIRLS ...
...CARE TO REST FOR A WHILE AT THE CAMP BEFORE YOU GO? WE'VE GOT COLD DRINKS.
YAAAY! THANKS!
THANK YOU SO MUCH.
MUCHAS GRACIAS.
SO THIS IS ANOTHER DEMON TOOL IN DWMA'S HANDS.

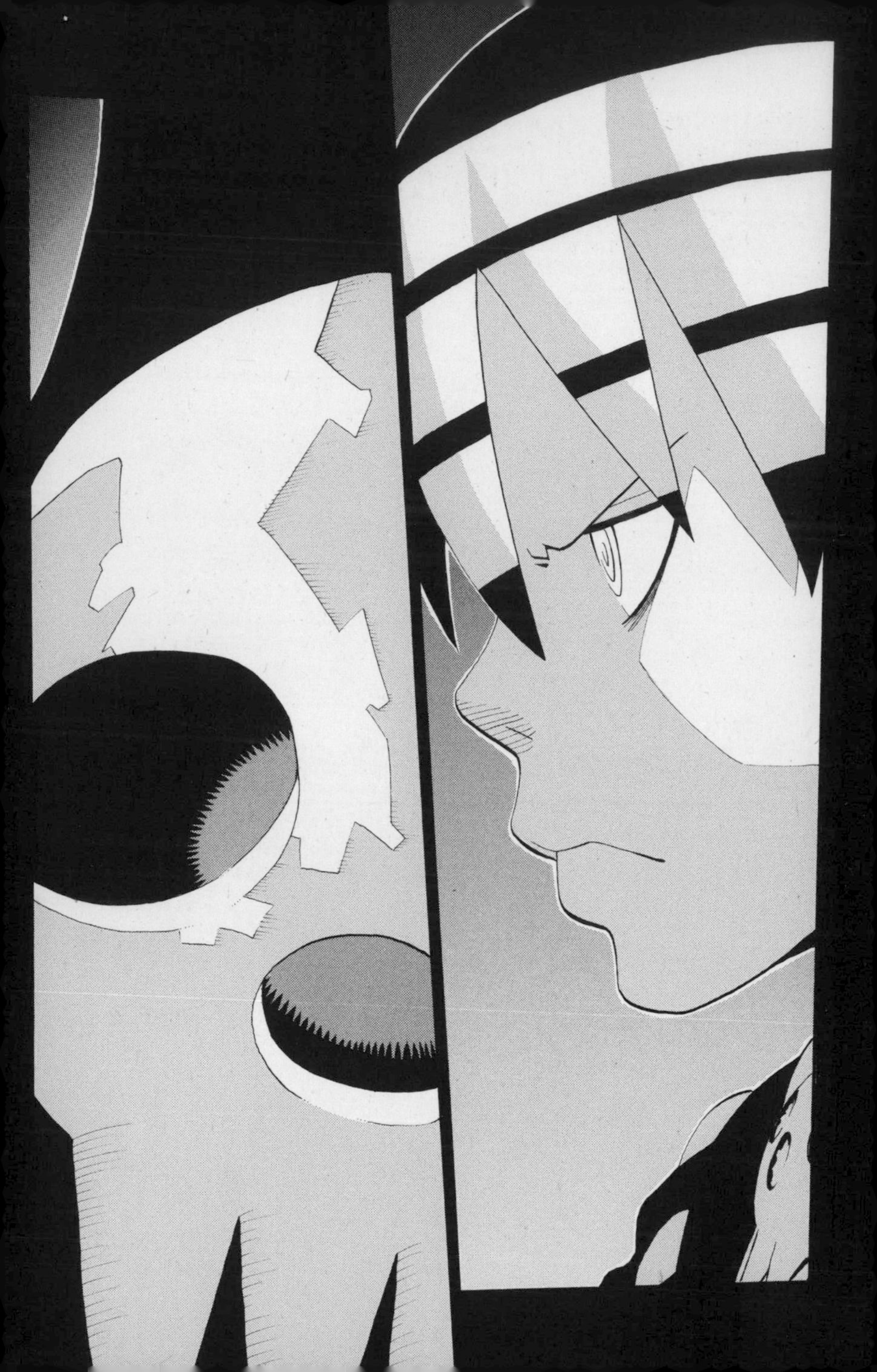

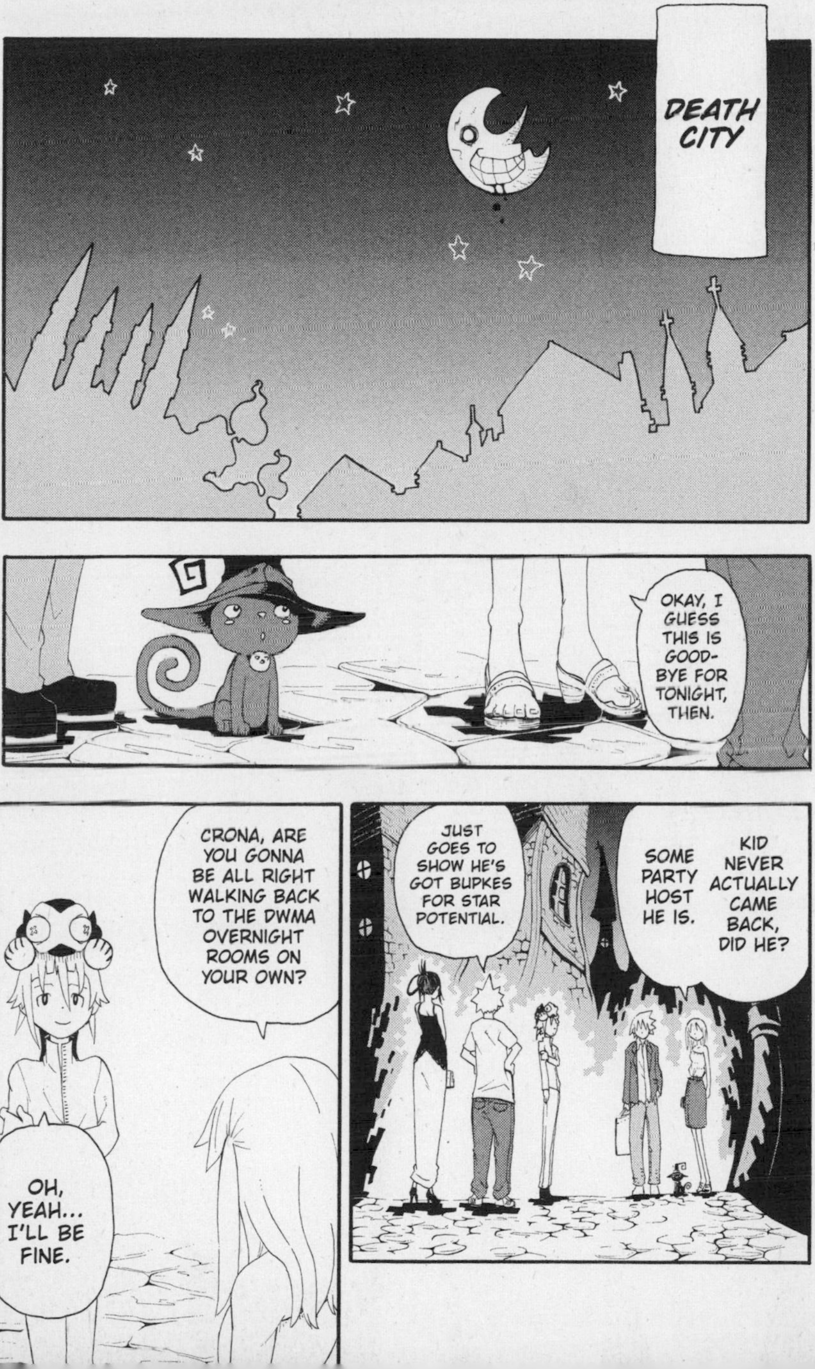
DEATH CITY
OKAY, I GUESS THIS IS GOOD-BYE FOR TONIGHT, THEN.
KID NEVER ACTUALLY CAME BACK, DID HE?
SOME PARTY HOST HE IS.
JUST GOES TO SHOW HE'S GOT BUPKES FOR STAR POTENTIAL.
CRONA, ARE YOU GONNA BE ALL RIGHT WALKING BACK TO THE DWMA OVERNIGHT ROOMS ON YOUR OWN?
OH, YEAH... I'LL BE FINE.

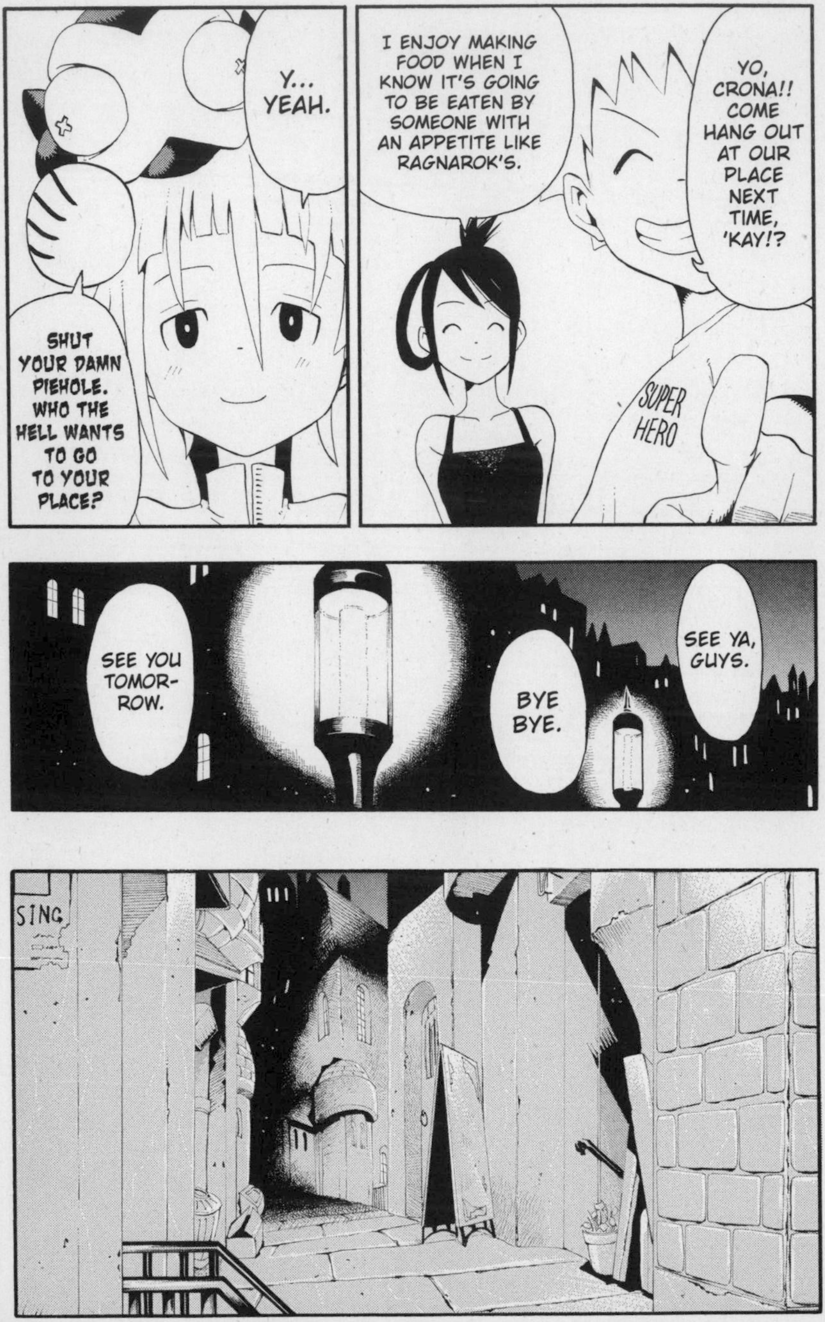
YO, CRONA!! COME HANG OUT AT OUR PLACE NEXT TIME, 'KAY!?
I ENJOY MAKING FOOD WHEN I KNOW IT'S GOING TO BE EATEN BY SOMEONE WITH AN APPETITE LIKE RAGNAROK'S.
SUPER HERO
Y... YEAH.
SHUT YOUR DAMN PIEHOLE. WHO THE HELL WANTS TO GO TO YOUR PLACE?
SEE YA, GUYS.
BYE BYE.
SEE YOU TOMOR-ROW.
SING

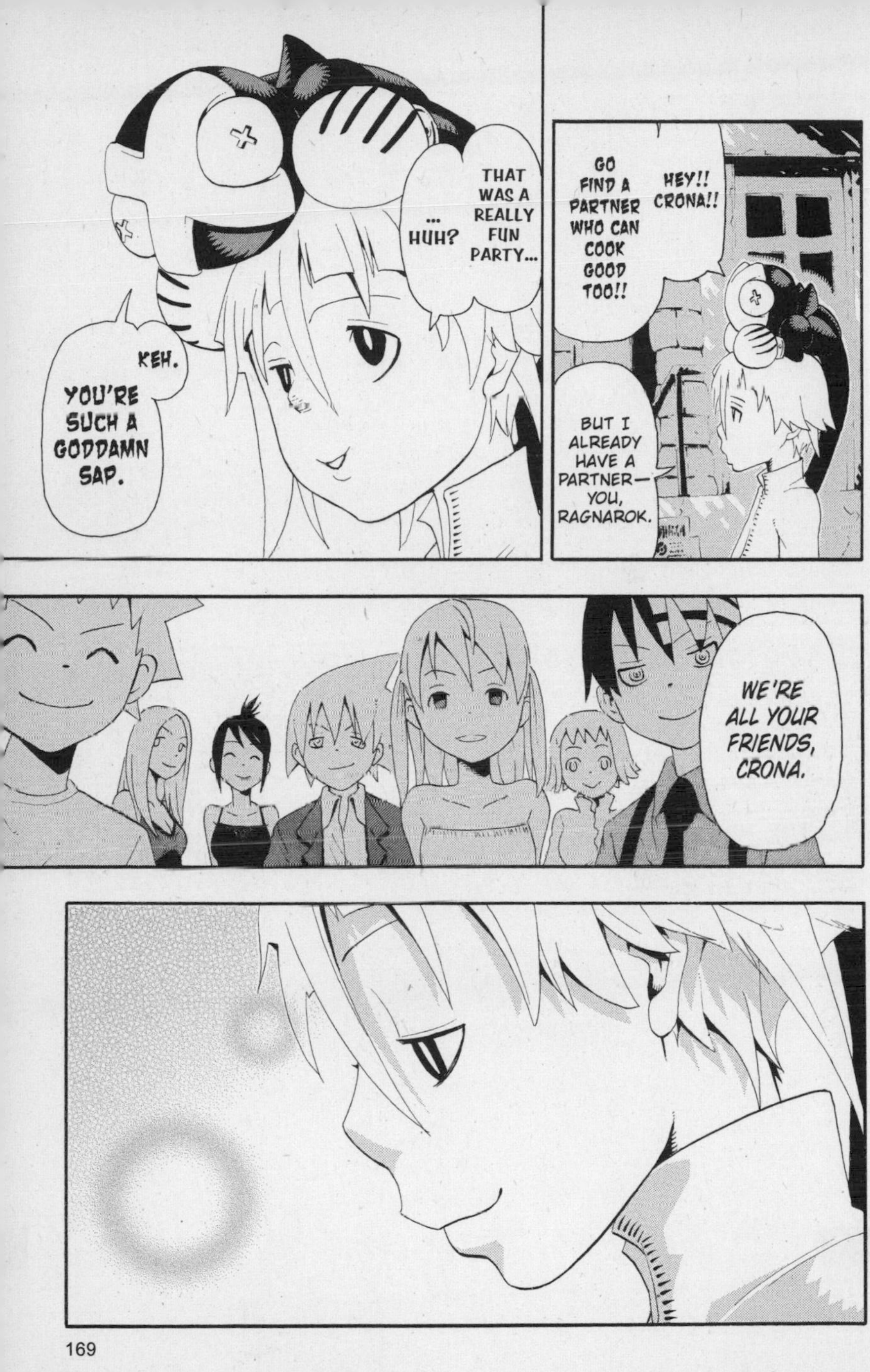
HEY!! CRONA!!
GO FIND A PARTNER WHO CAN COOK GOOD TOO!!
BUT I ALREADY HAVE A PARTNER— YOU, RAGNAROK.
THAT WAS A REALLY FUN PARTY...
... HUH?
KEH.
YOU'RE SUCH A GODDAMN SAP.
WE'RE ALL YOUR FRIENDS, CRONA.

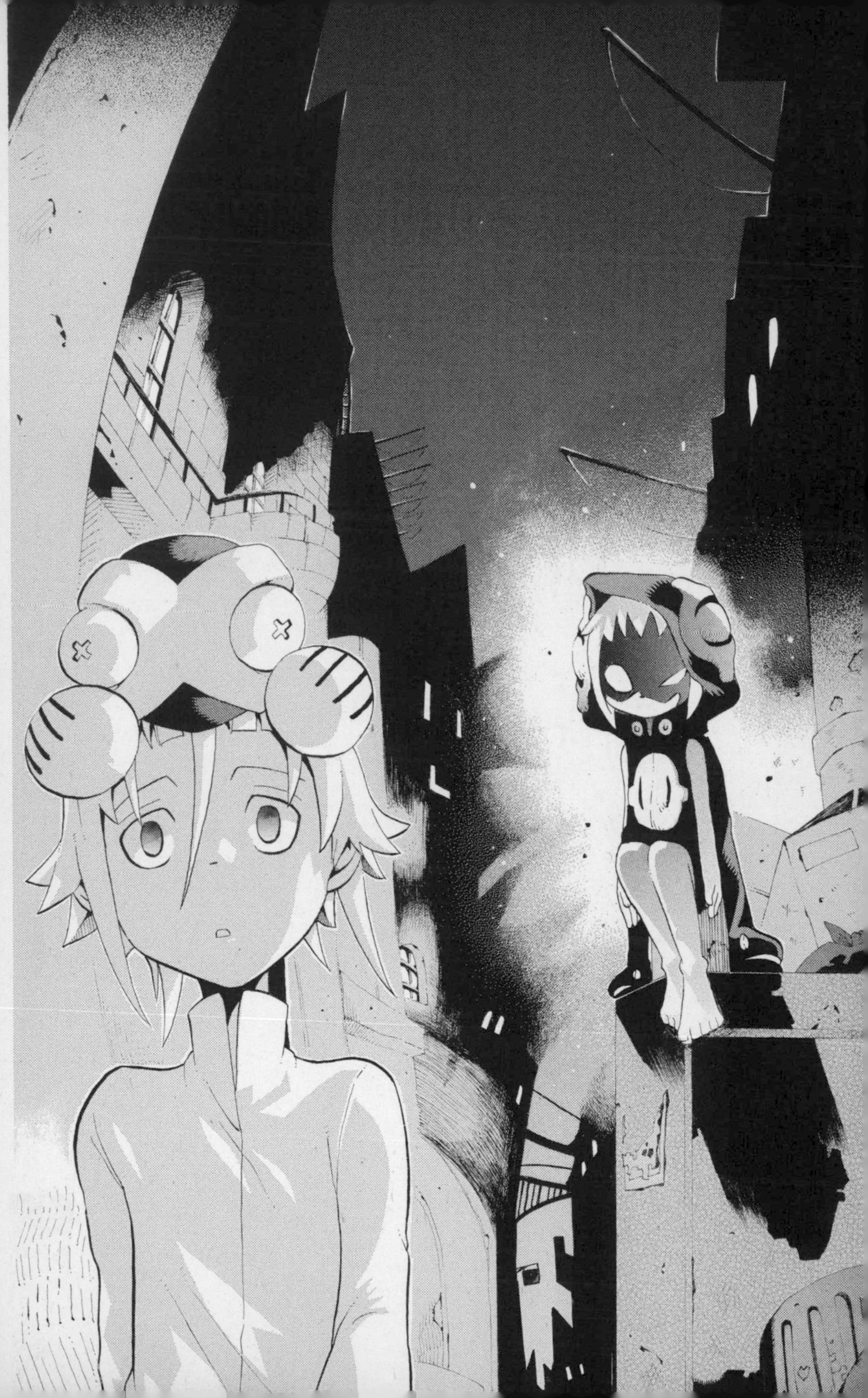

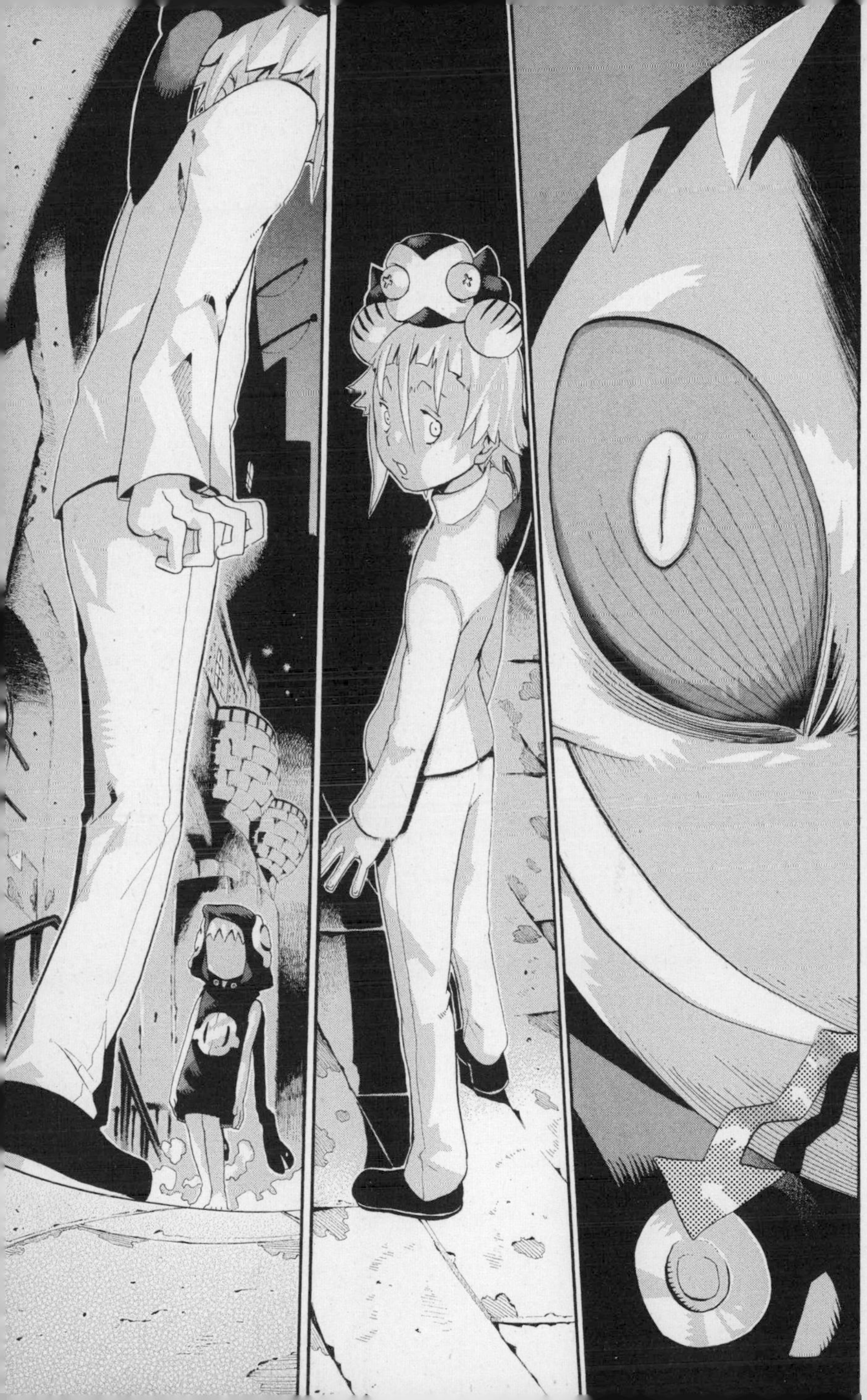

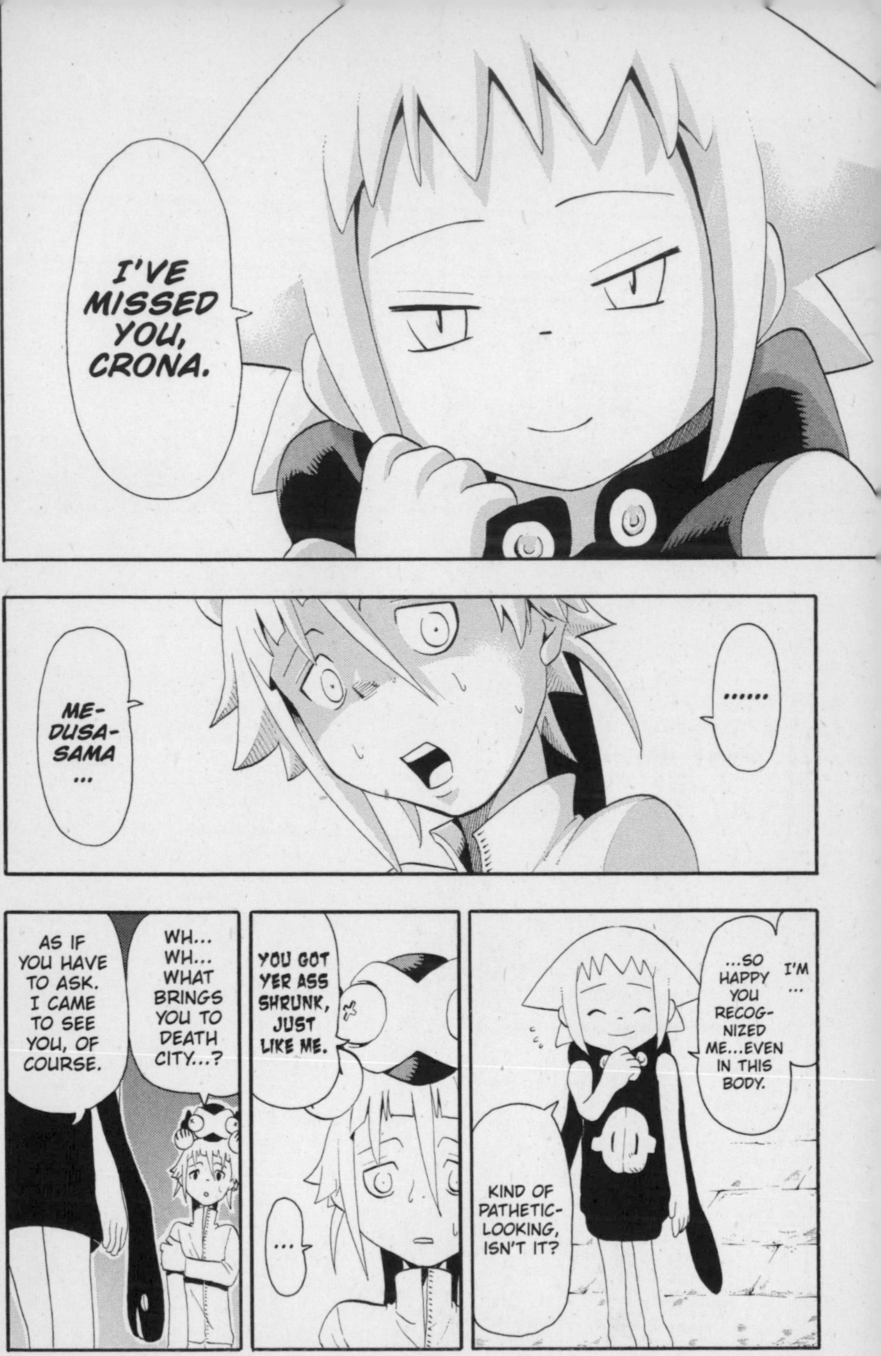
I'VE MISSED YOU, CRONA.
......
ME-DUSA-SAMA...
I'M ...
...SO HAPPY YOU RECOGNIZED ME...EVEN IN THIS BODY.
KIND OF PATHETIC-LOOKING, ISN'T IT?
YOU GOT YER ASS SHRUNK, JUST LIKE ME.
...
WH... WH... WHAT BRINGS YOU TO DEATH CITY...?
AS IF YOU HAVE TO ASK. I CAME TO SEE YOU, OF COURSE.

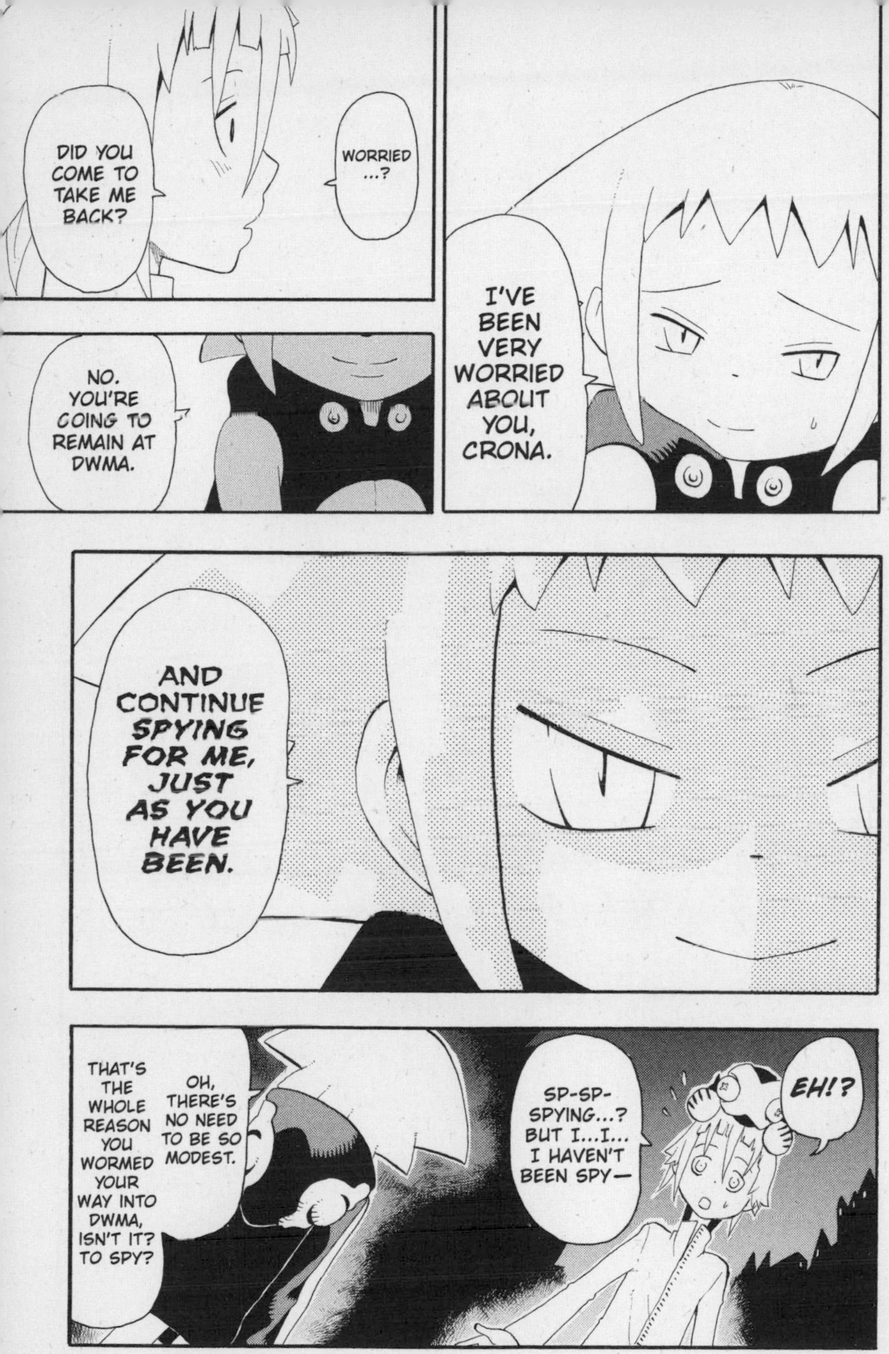
I'VE BEEN VERY WORRIED ABOUT YOU, CRONA.
WORRIED ...?
DID YOU COME TO TAKE ME BACK?
NO. YOU'RE GOING TO REMAIN AT DWMA.
AND CONTINUE SPYING FOR ME, JUST AS YOU HAVE BEEN.
EH!?
SP-SP-SPYING...? BUT I...I... I HAVEN'T BEEN SPY—
OH, THERE'S NO NEED TO BE SO MODEST.
THAT'S THE WHOLE REASON YOU WORMED YOUR WAY INTO DWMA, ISN'T IT? TO SPY?

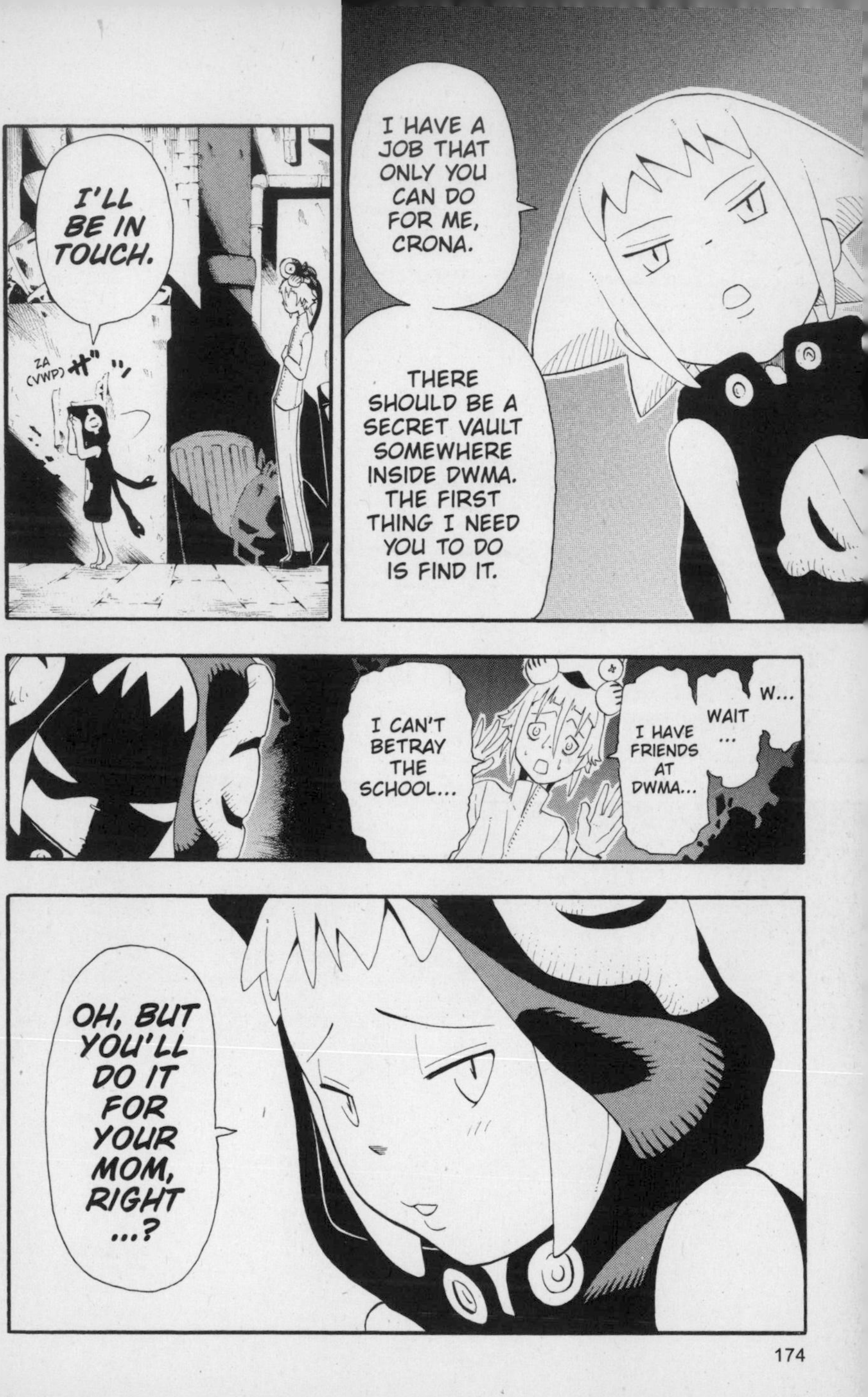
I HAVE A JOB THAT ONLY YOU CAN DO FOR ME, CRONA.
THERE SHOULD BE A SECRET VAULT SOMEWHERE INSIDE DWMA. THE FIRST THING I NEED YOU TO DO IS FIND IT.
I'LL BE IN TOUCH.
ZA (VWP)
W... WAIT ...
I HAVE FRIENDS AT DWMA...
I CAN'T BETRAY THE SCHOOL...
OH, BUT YOU'LL DO IT FOR YOUR MOM, RIGHT ...?

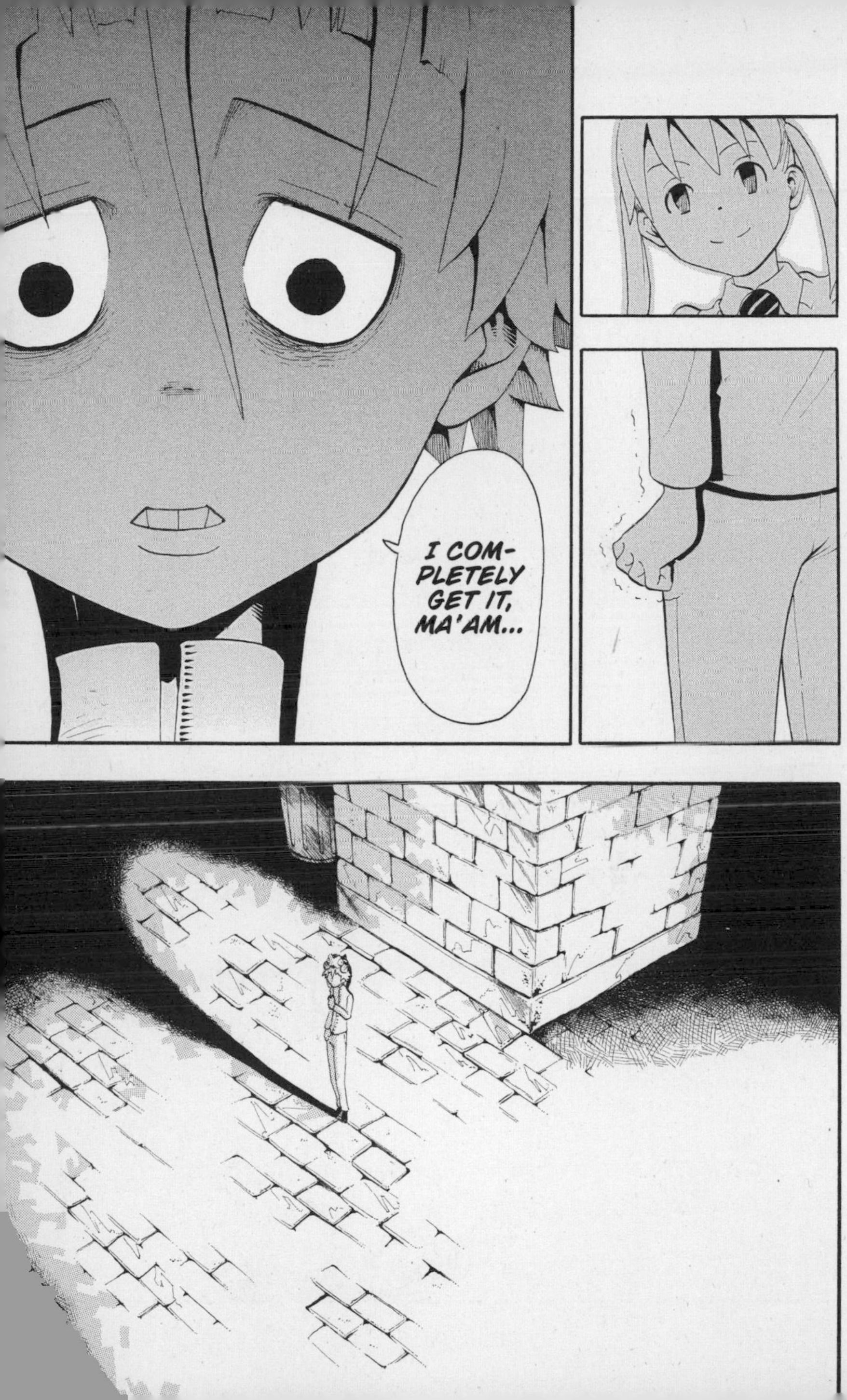
I COMPLETELY GET IT, MA'AM...

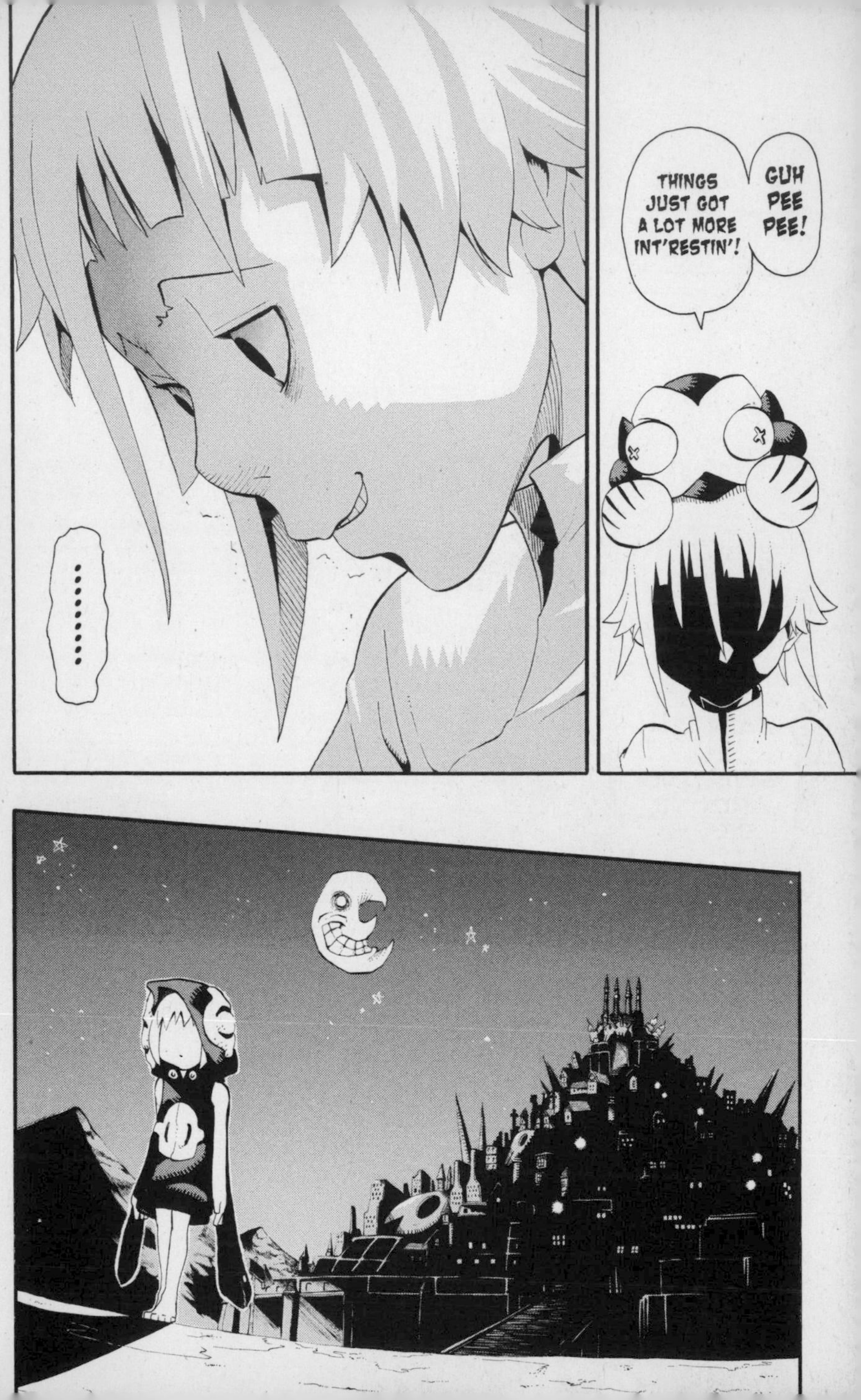
GUH PEE PEE!
THINGS JUST GOT A LOT MORE INT'RESTIN'!
....

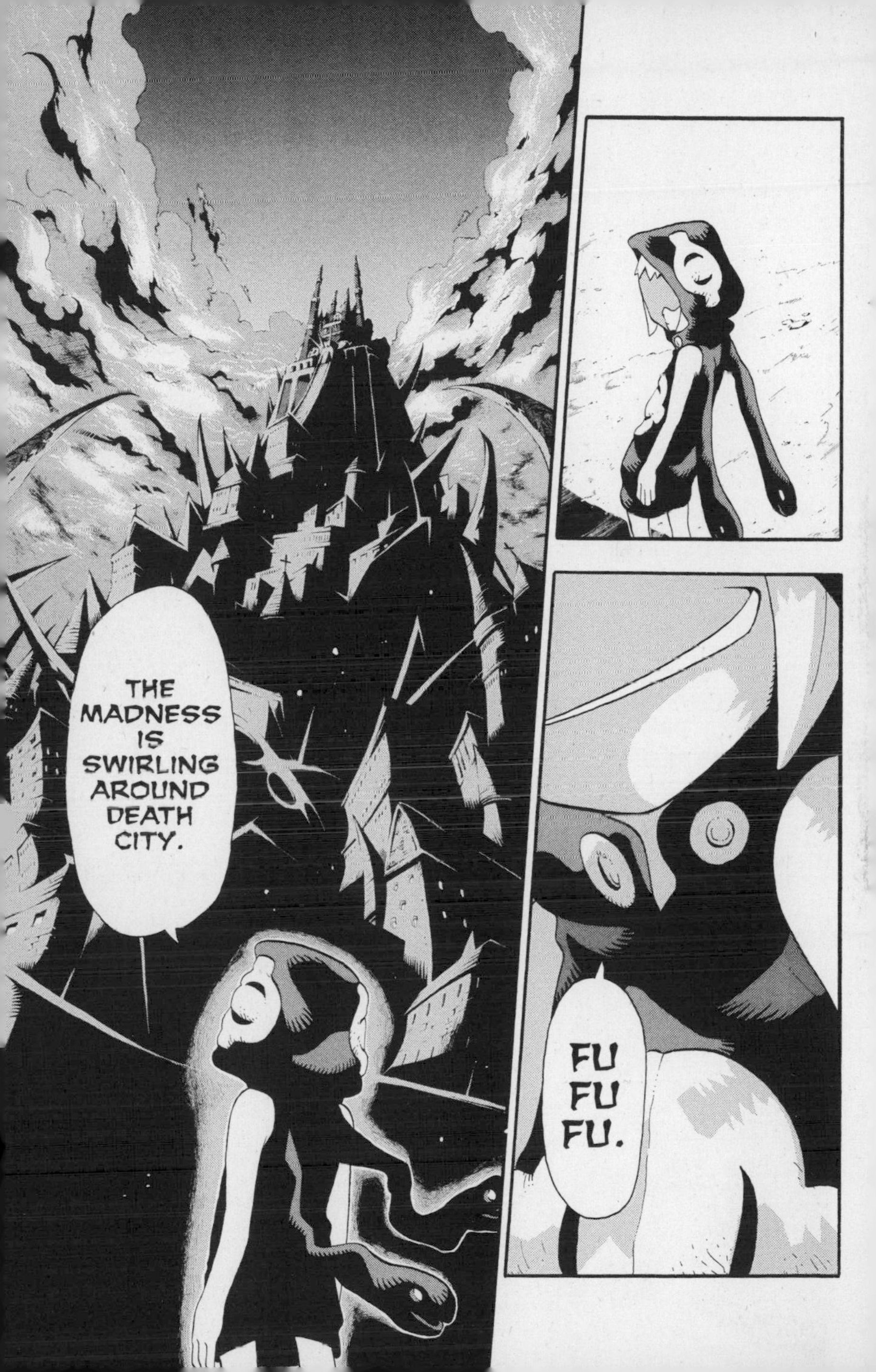
FU FU FU.
THE MADNESS IS SWIRLING AROUND DEATH CITY.

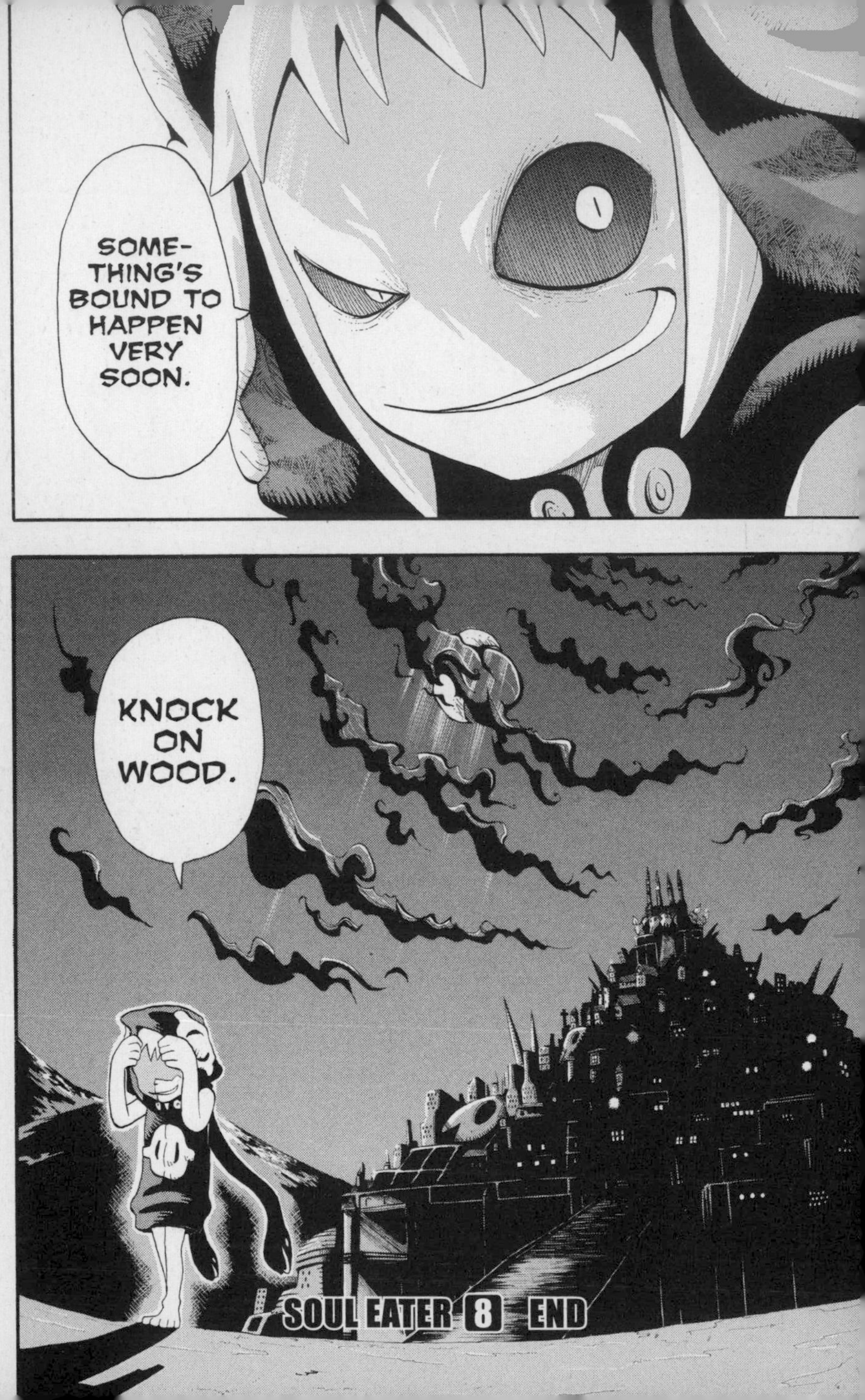
SOME-THING'S BOUND TO HAPPEN VERY SOON.
KNOCK ON WOOD.
SOUL EATER 8 END

SOUL EATER

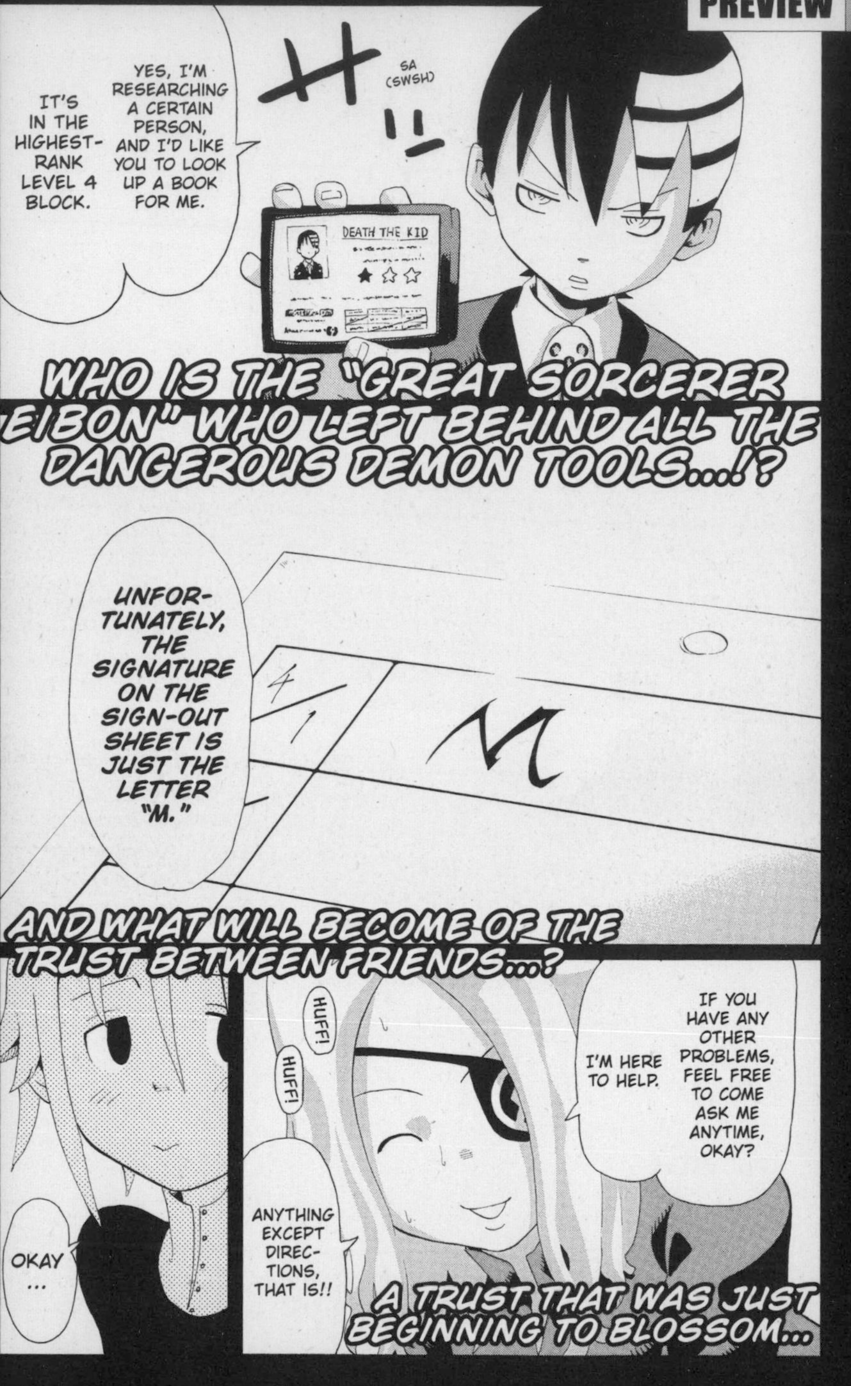
SA (SWSH)
YES, I'M RESEARCHING A CERTAIN PERSON, AND I'D LIKE YOU TO LOOK UP A BOOK FOR ME.
IT'S IN THE HIGHEST-RANK LEVEL 4 BLOCK.
DEATH THE KID
WHO IS THE "GREAT SORCERER EIBON" WHO LEFT BEHIND ALL THE DANGEROUS DEMON TOOLS...!?
UNFOR-TUNATELY, THE SIGNATURE ON THE SIGN-OUT SHEET IS JUST THE LETTER "M."
AND WHAT WILL BECOME OF THE TRUST BETWEEN FRIENDS...?
IF YOU HAVE ANY OTHER PROBLEMS, FEEL FREE TO COME ASK ME ANYTIME, OKAY?
I'M HERE TO HELP.
HUFF!
HUFF!
ANYTHING EXCEPT DIREC-TIONS, THAT IS!!
OKAY ...
A TRUST THAT WAS JUST BEGINNING TO BLOSSOM...

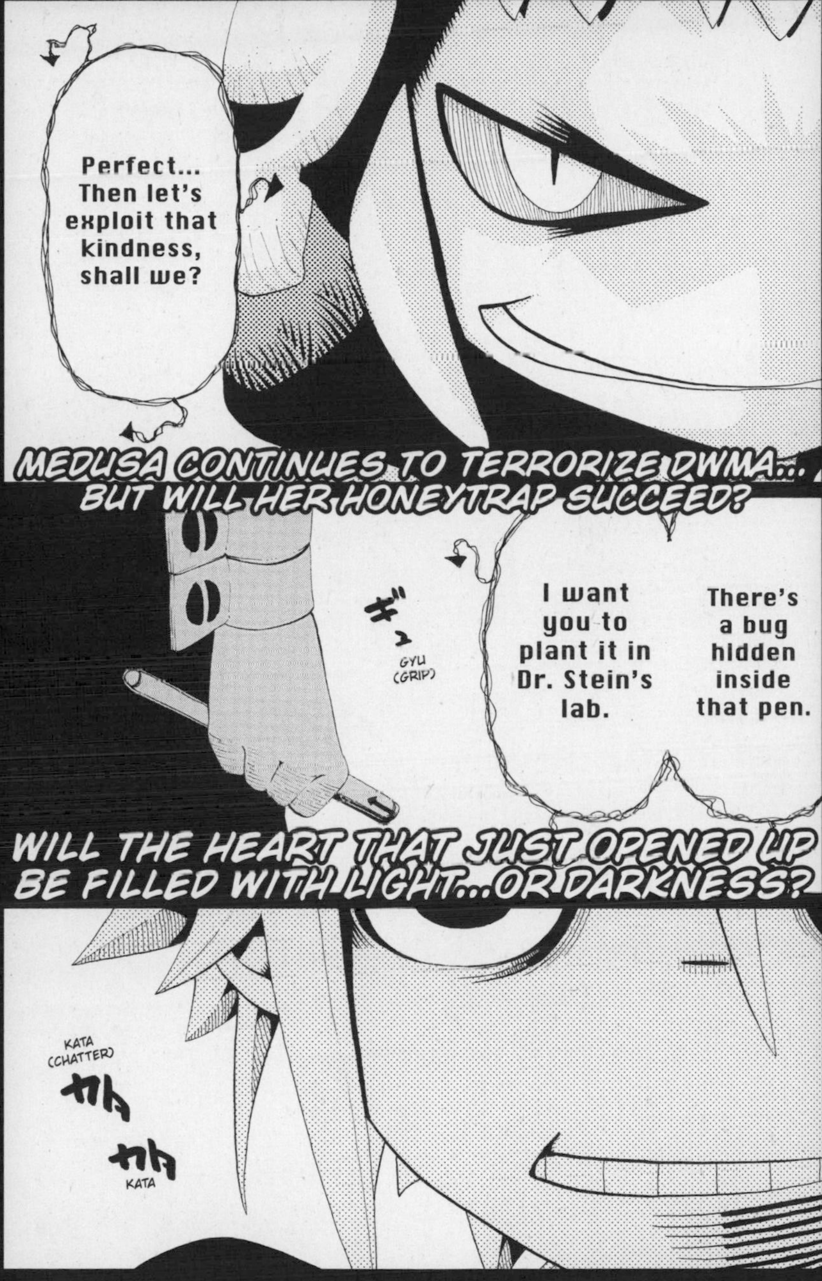
Perfect... Then let's exploit that kindness, shall we?
MEDUSA CONTINUES TO TERRORIZE DWMA... BUT WILL HER HONEYTRAP SUCCEED?
There's a bug hidden inside that pen.
I want you to plant it in Dr. Stein's lab.
ギュ
GYU (GRIP)
WILL THE HEART THAT JUST OPENED UP BE FILLED WITH LIGHT...OR DARKNESS?
KATA (CHATTER)
カタ
カタ
KATA

Continued in Soul Eater Volume 9!!

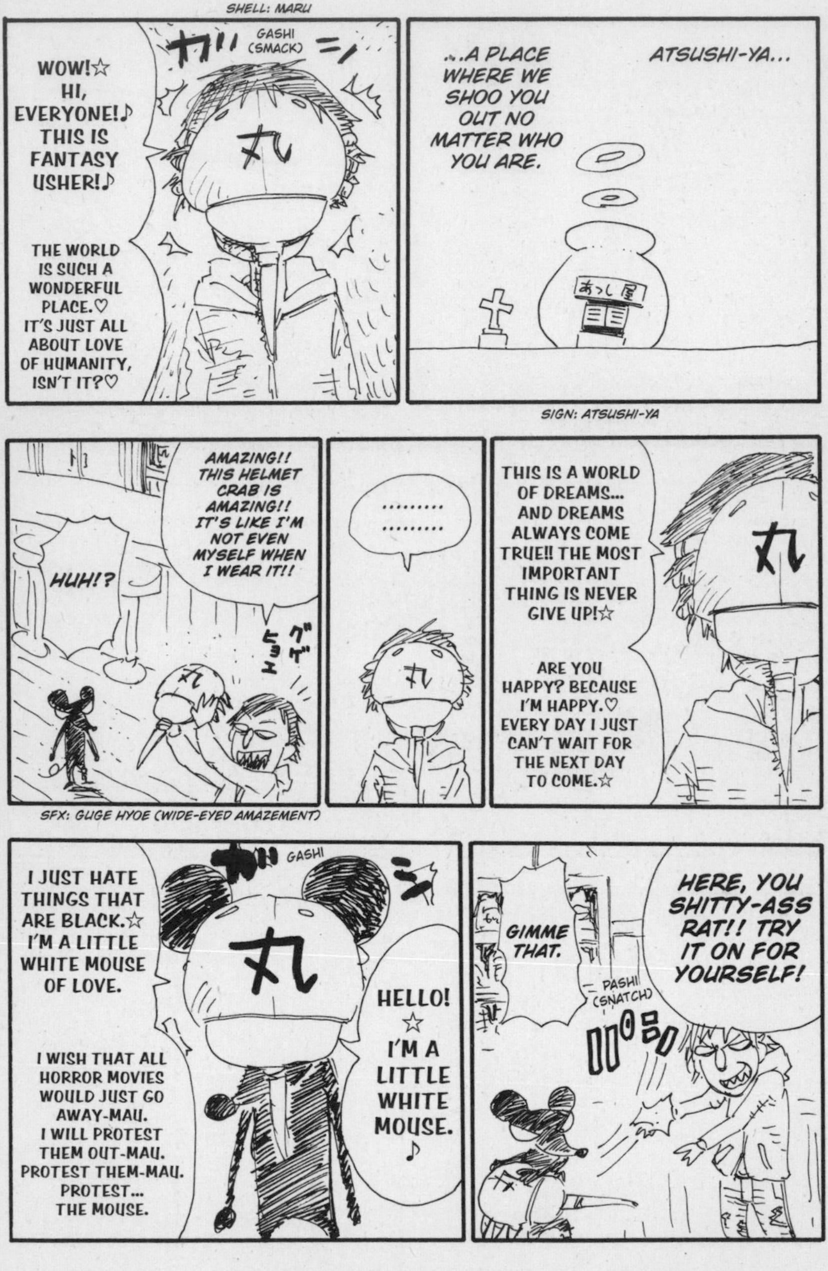
ATSUSHI-YA...
...A PLACE WHERE WE SHOO YOU OUT NO MATTER WHO YOU ARE.
SIGN: ATSUSHI-YA
SHELL: MARU
GASHI (SMACK)
WOW!☆ HI, EVERYONE!♪ THIS IS FANTASY USHER!♪
THE WORLD IS SUCH A WONDERFUL PLACE.♡ IT'S JUST ALL ABOUT LOVE OF HUMANITY, ISN'T IT?♡
THIS IS A WORLD OF DREAMS... AND DREAMS ALWAYS COME TRUE!! THE MOST IMPORTANT THING IS NEVER GIVE UP!☆
ARE YOU HAPPY? BECAUSE I'M HAPPY.♡ EVERY DAY I JUST CAN'T WAIT FOR THE NEXT DAY TO COME.☆
....
AMAZING!! THIS HELMET CRAB IS AMAZING!! IT'S LIKE I'M NOT EVEN MYSELF WHEN I WEAR IT!!
HUH!?
SFX: GUGE HYOE (WIDE-EYED AMAZEMENT)
HERE, YOU SHITTY-ASS RAT!! TRY IT ON FOR YOURSELF!
PASHI (SNATCH)
GIMME THAT.
GASHI
HELLO! ☆ I'M A LITTLE WHITE MOUSE. ♪
I JUST HATE THINGS THAT ARE BLACK.☆ I'M A LITTLE WHITE MOUSE OF LOVE.
I WISH THAT ALL HORROR MOVIES WOULD JUST GO AWAY-MAU. I WILL PROTEST THEM OUT-MAU. PROTEST THEM-MAU. PROTEST... THE MOUSE.

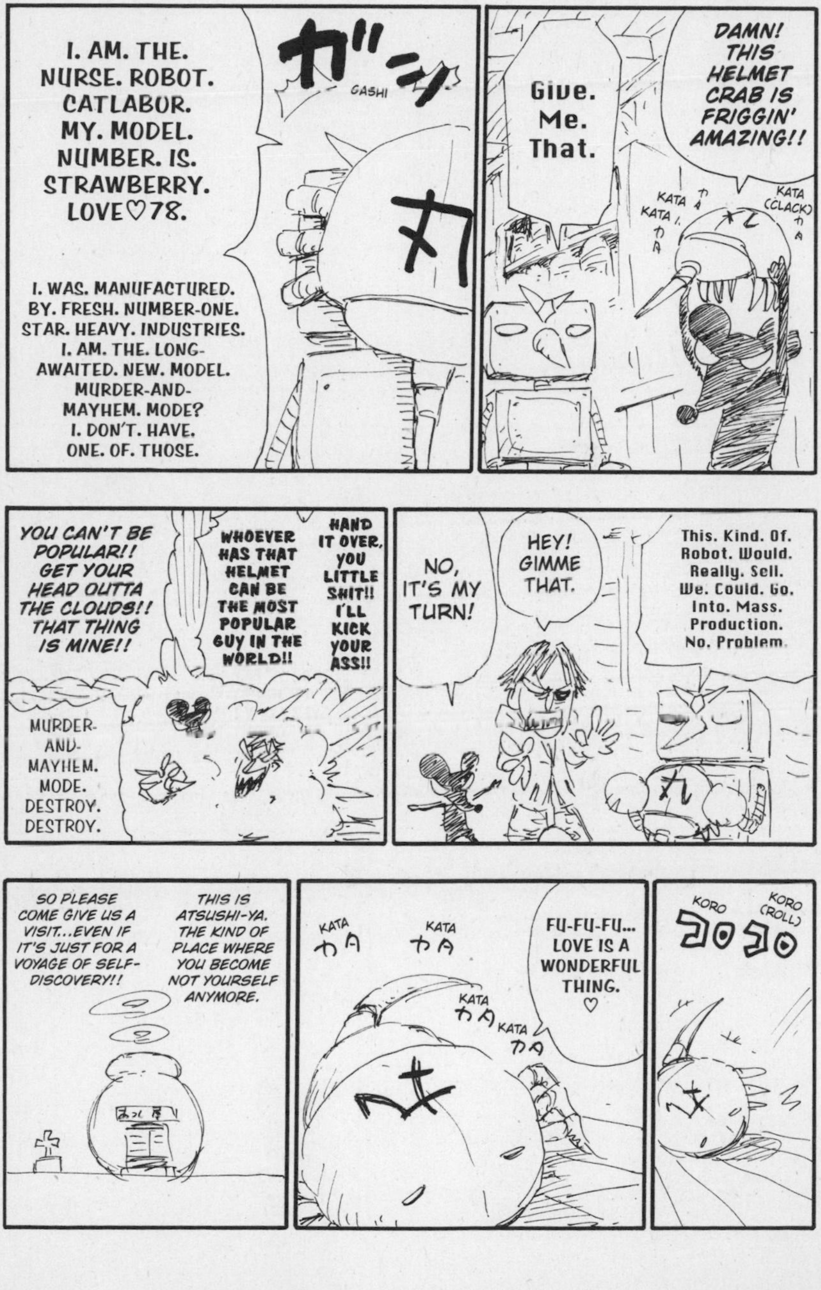
DAMN! THIS HELMET CRAB IS FRIGGIN' AMAZING!!
KATA KATA
KATA (CLACK)
Give. Me. That.
GASHI
I. AM. THE. NURSE. ROBOT. CATLABOR. MY. MODEL. NUMBER. IS. STRAWBERRY. LOVE♡78.
I. WAS. MANUFACTURED. BY. FRESH. NUMBER-ONE. STAR. HEAVY. INDUSTRIES. I. AM. THE. LONG-AWAITED. NEW. MODEL. MURDER-AND-MAYHEM. MODE? I. DON'T. HAVE. ONE. OF. THOSE.
This. Kind. Of. Robot. Would. Really. Sell. We. Could. Go. Into. Mass. Production. No. Problem.
HEY! GIMME THAT.
NO, IT'S MY TURN!
HAND IT OVER, YOU LITTLE SHIT!! I'LL KICK YOUR ASS!!
WHOEVER HAS THAT HELMET CAN BE THE MOST POPULAR GUY IN THE WORLD!!
YOU CAN'T BE POPULAR!! GET YOUR HEAD OUTTA THE CLOUDS!! THAT THING IS MINE!!
MURDER-AND-MAYHEM. MODE. DESTROY. DESTROY.
KORO KORO (ROLL)
FU-FU-FU... LOVE IS A WONDERFUL THING. ♡
KATA KATA
KATA KATA
THIS IS ATSUSHI-YA. THE KIND OF PLACE WHERE YOU BECOME NOT YOURSELF ANYMORE.
SO PLEASE COME GIVE US A VISIT...EVEN IF IT'S JUST FOR A VOYAGE OF SELF-DISCOVERY!!

Translation Notes

Common Honorifics

no honorific: Indicates familiarity or closeness; if used without permission or reason, addressing someone in this manner would constitute an insult.

-san: The Japanese equivalent of Mr./Mrs./Miss. If a situation calls for politeness, this is the fail-safe honorific.

-sama: Conveys great respect; may also indicate that the social status of the speaker is lower than that of the addressee.

-kun: Used most often when referring to boys, this indicates affection or familiarity. Occasionally used by older men among their peers, but it may also be used by anyone referring to a person of lower standing.

-chan: An affectionate honorific indicating familiarity used mostly in reference to girls; also used in reference to cute persons or animals of either gender.

-senpai: A suffix used to address upperclassmen or more experienced coworkers.

-sensei: A respectful term for teachers, artists, or high-level professionals.

Page 30
Marlon De Niro's name is a reference to Robert De Niro and Marlon Brando, both actors who played the role of Don Vito Corleone in the *Godfather* movies. (Brando played the old Vito in the first film, and De Niro played the young-adult Vito in the second film.)

Page 44
When Black☆Star refers to Minfune as a "**'sweet' samurai**," he uses the word *amai*, which literally means "sweet," but can also be used in the sense of "indulgent." Black☆Star is calling Mifune sweet-hearted but is also expressing his frustration at Mifune's patronizing attitude toward him.

Page 46
When Black☆Star refers to a "**bitter pill**," the word used in Japanese is *shoppai*, which means "salty" but is also wrestling (especially sumo) slang for "weak" or "pathetic." (Because the wrestlers toss salt into the ring before each bout, a losing wrestler who spends a lot of time on the floor ends up covered in salt.)

Page 61
"Hasta la vista, baby!"—and the whole TV sequence on this page—is an obvious parody of the movie *Terminator 2: Judgment Day*.

Page 73
Here Black☆Star uses *–neechan* (literally "big sis") as an honorific for Marie. This usage is similar to that of the more standard *onee-san* (same meaning), which is a common term of casual address for young to middle-aged adult women. However, he should be using *–sensei* in this case (and he sounds a little impudent for not doing so).

Page 139
Fisher King's taunts about his "rod and tackle" sound more blatantly sexual in Japanese, where the line is "*sao to tama*" (literally "fishing pole and balls").

DING-DONG!

DEAD-DONG!

DON'T BE LATE FOR THE N.O.T. CLASS AT DEATH WEAPON MEISTER ACADEMY!

OLDER TEEN
OT

Yen Press

SOUL EATER NOT!

ATSUSHI OHKUBO

Can't wait for the next volume? You don't have to!

Keep up with the latest chapters of some of your favorite manga every month online in the pages of YEN PLUS!

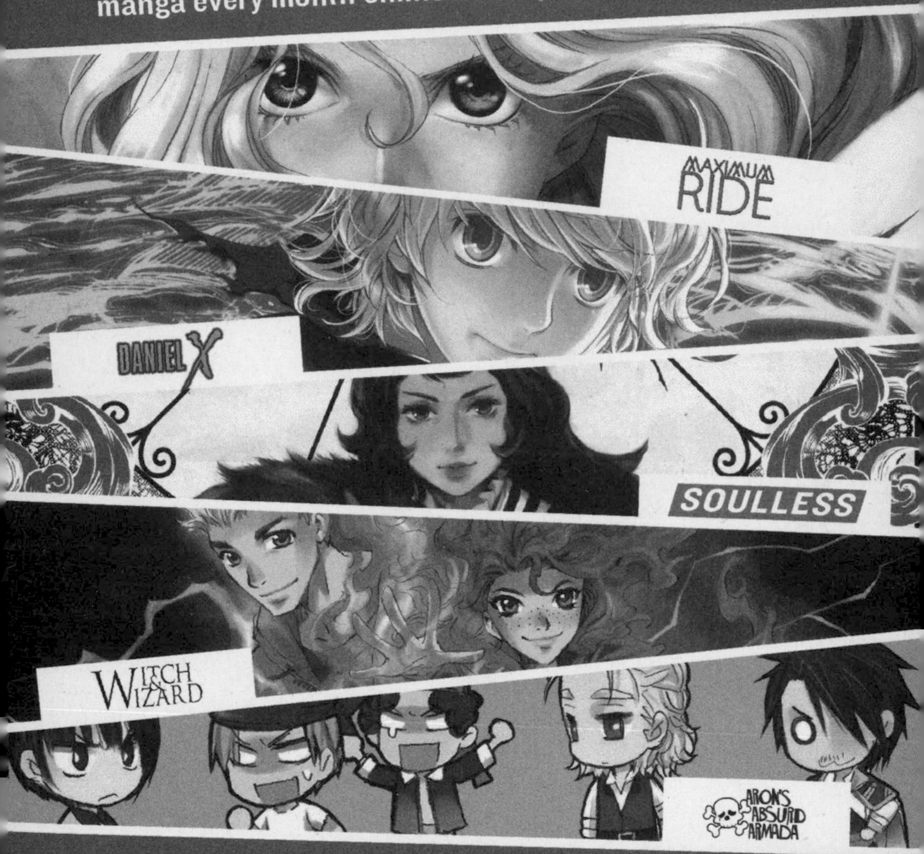
MAXIMUM RIDE
DANIEL X
SOULLESS
WITCH & WIZARD
ARON'S ABSURD ARMADA

Visit us at www.yenplus.com for details!

YEN+ Plus

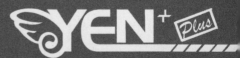

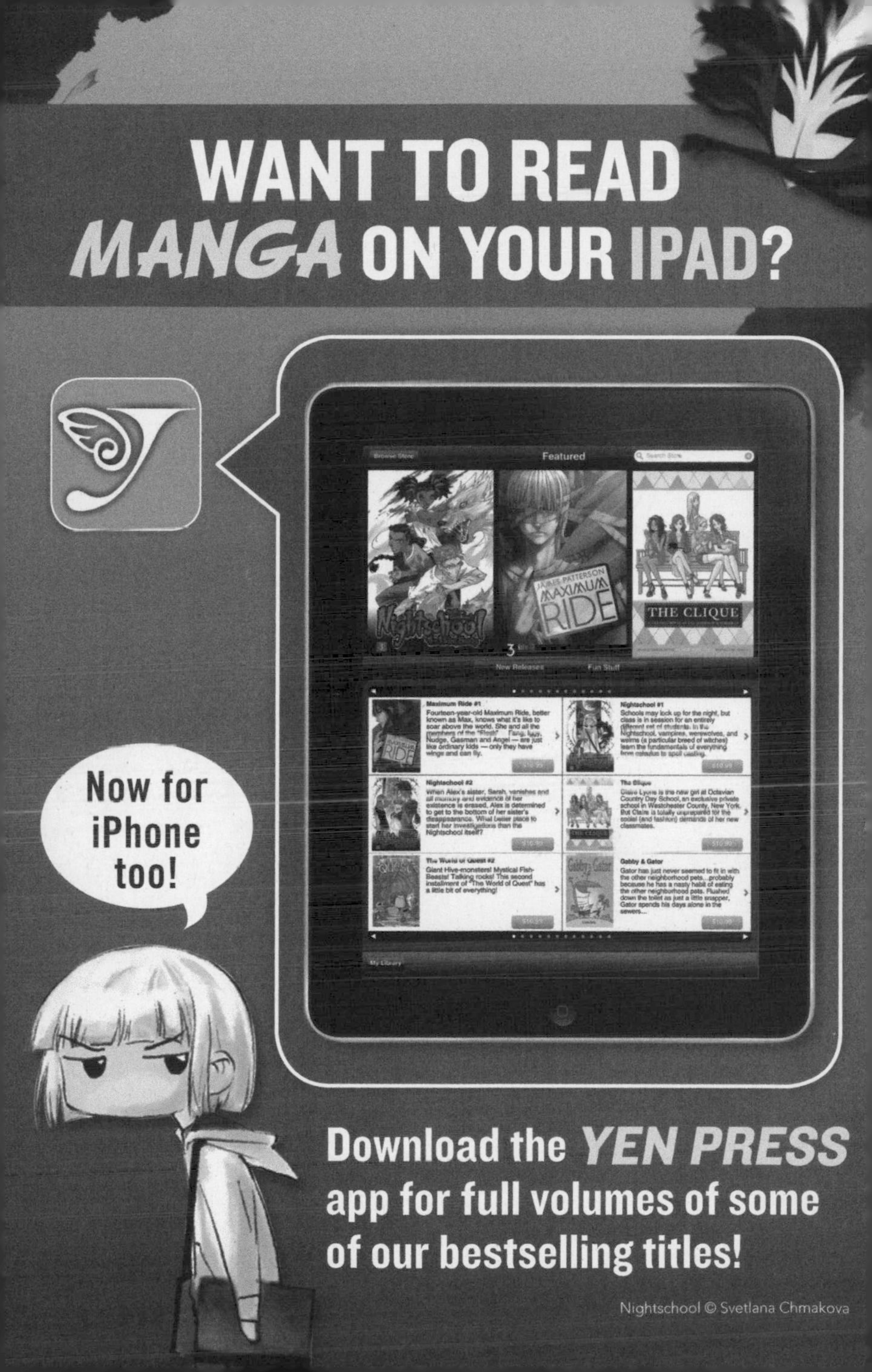
WANT TO READ
MANGA ON YOUR IPAD?
Now for iPhone too!
Featured
Download the YEN PRESS app for full volumes of some of our bestselling titles!
Nightschool © Svetlana Chmakova

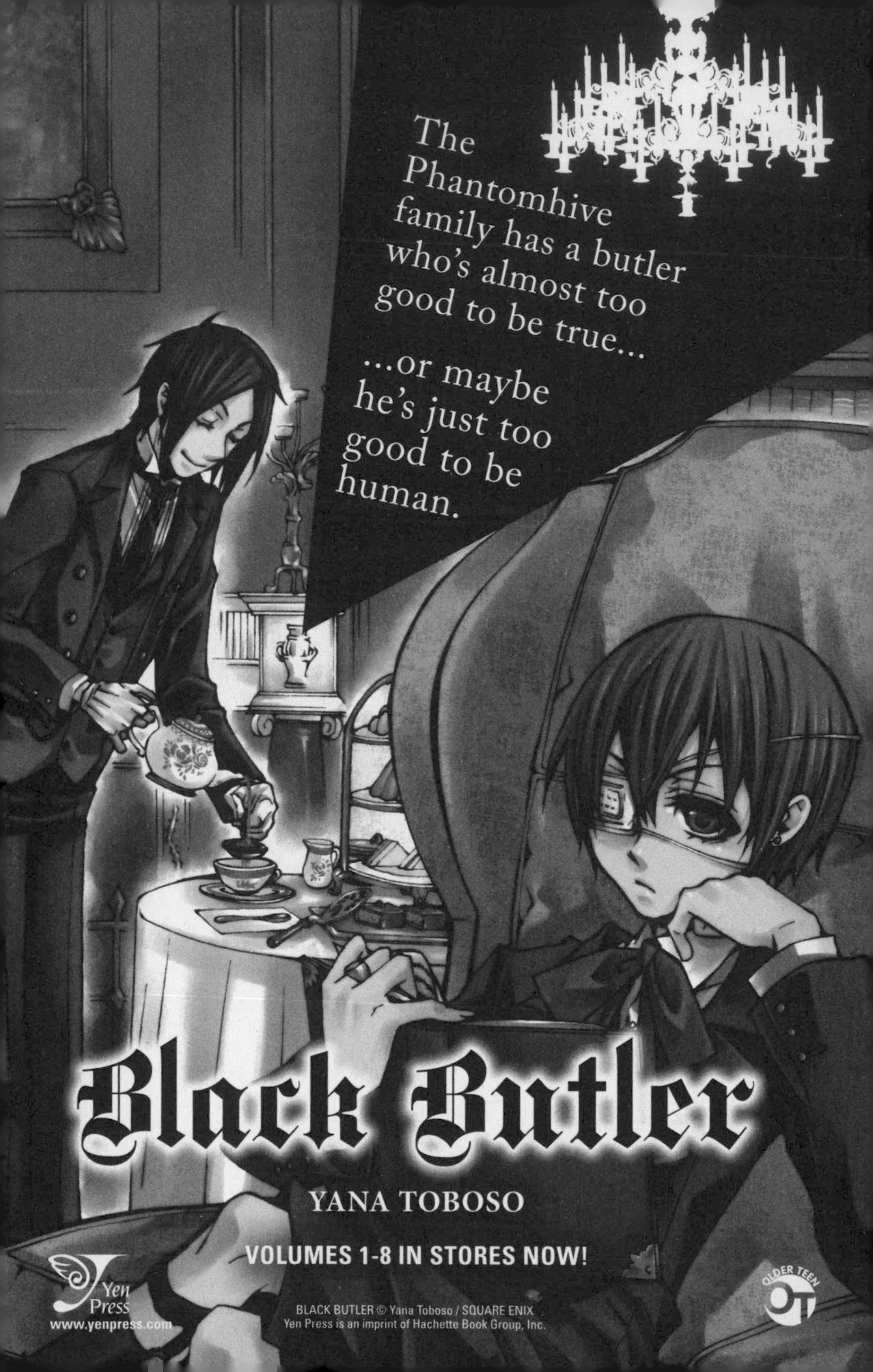
The Phantomhive family has a butler who's almost too good to be true...
...or maybe he's just too good to be human.
Black Butler
YANA TOBOSO
VOLUMES 1-8 IN STORES NOW!
Yen Press
www.yenpress.com
BLACK BUTLER © Yana Toboso / SQUARE ENIX
Yen Press is an imprint of Hachette Book Group, Inc.
OLDER TEEN
OT

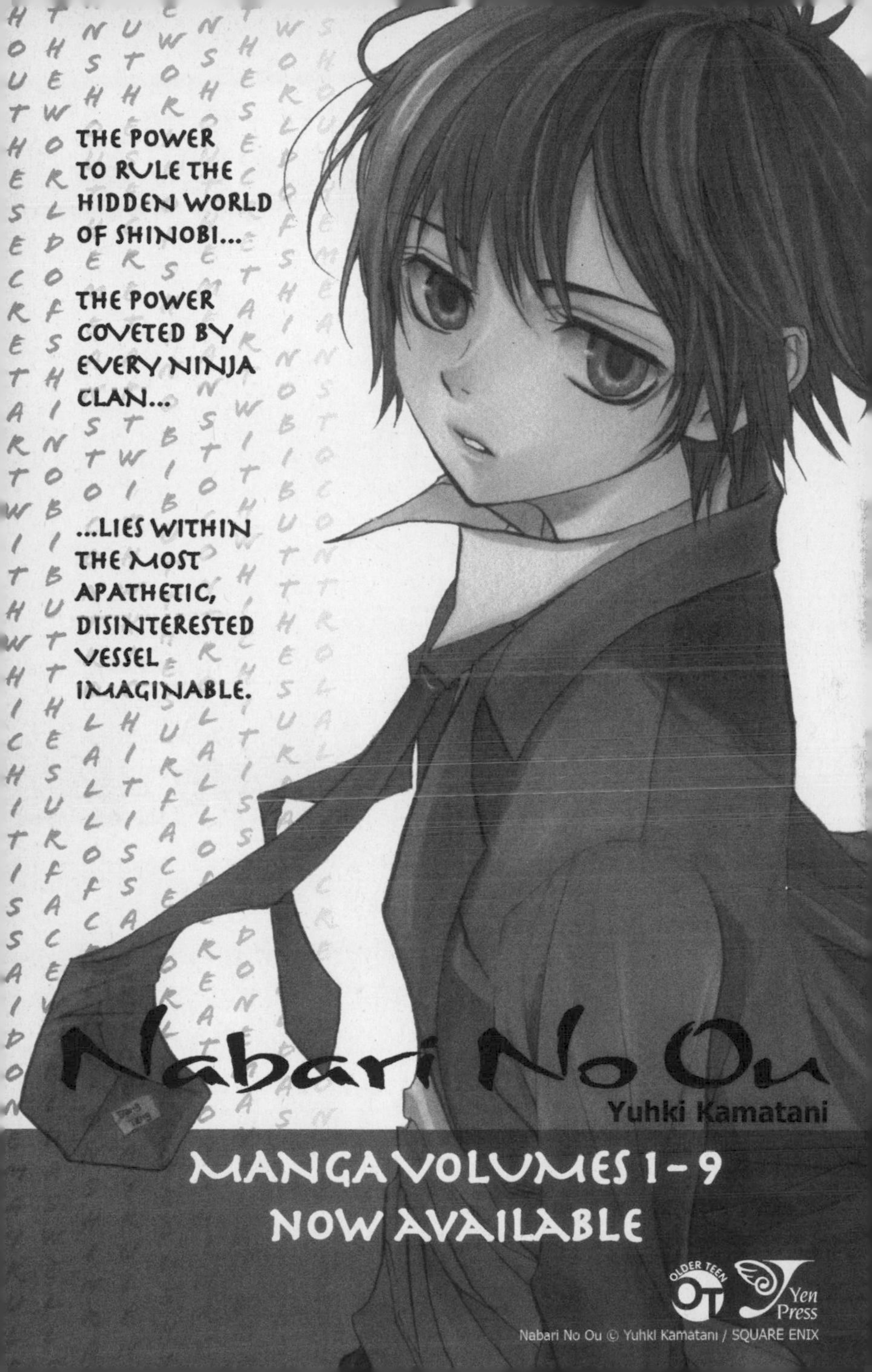
THE POWER TO RULE THE HIDDEN WORLD OF SHINOBI...
THE POWER COVETED BY EVERY NINJA CLAN...
...LIES WITHIN THE MOST APATHETIC, DISINTERESTED VESSEL IMAGINABLE.
Nabari No Ou
Yuhki Kamatani
MANGA VOLUMES 1-9
NOW AVAILABLE
OLDER TEEN
OT
Yen Press
Nabari No Ou © Yuhki Kamatani / SQUARE ENIX

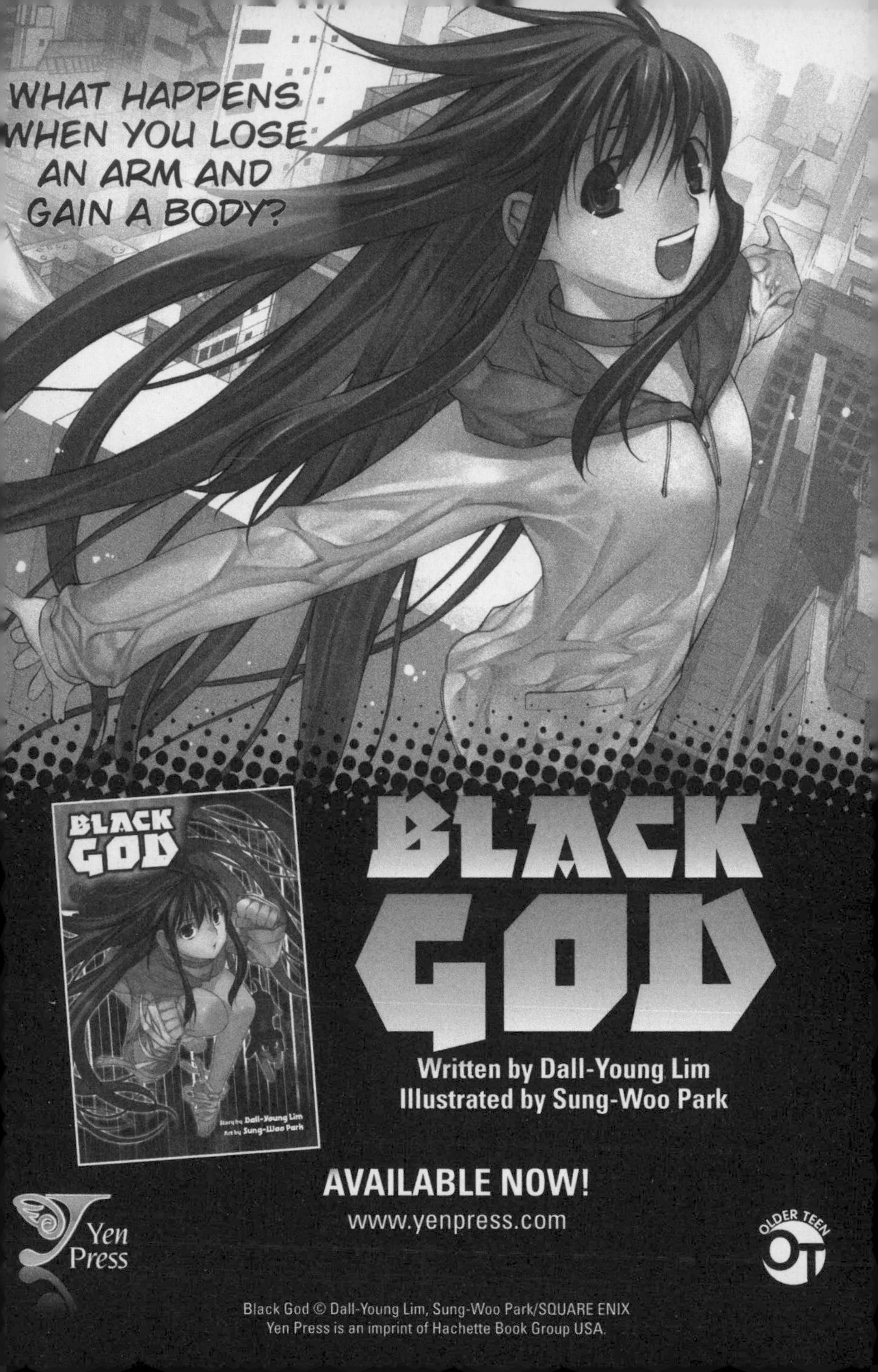
WHAT HAPPENS WHEN YOU LOSE AN ARM AND GAIN A BODY?
BLACK GOD
BLACK GOD
Written by Dall-Young Lim
Illustrated by Sung-Woo Park
AVAILABLE NOW!
www.yenpress.com
Yen Press
OLDER TEEN
OT
Black God © Dall-Young Lim, Sung-Woo Park/SQUARE ENIX
Yen Press is an imprint of Hachette Book Group USA.

SOUL EATER ⑧

ATSUSHI OHKUBO

Translation: Jack Wiedrick

Lettering: Alexis Eckerman

SOUL EATER Vol. 8 © 2007 Atsushi Ohkubo / SQUARE ENIX. All rights reserved. First published in Japan in 2007 by SQUARE ENIX CO., LTD. English translation rights arranged with SQUARE ENIX CO., LTD. and Hachette Book Group through Tuttle-Mori Agency, Inc.

Translation © 2012 by SQUARE ENIX CO., LTD.

Yen Press
Hachette Book Group
237 Park Avenue, New York, NY 10017

www.HachetteBookGroup.com
www.YenPress.com

Yen Press is an imprint of Hachette Book Group, Inc. The Yen Press name and logo are trademarks of Hachette Book Group, Inc.

First Yen Press Edition: February 2012

ISBN: 978-0-316-07112-3

10 9 8 7 6 5 4 3 2 1

BVG

Printed in the United States of America